Knowledge, Values and Educa

Education poses some of the most challenging questions of any profession. Whether we are teachers, policy makers or researchers, the complexity of the practices and policies that we encounter demands careful thought and reflection. The **Critical Perspectives on Education** series includes volumes designed to provoke the kind of thinking that will lead readers to re-evaluate their practices and consider how best they can be justified and improved.

Knowledge, Values and Educational Policy focuses on what schools are for and what should be taught in them, how learning is possible across boundaries, and issues of diversity and equity. Finally policies and practices relating to schools are considered.

Within this volume, internationally renowned contributors address a number of fundamental questions designed to take the reader to the heart of current debates around curriculum, knowledge transfer, equity and social justice, and system reform, such as:

- What are schools and what are they for?
- What knowledge should schools teach?
- How are learners different from each other and how are groups of learners different from one another, in terms of social class, gender, ethnicity and disability?
- What influence does educational policy have on improving schools?
- What influence does research have on our understanding of education and schooling?

To help with reflection, many of the chapters also include questions for debate and a guide to further reading.

Read alongside its companion volume, *Educational Theories, Cultures and Learning*, this book will encourage readers to reflect on some of the key issues facing education and education-ists today.

Harry Daniels is Professor of Education: Culture and Pedagogy, Head of the Learning as Cultural and Social Practice Research Programme, and Director of the Centre for Sociocultural and Activity Theory Research at the University of Bath, UK.

Hugh Lauder is Professor of Education and Political Economy, and Head of the Policy and Management Research Group, at the University of Bath, UK.

Jill Porter is Senior Lecturer in Research Methods and Special Education at the University of Bath, UK.

Critical Perspectives on Education

Education poses some of the most challenging questions of any profession. Whether we are teachers, policy makers or researchers, the complexity of the practices and policies that we encounter demands careful thought and reflection. The **Critical Perspectives on Education** series includes volumes designed to provoke the kind of thinking that will lead readers to re-evaluate their practices and consider how best they can be justified and improved.

Educational Theories, Cultures and Learning
A critical perspective
Edited by Harry Daniels, Hugh Lauder and Jill Porter

Knowledge, Values and Educational Policy
A critical perspective
Edited by Harry Daniels, Hugh Lauder and Jill Porter

Knowledge, Values and Educational Policy

A critical perspective

**Edited by
Harry Daniels
Hugh Lauder
Jill Porter**

with Sarah Hartshorn

Routledge
Taylor & Francis Group.

LONDON AND NEW YORK

First published 2009
by Routledge
2 Park Square, Milton Park, Abingdon, Oxfordshire OX14 4RN

Simultaneously published in the USA and Canada
by Routledge
711 Third Avenue, New York, NY 10017

Routledge is an imprint of the Taylor & Francis Group, an informa business

First issued in paperback 2011

© 2009 Harry Daniels, Hugh Lauder and Jill Porter for editorial selection
and material; individual chapters, the contributors

Typeset in Galliard by
Bookcraft Ltd, Stroud, Gloucestershire

British Library Cataloguing in Publication Data
A catalogue record for this book is available from the British Library

Library of Congress Cataloging in Publication Data
Knowledge, values, and educational policy : a critical perspective / edited
by Harry Daniels, Hugh Lauder, and Jill Porter.
    p. cm.
    Includes bibliographical references and index.
    1. Education—Aims and objectives. 2. Education—Social aspects.
    3. Education and state. I. Daniels, Harry. II. Lauder, Hugh.
    III. Porter, Jill.
LB41.K557 2009
370.1–dc22   2008043449

ISBN13: 978-0-415-49119-8 (hbk)
ISBN13: 978-0-415-68652-5 (pbk)

Contents

Contributors

Maria Balarin is a Lecturer in the Department of Education of the University of Bath, UK.

Harry Daniels is Professor of Education: Culture and Pedagogy and Director of the Centre for Sociocultural and Activity Theory Research at the University of Bath, UK.

Jo-Anne Dillabough is Reader in the Faculty of Education, University of Cambridge, UK.

Alaster Douglas has worked as a teacher and senior manager in four secondary schools and completed an MA in Education (Publishing) and an MSc in Educational Research Methodology before his current position as a full-time research student working on a doctorate at the University of Oxford, UK.

Yrjö Engeström is Professor of Adult Education and Director of the Centre for Activity Theory and Developmental Work Research at the University of Helsinki in Finland.

Michael Eraut is Professor Emeritus at the University of Sussex, UK.

Lani Florian is Professor of Social and Educational Inclusion at the University of Aberdeen in Scotland, UK.

Kris D. Gutiérrez is Professor at the University of California, Los Angeles, Graduate School of Education and Information Studies.

Mariane Hedegaard is head of the PPUK (Person, Practice, Development, Culture) research centre at the University of Copenhagen, Denmark, where she holds a chair in psychology.

Eva Hjörne completed her PhD in Education at the University of Gothenburg, Sweden, in 2004.

David Hopkins is the inaugural HSBC Chair in International Leadership, where he supports the work of iNet, the International arm of the Specialist Schools and Academies Trust and the Leadership Centre at the Institute of Education, University of London, UK.

Ruth Kershner is a Lecturer in the Psychology of Education in the Faculty of Education at the University of Cambridge, UK.

Hugh Lauder is Professor of Education and Political Economy at the University of Bath, UK.

Clare Morris is currently completing her EdD at the Institute of Education, University of London, UK.

Roy Nash died in October 2006 after a distinguished academic career at Massey University, New Zealand, as a sociologist of education with a speciality in the explanation of social disparities in educational achievement.

Sarah O'Flynn completed her doctoral studies at Cardiff University, UK, and works full-time as a deputy head teacher in a London Authority's Pupil Referral Unit.

Annemarie Sullivan Palincsar is the Jean and Charles Walgreen Jr. Chair of Reading and Literacy and a teacher educator at the University of Michigan, USA.

Jill Porter is Senior Lecturer in Research Methods and Special Education at the University of Bath, UK..

Naz Rassool is a Professor at the Institute of Education at the University of Reading, UK.

Viviane M.J. Robinson completed her doctoral study at Harvard University and is now Professor in the Faculty of Education at the University of Auckland, New Zealand.

Barbara Rogoff is UCSC Foundation Professor of Psychology, University of California, Santa Cruz, USA.

Roger Säljö is Professor of Education and Educational Psychology at the Department of Education, University of Gothenburg, Sweden, and Director of LinCS, the Linnaeus Centre for Research on Learning, Interaction and Mediated Communication in Contemporary Society.

Sarah E. Scott is an Assistant Professor of Reading Education in the Department of Instruction and Learning at the University of Pittsburgh.

Tom Shakespeare is a social scientist and bioethicist, who has researched and taught at the universities of Cambridge, Sunderland, Leeds and Newcastle in the UK.

Andrew Stables is Professor of Education and Philosophy at the University of Bath, UK.

Hanna Toiviainen is a post-doctoral researcher in the Centre for Activity Theory and Developmental Work Research, Department of Education, University of Helsinki, Finland.

Harry Torrance is Professor of Education and Director of the Education and Social Research Institute, Manchester Metropolitan University, UK.

Paul Warmington is a Senior Lecturer at the School of Education, University of Birmingham, UK.

Michael Young is a Professor of Education at the Institute of Education, University of London, UK, and at the University of Bath and an Honorary Professor at the Universities of Pretoria and Witwatersrand and Capital Normal University (Beijing).

Acknowledgements

Cartoons by Ros Asquith from the LINES series originally published in *Guardian Education*. Reprinted by permission of the artist.

2.1: 'Transfer of knowledge between education and workplace settings', by Michael Eraut: from *Workplace Learning in Context*, edited by Helen Rainbird, Alison Fuller and Anne Munro, © 2004 Routledge. Reproduced by permission of Taylor & Francis Books UK.

3.1: 'Cultural ways of learning', by Kris D. Gutiérrez and Barbara Rogoff: reproduced with permission of Sage Publications Inc. Journals from *Educational Researcher*, 2003, 32(5), pp. 19–25; permission conveyed through Copyright Clearance Centre, Inc.

3.3: 'Gender theory and research in education', by Jo-Anne Dillabough: reproduced with kind permission of Open University Press from *Investigating Gender: Modernist Traditions and Emerging Contemporary Themes*, edited by B. Francis and C. Skelton (Milton Keynes, Open University Press, 2001, pp. 11–26).

3.4: 'Symptoms, categories, and the process of invoking labels', by Roger Säljö and Eva Hjörne: reproduced with permission of Taylor & Francis (www.informaworld.com) from *Journal of Language, Identity and Education*, 2004, 3(1), pp. 1–24.

3.6: 'Disability: a complex interaction', by Tom Shakespeare: reproduced with permission of Routledge from *Disability Rights and Wrongs*, by Tom Shakespeare (London, Routledge, 2006, pp. 54–67).

Introduction

From Plato to Monday morning

Harry Daniels, Hugh Lauder and Jill Porter

Education poses some of the most challenging questions of any profession. Whether as teachers, policy makers or researchers, the complexity of the practices and policies that we encounter demands careful reflection. *Educational Theories, Cultures and Learning* and its companion volume *Knowledge, Values and Educational Policy* (two volumes in the Critical Perspectives on Education series) are designed to provoke the kind of thinking that will do justice to such complexity. In a world in which policy makers often seek the comforts of magic bullets that solve educational problems with one simple solution, and where commercial companies seek to solve the pressure on teachers' time with off-the-shelf curricula and school improvement packages, these volumes seek to do the opposite: there is no recipe book.

In the daily struggle to keep up with new policy initiatives and increased demands for accountability and the related mountain of paperwork, the fundamental questions that give us our professional moral and practical compass are sometimes overlooked. It is by returning to these questions that we can re-evaluate our practices and consider how best we can justify and improve them.

Within these two volumes we address a number of questions that may appear simple, but very quickly readers will find themselves immersed in debates with themselves and with others. To help with such reflection each chapter poses questions and offers an initial guide to further reading. Many of these questions have been debated from Plato onwards, but they are no less valid now than when first raised. The following are the questions that are addressed in a variety of ways both within and across the sections of the two volumes.

In *Educational Theories, Cultures and Learning*, we ask:

- What role does culture play in our understanding of pedagogy?
- What role do global influences, especially economic, cultural and social, have in shaping our understanding of education?
- What role does language play in influencing our thinking about education?
- How can we best understand childhood? What implications does our view of childhood have for education?
- How do we know what learners know?
- How do learners negotiate the transition between the different phases of education?
- How best can children learn the knowledge we believe should be taught?
- What is a teacher?
- How do teachers learn?
- How do we understand learners, their minds, identity and development?

And in *Knowledge, Values and Educational Policy*, we ask:

- What are schools and what are they for?
- What knowledge should schools teach?
- How are learners different from each other, and how are groups of learners different from one another, in terms of social class, gender, ethnicity and disability?
- What influence does educational policy have on improving schools?
- What influence does research have on our understanding of education and schooling?

These questions are designed to provide a framework for reflection; it is not exhaustive but it attempts to provide what we consider the bedrock questions for educationists. There is one obvious omission and that is values: education always presupposes values. These values are implicit in the systems of education within which we work and in our own practices. In relation to systems of education Allan Bloom (1997, pp. 498–9) makes the point that:

> Every education system has a moral goal that it tries to attain. It wants to produce a certain kind of human being. This intention is more or less explicit, more or less a result of reflection; but even the neutral subjects, like reading, writing and arithmetic, take their place in their vision of the educated person ... Always important is the political regime, which needs citizens who are in accord with its fundamental principles.

These remarks identify why education is seen as so central to modern societies and so controversial. Educational systems make certain assumptions about the nature of the society, human nature and how it develops, and how education can help to foster the dispositions and skills that are considered desirable. Currently, much of the focus in education is on what Grubb and Lazerson (2006) call 'the Educational Gospel', that is the view that the fundamental task of education is to provide the economic skills for future workers. While some of the issues relating to this question are addressed in the section on 'Learning across boundaries' in *Knowledge, Values and Educational Policy*, it will be clear from other sections in the two companion volumes that education is about much more than just the 'delivery' of workers into the labour market.

The values of an educational system are not always consistent with the practitioners within it, and many teachers reject the idea that their fundamental purpose is to make young people 'fit' for the economy at the expense of aims of individual well-being or social citizenship; this can cause conflicts which raise questions about the purposes of education and the role of the teacher. Here questions about the influence of globalisation and economic competitiveness loom large in policy makers' justifications for educational change.

But if values are caught up in these issues then so is power. Education is often portrayed as a technical matter in which if practice was only improved so many more students could pass their exams. But we know that some groups in society are systematically disadvantaged by education: the progressive expansion of educational systems has not consistently addressed the issues of unequal power and inequality of outcomes in education. In this volume we look at the theoretical and practical issues involved in such inequalities of power in relation to education, asking what progress teachers can make to help redress the problems of inequality they confront. While education may be part of the problem, the asymmetries of power often have their sources in the wider society and in the role of the state; but that insight does not help the teacher on Monday morning[1] when she has to confront the hopelessness and lack of faith that children bring to school as the consequences of inequality.

If education systems presuppose a view of human nature and how it can be changed and developed, then the same is true of the theories and practices of learning. Various theories or approaches to learning have been adopted by state education systems since their inception. This book largely focuses on sociocultural theories of learning, in part because they are assuming an increasingly important position in understanding how children learn. Indeed, learning itself has now taken a central position in education, because where once learners were seen as passive recipients of knowledge now it is recognised that students and teachers are active in the construction of what they learn and the way they come to understand knowledge. This view is consistent with the developing individualisation of society – that is, as individuals break away from established social rules and conventions so they have the possibility of becoming more active in the construction of their lives. But there is also a cultural element to this theory in that culture may be understood as a repository of tools and understandings which, once acquired by individuals, enable new forms of engagement with the world. Access to these cultural tools (words, machines, theories and so on) may be seen as the primary function of schooling. We do not construct knowledge and understanding from some kind of epistemological 'Year 0'; rather, we use our cultural historical legacies as the means of moving beyond our immediate experience of the world. Such a social cultural or cultural historical argument is witnessed in many of the chapters in this book. We have asked contributors to be clear about the assumptions which underpin their chapters. This is of particular importance at a time when it appears as if 'we are all sociocultural theorists now'. As ever, underneath this one 'catch-all' descriptor there lies a myriad of different positions.

There have been recent attempts to reduce the professionalism of teachers to that of advanced technicians. For example, in England it can be argued that the state has mandated a particular theory of learning centred on testing and accountability. Under such a system the values and ends of education are set by the state, and there is little need for the kind of intellectual and professional reflection that this book encourages. However, state-mandated policies that have used business models as their guide do not have a history of success (Callahan, 1962), and even as we write it seems clear that this model is now under threat.

The questions raised above can only be addressed if we make fundamental assumptions about human nature, learners and the role of institutions such as education. But if we are to achieve coherent and consistent views about these assumptions and how they relate to one another we need to embrace the key theories that seek to understand and explain how education 'works': that is, how views of the learner, pedagogy and schools interact to produce students' identities and outcomes.

There are many different ways in which the idea of a 'theory' can be understood. But the list of questions above provides a good starting point for understanding how we are using the concept. What theories in education do is take some of these questions and show how they can be addressed through a coherent view or perspective. Indeed, at the heart of a well-formed theory lies a world-view of the role of education in society and the way individuals best learn. For example, there are many theories of learning, each taking a quite different view of human nature. In the work of the celebrated behaviourist B.F. Skinner, human beings were assumed to have no free will but rather learned through a system of environmental stimuli and responses. In his novel *Walden II* he imagined how a utopia could be built from his theory. In contrast, sociocultural theory sees individuals as a product of their history and culture and argues that learning is about building on the engagement with both. In this context human beings are active in the construction of their learning in ways that would have been totally rejected by Skinner. To take a different example, the idea of the Education Gospel assumes that schools are primarily there to socialise students into the world of paid work and to be provide them with the associated skills. But such a view takes no account of the nature of paid work, whether it is exploitative of either individuals or the environment, and it raises questions about whether a focus on paid work precludes the development of critical perspectives that might challenge such a view of schooling.

In contrast to the ambitions of natural scientists, who are seeking a unified theory of everything to explain the origins of the universe, there is no one theory that can provide a full or indeed convincing account of the very many elements that comprise education: it is just too complex for that. Rather, the fundamental task we as educators have to confront is to develop theories in the particular area that is of interest to us, compare them to others and make judgements as to which theories appear the most plausible. Theories typically are in competition with one another. To take the example of behaviourism and sociocultural theory, they make fundamentally different assumptions about human nature. Behaviourism sees human beings as fundamentally passive, determined by the putative laws of stimulus and response. In contrast sociocultural theories see human beings as active but within the context of a particular moment in history. Equally, theories that see schools as fundamentally having an economic function of providing individuals with the skills and outlook to be employable will be quite different from those that argue that such theories uncritically reproduce existing inequalities and forms of exploitation.

In looking at the theories and perspectives adopted in these two companion volumes it will be apparent that theories have different roles. In particular:

- They can guide practice by providing insights, challenging our preconceptions and provoking us to think about education in different ways.
- They can provide explanations.

It would be hoped that we would start by looking at the most plausible explanations for those aspects of education that we are interested in and use those as a basis for guiding our practice, whether as teachers, researchers or policy makers.

How then do we choose which theories to work with? And how do we know which is the best theory in explaining educational relationships at any given moment? These are rather different but related questions. We may choose theories because they provide the best explanations at any given moment, but they may not always give us the insights and the ways of thinking about educational problems that we personally need. In these cases we may choose theories on the basis of our personal view of the world and our values. However, when it comes to competing explanations such as those between different conceptions of learning then there are several questions that we can ask and they centre on the question of how well-formed an explanatory theory is. These include:

- Does the theory provide a particular world-view as to the educational relationships we are interested in explaining?
- How plausible are its fundamental assumptions as regards human nature, society and education?
- Does it give rise to claims that can be empirically researched and tested?
- What is the evidential basis for the theory?
- What are the value implications of holding this theory?

In making judgements about theories, all these questions come into play. Empirical evidence is important, but in studying something as complex as education it is not always clear that the empirical evidence will provide a decisive test of a theory's plausibility, especially in social contexts different from where the theory was originally tested. Therefore, other factors need to be considered, such as the fundamental assumptions a theory makes and the value implications. To return to B.F. Skinner's theory of behaviourism, one of the reasons why it has been treated with scepticism is that it assumes human beings have no free will, with the value implication that they should be treated in a rather paternalistic way in which the environment for their learning is highly structured.

Of course, there are now many computer-based learning programmes that have incorporated elements of Skinner's theory which their proponents will claim are successful – in which case the view of human nature and the value position taken need to be weighed against the empirical evidence. Of course a competing theory may be able to provide a better explanation for the same learning strategies and practices. It is for these reasons that educational issues will always be a matter of debate and analysis.

The structure of the two volumes

Any critical analysis in education will need to take on board the account of theory and its uses that we have given. When reading the chapters in these two volumes, use the questions that we have raised as a guide to understanding and evaluating them.

Educational Theories, Cultures and Learning is divided into three sections. Section 1 presents chapters on the theme of how education is understood in different cultures. The primary purpose of this section is to raise questions about the assumptions we make about education in our own cultures. We often assume that education and our experience are simply a given, that it can be no other way. But the moment we see that education can be understood quite differently a fundamental challenge is posed to the taken-for-granted assumptions we often make about it. In Section 2, the chapters deal with the theories and related assumptions we make about learners and students and how we think about them. Here, readers will find, for example, contrasting chapters on the role of neuroscience in understanding learners and how children are socially constructed. Section 3 looks more explicitly at how we can understand the principal actors in education – learners and teachers.

Knowledge, Values and Educational Policy is divided into five sections. Section 1 asks fundamental questions about what schools are for and what should be taught in them. There are many ways of approaching such questions, and here philosophical, psychological and sociological theories are brought to bear. Section 2 presents chapters on one of the newest areas of interest: learning across boundaries. The more learning is seen not only as the preserve of education but as an activity which is as important at work or in the home the more the question of how we might learn across boundaries assumes significance. Section 3 examines issues of diversity and equity. One of the best-documented facts about the outcomes of education is that they are unequal in relation to social class, gender, ethnicity and disability. Here there are two issues: why do these patterns of inequality exist, and how can they best be addressed? The chapters in this section take a range of perspectives on these issues from the global trends identified by Raz Rassool through to the more specific questions of pedagogy identified by Kris Gutiérrez and Barbara Rogoff. Section 4 locates these issues in terms of policies and practices within school. This section presents a range of conflicting perspectives on the nature of policy and its effects on school. On the one hand, David Hopkins takes the view that government policies provide the levers for school improvement or have done up to a point, whereas Harry Torrance argues the opposing case, while Vivianne Robinson puzzles as to why policies fail. Andrew Stables does not consider schools to be the kind of institution to which policy levers of the kind championed by David Hopkins are applicable. Finally, Section 5 presents a series of reflections on the importance of theory for guiding educational practice and for developing research in education.

These two companion volumes can be seen as an aid to a personal and moral professional journey; it is hoped that they will provide a guide to reflection on the route to be taken.

Note

1 The idea of what teachers should do on Monday morning is taken from Paul Willis (1977). For a discussion of these issues see Lauder *et al.* (2006).

References

Bloom, A. (1997) 'On virtue (Introduction to *The Closing of the American Mind*)', in Halsey, A.H., Lauder, H., Brown, P. and Stuart Wells, A., *Education, Culture, Economy and Society*, Oxford, Oxford University Press.

Callahan, R. (1962) *Education and the Cult of Efficiency*, Chicago, University of Chicago Press.

Grubb, N. and Lazerson, M. (2006) 'The globalization of rhetoric and practice: the educational gospel and vocationalism', in Lauder, H., Brown, P., Dillabough J.-A., and Halsey, A.H. (eds), *Education, Globalization and Social Change*, Oxford, Oxford University Press.

Lauder, H., Brown, P., Dillabough, J.-A., and Halsey, A.H. (eds) (2006) *Education, Globalization and Social Change*, Oxford, Oxford University Press.

Willis, P. (1977) *Learning to Labour*, Farnborough, Saxon House

Section 1

Knowledge for teaching and learning

Introduction

Hugh Lauder

(Cartoon by Ros Asquith)

This section examines one of the fundamental puzzles in education. In terms of knowledge there is a robust view which sees knowledge as being what our best theories tell us about the world (Haig, 1987). These theories are often embedded in socially and historically constructed disciplines, such as chemistry, mathematics or sociology, although increasingly they cross disciplinary boundaries. In contrast, the best theories of learning currently available suggest that learners, in some sense, construct knowledge. As Palincsar and Scott in Chapter 1.3 put it, 'we create our understanding through our experiences and that the character of our experiences is influenced profoundly by the lenses we bring to those experiences'.

The puzzle is this: on the one hand we have theories that have logical structures and ways of gathering and interpreting evidence that are objective, and arguably students need to comprehend if they are to develop a deeper understanding of the natural and social worlds we inhabit; and on the other a view of learning which involves students' construction of knowledge. How then can these two positions be reconciled?

We need to start with the idea that (i) there are forms of knowledge as expressed through theories and related disciplines which are objective in the sense that they are independent of any individual and open to inspection and discussion through language and other symbolic systems, for example maths; and, (ii) that these forms of knowledge should be taught in schools and universities. The chapters by Michael Young and Roy Nash approach these questions from different perspectives but come to remarkably similar conclusions. Both acknowledge that there are social foundations to knowledge, that is to say that there are no certain foundations to knowledge or techniques which enable us to be certain about our knowledge claims. However, it can be argued that we can make judgements about which is the best theory at any given moment in history, and it is on this basis that knowledge advances and gives us the power to comprehend the world.

Michael Young begins by asking the fundamental question and one that is often taken for granted, 'what are schools for?'. Schools are often seen as the solution to all society's ills, from teaching about finance, to sex education and environmental sustainability. But Young argues that their primary purpose is to impart the kind of formal knowledge represented by academic disciplines and theories. This claim immediately raises a series of policy and pedagogical questions. 'Knowledge' as he uses the word has, he notes, been absent from much educational policy discourse because the focus has been on developing student competencies and qualifications. He acknowledges that the kind of knowledge he is advocating may be problematic in a pedagogical sense for working-class students to acquire because it goes beyond any common-sense understanding of their world and may in the sciences be counter to common sense. In this respect, such knowledge has often been identified as that of the professional middle class. But Young draws a distinction between 'knowledge of the powerful' and 'powerful knowledge'. While formal knowledge has often been associated with the culture and norms of the powerful he sees it as also being necessary for working-class and other dominated groups because it provides ways of systematic thinking and tools for practice that enable them to be active in the construction of their destinies. For example, it could be argued that some understanding of statistics is necessary for reasons of personal health, to understand the problems of environmental sustainability and social deprivation.

Nash's chapter tackles the issue of knowledge of the powerful and powerful knowledge head-on. He discusses the theories of one of the leading sociologists in the past century, Pierre Bourdieu, who sought to explain the significant advantage that professional middle-class children have in education. Part of his explanation lies in observing that the culture of middle-class homes and that of schools is similar: both have an emphasis on literacy and the importance of books and appeal to the merits of high culture. Bourdieu views this culture and the knowledge that it embodies as a form of symbolic violence against working-class students. He is able to make this claim, in at least one version of his theory, because he sees knowledge as culturally arbitrary and tied to class interests. However, Nash argues that some forms of knowledge should be taught as necessary, not arbitrary, if we are to flourish as human beings, because it is 'a gateway to an autonomous form of life'.

The chapters by Young and Nash raise fundamental problems of pedagogy and learning since abstract symbol systems such as those found in science, maths or literature are more consistent with life in professional middle-class families. But this practical problem also meets the theoretical problem of how children learn head-on. One of the dominant approaches to how children learn is that of constructivism: that is, children construct their own knowledge. Commenting on a constructivist position developed by Rudolph (2000), Nash argues that:

> students often possess naive realist perceptions of the nature of science and privilege demonstration and experimentation over other forms of reasoning, and if this is so then far from being 'a bad thing' it might provide a sound basis for a scientific education. Is it self-evident that the sort of idealism students might pick up from some constructivist teaching, which is unlikely to be a highly sophisticated understanding, is superior to

'naive realism'? The realism considered so naive may more likely be grounded in a robust materialism, which is a philosophy with a long history in working-class radicalism.

This view is contrary to that taken by Annemarie Sullivan Palincsar and Sarah Scott, who are committed to a particular version of what is the broad church of constructivism. They take constructivism to be first and foremost a theory of knowledge (an epistemology) which has implications for pedagogy and learning. However, their chapter is largely taken up with a discussion of theories of learning and in particular the way children construct their learning. Such an approach sees the child as active, rather than passive as some previous theories of learning have assumed. Moreover, it is clear from their chapter that they do not see children's learning as a kind of 'free-for-all' in which it is possible for every child to have different views of the world. For example, in enlisting Vygotsky's theory in the constructionists' cause they note that teachers are seeking particular forms of competence from children, which suggests a pre-existing social set of standards or competences that teachers are aiming for. Equally, in discussing reasoning in science they refer to forms of evidence which are different from those used in history.

Mariane Hedegaard's chapter addresses one of the key issues arising out of the work of Young, Nash and Palincsar and Scott in that she is seeking to help students make the transition from everyday categories of thought to the more abstract and theoretical. Her approach is in the tradition of learning theories developed by Vygotsky. Her proposal for a 'double move in teaching' exemplifies the application of Vygotsky's and his co-workers' understandings about the nature of theoretical knowledge and its relation to common-sense knowledge in learning. Her concern is that too much of the activity that is organised in schools is oriented only to empirical knowledge and that it fails to connect with the systematicity of abstract knowledge. Her recent extension of this 'within-school' analysis has been to focus also on the relation between the knowledge traditions in the local community and general theoretical knowledge of social matters. In this way the 'double move' seeks to engage local and personal experience with the broader tools for thinking and their basis in historical development that we use when we embark on any act of learning.

References

Haig, B. (1987) 'Scientific problems and the conduct of research', *Educational Philosophy and Theory*, 19(2), pp. 22–32.

Rudolph, J.L. (2000) 'Reconsidering the "nature of science" as a curriculum component', *Journal of Curriculum Studies*, 32(3), pp. 402–19.

1.1 What are schools for?

Michael Young

Introduction

Every parent and teacher needs to ask the question 'what are schools for?' They are not, of course, the only institutions with purposes that we should question, but they are a special case. Like families they have a unique role in reproducing human societies and in providing the conditions which enable them to innovate and change. Without schools each generation would have to begin from scratch or – like societies which existed before there were schools – remain largely unchanged for centuries. There are, however, more specific reasons why it is important to ask the question 'what are schools for?' today. Since the 1970s, radical educators and many critical sociologists have questioned the role of schools and have seen them in largely negative terms. I shall argue that despite having an element of truth which we should do well not to forget, these critiques are fundamentally misconceived. More recently, John White, the philosopher of education, has offered a critical but explicitly positive answer to the question (White, 2007). However, like the negative critiques, by failing to specify what is distinctive about the role of schools, he does not take us very far. I begin this chapter therefore by reviewing these two kinds of answer. I then go on to explore the implications of an alternative approach that locates schools as institutions with the very specific purpose of promoting the acquisition of knowledge.

For rather different reasons, the question of knowledge and the role of schools in its acquisition has been neglected by both policy makers and by educational researchers, especially sociologists of education. For the former, a focus on the acquisition of knowledge is at odds with the more instrumental purposes that are increasingly supported by governments. For many educational researchers a focus on knowledge masks the extent to which those with power define what counts as knowledge. However, there is no contradiction, I shall argue, between ideas of democracy and social justice and the idea that schools should promote the acquisition of knowledge.

The 1970s and 1980s critics of schools

In the 1970s negative views of schooling came largely from the left and were given considerable support by researchers in my own field – the sociology of education. The idea that the primary role of schools in capitalist societies was to teach the working class their place was widely accepted within the sociology of education (Althusser, 1971; Bowles and Gintis, 1976; and Willis, 1977). The few working-class students that did progress to university were seen as legitimating the fundamental inequalities of the education system as a whole. In the 1980s and 1990s this analysis was extended to refer to the subordination of women and ethnic and other minorities. However, these analyses rarely went beyond critiques and presented little idea of what schools might be like in socialist, non-patriarchal, non-racist societies. Radical critics such as such as Ivan Illich (1971) went even further and claimed that real learning would only be possible if schools were abolished altogether.

The post-structuralist turn in the social sciences

In the late 1980s and the 1990s, under the influence of post-modernist and post-structuralist ideas and the collapse of the communist system in Eastern Europe, Marxism and other grand narratives foretelling the end of capitalism (and even of schooling) lost their credibility. As a consequence, the critiques of schooling changed, but more in style than substance. They drew much on the work of the French philosopher Michel Foucault, who grouped schools with hospitals, prisons and asylums as institutions of surveillance and control; they disciplined pupils and normalised knowledge as subjects. The difference between thinkers such as Foucault and the left-wing ideas of earlier decades was that the 'post-Marxist' theorists dispensed with the idea of progress and any idea of a specific agency of change such as the working class. For Foucault there was no alternative to schooling as surveillance – all social scientists and educational researchers could do was to offer critiques. He expressed this point in the following terms:

> I absolutely will not play the part of one who prescribes solutions. I hold that the role of the intellectual today … is not to prophesy or propose solutions since by doing so one can only contribute to the determinate situation of power that must be critiqued.
>
> (Foucault, 1991, quoted in Muller, 2000)

It is not surprising, therefore, that these critiques were not listened to by policy makers – they really had little to say about schools, except to other social scientists.

Governments' responses

At the same time as the emergence of post-structuralist ideas, another set of ideas – neo-liberalism – came to dominate economics and government and, indirectly, education. Neo-liberals argued that the economy should be left to the market and governments should give up trying to have economic or industrial policies. The logic of this position was followed through with enthusiasm by governments of both main parties in the UK, with profound implications for schools. While ceding to the free market any role in the economy (with the exception of the control of interest rates), governments devoted their efforts to reforming the school system or improving 'human capital'. New Labour went even further than the Tories; they argued that the market offered the best solution for improving the public as well as the private sector – and education in particular. This had two consequences that are relevant to the question 'what are schools for?' One has been the attempt to gear the outcomes of schools to what are seen to be the 'needs of the economy' – a kind of mass vocationalism. The control of much post-compulsory education and even some schools and local education authorities has been put in the hands of sometimes willing but often reluctant private employers. The other consequence has been to turn education itself into a market (or at least a quasi-market), in which schools are forced to compete for students and funds. I call this the *de-differentiation of schooling*. Schools are treated as a type of delivery agency, required to concentrate on outcomes and pay little attention to the process or content of delivery. As a result, the purposes of schooling are defined in increasingly instrumental terms – as a means to other ends. With schools driven by targets, assignments and league tables, it is no wonder that pupils become bored and teachers experience 'burnout'.

New goals for old?

In seeking to reassert the distinctive purposes of schools, I want to consider two alternative answers to my starting question. The first can be found in John White's recent paper for the Philosophy of Education Society of Great Britain. It is called *What Are Schools for and Why?* (White 2007). No one could take issue with his claim that schools should promote human happiness and well-being. The problem is that such goals apply equally to all institutions (except perhaps prisons) and they say nothing specific about what schools are for and what distinguishes their role from that of other institutions. In his paper White is dismissive of the idea that subjects or disciplines might define the purposes of schools. He makes the curious argument that the subject-based curriculum was a middle-class device designed in the eighteenth century to promote the interests of the rising bourgeoisie of the time. It is inconceivable, he argues, that a curriculum with such origins could be the basis for schools for all in the twenty-first century. In my view his argument is deeply flawed for two reasons. First, as Baker and LeTendre (2005) have shown, the contemporary curriculum in the UK is remarkably similar to that found in most developed countries, despite their very different histories. Furthermore, the historical fact that this curriculum was developed by a particular fraction of the middle class in the late eighteenth/early nineteenth century is no grounds for describing it as a middle-class curriculum. It would be equally flawed to describe Boyle's law as a middle-class law on the grounds that Boyle was an eighteenth-century upper-middle-class gentleman! The particular historical origins of scientific discoveries are interesting, as are the historical origins of scientific laws; however, these origins have nothing to say about the truth of a scientific law or about the merits of a particular curriculum.

My second reason for rejecting White's argument is that it does not address the question why parents, sometimes at great sacrifice, especially in developing countries, have historically tried to keep their children at school for longer and longer periods. Nor does it tell us what parents expect as a result of these sacrifices. Despite asking the question 'what are schools for?' White also ends up, like the government and the post-structuralists, in de-differentiating the goals of schools. As a result we have surveillance for Foucault, employability for New Labour and happiness and well-being for John White. I certainly prefer the last but it is hardly a guide for those responsible for the curriculum.

Let us go back to Foucault for a moment. When he puts schools in the same category as prisons, asylums and hospitals, he misses both the history of the political struggle over mass schooling and what is distinctive about schools. I want to focus briefly on the first of these points and develop an argument about the implications of the distinctive purposes of schools.

Struggles over the purposes of schools

The historical struggle over the purposes of schooling can be seen in terms of two tensions. The first is between the goals of *emancipation* and *domination*. Since the Chartists in this country in the nineteenth century and more recently in the case of Bantu education in South Africa, dominant and subordinate classes have attempted to use schools to realise their widely different purposes. One only has to remember that Nelson Mandela was a product of the schools for Africans that predated Bantu education to be reminded that even the most oppressive school systems can be used by some as instruments of emancipation. The second tension is between the question 'who gets schooling?' and the question 'what do they get?' The struggle over schools in this country has, with a few exceptions, taken the second question as given and focused on the first. The terms in which each of these questions has been debated have of course changed. The 'access' question began with the campaign for free elementary schooling in the nineteenth century, led to struggles over the 11-plus and selection and now is expressed in terms of the goals of promoting social inclusion and widening participation. Interestingly the idea of a struggle over access has been replaced by a largely top-down approach associated with government policies for 'widening participation'. Debates over the question 'what do they get?' also go back to the Chartists in the nineteenth century and their famous slogan 'really useful knowledge'. This was an attack on the domination of the curriculum by Scripture. The Chartists' idea was revived on the left in the 1970s but such questions are far less widely debated today.

The legacy of earlier debates can be seen in two contrasting concepts of education that underlie present-day government policies. One might be called 'education as outcomes'. In this approach to education policy, teaching and learning become dominated by the setting, assessing and attaining of targets and the preparing of students for tests and examinations. Less visible is a very different idea of education that still finds expression in the idea of subject syllabuses. It is the idea that the primary purpose of education is for students to gain access to different specialist fields of knowledge. The idea of education as the transmission of knowledge has, with some justification, been heavily criticised by educational researchers. However, my argument is that these criticisms miss a crucial point. They focus on the mechanical one-way and passive model of learning implied by the 'transmission' metaphor and its association with a very conservative view of education and the purposes of schools. At the same time, they forget that the idea of schooling as the 'transmission of knowledge' gives transmission a quite different meaning and explicitly presupposes the active involvement of the learner in the process of acquiring knowledge. The idea that the school is primarily an agency of cultural or knowledge transmission raises the question 'what knowledge?' and in particular what is the knowledge that it is the schools' responsibility to transmit? If it is accepted that schools have this role, then it implies that types of knowledge are differentiated. In other words, for educational purposes, some types of knowledge are more worthwhile than others, and their differences form the basis for the difference between school or curriculum knowledge and non-school knowledge. What is it about school knowledge or the curriculum that makes the acquisition of some types of knowledge possible? My answer to the question 'what are schools for?' is, therefore, that schools enable or can enable young people to acquire the knowledge that for most of them cannot be acquired at home or in the community, or, for adults, in workplaces. The rest of this chapter is concerned with exploring the implications of this assertion.

What knowledge?

In using the very general word 'knowledge' I find it useful to distinguish between two ideas – '*knowledge of the powerful*' and '*powerful knowledge*'. 'Knowledge of the powerful' refers to who defines 'what counts as knowledge' and has access to it. Historically and even today when we look at the distribution of access to university, it is those with more power in society who have access to certain kinds of knowledge. It is this that I refer to as 'knowledge of the powerful'. It is understandable that many sociological critiques of school knowledge have equated school knowledge and the curriculum with 'knowledge of the powerful'. It was, after all the upper classes in the early nineteenth century who gave up their private tutors and sent their children to the Public Schools to acquire powerful knowledge (as well as, of course, to acquire powerful friends). However, the fact that some knowledge is 'knowledge of the powerful', or high-status knowledge as I once expressed it (Young, 1971, 1998), tells us nothing about the knowledge itself. We therefore need another concept in conceptualising the curriculum that I want to refer to as 'powerful knowledge'. This refers not to who has most access to the knowledge or who gives it legitimacy, although both are important issues; it refers to what the knowledge can do – for example, whether it provides reliable explanations or new ways of thinking about the world. This was what the Chartists were calling for with their slogan 'really useful knowledge'. It is also, if not always consciously, what parents hope for in making sacrifices to keep their children at school: that they will acquire powerful knowledge that is not available to them at home.

Powerful knowledge in modern societies in the sense that I have used the term is, increasingly, specialist knowledge. It follows therefore that schools need teachers with that specialist knowledge. Furthermore, if the goal for schools is to 'transmit powerful knowledge', it follows that teacher–pupil relations will have certain distinctive features that arise from that goal. For example:

- they will be different from relations between peers and will inevitably be hierarchical;
- they will not be based, as some recent government policies imply, on learner choice, because in most cases, learners will lack the prior knowledge to make such choices.

This does not mean that schools should not take the knowledge that pupils bring to school seriously or that pedagogic authority does not need to be challenged. It does mean that some form of authority relations are intrinsic to pedagogy and to schools. The questions of pedagogic authority and responsibility raise important issues, especially for teacher educators, which are beyond the scope of this chapter. The next section turns to the issue of knowledge differentiation.

Knowledge differentiation and school knowledge

The key issues about knowledge, for both teachers and educational researchers, are not primarily the philosophical questions such as 'what is knowledge?' or 'how do we know at all?' The educational issues about knowledge concern how school knowledge is and should be different from non-school knowledge and the basis on which this differentiation is made. Although the philosophical issues are involved, school/non-school knowledge differences raise primarily sociological and pedagogic questions.

Schooling is about providing access to the specialised knowledge that is embodied in different domains. The key curriculum questions will be concerned with:

- the differences between different forms of specialist knowledge and the relations between them;
- how this specialist knowledge differs from the knowledge people acquire in everyday life;
- how specialist and everyday knowledge relate to each other; and
- how specialist knowledge is pedagogised.

In other words, how it is paced , selected and sequenced for different groups of learners.

Differentiation, therefore, in the sense I am using it here, refers to:

- the differences between school and everyday knowledge;
- the differences between and relations between knowledge domains;
- the differences between specialist knowledge (e.g. physics or history) and pedagogised knowledge (school physics or school history for different groups of learners).

Underlying these differences is a more basic difference between two types of knowledge. One is the *context-dependent* knowledge that is developed in the course of solving specific problems in everyday life. It can be *practical* – like knowing how to repair a mechanical or electrical fault or how to find a route on a map. It can also be *procedural*, like a handbook or set of regulations for health and safety. Context-dependent knowledge tells the individual how to do specific things. It does not explain or generalise; it deals with particulars. The second type of knowledge is *context-independent* or *theoretical knowledge*. This is knowledge that is developed to provide generalisations and makes claims to universality; it provides a basis for making judgements and is usually, but not solely, associated with the sciences. It is context-independent knowledge that is at least potentially acquired in school, and is what I referred to earlier as *powerful knowledge*.

 Inevitably schools are not always successful in enabling pupils to acquire powerful knowledge. It is also true that schools are more successful with some pupils than others. The success of pupils is highly dependent on the culture that they bring to school. Elite cultures that are less constrained by the material exigencies of life, are, not surprisingly, far more congruent with acquiring context-independent knowledge than disadvantaged and subordinate cultures. This means that if schools are to play a major role in promoting social equality, they have to take the knowledge base of the curriculum very seriously – even when this appears to go against the immediate demands of pupils (and sometimes their parents). They have to ask the question 'is this curriculum a means by which pupils can acquire powerful knowledge?' For children from disadvantaged homes, active participation in school may be the only opportunity that they have to acquire powerful knowledge and be able to move, intellectually at least, beyond their local and the particular circumstances. It does them no service to construct a curriculum around their experience on the grounds that it needs to be validated, and as a result leave them there.

Conceptualising school knowledge

The most sustained and original attempt to conceptualise school knowledge is that developed by the English sociologist Basil Bernstein (Bernstein, 1971, 2000). His distinctive insight was to emphasise the key role of knowledge boundaries, both as a condition for the acquisition of knowledge and as embodying the power relations that are necessarily involved in pedagogy. Bernstein begins by conceptualising boundaries in terms of two dimensions. First he distinguished between the *classification* of knowledge – or the degree of insulation between knowledge domains – and the *framing* of knowledge – the degree of insulation between school knowledge or the curriculum and the everyday knowledge that pupils bring to school. Second, he proposed that classification of knowledge can be *strong* – when domains are highly insulated from each other (as in the case of physics and history) – or *weak* – when there are low levels of insulation between domains (as in humanities or science curricula). Likewise, framing can be *strong,* when school and non-school knowledge are insulated from each other, or *weak*, when the boundaries between school and non-school knowledge are blurred (as in the case of many programmes in adult education and some curricula designed for less able pupils). In his later work Bernstein (2000) moves from a focus on *relations between* domains to the *structure of the domains* themselves by introducing a distinction between vertical and horizontal knowledge structures. This distinction refers to the way that different domains of knowledge embody different ideas of how knowledge progresses. Whereas in vertical knowledge structures (typically the natural sciences) knowledge progresses towards higher levels of abstraction (for example, from Newton's laws of gravity to Einstein's theory of relativity), in horizontal (or as Bernstein expresses it, segmental) knowledge structures like the social sciences and humanities, knowledge progresses by developing new languages which pose new problems. Examples are innovations in literary theory or approaches to the relationship between mind and brain. Bernstein's primary interest was in developing a language for thinking about different curriculum possibilities and their implications. His second crucial argument was to make the link that between knowledge structures, boundaries and learner identities. His hypothesis was that strong boundaries between knowledge domains and between school and non-school knowledge play a critical role in supporting learner identities and therefore are a condition for learners to progress. There are, however, a number of distinctive aspects to how Bernstein uses the idea of boundary, all of which can be traced back to Durkheim (Moore, 2004). First, boundaries refer to *relations between contents* not the *knowledge contents themselves*. Second, although strong boundaries have traditionally been expressed in disciplines and subjects, from Bernstein's perspective, this is a historical fact, and the disciplines and subjects that we know are not the only form that strong boundaries can take. Third, strong boundaries between contents will have distributional consequences; in other words they will be associated with certain inequalities of outcomes. Fourth, whether it is associated with creating new knowledge (in the university) or extending the acquisition of powerful knowledge to new groups of learners, innovation will involve crossing boundaries and calling identities into question. In other words school improvement from this perspective will involve both stability and change, or, in the terms set out in this chapter, the inter-relation between boundary maintenance and boundary crossing.

Conclusions

This chapter has argued that whatever their specific theoretical priorities, their policy concerns or their practical educational problems, educational researchers, policy makers and teachers must address the question 'what are schools for?' This means asking how and why school have emerged historically, at different times and in very different societies, as distinctive institutions with the specific purpose of enabling pupils to acquire knowledge not available to them at home or in their everyday life.[1] It follows, I have argued, that the key concept for the sociology of education (and for educators more generally) is *knowledge differentiation*.[2]

The concept of knowledge differentiation implies that much knowledge that it is important for pupils to acquire will be non-local and counter to their experience. Hence pedagogy will always involve an element of what the French sociologist Pierre Bourdieu refers to, over-evocatively and I think misleadingly, as *symbolic violence*. The curriculum has to take account of the everyday local knowledge that pupils bring to school, but such knowledge can never be a basis for the curriculum. The structure of local knowledge is designed to relate to the particular; it cannot provide the basis for any generalisable principles. To provide access to such principles is a major reason why all countries have schools.

The concept of *knowledge differentiation* sets a threefold agenda for schools and teachers, for educational policy makers and for educational researchers. First, each group (separately and together) must explore the relationship between the purpose of schools[3] to create the conditions for learners to acquire powerful knowledge and both their *internal structures* – such as subject divisions – and their *external structures* – such as the boundaries between schools and professional and academic 'knowledge producing communities' and between schools and the everyday knowledge of local communities.

Second, if schools are to help learners to acquire powerful knowledge, local, national and international groups of specialist teachers will need to be involved with university-based and other specialists in the ongoing selection, sequencing and inter-relating of knowledge in different domains. Schools therefore will need the autonomy to develop this professional knowledge; it is the basis of their authority as teachers and the trust that society places in them as professionals. This trust may at times be abused; however, any form of accountability must support that trust rather than try to be a substitute for it.

Third, educational researchers will need to address the tension in the essentially *conservative* role of schools as institutions with responsibility for knowledge transmission in society – especially as this aspect of their role is highlighted in a world increasingly driven by the instabilities of the market. However, 'conservative' has two very different meanings in relation to schools. It can mean preserving the stable conditions for acquiring 'powerful knowledge' and resisting the political or economic pressures for flexibility. A good example is how curricular continuity and coherence can be undermined by modularisation and the breaking up of the curriculum into so-called 'bite-sized chunks'. The 'conservatism' of educational institutions can also mean giving priority to the preservation of particular privileges and interests, such as those of students of a particular social class or of teachers as a professional group. Radicals and some sociologists of education have in the past tended to focus on this form of conservatism in schools and assume that if schools are to improve they have to become more like the non-school world –or more specifically the market. This takes us back to the tension between differentiation and de-differentiation of institutions that I referred to earlier in this chapter.

This chapter has made three related arguments. The first is that although answers to the question 'what are schools for?' will inevitably express tensions and conflicts of interests within the wider society, nevertheless educational policy makers, practising teachers and educational researchers need to address the distinctive purposes of schools. My second argument has been that there is a link between the emancipatory hopes associated with the expansion of schooling and the opportunity that schools provide for learners to acquire 'powerful knowledge' that they rarely have access to at home. Third, I introduce the concept of *knowledge differentiation* as a principled way of distinguishing between school and non-school knowledge. Contemporary forms of accountability are tending to weaken the boundaries between school and non-school knowledge on the grounds that they inhibit a more accessible and more economically relevant curriculum. I have drawn on Basil Bernstein's analysis to suggest that to follow this path may be to deny the conditions for acquiring powerful knowledge to the very pupils who are already disadvantaged by their social circumstances. Resolving this tension between political demands and educational realities is, I would argue, one of the major educational questions of our time.

Notes

1 If set in a broader theoretical context this chapter can be seen as locating the role of schools in the links between modernisation and social justice.

2 In beginning with a *theory of knowledge differences* and not just the fact of differences, the concept of *knowledge differentiation* is quite distinct from (and a critique of) the superficially similar idea that there are different types of knowledge.

3 Here, 'schools' is shorthand for *all* formal educational institutions.

References

Althusser, L. (1971) *Lenin and Philosophy and Other Essays*, New York, Monthly Review Press.

Baker, D.P. and LeTendre, G.K. (2005) *National Differences, Global Similarities: World Culture and the Future of Schooling*, Stanford University Press.

Bernstein, B. (1971) *Class, Codes and Control*, volume 1, London, Routledge and Kegan Paul.

—— (2000) *Pedagogy, Symbolic Control and Identity: Theory, Research, Critique*, 2nd edition, Oxford, Rowman & Littlefield.

Bowles, S. and Gintis, H. (1976) *Schooling in Capitalist America*, New York, Basic Books.

Foucault, M. (1991) *Remarks on Marx*, New York, Semiotext(e).

Illich, I. (1971) *Deschooling Society*, Harmondsworth, Penguin Books.

Moore, R. (2004) *Education and Society*, London, Polity Press.

Muller, J. (2000) *Reclaiming Knowledge: Social Theory, Curriculum and Education Policy*, London, RoutledgeFalmer.

White, J. (2007) *What Schools Are for and Why?* Impact Paper, Philosophy of Education Society of Great Britain.

Willis, P. (1977) *Learning to Labour*, New York, Columbia University Press.

Young, M. (1971) *Knowledge and Control: New Directions for the Sociology of Education*, London, Collier Macmillan.

—— (1998) *The Curriculum of the Future*, London, Falmer.

Reflective questions

1   How far do you think that the primary purpose of schools is to provide the conditions for pupils to acquire knowledge that takes them beyond their experience?
2   The purpose of schools has always been a 'contested idea'. Discuss.
3   The distinction between theoretical and everyday knowledge is the starting point of any curriculum. Discuss.

Further reading

Bernstein, B. (2000) *Pedagogy, Symbolic Control and Identity: Theory, Research, Critique*, 2nd edition, Oxford, Rowman & Littlefield.

Moore, R. (2004) *Education and Society*, London, Polity Press.

Muller, J. (2000) *Reclaiming Knowledge: Social Theory, Curriculum and Education Policy*, London, RoutledgeFalmer.

Young, M. (2007) *Bringing Knowledge Back In: From Social Constructivism to Social Realism in the Sociology of Education*, London, Routledge.

Young, M. and Gamble, J. (2006) *Knowledge, Curriculum and Qualifications for South African Further Education*, Pretoria, South Africa, HSRC Press.

Young, M. and Whitty, G. (1976) *Explorations in the Politics of School Knowledge*, Driffield, Yorks, Nafferton Books.

1.2 The school curriculum, theories of reproduction and necessary knowledge

Roy Nash

Introduction

In most school systems, after decades of 'reform', the curriculum is now so tightly regulated, the teaching methods so minutely prescribed, and the modes of evaluation so closely monitored, that a teacher might be forgiven for thinking a philosophical enquiry into the nature of knowledge to be concerned with a matter somewhere near the bottom of his or her day-to-day priorities. Those of us concerned with education, however, cannot opt out of the effort to understand why we do what we do and what consequences follow. It is one thing, in fact, to know what we are doing and quite another, as Bourdieu puts it, to know what what we do does. Such knowledge is a prerequisite for engagement in the struggle to strengthen the professional autonomy of teachers as educators.

What should school students learn? At one time they learned an English defined by its grammar, a geography of 'capes and bays', a geometry codified by Euclid, and a history of kings, queens and presidents. Many of the schools built in that era remain in use, but what they teach, and how they teach, may fairly be said to have changed. What we have now will also surely change. Through all this process of transformation, however, it is possible to detect an underlying continuity, for it may be argued that the modem school, established for at least 250 years, has privileged abstract logical thought and recognised the authority of the general principles of theoretical science. This, I will suggest, is the necessary core of the school curriculum. It is necessary for at least two reasons: first, it will be asserted that human beings are endowed with a capacity to learn about the nature of the world and that in the fulfilment of these capacities people are thus able to become what that they are capable of being; second, that the social tools of logic and science (a form of cultural heritage not to be lost) are, as a matter of fact, best suited to obtaining knowledge about the real structures of the social world. These theses, although here tied together, are usually treated independently and their distinct origins will be discussed.

Theories of differential access to education

It is important to explain that although the arguments are basically philosophical, the discussion is actually with the sociology of education and for students confronted with one of its central arguments. The definitive task of this sub-discipline is to provide explanations of the causes of social disparities in educational achievement and subsequent occupational status. This is the common problem of origins and destinations, of social mobility, of the creation of an 'inclusive society' (Halsey, Heath and Ridge, 1980). The relative odds of the son of a manual worker being promoted to a professional occupation, compared with those of the son of a professional being relegated to manual work, seem to have altered little for a generation or more (Goldthorpe, 2000). These historical comparisons are more easily made in the case of men rather than women because of recent changes in women's occupational patterns. Of course, there is a considerable degree of social mobility in developed states, perhaps as many working-class children better their parents' position as maintain it, and most of the mobility observed is actually achieved through the educational system. There is no need either to overestimate or underestimate the extent of class disparities in education.

The construction of accurate, or even plausible, theories to explain the extent of inequality/ difference, as it might be called, is more difficult than might be supposed. Most accounts turn out to be 'list theories' in which a number of 'factors' or 'variables' are described – and in their statistical version given an estimate of their contribution to the effect to be explained – with little or no theoretical integrity. In this context, it is understandable that many sociologists of education should turn to theories of cultural and social reproduction with an uncompromised pedigree in the genealogy of social science. If we can account for the maintenance of structural relations, above all those between social classes, largely in terms of the distribution of classed knowledge by the educational system, then school achievement disparities between classes are to that extent explained. Such theories are, as it happens, almost entirely resistant to empirical test, for the existence of differential class access to knowledge and a substantial degree of inter-generational class reproduction is generally considered enough to sustain the hypothesis, and their inherent weaknesses have not prevented social reproduction theories from being widely accepted by sociologists of education. The most influential of such theories is that derived from Bourdieu (Bourdieu and Passeron, 1977).

Bourdieu and the cultural arbitrary

A representative introduction to the 'dialectical perspective' in the sociology of education not unexpectedly places Bourdieu's concepts of 'cultural arbitrariness' and 'symbolic violence' at the heart of his account of the processes of educational differentiation (Izquierdo and Minguez, 2003). These authors explain that Bourdieu defends the argument that all academic culture is arbitrary on the grounds that 'its validity comes solely from the fact that it is the culture of the ruling classes, imposed on the whole society as if it were the only form of objective knowledge' (p. 27). Bourdieu's works, they add, 'stress the fact that academic culture is not neutral, since through cultural arbitrariness and symbolic violence incorporated into teaching, the concept of domination linked to teaching is concealed, thus contributing to the reproduction of class inequalities' (p. 28). Such might be called the standard position on Bourdieu. These concepts of symbolic violence and arbitrariness are closely related, for the imposition of a cultural arbitrary is a passable working definition of symbolic violence, in as much as a group exposed to knowledge, which it may accept or reject, that is not its own and likely, given the relations of power involved, to be against its interests, suffers an act of symbolic violence. The concept of arbitrariness, then, is the key to this aspect of Bourdieu's theory. The argument, somewhat simplified, is this: the educational system, being controlled by the dominant class, requires all its students to master an arbitrary class knowledge. The skills necessary to acquire that knowledge are, however, possessed by virtue of their family socialisation, and largely, therefore, by children of the dominant class and, in these circumstances, the typical experience for working-class children is relative educational failure and exclusion from the system.

The argument has not convinced all sociologists of education. Lynch (2000, p. 95), having outlined the standard view observes, '[t]his is not to suggest that all education in schools is, to use Bourdieu's phrase, a system of "symbolic violence" for it is patently not; there are aspects of curricula which are owned by all groups (literacy, numeracy, critical analysis, scientific method, etc.).' The critique of Bourdieu's concept needs, however, to go a little further than the simple assertion that some aspects of the school curriculum should not be recognised as arbitrary. What justification can be offered for the statement, other than it being 'patently' obvious, that literacy, numeracy, critical analysis, scientific method, and so on, are 'owned by all groups'? In a statistical sense it might be argued that this is not so; moreover, it is not so because of the actions of the school, which as a matter of fact controls the curriculum and determines the conditions of its access. Here the 'ownership' Lynch refers to must be one of human right rather than a sociological description of what is so. The attempt to argue that case is the principal goal of this chapter.

The anthropological narrative of human society is one of arbitrary difference. Whether family social relations in a traditional society are organised by matrilocality or patrilocality, by endogamy or exogamy, by filial or non-filial inheritance, is arbitrary in the sense that one will function as well as another, and the selection is emphatically grounded in a cultural rather than a genetic code. This central concept of anthropological theory plays so large a part in Bourdieu's discourse, for he was trained as an anthropologist, that LiPuma (1993) has identified in his theory three distinct references:

> any practice is arbitrary from a class-cultural standpoint in the sense that things could be otherwise, the social valuation afforded any practice within a given culture is arbitrary, and any practice will serve thus as an arbitrary symbolic marker of distinction.

These several usages, which Bourdieu does not openly acknowledge, contribute to the complexity of his conceptual framework and pose a series of problems that require particular resolutions. Bourdieu's concept of cultural capital, for example, is at once relative and normalised: it is relative in the sense that what counts as cultural capital is arbitrary, that is specific to a type of society, and normalised in the sense that in modern class-based societies people with the habits of a literate culture possess a symbolic capital that is recognised and legitimated in certain fields of practice. In this perspective, therefore, the relations between social class, knowledge and the world itself must be regarded as finally arbitrary.

The basic idea is brought out particularly clearly in the words of one of Bourdieu's American co-workers, Wacquant (2000, p. 115), in a structuralist analysis that melds all three of LiPuma's distinctions into a single argument:

> To uncover the social logic of consumption thus requires establishing, not a direct link between a given practice and a particular class category (e.g., horseback riding and the gentry), but the structural correspondences that obtain between two constellations of relations, the space of lifestyles and the space of social positions occupied by the different groups.

This passage is useful because it almost begs for critique. Wacquant makes the point, following Bourdieu, that the field of practice ('the space of lifestyles and the space of social positions') in which consumption is enjoyed, is informed by a 'logic' (a system of meaning at the level of cultural forms structural analysis attempts to reveal) that structures the 'choices' of, in this case, the 'gentry' to engage in horse riding. The common-sense idea that horse riding is a pastime of the upper classes whereas, say, dog racing is a pastime of the working classes (the sport is quite popular in parts of England) for historical and financial reasons is explicitly discounted by this form of analysis. No more than a hundred years separate us from the days of the elite cavalry regiments, themselves the conscious heirs of the medieval knights (almost invariably from the landed classes), bearers of an age-old tradition, and to overlook all this requires an act of 'forgetting' on a grand scale. In this context, only the slavish adherence to the imperatives of 'theory' is capable of allowing such forgetting. This is how structural theory dictates that its analyses proceed. But whether a particular analysis provides any insights worth having is another matter.

The standard reading of Bourdieu is arguably justified. His most influential statements (Bourdieu, 1984) see differences in socially conditioned intellectual aptitudes as arbitrary forms of mentality treated by the school as unequal 'gifts of nature' and transformed by its institutional power into actual differences in objective educational qualifications. And yet, at the same time, Bourdieu saw no reason why he should become a 'Bourdieusian' at the cost of his commitments to the central values of the school, which, arbitrary or not, he supported for intellectual and political reasons. One of his earliest papers advocates a 'universal pedagogy' (Bourdieu, 1974) and a late book, *Pascalian Meditations* (Bourdieu, 2000, p. 233) insists, against the grain of contemporary radicalism, on the grim realities and depressed potentials of working-class life.

In this context, the advocacy of a 'universal pedagogy' designed to enable children of all origins to access the school curriculum is interesting. Although Bourdieu only hinted at the nature of such a curriculum – regarding its creation and implementation, no doubt, as a matter of pedagogical expertise – the position is not easily compatible with the view that school knowledge must be seen as a class arbitrary. Bourdieu, furthermore, explicitly rejected 'radical' calls for the construction of a 'working-class' curriculum, a parallel system of knowledge, which he believed would simply deny working-class children what few opportunities the system allows them and undermine the efforts, small as their system effects must be, of dedicated teachers working to widen class access through their own 'universal pedagogy'.

Bourdieu was rather sharp in his contempt for certain 'romantic' theses on working-class education. The discussion in *Pascalian Meditations* is worth some reflection. Commenting on the almost inevitable responses, particularly those by youth, to the conditions of working-class life at its most dominated, Bourdieu dismisses in scathing terms the 'populist illusion nourished by a simplistic rhetoric of "resistance" to conceal one of the most tragic effects of the condition of the dominated – the inclination to violence'. We see working-class youths, he observes, without the prospects of permanent employment, drawn to 'acts of violence, death-defying games with cars, as a desperate way of existing in the eyes of others, achieving a recognised form of social existence, or simply making something happen rather than nothing' (p. 233). The entire context of this discussion makes it clear that Bourdieu, expressing himself with understandable caution, recognises that in such conditions of life one's dispositions to learn, that 'conditionability in the sense of a capacity to acquire non-natural, arbitrary capacities' (p. 136), including, of course, cognitive capacities, are likely to be unrealised. Bourdieu cannot be described as a scientific realist, his thought arises from other sources and bears other commitments, but his investigations always attempted to be true to the nature of social reality.

The case for necessary knowledge

The case for necessary knowledge is asserted rather than argued by Bourdieu, and in a context where his formal theory seems to lead to a different conclusion, this is hardly surprising. We must look elsewhere for the concepts to defend the idea of necessary knowledge. The bases of the argument are these: necessary knowledge is important to human flourishing and to a sound grasp of the nature of reality. Human well-being, human flourishing, is a value to which we should be committed. This is a frank statement of belief. There is an ancient discussion – the argument is at least as old as Aristotle – about whether 'ought' can be derived from 'is' (Anscombe, 1969). In the contemporary literature, Bhaskar (1993) argues that the move is legitimate (we make it whenever we see a child crying of hunger and say that its mother should feed it), whereas Flynn (2000) argues that the attempt always involves some casuistry (that children should be fed is not binding on those who think otherwise, and systematic starvation has been a policy even of democratic states). We need only argue, then, our belief that human beings are such that their individual and collective well-being is met when their intellectual capacities are developed to their fullest extent. Just as everyone has a specific genetic potential (genotype) to develop a certain physique, one that may or may not be realised in the environment available (phenotype), so do we have a potential to develop our powers of cognition. In the case of literacy-based skills, moreover, these cognitive powers are, almost certainly, very largely dependent on the social environment. There is no need to insist that this ontological foundation – one that rests on the nature of human beings – is demonstrated by this account of human being. It may be better, as Flynn suggests, to accept that arguments for the move from is to ought cannot be given the status of facts established by natural science. But if we are, in principle, committed to the idea that we should be all that we can be, then the case may be accepted.

The second argument maintains that necessary knowledge is all but defined as that which gives access to the nature of reality. This involves stating the case for scientific realism. Like most philosophical doctrines, realism comes in a number of varieties, but the basis of scientific realism is just an acceptance that things in the series, atoms, molecules, grains of sand, sand-castles, beaches and so on, are real entities. A physicist's model of a molecule (a thing of plastic spheres and connecting rods depicting its atomic structure) and an environmental engineer's model of a beach (a 100th-scale model in a tank where its stability can be tested under different conditions) are representations of real, and actual, things. This doctrine is opposed to idealist perspectives, some of which regard all metaphysical discussions of reality as meaningless, whereas others are content to dismiss them as naive. Scientific realism accepts the emergence of properties at different levels of being: a molecule, such as water, has properties, like being wet, that are not possessed by its component atoms hydrogen and oxygen. There is no good reason, in the view of many philosophers, why reality should not be denied to social systems as emergent properties of social entities (Bunge, 1996). The child building the sand-castle is a member of a family, that is a social organisation constituted by its members as a system, within a larger society. It is, moreover, a particular organisation of that larger society, the local district council, responsible among other things for the maintenance of the beach, that has commissioned an engineer's report, and its actions may well determine whether there is any sand to build with in years to come. And so it is possible to argue for the reality of the social as emergent properties of organised human groups. It is the task of sociology to discover the nature of such social properties and study their effects.

As realists we can say this: the world exists; that we are beings so constituted by the capacities of our senses and cognitive capacities to know that it exists and to form theories about what it is like; that we are able to check some, at least, of these theories against what the world is actually like and so gain accurate knowledge of it; and, therefore, may maintain that the demonstrated knowledge of science and the social tools of its production should be given a central place in the school curriculum. The continual interrogation of the curriculum in these terms does not entail commitment to non-realist concepts of knowledge and truth. That French schools teach a literature of Molière and Stendhal and English schools a literature of Shakespeare and Dickens is an anthropological arbitrary at the level of their nationhood; that they both teach differential calculus is an anthropological arbitrary at the level of their existence as modern states dependent for their survival upon a sophisticated technology; that they teach literature and mathematics, however, is also a matter of universal necessity given that the purpose of education is to enable students to learn how the physical and social world is constituted and how it operates.

If this section reads like common sense, then so much the better. There is often little wrong with common sense. If realism is right, then what we know to be real, about physical and social entities, ought to be at the heart of the school curriculum. This is another of those is/ought moves that can bring so much difficulty. Once again, it need only be declared that realism is a commitment and, as has already been pointed out, not one shared by everyone. Nevertheless, in a democratic polity there might be a case to be made for resolving this matter by the ordinary processes of collective decision-making. If the decision stands with the idealists, then so be it, but that outcome seems unlikely, even though there are specific areas where non-realist positions, such as the doctrinal resistance to Darwinism, are widely adopted. This chapter argues that modern science has been successful in investigating and demonstrating the nature of reality, for as Bhaskar points out, were it not basically correct our telecommunications would not operate, our bridges would not stand, and our aeroplanes would never get off the ground. This argument, that things must be real or our technology would fail, may put things the wrong way round, for one might better say that because things are real our technology works by virtue of being based on a science that has got it right. In any event, it is argued here on realist grounds that the logic and methods of science should be at the core of the schools' curriculum in necessary knowledge.

One might say that an accurate knowledge of the world is the gateway to an autonomous form of life. Durkheim (1957, p. 91), a realist of a certain variety with respect to social forces and yet not a scientific realist in the contemporary sense, seems to have taken the same viewpoint:

> To be autonomous means, for a human being, to understand the necessities he has and to bow to and accept them with full knowledge of the facts. Nothing that we can do can make the laws of things other than they are, but we free ourselves of them in thinking them, that is, in making them ours by thought.

These words from *Professional Ethics and Civic Morals* (1957), addressed principally to teachers a century ago, from a sociologist strongly influenced by idealist philosophies, might be considered somewhat provocative in this context, but the strains in Bourdieu's argument, the apparent contradiction between the formal theory and the personal commitment to the principles of logic and science as the essential tools of intellectual practice, have deep roots. It is no accident that Durkheim and Bourdieu share the Enlightenment values of French republican ideology (Lane, 2000). These arguments, with their distinctly abstract quality, may be placed in a more practical context with reference to the teaching of realist science.

On the teaching of realist science

Teachers should want students to learn what the world is actually like. Scientists do that by observation, developing theories, formulating hypotheses, carrying out experiments and so on. This is how scientists construct knowledge. It seems reasonable, therefore, to design a science curriculum in which school students can do much the same. They will learn science by doing science as scientists do. Of course, they will not be smashing atoms, but they can weigh things in and out of water, roll marbles down inclined planes and so on, and with some unobtrusive guidance from the teacher they might get as far as the science of Archimedes and Galileo. The idea has certain attractions. It means, at the very least, that the curriculum will be full of purposeful activity directed at discovering something about the properties of material objects, and in practice this is probably how such a curriculum operates (Osborne, 1997). Nevertheless, the project is rhetorically embedded in a discourse that Matthews (1995) is not alone in finding objectionable. If students are to act as scientists, the argument goes, then the theories they construct as a result of their observations and experiments should be taken seriously as their science. In principle, their scientific theories of specific gravity or momentum, for example, are as meaningful, considered as systems of discourse, as those of any other scientists. If students are to act as scientists, then their activities should be guided only in the most general methodological sense by the teacher, who should certainly not impose her own theories. Indeed, it is even possible to argue that an individual completely ignorant of 'standard' scientific theories might be the ideal teacher for a constructivist classroom. This discourse is grievously in error. It is wrong in suggesting, if not actually stating, that one theory is as good as another; wrong in thinking that school children can, in fact, rediscover Galilean science (which is highly sophisticated and actually contrary to common sense); and wrong about the appropriate role of the science teacher. Anti-realist conceptions of science, moreover, undermine the scientific project itself by downgrading the significance of demonstration and the possibility of more or less accurate knowledge.

To know the world as it is should be recognised as being in itself a form of power: not a power over nature but over oneself in relation to nature. Where such knowledge and this sense of its worth is not part of the taken-for-granted cultural framework within students' families, then the school may need to assume the responsibility to provide such contextualisation. But it may be argued that working-class families generally do recognise the practical value of knowledge, in craft expertise, for example, and the foundations of working-class thought in a realist and practical conception of knowledge are secure. It is in this area that the constructivist influence on education might bear some reconsideration. Rudolph (2000, p. 412) notes that 'students often possess naive realist perceptions of the nature of science' and 'privilege demonstration and experimentation over other forms of reasoning', and if this is so then far from being 'a bad thing' it might provide a sound basis for a scientific education. Is it self-evident that the sort of idealism students might pick up from some constructivist teaching, which is unlikely to be a highly sophisticated understanding, is superior to 'naive realism'? The realism considered so naive may more likely be grounded in a robust materialism, which is a philosophy with a long history in working-class radicalism.

Many students, particularly those from working-class families, have only the sketchiest outline of the great range of technical and scientific occupations available in the contemporary economy. School students might think of medicine or pharmacy, but rarely of biochemistry, food technology, meteorology, metallurgy or any of the huge range of available scientific occupations. Bringing together the sciences in terms of their value, giving some attention to their history and demonstrating to students the critical value of such knowledge would provide a contextualisation of great benefit. Through video production, debates, scientific clubs, magazines and other activities designed to demonstrate the fundamental unity of science and the practical integration of its fields of application, students might gain a fuller appreciation of the value of their scientific education. It may be important that teachers and others who work in schools should give students an elaborated sense of the career opportunities open to them as people who have mastered a body of scientific knowledge. The reason, after all, why mathematics with calculus is valued more highly than alternative mathematics is precisely because it is more useful to any one of the myriad technologies that sustain industrial civilisation than so-called 'alternative mathematics'. Students may need to understand, moreover, that mathematical and scientific knowledge is valuable, that is applicable in the most direct sense, to fields other than the strictly vocational. An informed participation in many areas of organised life, as a citizen and as a member of different communities, can only be enhanced by a scientific education. Debates about environmental and planning issues, often hotly contested, are effectively closed at the highest level to those with an uncertain grasp of the concepts and methods of modern science.

Conclusion

Bourdieu's theory of reproduction has been subjected to critique in this chapter. The critique, however, should be interpreted as an argument with Bourdieu rather than against Bourdieu. It is worth arguing with Bourdieu for the simple reason that he has something worthwhile to say. In the broad anthropological sense, accepted by Bourdieu, all knowledge can be regarded as arbitrary within a given society. The practices that constitute and reproduce society are analysed in terms of their fundamental principles that are naturally acquired through the process of socialisation and thus maintained as learned habits. Bourdieu, as any introductory text will point out, refers to such dispositions to act as constituting the habitus. These core principles will – it is possible to say almost necessarily – be transmitted from generation to generation as embodied dispositions. Such knowledge, moreover, has the property of symbolic violence in as much as it is the cultural property of a particular group and mobilised in the struggle for dominance. There is no need to suppose that school knowledge is organised and taught with the conscious intention of excluding those with an inferior habitus; nevertheless, as Bourdieu (1974) argues, it effectively achieves that end. This concept of the arbitrary, therefore, drawing further support from the concept of symbolic violence, has become the basis of the widely accepted argument that the cause of inequality/difference, within the school, is the classed and culturally arbitrary curriculum. This theory is interesting and not self-evidently wrong.

Nevertheless, the standard Bourdieusian narrative of educational reproduction, for all that it might seem impeccably derived from Bourdieu's conceptual framework, is questioned even by Bourdieu. His advocacy of a universal pedagogy and his outright rejection of 'populist illusions' are derived from ideological commitments more important to him than unreflective conformity to the imperatives of theory. Bourdieu saw theory as a tool, to be applied when it was useful to the task in hand and put aside when it was not, and the idea of selecting the task according the tools available never occurred to him. These inconsistencies, all the same, continue to be a source of strain in his theory and practice.

It will be no contradiction, therefore, having argued for the placement of necessary knowledge at the heart of the school curriculum, to conclude this chapter with an appeal not to dismiss Bourdieu's critique of arbitrary knowledge and symbolic violence but, on the contrary, to continue to investigate the nature of the school. For while it is arguable that the most flagrant elements of classed knowledge (Latin being a prime example) have been removed as a result of democratic pressure, there remain areas of knowledge where the class basis of its selection and organisation is little disguised. It is right that these should be subject to continual critical attention. This essay will have misled readers if it is taken as support for the status quo or as a denial that working-class school students are free from subjection to the symbolic violence of a class arbitrary. To argue that the school's curriculum should be founded on a realist science and a moral concept of human flourishing is to say nothing at all about the nature of the contemporary school. Even so, what the school is like, in this respect as in any other, should be a matter for theoretical and empirical investigation, and not 'read off' from Bourdieu's theory, for in this area also the principles of logic and science are there to be applied, and not passed aside on the basis of theoretical pronouncements thus endowed with the power to constitute the given.

References

Anscombe, G.E.M. (1969) 'Modern moral philosophy', in Hudson, W.H. (ed.), *The Is–ought Question: A Collection of Papers on the Central Problem in Moral Philosophy*, London, Macmillan, pp. 175–95.

Bhaskar, R. (1993) *Dialectic: The Pulse of Freedom*, London, Verso.

Bourdieu, P. (1974) 'The school as a conservative force: scholastic and cultural inequalities', in Eggleston, J. (ed.), *Contemporary Research in the Sociology of Education*, London, Methuen, pp. 32–46.

—— (1984) *Distinction: A Social Critique of the Judgement of Taste*, trans. R. Nice, Cambridge, MA, Harvard University.

—— (2000) *Pascalian Meditations*, trans. R. Nice, Cambridge, Polity Press.

Bourdieu, P. and Passeron, J.-C. (1977) *Reproduction in Education, Society and Culture*, trans. R. Nice, London, Sage.

Bunge, M. (1996) *Finding Philosophy in Social Science*, New Haven, Yale University Press.

Durkheim, E. (1957) *Professional Ethics and Civic Morals*, London, Routledge & Kegan Paul.

Flynn, J.R. (2000) *How to Defend Humane Ideals: Substitutes for Objectivity*, Lincoln, NB and London, University of Nebraska Press.

Goldthorpe, J.H. (2000) *On Sociology: Numbers, Narratives, and the Integration of Theory and Research*, Oxford, Oxford University Press.

Halsey, A.H., Heath, A.F. and Ridge, J.M. (1980) *Origins and Destinations: Family, Class, and Education in Modern Britain*, Oxford, Clarendon Press.

Izquierdo, M.M. and Minguez, A.M. (2003) 'Sociological theory of education in the dialectical perspective', in Torres, C.A. and Antikainen, A. (eds), *The International Handbook on the Sociology of Education: An International Assessment of New Research and Theory*, Lanham, Rowman & Littlefield.

Lane, J.F. (2000) *Pierre Bourdieu: A Critical Introduction*, London, Pluto.

LiPuma, E. (1993) 'Culture and the concept of culture in a theory of practice', in Calhoun, C., LiPuma, E. and Postone, M. (eds), *Bourdieu: Critical Perspectives*, Cambridge,, Polity Press, pp. 14–34.

Lynch, K. (2000) 'Research and theory on equality and education', in Hallinan, M.T. (ed.), *Handbook of the Sociology of Education*, New York, Kluwer Academic/Plenum, pp. 85–105.

Matthews, M.R. (1995) *Challenging New Zealand Science Education*, Palmerston North, Dunmore Press.

Osborne, M.D. (1997) 'Balancing the individual and the group: a dilemma for the constructivist teacher', *Journal of Curriculum Studies*, 29(2), pp. 183–96.

Rudolph, J.L. (2000) 'Reconsidering the "nature of science" as a curriculum component', *Journal of Curriculum Studies*, 32(3), pp. 402–19.

Wacquant, L. (2000) 'Durkheim and Bourdieu: the common plinth and its cracks', in Fowler, B. (ed.), *Reading Bourdieu on Society and Culture*, Oxford, Blackwell.

Reflective questions

1   Are some forms of knowledge necessary?
2   Bourdieu argues that these forms of knowledge have been appropriated by the profes-
    sional middle class in that the cultural capital of the home, in the form of books, reading,
    etc., is consistent with the disciplines and expectations of the school. If this is so then
    how can working-class children access these forms of knowledge?
3   Can the inequality in life chances between different classes be explained by inequalities
    in knowledge?

Further reading

Bourdieu, P. (1974) 'The school as a conservative force: scholastic and cultural inequalities', in Eggleston, J.
    (ed.), *Contemporary Research in the Sociology of Education*, London, Methuen, pp. 32–46.
—— (2000) *Pascalian Meditations*, trans. R. Nice, Cambridge, Polity Press.
Bourdieu, P. and Passeron, J.-C. (1977) *Reproduction in Education, Society and Culture*, trans. R. Nice,
    London, Sage.
Dale, R. (2009) 'Pedagogy and cultural convergence', in Daniels, H., Lauder, H. and Porter, J. (eds),
    Educational Theories, Cultures and Learning, London, Routledge, pp. 27–38.
Young, M., chapter 1.1, this volume.

1.3 The influence of constructivism on teaching and learning in classrooms

Sarah E. Scott and
Annemarie Sullivan Palincsar

The Blindmen and the Elephant

It was six men of Hindustan
To learning much inclined,
Who went to see the Elephant
(Though all of them were blind)
That each by observation
Might satisfy the mind.

The first approached the Elephant
And happening to fall
Against his broad and sturdy side
At once began to bawl:
'Bless me, it seems the Elephant
Is very like a wall'.

The second, feeling of his tusk,
Cried, 'Ho! What have we here
So very round and smooth and sharp?
To me 'tis mighty clear
This wonder of an Elephant
Is very like a spear'.

The third approached the animal,
And happening to take
The squirming trunk within his hands,
Then boldly up and spake:
'I see,' quoth he, 'the Elephant
Is very like a snake.'

The Fourth reached out an eager hand,
And felt about the knee.
'What most this wondrous beast is like
Is mighty plain,' quoth he;
''Tis clear enough the Elephant
Is very like a tree!'

The Fifth, who chanced to touch the ear,
Said: 'E'en the blindest man
Can tell what this resembles most;
Deny the fact who can,
This marvel of an Elephant
Is very like a fan!'

The Sixth no sooner had begun
About the beast to grope,
Than, seizing on the swinging tail
That fell within his scope,
'I see,' quoth he, 'the Elephant
Is very like a rope!'

And so these men of Hindustan
Disputed loud and long,
Each in his own opinion
Exceeding stiff and strong,
Though each was partly in the right
And all were in the wrong.

So oft in theologic wars,
The disputants, I ween,
Rail on in utter ignorance
Of what each other mean,
And prate about an Elephant
Not one of them has seen!

John Godfrey Saxe[1]

Introduction

This poem is typically used to illustrate the fact that one's perspective shapes one's reality, and, furthermore, that even though we may have access to only a tiny portion of reality, our inclination is to extrapolate from that understanding as though our sense-making were both accurate and complete. We think this is a fitting story for introducing the reader to constructivism. At its core, constructivist theory suggests that we create our understanding through our experiences, and that the character of our experiences is influenced profoundly by the lenses we bring to those experiences.

Constructivism is a theory of knowledge, not a theory of pedagogy. However, constructivist theory has numerous implications for learning and teaching. In this chapter we will characterize the features of this theory and provide a brief history of its development. Then, as befits the title, we will devote most of our attention to describing how this theory has influenced conceptions of classroom activity, including the roles of teachers and learners in classrooms and the nature of the curriculum.

The features of constructivist theory

Constructivist theory has captured the attention of writers and researchers in the social sciences, natural sciences and humanities for decades. It is a perspective that has played a significant role in efforts to transform education. The literature on constructivism is vast and has been growing exponentially over the past several decades. In the literature you will find at least six alternative core paradigms of constructivism: social, radical, social constructionism, information processing constructivism, cybernetic systems and sociocultural approaches to mediated action (see Steffe and Gale, 1995, for a helpful presentation and discussion of these paradigms). Hence, constructivism refers to many ideas, and, as Burbules (2000) notes, these ideas are joined by the merest thread of family resemblance and often express quite contradictory views. It is probably safe to say that what unifies constructivist perspectives is a rejection of the view that the locus of knowledge is in the individual; learning and under-standing are regarded as inherently social; cultural activities and tools (ranging from symbol systems to artifacts to language) are regarded as integral to conceptual development.

It would be impossible to write a chapter on constructivism that satisfied the vast and complex terrain of this theory. That said, to give the reader a more complete sense of constructivism, we present a number of characterizations from the vast literature. We hope that these characterizations will be useful to the reader in constructing a meaningful and useful notion of constructivism.

- Constructivists argue that there is no such thing as ready-made knowledge; regardless of what a teacher does, learners construct their own knowledge. All learning, whether it entails evaluating new ideas, generating an explanation, acquiring a specific skill, or even commit-ting something to memory, requires reinterpreting the information to be learned or used in light of one's existing understandings and abilities. A corollary to this claim is that no two people learn the 'same' material in precisely the same way (see Burbules, 2000).
- Constructivism is typically contrasted with a Cartesian view of knowledge and coming to know. The Cartesian model assumes that there is a fundamental division – or dualism – between body and mind. The primary dualism is that the mind is isolated from the world and from the body. This means that, according to this model, knowledge cannot come from the actions of the body, but, must either be innate or be received from the outside by perceptual input. You may recall that Descartes coined the expression: 'I think, therefore I am.' In contrast, John Sealy Brown, speaking from a construc-tivist perspective, offers the expression, 'We participate and therefore we are.' From a constructivist perspective, mind does not reside solely in the individual, but rather is an attribute of a system with multiple individuals interacting with one another and with tools; these tools include language, ideas that have been generated across time, computers, personal digital assistants, rulers, and the like.
- Constructivists are often contrasted with realists. Realists conceive of knowledge as objective, complete and unchanging; furthermore, they argue that knowledge disputes can be settled by appeals to 'the way the world is'. Constructivists, in contrast, are more likely to think that knowledge is partial, provisional, and imperfect, and that knowledge disputes are often intractable because strongly held beliefs are intertwined with other social and cultural elements that groups may be reluctant to give up or change (Bredo, 2000; Phillips, 2000).
- Relatedly, constructivists view disciplines such as mathematics, history, science, and literary studies as socially constructed human activities. Each domain has a history, a

tradition, and a culture. As students are provided with access to the norms and conventions that are associated with these disciplines, they ultimately construct their own appreciation of and understanding of these fields (Richards, 1991).

What is the evidence for constructivism?

Evidence for constructivism arises from research on student thinking which suggests that simply telling students something will not necessarily result in understanding or learning. Over the past six decades literally thousands of research articles have been published on the topic of students' conceptions on various topics. Broadly speaking, this research suggests that people: (a) develop ideas about their world, (b) develop meanings for unfamiliar terms, and (c) develop strategies to generate explanations for how and why things behave as they do (Osborne and Wittrock, 1983). Importantly, research has also shown that these conceptions emerge before students ever receive formal instruction on the topic and that students' conceptions are resistant to change even with instructional intervention.

Take, for example, the relationship between force and acceleration. Researchers who have investigated students' understanding of this basic principle of science have found that students often explain that 'motion implies a force' – a preconception that students develop prior to formal instruction in physics and an idea that is resistant to change (Clement, 1982). The task of teaching students about Newton's first and second laws, then, from a constructivist perspective means taking into consideration the preconceptions and (mis)understandings, or naive conceptions, that students bring to the science classroom.

What is the history of constructivism?

Presenting a definitive historical account of constructivism is a difficult task. The many and varied roots of contemporary constructivism are united by the view that the individual is an active participant in constructing reality and not just a blank slate to be written on by more knowledgeable others.

Constructivism is often presented as a response to behaviorism. The behaviorist tradition is marked by an antimentalistic stance toward thinking; behaviorists pay no heed to individuals' intentions, cognitive structures, or maturation. From a behaviorist perspective, evidence for learning is a change in the probability of a specific observed response, and that probability is determined by the deployment of learning mechanisms, such as reinforcement, punishment, discrimination, generalization, and extinction. The instructional model that best reflects the tenets of behaviorism is referred to as direct instruction teaching. The hallmark of direct instruction is the active and directive role assumed by the teacher, who maintains control of the pace, sequence, and content of the lesson:

> The teacher, in a face-to-face, reasonably formal manner, tells, shows, models, demonstrates, teaches the skill to be learned. The key word here is teacher, for it is the teacher who is in command of the learning situation and leads the lesson, as opposed to having instruction 'directed' by a worksheet, kit, learning center, or workbook.
>
> (Baumann, 1988, p. 714)

The research regarding direct instruction suggests that, while it is an effective means of teaching factual content, there is less evidence that this instruction transfers to higher-order cognitive skills such as reasoning and problem solving, nor is there sufficient evidence that direct instruction teaching results in the flexibility necessary for students to use the targeted strategies in novel contexts (Peterson and Walberg, 1979).

Immanuel Kant and Jean Piaget had considerable influence on constructivist theory writ large, and Piaget and Lev Vygotsky are often cited as the key scholars in constructivist learning theory. Immanuel Kant, who significantly influenced Piaget's thinking, proposed that it is the mind that provides the categories of knowing, while experience yields the content. Piaget (1955) argued that it is through the child's experiences manipulating and changing the world that the child acquires knowledge about relations within and between people and objects. Piaget was interested in the logical structures that the child uses to organize the world he or she experiences. He investigated these structures through a series of experiments in which he probed the child's thinking through interviews. Often the child's incorrect answers provided a powerful window into children's ways of making sense of the world. These ways of viewing the world were qualitatively different than the ways in which adults view the world. Furthermore, he claimed that these structures developed in stages that transpire from birth through the first 19 years of life.

Russian psychologist Lev Vygotsky (1978) was the theorist who added the importance of social context to constructivist epistemology. Vygotsky suggested: 'The social dimension of consciousness is primary in time and in fact. The individual dimension of consciousness is derivative and secondary' (Vygotsky, 1978, p. 30, cited in Wertsch and Bivens, 1992). From this perspective, mental functioning of the individual is not simply derived from social interaction; rather, the specific structures and processes revealed by individuals can be traced to their interactions with others. This tenet has been illustrated by examining the interactions between individuals with disparate knowledge levels; for example, children and their caregivers or experts and novices. Illustrative is the cross-cultural research of Rogoff who studied the supportive contexts in which Mayan children acquire knowledge and strategies:

> The routine arrangements and interactions between children and their caregivers and companions provide children with thousands of opportunities to observe and participate in the skilled activities of their culture. Through repeated and varied experience in supported routine and challenging situations, children become skilled practitioners in the specific cognitive activities in their communities.
>
> (Rogoff, 1991, p. 351)

Vygotsky was critical of Piaget's theory in which 'maturation is viewed as a precondition of learning but never the result of it' (Vygotsky, 1978, p. 80). In contrast, Vygotsky proposed:

> Learning awakens a variety of internal developmental processes that are able to operate only when the child is interacting with people in his environment and with his peers … learning is not development; however, properly organized learning results in mental development and sets in motion a variety of developmental processes that would be impossible apart from learning. Thus learning is a necessary and universal aspect of the process of developing culturally organized, specifically human, psychological functions.
>
> (p. 90)

In support of this perspective, Vygotsky (1978) introduced the construct of the *zone of proximal development* (ZPD) as a fundamentally new approach to the problem that learning should be matched in some manner with the child's level of development. He argued that to understand the relationship between development and learning, we must distinguish between two developmental levels: the actual and the potential levels of development. The actual refers to those accomplishments a child can demonstrate alone or perform independently; in contrast to potential levels of development as suggested by the ZPD – what children can do with assistance: 'the distance between the actual developmental level as determined by independent problem solving and the level of potential development as determined through problem solving under adult guidance or in collaboration with more capable peers' (p. 85). The ZPD was regarded as a better, more dynamic and relative indicator of cognitive development than what children accomplished alone.

In summary, from this perspective, productive interactions are those which orient instruction toward the ZPD; otherwise, instruction lags behind the development of the child. 'The only good learning is that which is in advance of development' (Vygotsky, 1978, p. 89). Hence, from a Vygotskian perspective, cognitive development is studied by examining the processes that one participates in when engaged in shared endeavors and how this engagement influences engagement in other activities. Development occurs as children learn general concepts and principles that can be applied to new tasks and problems; whereas from a Piagetian perspective, learning is constrained by development. This is a helpful example of how the particular 'strain' of constructivism that one embraces can result in different pedagogical decisions. Influenced by Piaget's stage theory, a teacher might refrain from engaging students in certain kinds of scientific inquiry experiences that call for children to, for example, design controlled experiments (Metz, 1995) guided by the belief that children – even in the middle school grades – do not have the intellectual wherewithal to engage in this type of scientific reasoning. However, from a Vygotskian perspective, a teacher would argue for the importance of students engaging in design work, recognizing that the teaching will be in anticipation of competence and altering the demands of the task and the level of support to accommodate individual differences among students.

What are the implications of constructivism for curriculum and pedagogy?

Konold (1995) has observed, and we agree, that: 'For all the differences among the various perspectives [on constructivism], the prescriptions offered for the classroom seem remarkably similar' (p. 181). Hence, rather than try to pair a particular perspective on constructivism with its implications for teaching and learning, we have chosen to illustrate the influence of constructivism on general notions of classroom culture, roles of teachers and students, and subject-matter specific curriculum and pedagogy. Before proceeding, several caveats are in order. Constructivism is a theory of knowledge; it is not a theory of teaching. Hence, what you are about to read are extrapolations from theory. A related caveat is that constructivist perspectives lend themselves to discussions of teaching for conceptual understanding, as opposed to learning from rote memory; hence, the researchers you will learn about aspire to fairly ambitious educational objectives. Finally, it is probably safe to say that many teachers have long operated as though guided – perhaps at an intuitive level – by constructivist notions; what constructivism does is to provide a solid conceptual basis for teacher decision making and activity. We will try, in each of our examples, to capture this conceptual basis.

There are literally hundreds of research efforts from which we could have drawn. Rather than provide a broad survey of approaches, we selected particular efforts for which there was empirical support and a clear set of principles that could be identified as constructivist in orientation. Furthermore, we have chosen examples that span the grades, as well as the content domains.

A constructivist window on the culture of the classroom

Fostering Communities of Learners (FCL) is an outstanding example of an educational reform effort influenced by 'constructivist pedagogy'. The developers, Ann Brown and Joseph Campione, worked closely with classroom teachers in upper-elementary and middle-school grades in urban settings. Although the original research was undertaken in science classrooms, the principles of FCL have been applied to learning in other domains (for example, see Mintrop, 2004, for discussion of an application in social studies classrooms and Whitcomb, 2004, for discussion of FCL in a high-school English language arts classroom).

The theoretical concepts most central to the design of FCL classrooms included a focus on zones of proximal development and a flexible curriculum that focused on developing deep understandings of a few key concepts. First, the classroom was conceived as being composed of multiple zones of proximal development (Vygotsky, 1978) through which participants navigated at various rates and through various routes. Second, teachers and peers engaged in 'seeding' the environment with ideas, knowledge, and other tools, which were appropriated by children in various ways as a function of the current zone of proximal development in which they were engaged. Finally, there was an ongoing process of mutual negotiation as members of the class engaged in shared activities and came to shared understandings of the activities in which they were engaged (Brown and Campione, 1994).

In addition to these theoretical principles, curriculum design was a feature key to understanding how activity unfolded in FCL contexts. The curricula were organized around thematic units; for example, biological themes included interdependence and adaptation; and environmental science themes included balance, competition, and cooperation. Children had access to a broad array of material to support their inquiry, including text, video, and a computer environment in which children corresponded with one another, as well as with expert consultants. Much of the activity in FCL classrooms occurred in the context of collaborative learning either using Reciprocal Teaching (Palincsar and Brown, 1984) or the jigsaw method (Aronson, 1978) in which children were assigned part of the topic of study to learn and subsequently to teach to others; hence becoming expert relative to different aspects of the topic under study and then sharing their expertise with their peers.

In addition to using traditional measures of achievement, the Brown and Campione team employed a variety of dynamic assessments (Brown and Campione, 1990), conducted primarily through clinical interviews in which interviewers would probe student reasoning about problems that were central to the curriculum, as well as problems that provided the opportunity to assess transfer. Results of these assessments, as well as analyses of classroom discourse, were used to inform the redesign of the curriculum and instruction.

In FCL, we see instruction designed to support an active role for the learners, who are encouraged to assume control of their activity and be reflective in the process, essentially becoming critics of their own learning process. To attain these goals of critical thinking and reflection, Brown and Campione were committed to deep disciplinary content as the grist for instruction, preferring to focus on the teaching of a few 'lithe and beautiful and immensely generative' ideas (Bruner, 1969, p. 121). In hand with rich content, Brown and Campione were keenly aware of the role that expert others played in advancing students' ability to engage with these ideas. In the absence of knowledgeable others, students were unlikely to be pushed to higher levels of understanding or to confront and correct misunderstandings. Recognizing the burden this places on classroom teachers, who are seldom subject-matter specialists (especially in the elementary grades), they expanded the expertise of the classroom community with the addition of content area experts, who were accessible through electronic media or in person.

The issue of transfer, or the capacity and inclination to apply learning to and in novel contexts, was central to FCL. Brown and Campione proposed that integral to promoting transfer in the classroom were opportunities for students to come to understand a variety of domain-specific concepts, as well as the more general processes useful to advancing new and continued learning. Such understanding would enable students to talk knowingly about these processes, as well as to use them flexibly. These tenets implied that instruction must first of all be about the task of mastering a rich domain of knowledge. In addition, instruction in this rich domain must include modeling that is designed to help students acquire the critical thinking and reflection activities that will guide their thinking as they enter new areas of learning. Finally, consistent with their belief in the social nature of cognition, Brown and Campione urged that students be provided with many occasions for explaining to others (and hence to themselves) the characteristics and limitations of what they are learning, and the reasons they are engaged in particular learning activities.

Teaching history from a constructivist perspective

The ability to make evidence-based claims is a central tenet of many disciplines, but what counts as evidence, and how one must interpret this evidence, differs across disciplines. History educator Susan Mosborg (2002) notes that historians are storytellers; but, in contrast to fictional narratives, the claims made in historical texts are subject to warrant. This is consistent with the writing of Perfetti, Britt, and Georgi (1995), who suggest that one of the important objectives in teaching history is inculcating in students an appreciation that while evidence counts, one must also evaluate the sources of evidence in order to evaluate the strength of the story.

Reflecting the spirit of constructivism, Mosborg (2002) points out that surfacing students' own *background narratives*, which she defines as 'the socially shared schema of historical events and ideas that appear to be activated by an encounter with a story on a given topic' (p. 333) is a powerful means of leading students to contrast the past and present, as well as to contrast their own views with those of others. In Mosborg's research, these background narratives were activated by engaging students in conversations about contemporary newspaper articles.

Sharing goals similar to those of Mosborg, another history educator, Robert Bain, sought to investigate how teachers could effectively use textbooks in the teaching of history, despite some of their limitations. Bain (2006) identified these limitations as: the 'objective' voice in which they are typically written, the tone of certainty, and the dry presentation of undocumented facts. In an approach that Bain describes as 'transforming ritualized interactions', Bain supported his secondary students to assume a critical stance in their reading of their history texts by preparing them to become experts on a particular historical topic (the fourteenth-century pandemic of bubonic plague). To do this, he provided the students with a broad array of documents, including a majority of primary documents from the European record, along with primary sources from China and the Muslim world. The textbook was not among the documents students consulted. Whole-class and small-group presentations and discussions provided the contexts in which students were supported to read, weigh, and corroborate evidence regarding such issues as how fourteenth-century citizens made sense of the plague and how families and institutions responded to the plague. Following these rich experiences, the students were invited to consider the textbook's account of the plague.

To assess what students learned though this activity, Bain asked his students to write letters to the textbook's authors. Bain documented that these secondary students, as a collective, identified the same set of historiographic shortcomings identified by professional historians who critiqued this textbook.

Developing complex reasoning in science: BioKIDS

Much like historians, scientists also rely on using evidence to make claims. Making sound scientific claims, however, relies on forms of evidence that differ from what would count as evidence in the field of history. In an effort to enculturate students into the deep reasoning skills associated with scientific inquiry, a group of science educators developed the BioKIDS curriculum, an upper-elementary and middle science curriculum focused on students' developing a deep understanding of scientific concepts (Songer, 2006).

The design of the BioKIDS curriculum is guided by the groundbreaking work of Karplus (1977) and others (e.g., Bruner, 1996) concerned with how to present learning opportunities to students in ways that promote deep understanding of the material. One important barrier to learning science, as mentioned earlier in this chapter, the conceptions that children form about their world that run counter to scientific theory. BioKIDS attempts to overcome these (mis)conceptions through sustained inquiry (a year-long curriculum), repeated interactions with various scientific concepts with increasing levels of complexity, and a genuine focus on inquiry rather than simple classification tasks or memorization of superficial characteristics of plants, animals, or the natural world.

Each BioKIDS unit is organized into four phases: engage, explore, explain and synthesize. In the first unit, a unit on biodiversity, students *engage* in close observation of their schoolyard for the purposes of identifying and describing the various habitats that are present in the schoolyard. This is followed by an opportunity to *explore*, in which students collect data on a specific part of the schoolyard (the schoolyard was divided into zones). Students use a handheld device in order to systematically collect data about the zone in which they were assigned. During the *explain* phase, students use the data collected in the previous phase to begin explaining the various patterns that are observable in the data, such as documenting the zone with the most biodiversity, and the zone with the least biodiversity. Finally, students are asked to *synthesize* what they have learned about their schoolyard in order to generate hypotheses regarding the relationship between habitat and a species' physical and behavioral characteristics.

In constructivist pedagogy, it is often suggested that the teacher plays a minimal role and students engage in 'discovery learning'. BioKIDS offers a glimpse into the key role that the teacher plays in inquiry-oriented learning opportunities. At each phase the teacher provides various levels of support, guidance, and prompts in order to frame the learning opportunities. The students are not simply 'discovering' science – they are engaging in systematic and guided inquiry in order to construct sound explanations and understandings of the natural world.

Leading with students' mathematical thinking: Cognitively Guided Instruction

When children begin school, many demonstrate the ability to solve mathematical problems, yet they have not received instruction in formal operations such as addition and subtraction. The fact that students come to school with conceptions about mathematical operations is the basis for Cognitively Guided Instruction (CGI), an approach to elementary mathematics instruction that leads with valuing students' thinking. CGI is guided by two key tenets. First, that children develop conceptions about mathematics prior to formal schooling and that these intuitive conceptions should play an important role in developing children's formal knowledge of mathematics. The second key tenet is that math instruction should focus on problem solving over the memorization of math facts and mastering rules (Carpenter *et al.*, 1989).

CGI is a not a specific curriculum. Rather, it is a program of professional development in which teachers focus on developing an understanding of the ways in which children think about numbers. Conversations about how students think about numbers and the common errors that children make as they master formal mathematical operations are paired with developing an understanding of the ways in which children's thinking can be incorporated into daily mathematics lessons. By understanding patterns of development in children's understanding of mathematics, CGI facilitates instruction that uses what children know as a basis for learning formal mathematical knowledge. Student errors, rather than being seen as mistakes, are viewed as an opportunity to understand what the child knows.

'Invented strategies' in coming to know mathematics

The term 'invented strategies' is common parlance in mathematics textbooks and evolved out of the work of CGI researchers. When children begin formal schooling, most are able to solve addition and subtraction problems using non-standard, or 'invented' strategies. Mathematics educators have investigated the systematic errors students make in adding and subtracting using formal algorithms (e.g., Brown and VanLehn, 1982). These researchers have hypothesized that one reason for these systematic errors is that students are executing the algorithms with rote understanding rather than a deep conceptual understanding of the procedures. Allowing students to use invented strategies promotes an understanding of the underlying concepts rather than focusing on rote memorization of rules.

Constructing 'third spaces' to promote literacy learning

Consistent with constructivist pedagogy, a number of literacy researchers (e.g., Lee, 2007; Moje *et al.*, 2004) are interested in the process of integrating the 'first space' of people's home, community, and peer networks with the 'second space', marked by the more formalized discourses encountered in school, to create a 'third space' (Bhabha, 2004; Gutiérrez, Baquedano-Lopez and Tejana, 1999). The goal of this research is to document the funds of knowledge (Moll, Veléz-Ibanéz, and Greenberg, 1989) and discourses (Gee, 1996) that shape students' interactions with texts in and out of school and use this knowledge to both build bridges between in- and out-of-school contexts and also expand and deepen understanding of the target content knowledge. This often requires classroom instruction to embrace traditionally marginalized forms of literacy.

Illustrative of this research is Carol Lee's Cultural Modeling Project, which is set in a predominantly African American school where a majority of students are speakers of African American English Vernacular (AAEV). Lee uses the AAEV practice of signifying – a form of everyday knowledge in the community of AAEV speakers that utilizes figurative language, persuasion, and double entendre to engage in insult – as an entrée into literary reasoning (Lee, 2007).

The cultural modeling project is organized around units of instruction that focus on interpretive problems. Instruction begins with cultural data sets – R&B or rap lyrics, rap videos, film clips, and television programs – that students might be familiar with. Examples from these popular cultural sources are used as an entrée into formal literary reasoning with more canonical texts.

For example, in a unit on symbolism with Toni Morrison's novel *Beloved* as the primary focus, students engaged in secondary readings that might be typical in English classrooms. For example, students read Lerone Bennett's (1964) text *Before the Mayflower* in order to gain background knowledge of America in an era of Jim Crow laws. However, students also engaged in discussion of texts that are less commonly valued in English classrooms, such as a rap songs, clips from television mini-series, and R&B lyrics, in order to understand more fully the literary tropes, such as symbolism and inverted chronology, that Morrison uses throughout the novel *Beloved* and that are also commonly used in texts that students encounter in their everyday lives. By using texts that students are familiar with, teachers in the cultural modeling project are able to make explicit the tacit knowledge that students possess around a particular literary problem – in short, helping students make connections between their out-of-school knowledge and the canonical, school-based problems they are expected to master. This approach also provides students with language with which to explain the processes they are already engaging, thus inducting them into the formal discipline of literary criticism.

Technology and constructivist pedagogy

Technology is relevant to our consideration of constructivist pedagogy in several respects. First, technology has the potential to expand learning communities well beyond the walls of a classroom; it is now possible for peers to be linked with peers, as well as experts, in the pursuit of knowledge building. A case in point is the Computer Supported Intentional Learning Environment (CSILE), also referred to as Knowledge Forum (KF), designed and investigated by Marlene Scardamalia, Carl Bereiter, and their colleagues (Scardamalia, Bereiter, and Lamon, 1994). Underlying the design of this environment is the tenet captured in the following quotation:

> Historically, learning has been an adequate objective for education because knowledge has not been thought of as growing, but rather in danger of being lost … the information revolution spells unprecedented growth in information … and requires staying up to date as a prerequisite to contributing in your own right to the cultural wealth of society. Preparing students for knowledge generation represents a radically different challenge for education.
>
> (Scardamalia, 2004)

Consistent with this perspective on learning, KF is designed as a multi-media community knowledge space, in which students are supported by an array of tools designed to foster an environment specifically designed to support inquiry, information searches, and creative work. These tools include:

- annotation, citation, and reference links;
- interconnected views through interlinking;
- author-assigned indices (keywords, titles, problem fields);
- automatically assigned indices (author, date, semantic field);
- knowledge scaffolding processes (supporting theory refinement and constructive criticism);
- 'rise above' notes (presenting new ideas that represent an advance over previous ideas).

In addition to reconfiguring learning communities, technology offers alternative ways for students to create, communicate, and represent their ideas. A new area of scholarship concerns itself with these processes and is aimed at encouraging educators to consider the alternative learning spaces, afforded by technology, that center on youth culture and new media (e.g., Alvermann, 2003; Hull, 2003; Leander and Lovvorn, 2006).

Reflections across these examples of constructivist pedagogy

As the examples above illustrate, teaching from a constructivist perspective is a complex enterprise. There are numerous demands on the teacher as she or he orchestrates the activity of students in the typical constructivist-oriented classroom. The teacher needs to have deep knowledge of the subject-matter in order to select and adapt curricula and design powerful activities that both elicit students' thinking and support students in attaining more complete, accurate, and generative understandings. Furthermore, the teacher is advantaged when knowledgeable about the typical naive conceptions that students bring to an area of inquiry. With content knowledge, as well as knowledge about the development of children's thinking, teachers are positioned to engage in the kinds of mediation that will enhance learners' understanding (see, for example, Lampert, 2001).

Research suggests that it is important for teachers to display a genuine curiosity in students' ideas and how they came to those ideas. One challenge, however, is that very few teachers have actually participated, as learners, in a constructivist learning environment where their own thinking and understanding were valued and probed. Given that teachers tend to teach as they were taught (Cohen, 1989; Lortie, 1975), this is an immense challenge to implementing constructivist pedagogy well.

Furthermore, teachers' best efforts to engage in constructivist pedagogy can be frustrated when there is a misalignment between the goals of constructivist teaching and the educational outcomes to which students are held accountable. If assessments are designed to measure the recall of factual information and teachers are held accountable for covering a curriculum that is 'a mile wide and an inch deep', these will serve as disincentives to undertaking the challenging pedagogy represented by constructivism. In addition, teachers have to deal with administrators', parents', and the general public's expectations of what effective teaching and learning look like. If constituents do not value the aims of constructivist pedagogy, they are unlikely to support the means, which seldom entail students sitting in an orderly fashion, following clearly specified directions.

Note

1   J. G. Saxe, 'The Blindmen and the Elephant', available online at http://en.wikisource.org/wiki/The_Blindmen_and_the_Elephant. While this poem was written by the nineteenth-century American poet John Godfrey Saxe, variations have been attributed to Jainists, Buddhists, Sufis and Hindus and can be traced to at least the thirteenth century.

References

Alvermann, D.E. and Xu, S.H. (2003) 'Children's everyday literacies: Intersections of popular culture and language arts instruction', *Language Arts*, 81(2), pp. 145–54.

Aronson, E. (1978) *The Jigsaw Classroom*, Beverley Hills, Sage Publications.

Bain, R.B. (2006) 'Rounding up unusual suspects: Facing the authority hidden in the history classroom', *Teachers College Record*, 108(10), pp. 2080–114.

Baumann, J. (1988) 'Direct instruction reconsidered', *Journal of Reading Behavior*, 31, pp. 712–18.

Bhabha, H.K. (1994) *The Location of Culture*, New York, Routledge.

Bredo, E. (2000) 'Reconsidering social constructivism: The relevance of George Herbert Mead's interactionism', in Phillips, D.C. (ed.), *Constructivism in Education: Opinions and Second Opinions on Controversial Issues: Ninety-ninth Yearbook of the National Society for the Study of Education*, part 1, Chicago, National Society for the Study of Education, pp. 127–57.

Brown, A.L. and Campione, J.C. (1990) 'Communities of learning and thinking, or a context by any other name', *Human Development*, 21, pp. 108–25.

—— (1994) 'Guided discovery in a community of learners', in K. McGilley (ed.), *Classroom Lessons: Integrating Cognitive Theory and Classroom Practice*, Cambridge, MA, MIT Press, pp. 229–72.

Brown, J.S., and VanLehn, K. (1982) 'Towards a generative theory of "bugs"', in T.P. Carpenter, J.M. Moser, and T.A. Romberg (eds), *Addition and Subtraction: A Cognitive Perspective*, Hillsdale, NJ, Erlbaum, pp. 117–35.

Bruner, J.S. (1969) *On Knowing: Essays for the Left Hand*, Cambridge, MA, Harvard University Press.

—— (1996) *The Culture of Education*, Cambridge, MA, Harvard University Press.

Burbules, N. (2000) 'Constructivism: Moving beyond the impasse', in D.C. Phillips (ed.), *Constructivism in Education: Opinions and Second Opinions on Controversial Issues: Ninety-ninth Yearbook of the National Society for the Study of Education*, Chicago, University of Chicago Press , pp. 302–30.

Carpenter, T.P., Fennema, E., Peterson, P.L. and Chiang, C.P. (1989) 'Using knowledge of children's mathematics thinking in classroom teaching: An experimental study', *American Education Research Journal*, 26, pp. 499–531.

Clement, J. (1982) 'Students' preconceptions in introductory mechanics', *American Journal of Physics*, 50, pp. 66–71.

—— (1982) 'Algebra word problem solutions: Analysis of a common misconception', *Journal for Research in Mathematics Education*, 13, pp. 16–30.

Cohen, D.K. (1989) 'Teaching practice: Plus que ça change', in P. W. Jackson (ed.), *Contributing to Educational Change: Perspectives on Research and Practice*, Berkeley, CA, McCutchan , pp. 27–84.

Gee, J.P. (1996) *Social Linguistics and Literacies: Ideology in Discourses*, 2nd edn, London, Taylor and Francis.

Gutiérrez, K., Baquedano-Lopez, P., and Tejeda, C. (1999) 'Rethinking diversity: Hybridity and hybrid language practices in the third space', *Mind, Culture, and Activity: An International Journal*, 6(4), pp. 286–303.

Hull, G.A. (2003) 'Youth culture and digital media: New literacies for new times', *Research in the Teaching of English*, 38(2), pp. 229–33.

Karplus, R. (1977) 'Science teaching and the development of reasoning', *Journal of Research in Science Education*, 14(2), pp. 169–75.

Konold, C. (1995) 'Social and cultural dimensions of knowledge and classroom teaching', in L. P. Steffe and J. Gale (eds), *Constructivism in Education*, Mahwah, NJ, Lawrence Erlbaum Associates, pp. 175–84.

Lampert, M. (2001) *Teaching Problems and the Problems of Teaching*, New Haven, CT, Yale University Press.

Leander, K. and Lovvorn, J. (2006) 'Literacy networks: Following the circulation of texts, bodies, and objects in the schooling and online gaming of one youth', *Cognition and Instruction*, 24(3), pp. 291–340.

Lee, C.D. (2007) *Culture, Literacy, and Learning: Blooming in the Midst of the Whirlwind*, New York, Teachers College Press.

Lortie, D. (1975) *Schoolteacher*, Chicago, University of Chicago Press.

McCloskey, M. (1983) 'Naive theories of motion', in D. Gentner and A.L. Stevens (eds), *Mental Models*, Hillsdale, NJ, Lawrence Erlbaum Associates, pp. 299–324.

Metz, K. (1995) 'Reassessment of developmental constraints on children's science instruction', *Review of Educational Research*, 65, pp. 93–127.

Mintrop, H. (2004) 'Fostering constructivist communities of learners in the amalgamated multi-discipline of social studies', *Journal of Curriculum Studies*, 36(2), pp. 141–58.

Moje, E.B., Ciechanowski, K.M., Kramer, K., Ellis, L., Carrillo, R., and Collazo, T. (2004) 'Working toward third space in content area literacy: An examination of everyday funds of knowledge and discourse', *Reading Research Quarterly*, 39(1), pp. 38–70.

Moll, L.C., Veléz-Ibanéz, C., and Greenberg, J. (1989) *Year One Progress Report: Community Knowledge and Classroom Practice: Combining Resources for Literacy Instruction*, (IARP Subcontract L-10, Development Associates), Tucson, AZ, University of Arizona.

Mosborg, S. (2002) 'Speaking of history: How adolescents use their knowledge of history in reading the daily news', *Cognition and Instruction*, 20, pp. 323–58.

Osborne, R.J. and Wittrock, M.C. (1983) 'Learning science: A generative process', *Science Education*, 67(4), pp. 498–508.

Palincsar, A.S. and Brown, A.L. (1984) 'Reciprocal teaching of comprehension-fostering and comprehension-monitoring activities', *Cognition and Instruction*, 1(2), pp. 117–75.

Perfetti, C., Britt, M.A., and Georgi, M.C. (1995) *Text-based Learning and Reasoning: Studies in History*, Hillsdale, NJ, Erlbaum.

Peterson, P., and Walberg, H.J. (1979) *Research in Teaching*, Berkeley, McCutchan.

Phillips, D.C. (2000) 'An opinionated account of the constructivist landscape', in D.C. Phillips (ed.), *Constructivism in Education: Opinions and Second Opinions on Controversial Issues: Ninety-ninth Yearbook of the National Society for the Study of Education*, part 1, Chicago, National Society for the Study of Education, pp. 1–16.

Piaget, J. (1955) *The Language and Thought of the Child* (M. Gabain, trans.), Cleveland, Meridian, (original work published in 1923).

Richards, J. (1991) 'Mathematical discussions', in E. von Glasersfeld (ed.), *Radical Constructivism in Mathematics Education*, Dordrecht, The Netherlands, Kluwer, pp. 21–47.

Rogoff, B. (1991) 'Guidance and participation in spatial planning', in L. Resnick, J. Levine, and S. Teasley (eds), *Perspectives on Socially Shared Cognition*, Washington, DC, American Psychological Association, pp. 349–83.

Scardamalia, M. (2004) 'CSILE/Knowledge Forum', in A. Kovalchick and K. Dawson (eds), *Education and Technology: An Encyclopedia*, Santa Barbara, ABC-CLIO, pp. 183–92.

Scardamalia, M., Bereiter, C., and Lamon, M. (1994) 'The CSILE project: Trying to bring the classroom into World 3', in K. McGilley (ed.), *Classroom Lessons: Integrating Cognitive Theory and Classroom Practice*, Cambridge, MA, MIT Press, pp. 201–28.

Songer, N.B. (2006) 'BioKIDS: An animated conversation on the development of curricular activity structures for inquiry science', in R. Keith Sawyer (ed.), *Cambridge Handbook of the Learning Sciences*, New York, Cambridge University Press, pp. 355–69.

Steffe, L.P. and Gale, J. (1995) *Constructivism in Education*, Hillsdale, NJ, Lawrence Erlbaum.

Vygotsky, L. (1978) *Mind in Society: The Development of Higher Psychological Processes*, ed. M. Cole, V. John-Steiner, S. Scribner, and E. Souberman, Cambridge, MA, Harvard University Press.

Wertsch, J.V. and Bivens, J.A. (1992) 'The social origins of individual mental functioning: Alternatives and perspectives', *The Quarterly Newsletter of the Laboratory of Comparative Human Cognition*, 14(2), pp. 35–44.

Whitcomb, J.A. (2004) 'Dilemmas of design and predicaments of practice: Adapting the "Fostering a Community of Learners" model in secondary school English language arts classrooms', *Journal of Curriculum Studies*, 36(2), pp. 183–206.

Reflective questions

1   In this chapter, we outline the features of constructivist theory and also offer illustrative examples of projects and programs that are grounded in constructivist theory. Consider an in-school or out-of-school learning experience you had that you would identify as 'constructivist'. What were the specific features of this experience for you as a learner?

2   Throughout the chapter we argue that constructivism is a theory of knowledge, not a theory of pedagogy. This means that any learning experience could be oriented around constructivist theory. Many would not identify a lecture as 'constructivist'. If you were to prepare a lecture, what could you do as you plan and deliver the lecture in order to orient it around constructivist theory?

Further reading

Brearley, M. and Hitchfield, E. (2006) *A Teacher's Guide to Reading Piaget*, London, Routledge.

Breault, D.A. and Breault, R. (eds) (2005) *Experiencing Dewey: Insights for Today's Classroom*, Indianapolis, Kappa Delta Pi.

Cohen, D. (1990) 'A revolution in one classroom: The case of Mrs Oublier', *Educational Evaluation and Policy Analysis*, 12(3), pp. 311–29.

National Research Council (2000) *How People Learn: Brain, Mind, Experience, and School*, Washington, DC, National Academy Press.

1.4 The double move in teaching

Developmental learning

Mariane Hedegaard

Introduction

Vygotsky (1998) conceptualised children's development from a holistic perspective within which children are seen as intentional and active in their engagement in interaction with other persons. The psychological and educational approach that Vygotsky started has been developed further by Elkonin (1999) and Leontiev (1978). Their contribution to this approach allows for an understanding of children's development as taking place within the culture of institutional practice. This practice has to be seen as a condition for children's development.

Vygotsky advanced the pedagogical argument that development takes place as a result of interaction between a child and more culturally competent persons (Vygotsky, 1982, 1998). This interaction results in a change in the child's relations to his surroundings. Not all kinds of learning lead to development according to Vygotsky, only the kind of learning that changes the child's 'zone of proximal development'. This principle that Vygotsky formulated has led to an interpretation of the zone of proximal development as a psychological space within which a child acquires new cognitive competence. Chaiklin (2003) argues, in line with Vygotsky (1982), that the child acquires not only new competence but that the zone of proximal development is related to qualitative changes in the child's overall functioning. This interpretation also allows one to see the development of a child's motives within a zone of proximal development and fits into Elkonin's (1999) theory in which cognition and motivation are conceptualised as being interwoven into developmental stages. Elkonin saw the child's engagement and motives as integrated with his/her cognitive development. He conceptualised development in relation to the child's acquisition of new leading motives. This concept is also proposed by Leontiev (1978) in his theory of personality development. A person's appropriation of a motive is seen as the key concept in personality development.

My theoretical approach has been to relate Vygotsky's idea of the zone of proximal development to Davydov and Elkonin's developmental teaching approach. This has resulted in several teaching experiments (Hedegaard, 1988, 1990, 1995, 1996, 2002; Hedegaard and Chaiklin, 2005; Hedegaard and Sigersted, 1992).

In my own work, I have especially focused on teaching in school as the basic condition for children's development. In the 1980s I became inspired by Elkonin and Davydov's experimental teaching approach, which had been developed in the 1950s and 1960s which they referred to as 'developmental teaching and learning' (Davydov, 1988). A small conference in Denmark in 1983 resulted in a publication *Learning and Teaching on a Scientific Basis* (Hedegaard *et al.*, 1984) which was based on Davydov's theoretical orientation. The 'developmental learning and teaching' approach had already been adapted by Joachim Lompscher in Berlin in the 1970s and became known as 'ascending from the abstract to the concrete' (Lompscher, 1982, 1984, 2000). In my version I have tried to accentuate Vygotsky's ideas of the zone of proximal development and the relation between children's everyday concepts and subject-matter concepts. I also tried to integrate this with the idea of the zone of proximal development for motives and interests. This gave rise to the term 'the double move in teaching', which means that teaching should move between children's everyday concepts and interests and the subject-matter concepts of the school and create a learning motive. Central to 'the double move in teaching' is the interrelation between children's motives and cognition, as seen in Elkonin's (1999, originally published in 1972) theory of child development.

Learning within the zone of proximal development

One of the dilemmas facing the teacher when teaching in the classroom is deciding how to gain insight into each child and their ideas, reflections and interests when s/he, as the teacher, must also work with the whole group of children and also engage with the central principles and content of the subject s/he is supposed to teach. The solution is a teaching approach that motivates the students to cooperate in planning and research activities which create a link between questions the children share and the problems that are central for the subject being taught. Such an approach may involve the children in active dialogue in the class about formulation and exploration of central themes in a subject area. In this way problems that the children can understand and formulate become the key between the child and the subject area. If this connection is established, it will be possible to create teaching within the children's zone of proximal development.

In the following sections I will present the ideas behind the double move in teaching and how it relates to developmental learning. To illustrate the principles of the double move in teaching I will draw on a teaching experiment I conducted in third- to fifth-grade classes in biology and history in the comprehensive school system in Denmark (see Hedegaard, 1988, 1990, 2002). The last part of the chapter relates the principles of the double move in teaching to fifth-grade history teaching, and focuses on one boy's learning through his shared relations with his classmates and the teacher.

The double move in teaching

The double move in teaching and developmental learning includes two core ideas taken from the version of developmental teaching in the mother tongue described by Aidarova (1982).[1] These are that students' engagement in learning activity is progressed by:

- student use of conceptual core models (germ-cell models) as tools for formulating subject-matter conceptual relations;
- student use of procedural models inspired by social science research methods for analysing their formulation of subject-matter conceptual relations.

I will argue that this type of involvement using models and research strategies leads both to motive and conceptual development.

Germ-cell/core models

The concept of a 'germ cell' has been formulated as the scientific abstraction of the key relations in the content of a subject area (Davydov, 1990, 1982). Examples of such an abstraction are the germ-cell model of biological evolution formulated by Darwin, which posits dialectical relations between ecology, species and population (Mayr, 1976). Another example of such an abstraction is the germ-cell model in Aidarova's core teaching experiment related to Vygotsky's theory of communication. The dialectical relations in this model are between the sender and the receiver, with the message as the mediating link. Other examples are the ones that were the inspiration for the teaching experiments I conducted. Darwin's germ cells from biology were transformed into a germ cell of palaeontology and the origins of mankind (Leakey and Lewin, 1978). In this germ-cell model the relation between nature and species was transformed into the relation between resources and way of life, and the relation between species and population was transformed into the relation between way of life and structure of the collective/the group. These models were formulated in such a way that they contained the ideal abstraction but also were accessible to children. Figure 1.4.1 shows the basic relations as they were transformed through the children's conceptualisation.

What is special about a germ-cell model is that it is the product of a real scientific research process, as in Darwin's research in biology, in Leakey's research in palaeontology and Marx's (1976) research in social science. Such germ cells can be recognised in everyday life activities. This idea of germ-cell models and research strategies builds on Davydov's theory of theoretical knowledge. Davydov characterised theoretical knowledge in this way:

> A theoretical idea or concept should bring *together* things that are *dissimilar*, *different*, *multifaceted*, and *not coincident*, and should indicate their proportion in this whole. Consequently the objective *connection* between the *universal* and the *isolated* (the integral and the distinct) emerges as the specific content of a theoretical concept. Such a concept, in contrast to an empirical one, does not find something identical in every particular object in a class, but traces the interconnection of particular objects within the whole, within the system in its formation.
>
> (1990, p. 255)

Davydov (1982, 1990) contrasts theoretical knowledge with empirical knowledge, though this is not an exclusive contrast since the categories of empirical knowledge enter into theoretical knowledge (Davydov, 1990, p. 258). Empirical knowledge brings together what can be found to be similar by abstracting shared attributes. Empirical knowledge is not problematic if it is related to its conditions and not seen as absolute facts. Practical activity in the form of experimentation in everyday productive activity as well as in research is the prototype for how activity transforms into theoretical knowledge. Visual models of the dialectical relations – germ-cell models – are used as the medium for communicating theoretical knowledge.

If we transfer Davydov's conceptions of theoretical knowledge to subject-matter knowledge, then subject-matter knowledge should be conceptualised as being located within a connected system. The articulation of a germ-cell model (seen as an ideal abstraction of a scientific problem area) is not always easy for a teacher or a researcher to accomplish.[2] It is difficult to be sure that the germ-cell model chosen is the most ideal abstraction,[3] therefore I prefer to call the teacher's and students' model of the central conceptual relation of a subject-matter area a core model. The term core model indicates that it is a model that one can argue for, but that there can be other core models that can also be argued for. The

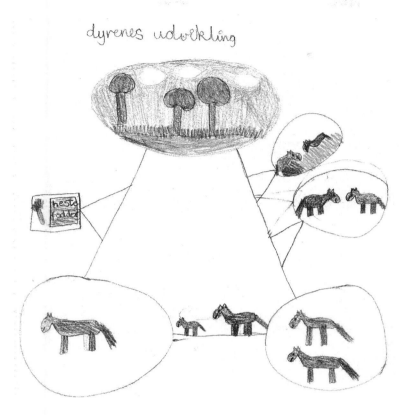

Figure 1.4.1 A child's model of 'animals' development'

Note Here development relates 'nature' (ecology) to a 'specific type of animal' (species) and to 'other animals of the same kind' (population), where 'nature' and 'animal' are related through food, and 'animal' and 'other animals' are related by living together and 'other animals' are related to 'nature' by parental care and defence against enemies.

students can have a core model of a problem area that is different from the germ-cell model of this problem area, but the student's model can be seen as a core model if they can reflect upon and argue for their model. The core model is the person's own ideal abstraction of a subject-matter area.

Core models can function both as a tool for the teacher in his/her preparatory work and as an aid to the students in their research activities. The main characteristic of core models is that gradually they can be extended from being a simple relationship between two or three basic concepts within a subject field to illustrate the relationships between the subject-matter's central concepts. For example, in biology this can be demonstrated when the conceptual relationships between animal and nature or between organism and context are elaborated. Such an elaboration will not only add to the core conceptual relation already modelled, but also influence and change the meaning of these conceptual relationships. Alternatively in the subject domain of evolution, the core relation of animal and nature was, in our experimental teaching within biology, changed and extended into models of relationships between the concepts of species, population and ecological niche (Hedegaard, 1990, 1996). The concept of species in this new relationship is a transformation of the concept of animal through its more complicated relations to population and ecological niche. In the same way the concept of ecological niche is a transformation of the concept of nature through its relation to population and species.[4] When this core model is applied to a concrete case, then it is possible to follow the effects of change in one aspect in the model on the other aspects (e.g., by using the model of evolution in the concrete case of the snow hare (Hedegaard, 1990), one can then predict that if the ecological niche of the hare changes, then both the species and the population will gradually change, as happened when the snow hare was introduced to the Faeroe Islands).

By using theoretical knowledge of a problem area, it becomes possible to organise the concrete experiences of the students around a conceptual core model and thereby link the students' everyday concepts and experience from research activity in the classroom into a connected system. By helping the child to do this (within the educational activity), the child acquires 'symbolic tools' that can be used to analyse and understand the complexity of different concrete practices.

Central method

The central method in an educational mediation of theoretical knowledge is 'experimentation'. In its most elementary form, experimentation can be characterised as observing the effect of making a change in one object in a connected system on the other objects in the system. In this method, an object of investigation can be a real change or an imaginary change. The method of imagined experimentation can be a valuable educational tool. An example of imagined experimentation can be seen in lesson in the third grade in biology (Hedegaard, 1990). The students were asked to imagine what would happen to the polar bear if it was moved to the Kalahari desert and the desert hare was moved to Greenland. Their answers showed that the students took the ecological niches of the polar bear and the desert hare into account in this 'mental experimentation'. From this 'imagined experimentation' the children could conclude that each species adapts to its special ecological niche. Later, when the children worked with how humans live under different climatic and environmental conditions, the teacher asked the children again to undertake an imagined change. In this case by imagining what would happen if a native member of the Kung tribe in the Kalahari desert boarded an aeroplane and moved to Greenland (Hedegaard, 1988). The answers this time were quite different and reflected the children's understanding of the new core model. The children argued that a Kung person could survive in Greenland if they obtained suitable clothes, housing and tools and were also taken care of socially. These examples illustrate the way in which theoretical methods of 'imagined experimentation' can become a tool in children's learning activity for analysing and reflecting on the content being investigated and thereby promote theoretical thinking.

Core models can help the teacher to formulate relevant problems for the children's exploratory activities. They can also help the children to gradually learn how to combine and sum up the various themes and concepts explored and introduced during the course of the teaching. As the assignments set by the teacher are governed by these concepts, the children, through their own research, will be able to formulate their own model which they can then develop still further and eventually use to evaluate what they are actually learning.

The core models, while resting on theoretical foundations in the specific subject-matter field in the experimental teaching of biology and history, also developed further during the specific projects. This became apparent during analysis of the children's learning processes, inasmuch as many new ideas arose during the teaching, and these then led to changes in and an expansion of the conceptual models.

Analogy to research methodology

In the teaching project a procedure was used in connection with the children's research activities that were inspired by research methods used in the social sciences (Lewin, 1935). The basic principles of this procedure were:

1 Formulation of the field of research.
2 What do we know and what do we not know about this field?
3 How can we produce a coherent model that relates what we do not know to what we do know?
4 What resources are available for exploring the model?
5 How do the results of our exploration relate to the central field of research?

The children got to know this procedure through time spent in each session when the teacher reviewed the class's work with the children and then evaluated the class's activities in relation to the problems posed initially for the course. A variant of this procedure was used to shape each session. Sessions were structured as follows:

1 Résumé of the previous session in the light of the goals of and the results the students had achieved through their research activities.
2 Discussions of how the children's results fitted into the core model of the subject field.
3 Formulation of the goals for the day's activities, on the basis of the problems they now needed to tackle in relation to the general problems for the course as a whole.
4 Carrying out various activities which could contribute to shedding light on the problems and goals set for that day.
5 Evaluation of the events of the day.

In the different subject-matters both in Aidarova's mother-tongue teaching and in the teaching of biology and history in Denmark several different methods directly related to the subject teaching were also introduced. In Aidarova's experiment a structural analysis model was used among others to analyse words so that the morphological and semantic structure became apparent. In the history teaching that will be exemplified later a conscious effort was made to acquaint the children with historical methodology. Timelines were used for different historical periods, reconstructions of findings in relation to the timelines and the conceptual models, and analogies were made to ways of living among primitive people of today.

Developmental learning

Three factors are crucial in the double move approach in which teaching can lead to developmental learning. These are:

- formulation of tasks that motivate the children and demand that the children work with the central conceptual relations and methods;
- social interaction, communication and cooperation between children;

- phases in teaching, which are based upon progressive and qualitative changes in the children's appropriation of motives and competencies.

Tasks and motivation

One of the goals of the teaching experiment was to use children's 'big' questions to formulate the overall questions for a subject-matter field. These questions are in the same category as those found in religion, philosophy, biology and social science – quintessential questions about humanity and life on earth, about life and death, about eternity and about the ever-changing world with all its creatures. Furthermore the idea was that involving the children in research activities would gradually promote their own formulation of versions of central problems that led to new motives for participating in the research process.

Besides starting with children's big questions of life an important way to create interest and shared experiences is to let the class participate together in events and thereby create shared experience and questions. This is done through visits to museums with workshops, use of films and role-play about the 'old days'. Looking at archive pictures and listening to stories were also seen as important events.

Social interaction, communication and cooperation between children

The importance of group work for cognitive development lies, among other factors, in the division of work among the children when they are researching and carrying out assignments in class. Group work makes it possible to break down the components of any one assignment by giving each child in the group a sub-assignment which forms a part of a larger entity to be solved by the whole group.

During the course of the teaching project, various tasks were assigned to various groups within the class and, as time went on, to different children within the groups.

Phases in the teaching

Developmental teaching is based on the assumption that each phase of the teaching process is dialectically linked to phases in the learning process. Three separate elements can be isolated in this process of learning: the formulation of goals; the learning process itself; and an evaluation of what has been learned (Davydov, 1982; Hedegaard, 2004).

1   The first main stage in the teaching is, therefore, to help the children to formulate goals for investigating and formulate a first core relation that comprises the main problem for the course.
2   The second main stage is characterised by the expansion of the thematic relationship in the core model, where the relationships within the core model are explored through various assignments.
3   The third main stage in the teaching has as its goal that the children should learn how to reflect on the conceptual relationships being investigated.

The principles for conducting the double move in teaching: a teaching experiment in history

The theme of the teaching experiment in the fifth grade was *historical change in societies*. The question that started the activities in the fifth grade was: 'How can it be that people have lived differently in different historical periods?' The problems and topics the children worked with throughout the fifth grade that will be drawn upon in this chapter can be seen in Figure 1.4.2. History teaching in the fifth grade consists of 36 three-hour teaching sessions over the year. The main characteristics of the 'double move in teaching' were:

- content analyses and formulation of germ-cell/core models;
- structuring the teaching along a historical timeline and its periods;
- phases in teaching.

Content analyses and formulation of germ-cell/core models

The subject-matter goal in the experimental history teaching was to give the students an understanding of the links between differences in resources, living conditions and characteristics of society during various periods of history, in order that they might gain an understanding of how conditions of life in modern society are a result of changes extending over a number of periods of history. A second goal was to give students an insight into the various forms of living conditions as seen in Danish society through time, but also between contemporary societies. The aim was to provide the children with a conceptual basis in the form of a coherent model which would give them a tool they could use and refine by analysing past societies, and which could also be used as a starting point for research into present society.

The subject content was provided through the formulation of central conceptual coherence that depicted the core relations between resources, production forms, ways of living and type of society. These conceptual pairings constituted the founding relationships in the core models which guided the teaching (see Figure 1.4.2) and the teacher's formulation of tasks and thereby became the guidelines for the 'core models' that the children constructed (see Figure 1.4.1).

Structuring the teaching along a historical timeline and its periods

A historical timeline and specific periods of history were used to structure the children's activities. During the fourth-grade phase of the experimental teaching project the class worked with the Stone Age, the Bronze Age, the Iron Age and the Viking Age. During the fifth grade, the historical periods were extended to encompass the Middle Ages, the Age of Enlightenment and the first phase of the Industrial Revolution. We used different conceptual relations of the germ-cell model for history to analyse the different historical periods.

For the Stone Age, the Bronze Age and the Iron Age, the teaching focused on the differences in the tools used during these three periods and the importance of these differences for the basic conditions of human life. However, in the case of the Iron Age the children also 'discovered' that new forms of tools led to a radical change in people's attitude to nature. Danes began to live in permanent settlements, and with this a more permanent disparity was established between groups as to the division of labour. During the Viking Age, this division of labour led to a society with a simple class system of freemen and slaves. The freemen (the Vikings) went off

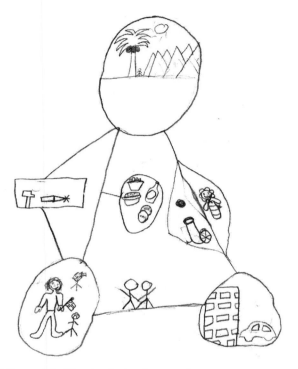

Figure 1.4.2 A child's model of 'society's development'

on expeditions while the slaves tended the fields. The attention given to this division of labour led the children to focus on the rules governing how these two classes lived together.

For the Middle Ages, the teaching focused on the influence of religion in the development of a special class of society. A distinction was made between four different classes of people: (1) clergy (priests and monks); (2) town residents (merchants and craftsmen); (3) castle residents (the nobility); and (4) village residents (bondsmen). The children tried to find out how these groups lived together, which resulted in a focusing on religion and the division of resources.

Dealing with the Age of Enlightenment led the children to work with class divisions and rules for the division of resources. Ownership and exploitation became central elements in analysing this period of history. The Age of Enlightenment also led the children in the class to engage in an analysis of the use and development of tools, of the increases in knowledge in many fields (e.g., navigation and geography) and of the development of reading and writing skills. Their work on the Age of Enlightenment meant that the children extended their historical horizons from Denmark to encompass a more global picture.

Phases in teaching

During the entire course of teaching, each phase was guided by the fact that the children had become model users. The change to a new historical period led to expansion of their models and to change in model use. These changes came to characterise the structure of the children's learning activity by means of the following phases: (1) problem formulation and model use; (2) model extension; (3) model evaluation (see Table 1.4.1).

Analysis of one student's participation in the double move teaching project in the fifth grade

In the following section I want to describe the social, motive and cognitive development of a student, Morten, to show how students' participation in teaching activity based on the principles of the double move approach can result in learning activity that leads to development.

At the start of the fifth grade Morten was easygoing with his classmates, but did not especially go out of his way to socialise with adults. Morten had developed a close friendship with his classmate Allan; the two boys were more often than not to be found in the same group and carried out many of the joint projects together.

Phase 1: problem and model formulation (sessions 1–10)

In the first sessions in this phase Morten finds himself in a dilemma: he wants to help and be with his classmates, but he also wants to work on his own assignments. For example, Morten did not want anybody to copy his drawings of core-model relations. In the first couple of sessions Allan, his best friend, was not allowed to read a book that Morten had borrowed from the class library and yet Morten was interested in and got permission to read Allan's book.

In the first session the students were given the task of evaluating what were good and bad questions to ask about the Viking Age and the Middle Ages. This task was referenced to a question sheet from a Viking museum that they had visited just before the end of last school year. In relation to this visit the children themselves also formulated questions using the concepts of the core model for the Viking Age and the Middle Ages. The evaluation of good and bad questions took place in workgroups of four children. This task did not engage Morten. He tried to get the work over and done as quickly as possible so that he could read books from the class library about castles, knights and weapons in the Middle Ages, which he found more exciting. In the following sessions, after discussion of their evaluation of the questions in the class, he started to become more interested, especially when the evaluation was related to the children's own formulation of questions about the Middle Ages. In extending their models Morten's involvement became more obvious. This could be seen by the determination with which he cooperated in making a model on a notice board. The teacher supported cooperation in the class by giving each workgroup of four children the task of integrating their individual models into a shared model to hang in the classroom. In this task Morten interacted with another member in his group to draw the one half of the model that related to societal beliefs and nature.

Morten's understanding of why society changed itself underwent a change. In the first session he said that it was due to changes in nature, in the same way as they had learned about in the evolution of species. But during the tenth session he suggested that the changes that occurred between the Viking Age and the Middle Ages were related to changes in society and in the invention of methods of defence, which also showed that he had reconceptualised the relations between society, ways of living and nature.

Table 1.4.1 Phases and activities in fifth grade

Phase 1: Problem Formulation – Model Transformation (teaching sessions 1–10)

Tasks:

- Reflection and résumé of the problems investigated and models drawn last year. Formulating goals for this year's activity.
- Sorting and analysing pictures depicting different cultural societies of today and of different historical periods in Denmark.
- Dramatic play about division of work in four historical periods.

Model transformation: the model became expanded by the formulation of the concept of society, division of work, beliefs and laws.

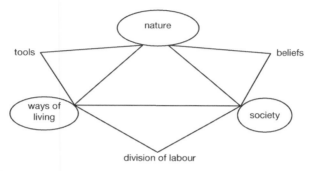

Research methods:

- The general research method – creation of posters of what we are investigating – what we know and – what we do not know

Phase 2: Model Use and Extension (teaching sessions 11–27)

Tasks:

- Comparison and evaluation of a museum-produced task with the students' own produced tasks of the Viking Age.
- Analyses of the effects of change in societal living from a novel that highlighted division of work and of rules in a Viking Settlement.
- Writing an essay about the structure of society in the Middle Ages from texts about four institutions in the Middle Ages.
- Formulating models and writing letters to other children in a school in New York City about their research work.

Model extension: Through these activities the concept of society is related to division of work and the concept 'ways of living' is related to need for work results

---

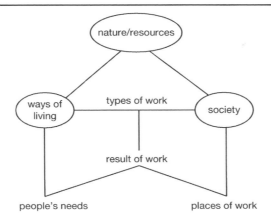

Research methods:

- Specific historical methods of interpretation of archaeological discoveries

Phase 3: Model Evaluation – Model Extension (teaching sessions 28–36)

Tasks:

- Analyses of movies about discovery of the New World.
- Planning and creating dramatic plays with focus on the concept of power and class.
- Creation of own tasks for analysing a craft industry museum exhibition.
- Playing a computer game: Island Survivors – given tasks to explore the contrasts in surviving in a modern society and a desert island.
- Analyses of the concepts demonstrated in the four different plays constructed and performed in the class. The plays were videotaped and replayed for the analyses.
- Final task: an essay about the Danish society of today and in the future.

Model extension:

1. beliefs – with power; 2. tools – with academic knowledge; 3. division of work – with classes

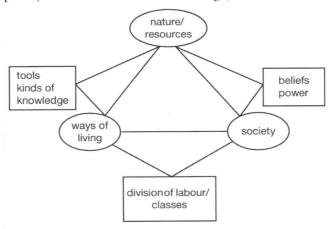

Research method:

- General and specific methods of transformation and reflection

Phase 2a: model extension phase for the Middle Ages. Focus on the concept of society (sessions 11–14)

In this phase the children took turns in adopting the role of the teacher and guided the first part of the class dialogue, which involved a résumé of the previous session and the object formulation for the current session. Morten was allocated the role of teacher, but he did not succeed so well when it became his turn, and could not remember the questions to ask his classmates, but he was motivated to repeat the activity in the following session. With the teacher's help he prepared himself to make a better job of it the second time around. This event was a turning point for Morten; he started to be engaged in taking the role of leader in group activities. Like the rest of his group, he was happy to work with tasks about the Middle Ages, especially because his group got the task of describing and drawing the different types of jobs found at a castle and the work people did. These drawings, together with drawings from the Stone Age, the Iron Age and the Viking Age, were to be presented in a book for children in a pen-pal class in New York City. In the various class discussions Morten appeared interested in trying to understand and explain the changes in society. Like the other children, Morten had problems coming to grips with the concept of society, though he did not confuse this with living conditions in the way several of the other children did.

Through the preparatory work on the book project for children in New York City he formed an overview of the four different class communities that existed during the Middle Ages, and came to understand the relationship between types of work, the results of work, and which needs were met by specific types of work.

Phase 2b: extension of the model by learning about the Age of Enlightenment and the New World and communicating with other children in the 'New World' (sessions 15–27)

Morten became increasingly motivated by the projects in history and discussions, so much so that, in contrast to previous phases, he showed considerable interest in solving the problems that the class was set. His level of involvement was perhaps linked to the development of his insight into how changes in society can be explained. The process of extending the model interested him whilst the class was constructing the book project with models and drawings for children in the pen-pal class in New York. Morten also really wanted to write a personal letter in English to one of the American children. However, after being criticised by Allan, his best friend, he lost his motivation, partly because he found using a bilingual dictionary difficult. But his friend got him back on track by offering him help, and later the teacher even encouraged Morten and Allan to try and help another classmate – an assignment the two friends attempted together. They had only had three months of English at school at the time the letters were written, so there must have been a high level of motivation in this project as almost every word would have had to be looked up in the dictionary.

Morten was in no doubt as to how he should use the model to create new hypotheses about themes from the period of history they had worked with. The model and its concepts had become an instrument of thought. The understanding that he, together with his classmates, had gained through their discussions could now be used in his work on changes in the picture of the world at the historical period of the Enlightenment and the developments in tool technology that came to dominate this period. Morten also showed that he was beginning to understand the connection between power and the division of labour, as, for example, in the manner in which some people were sold into slavery in the historical period of the Enlightenment.

Phase 3: using the historical model of society to go beyond the study of history (sessions 28–36)

The children in the class were divided into four groups which each had to make a play about central themes in the historical period of the Enlightenment. Morten was the leading force in working out a theme in his group, deciding on the roles and ensuring that there was a unity in the planning of the play. He was also the key figure in carrying it out. Morten adhered to both the content and the procedure the teacher had described when planning the play. He used the map to help him when in doubt.

Morten's motivation to work with the group and his motivation to put together a good play within the framework of the subjects they had been studying were interconnected. He used the teamwork with his classmates to carry out the class assignments, jointly resolving both social and academic problems.

He could apply a procedure in the computer game, 'Island Survivors', that was used for experimentation with living conditions by keeping one factor of supplies constant to monitor its effect on how animal species and humans survived on the desert island. The concepts from the model were used quite naturally in the computer game, and these concepts resurfaced in the essay: nature, tools/technology and division of labour. Morten was also able to use the concepts of the model to analyse transitions in society through different time periods and how society has changed into the 'modern' form both in writing a short essay and illustrating this with a drawing (see Figure 1.4.3).

Morten's development in the fifth grade

At the outset of the fifth grade Morten was incapable of combining his readiness to help others with his desire to be proficient in class. In conflict situations others had to help him rejoin social activities, and he had difficulty accepting criticism, i.e., about his approach to translation. However, during the last part of the year he became able to take criticism and initial failure in a completely different way and became able to solve social conflicts by himself. His motive for social cooperation had therefore developed from a motive of 'being together' and demonstrating his academic capacities to his friends to a motive of working together in joint problem solving of the history-based assignments. This change became apparent after he had taken on the role of teacher during the class résumé. Here he discovered that he could be very active in a social situation and at the same time be appreciated for his academic efforts.

Conclusion

The double move teaching approach includes three phases: a problem and model formulation phase, a phase of model and extension in relation to use in relation to a variety of tasks within the subject-matter field and a phase of reflection about the conceptual relations through a challenge to use them in other situations than those where they were acquired. In this process children's cognitive development has to be seen as interrelated with their development of motives. This was what I wanted to demonstrate with the concrete case about Morten's development of a motive for social cooperation and competence in his effort to come to formulate and use core models. Knowledge as well as motives are always culturally created and they are connected to the practice area in which they evolve.

Children acquire competencies through schooling, but for competencies to be relevant

Figure 1.4.3 Morten's description of Danish society today

1 'Farm country.'
2 'It is democratic.'
3 'Our climate varies, but not so much any more since we spoilt the ozone cover: Hello neighbour. Dead because of cancer.'
4 'We live off: potatoes, brown gravy, meatballs (and beer).'

outside school they have to complement children's everyday concepts with the systema-ticity that one finds in subject-matter concepts. They can transform their everyday concepts so they become functional concepts outside the situation in which they are learned when both children's everyday knowledge and motives are taking into consideration when plan-ning teaching. Subject-matter concepts should enrich children's competencies so that they become able to use them outside the immediate situation in which they are acquired. This is what I have tried to demonstrate within the experimental teaching project using the teaching approach of the double move. The finding that the children were able to transcend their learning situation has to be anchored in their engagement with the task. This is exempli-fied through the analyses of Morten's learning activity in the fifth grade. How the teaching proceeded to create motivation and cooperation can be seen in relation to the demands in the last teaching phase. Here children have to be able to reflect upon what they learned and their own competencies. Morten, as well as the other children in the class, had an interested adult visitor from a school in New York City. This led the children to want to communi-cate with children in this school about what they have learned and about their models. Another example from this phase was Morten's and his classmates' experimentation with the concepts of the model in the computer game 'Island Survivors'. A third example was the essay they accomplished about the difference between modern society and earlier societies in Denmark.

In the project of experimental teaching I chose to focus on history teaching mostly because critiques of teaching from the cultural historical perspective have been related to math-ematics and literacy (Aidarova, 1982; Freire, 1970; Davydov, 1990; Lave, 1988; Scribner and Cole; 1981; Scribner and Stevens, 1989). It is also important to find a way to improve teaching within the social science curriculum. Children need competencies related to this field as they grow up in a modern society, a view that has also been reflected in later research work (Leinhardt, Stainton and Virji, 1994; Spoehr and Spoehr; 1994 Tulviste and Wertsch, 1993; Wertsch, 1994). For children to appropriate subject-matter knowledge and a motive to engage in social science subject-matter activities they have to be related both to the everyday concepts that children have when introducing the subject to them as well as to the motives and interest that dominate the age group.

Subject-matter knowledge is related to knowledge within a scientific research field. Knowledge within a scientific research field can be seen as developed from pressing societal problems (Jensen, 1986; Wartofsky, 1979). The societal needs influence how a scientific area develops and which subject-matter is favoured in school. Perhaps history has not been given enough attention because technical matters have been the most obvious problems in modern society and therefore have dominated education. Perhaps educators need to be more aware of societal problems and give more room to educational experimentation in social science teaching. Society needs young people who can work with pressing societal problems in the creation of a cohesive democratic society. To be able to think about present society one has to know about the past, but to think about the past one also has to be aware that one has a posi-tion in today's society and use concepts derived from that society (Hermans, Kempen and van Loon, 1992; Kjelstadli, 1992). This is not what has been reflected in history teaching in school in Denmark (for an overview of history teaching traditions see Hedegaard, 1998).

The ideas that Elkonin and Davydov formulated for teaching theoretical knowledge have developed within a range of subject areas in the Russian educational tradition and have started to provide a robust approach to teaching and learning in school. This project has also evolved within the approach I have formulated as the double move in teaching. It has proved itself useful within social science teaching within a multicultural, diverse society in which history is important and where personal perspectives on history are vital (se also Zinn, 1980; Østergaard, 1992). This led me, together with Seth Chaiklin, to extend the ideas of the double move in teaching which focus on the relation between everyday concepts and subject-matter concepts to include the relation between the knowledge traditions in the local community and general theoretical knowledge about different societal matters. This is an approach we have characterised as 'radical local teaching and learning' (see Hedegaard and Chaiklin, 2005).

Notes

1   Lade Aidarova's teaching was connected with Elkonin and Davydov's developmental teaching project.
2   A germ-cell can also vary with the scientific epistemology of the researcher.
3   For a discussion of this, see Chaiklin (1999).
4   When a new element is introduced into a relationship the earlier elements change their conceptual meaning.

References

Aidarova, L. (1982) *Child Development and Education*, Moscow, Progress.
Bruner, J.S. (1996) *The Culture of Education*, Cambridge, MA, Harvard University Press.
Chaiklin, S. (2000) 'Developmental teaching in upper-secondary school', in M. Hedegaard and J. Lompscher (eds), *Learning Activity and Development,* Aarhus, Aarhus University Press.
—— (2003) 'The zone of proximal development in Vygotsky's analysis of learning and instruction', in A. Kozulin, B. Gindis, V. S. Ageyev and S. M. Miller (eds), *Vygotsky's Educational Theory and Practice in Cultural Context*, Cambridge, Cambridge University Press, pp. 39–64.
Davydov, V.V. (1982) 'Ausbildung der Lerntätigkeit (Development of learning activity)', in V.V. Davydov, J. Lompsher and A. K. Markova (eds), *Ausbildung der Lerntätigkeit bei Schülern*, Berlin, Volk und Wissen.
—— (1988) 'Problems of development teaching', *Soviet Education*, 30, nos. 8, 9, 10.
—— (1990) *Types of Generalization in Instruction: Logical and Psychological Problems in the Structuring of School Curricula*, Soviet studies in mathematics education, vol. 2. Reston, VA, National Council of Teachers of Mathematics.
Elkonin, D.B. (1999) 'Toward the problem of stages in the mental development of the child', *East European Soviet Psychology*, 10, pp. 538–653.
Freire, P. (1970) *Pedagogy of the Oppressed,* New York, Seabury (originally published 1968).
Hedegaard, M. (1988) *Skolebørns Personlighedsudvikling set Gennem Orienteringsfagene* (The development of schoolchildren's personality viewed through social science subjects), Aarhus, Aarhus University Press.
—— (1990) 'The zone of proximal development as basis for instruction', in L. Moll (ed.), *Vygotsky and Education: Instructional Implications and Applications of Sociohistorical Psychology*, New York, Cambridge University Press.
—— (1995) 'The qualitative analyses of the development of a child's theoretical knowledge and thinking', in L. Martin, K. Nelson and E. Toback (eds), *Sociocultural Psychology. Theory and Practice of Doing and Knowing*, New York, Cambridge University Press.
—— (1996) 'How instruction influences children's concepts of evolution', *Mind, Culture, and Activity: An International Journal*, 3, pp. 11–24.
—— (1998) 'History education and didactics', in Y. Engeström, R. Miettinen and R.L. Punamäki (eds), *Perspectives on Activity Theory*, New York, Cambridge University Press.
—— (2002) *Learning and Child Development*, Aarhus, Aarhus University Press.
—— (2004) 'A cultural-historical approach to learning in classrooms', *Outlines: Critical Social Studies*, 6, pp. 21–34.

Hedegaard, M. and Chaiklin, S. (2005) *Radical Local Teaching and Learning*, Aarhus, Aarhus University Press.

Hedegaard, M., Hakkarainen, P. and Engeström, Y. (1984) *Learning and Teaching on a Scientific Basis*, Aarhus, Department of Psychology, Aarhus University.

Hedegaard, M. and Sigersted, G. (1992) *Undervisning i Samfundshistorie* (Teaching social science), Aarhus, Aarhus University Press.

Hermans, H.J., Kempen, J.G. and van Loon, R.J.P. (1992) 'The dialogical self', *American Psychologist*, 47, pp. 23–33.

Jensen, U. (1986) *Practice and Progress: A Theory for the Modern Healthcare Systems*, Oxford, Blackwell Scientific Publishing.

Kjelstadli, K. (1992) *Fortida er ikke hva den en gang var* (The past is not what it used to be), Oslo, Universitets-forlaget.

Lave, J. (1988) *Cognition in Practice: Mind, Mathematics, and Culture in Everyday Life*, New York, Cambridge University Press.

Leakey, R. and Lewin, R. (1978) *People of the Lake: Mankind and its Beginning*, Garden City, NY, Anchor Press/Doubleday.

Leinhardt, G., Stainton, C. and Virji, S.M. (1994) 'A sense of history', *Educational Psychologist*, 29, pp. 78–88.

Leontiev, A.N. (1978) *Activity, Consciousness and Personality*, Englewood Cliffs, NJ, Prentice Hall.

Lewin, K. (1935) *A Dynamic Theory of Personality: Selected Papers*, New York, McGraw Hill.

Lompscher, J. (1982) 'Analyse und Gestaltung von Lernanforderungen' (Analysis and working out of learning demands), in V.V. Davydov, J. Lompsher and A.K. Markova (eds), *Ausbildung der Lerntätigkeit bei Schülern*, Berlin, Volk und Wissen

—— (1984) 'Problems and results of experimental research on the formation of theoretical thinking through instruction', in M. Hedegaard, P. Hakkarainen and Y. Engeström (eds), *Learning and Teaching on a Scientific Basis*, Aarhus, Aarhus University, Department of Psychology.

—— (2000) 'Learning activity and its formation: Ascending from the abstract to the concrete', in M. Hedegaard and J. Lompscher (eds), *Learning Activity and Development*, Aarhus, Aarhus University Press.

Marx, K. (1976) *Capital*, vol. 1, London, Penguin Books.

Mayr, E. (1976) *Evolution and the Diversity of Life*, Cambridge, MA, Harvard University Press.

Østergaard, U. (1992) 'Nationale minoriteter: Et historieforskningsperspektiv' (National minorities: A historical research perspective), in H. Krag and M. Warburg (eds), *Minoriteter*, Copenhagen, Spektrum.

Scribner, S. and Cole, M. (1981) *The Psychology of Literacy*, Cambridge, MA, Harvard University Press.

Scribner, S. and Stevens, J. (1989) *Experimental Studies on the Relationship of School Math and Work Math*, Teachers College, Columbia University, Technical Paper Series, no. 4.

Spoehr, K. and Spoehr, L.W. (1994) 'Learning to think historically', *Educational Psychologist*, 29, pp. 71–7.

Tulviste, P. and Wertsch, J. (1994) 'Official and unofficial histories: The case of Estonia', *Journal of Narrative and Life History*, 4, pp. 311–29.

Wartofsky, M. (1979) *Models: Representations and the Scientific Understanding*, Dordrecht and Boston, D. Reidel.

Wertsch, J.V. (1994) 'Struggling with the past: Some dynamics of historical representation', in M. Carretero and J. Voss (eds), *Cognitive and Instructional Processes in History and Social Sciences*. Hillsdale, NJ, Erlbaum.

Vygotsky, L.S. (1982) *Om Barnets Psykiske Udvikling* (About the child's psychic development), Copenhagen, Nyt Nordisk Forlag.

—— (1998) 'Development of thinking and formation of concepts in the adolescent', in *The Collected Work of L. S. Vygotsky*, vol. 5, *Child Psychology*, New York, Plenum, pp. 29–82.

Zinn, H. (1980) *A People's History of the United States*, New York, Harper and Row.

Reflective questions

1   I have argued for the importance of theoretical knowledge in the form of core models that can relate subject-matter knowledge to everyday knowledge. Can you give examples of how you have worked with conceptual relations in your own activity (i.e., teaching or learning) and how your understanding of these relations enabled you to analyse concrete cases, and how these analyses worked back on your conceptual understanding?
2   I have argued for the interconnection between cognitive and motivational learning and development. Can you give examples from your own learning activity that have challenged you to change or develop your motive?

Further reading

Aidarova, L. (1982) *Child Development and Education*, Moscow, Progress.
Hedegaard, M. (2002) *Learning and Child Development*, Aarhus, Aarhus University Press.
Hedegaard, M. and Chaiklin, S. (2005) *Radical Local Teaching and Learning*, Aarhus, Aarhus University Press.

Section 2
Learning across boundaries
Introduction

Harry Daniels

(Cartoon by Ros Asquith)

In this short but important section, we have placed three chapters which discuss notions of transfer from one setting to another and the practices which allow boundaries between contexts to be crossed. These issues have been a particular concern for researchers and practitioners in fields where the movement between education and practice is in the foreground. Vocational education, apprenticeship, continuing professional development and work-based learning all demand close scrutiny of the relation between formal and informal learning. Such considerations also bring distinctions between tacit and implicit learning in the workplace into question.

In the first chapter in the section Michael Eraut analyses the different knowledge cultures of higher education and the workplace, contrasting the kinds of knowledge that are valued and the manner in which they are acquired and used. He discusses the ways several different forms of knowledge and skill are integrated in the workplace when the conditions allow for a form of analytical and deliberative engagement. He considers the place of tacit knowledge, particularly with respect to how more formal, explicit knowledge is used in specific settings. He also discusses transfer as a learning process that requires both understanding and positive commitment from individual learners, formal education, employers and local workplace managers. He cautions that the neglect of transfer and the downplaying of the gap between formal education and the workplace offer significant barriers to improvement.

In the second chapter Paul Warmington engages with the demands that transformations in the workplace bring in terms of professional learning and for the changed circumstances. His focus is on the formation of multiagency teams in a newly conceived notion of Children's Services in England. He gives an overview of a project that has drawn on the methodology developed in Helsinki, which is discussed in the third chapter. An outline of the preliminary findings gives insight into the complexities of the patterns of learning that are invoked as practitioners learn to cross what have been strong boundaries in the workplace, i.e. between education and social work.

In the final chapter, Hanna Toiviainen and Yrjö Engeström from the Centre for Developmental Work Research in Helsinki introduce another type of learning into this framework. They discuss expansive learning, which may be thought of in terms of learning that leads to new formulations and possibilities for activity. In a sense it is the kind of learning that is involved in the transformation of the workplace. The analysis is based on a consideration of learning that does not rest on a model of the individual learner but reflects on the way in which systems may be thought of in terms of collective learning and transformation. Their chapter introduces the interventionist research approach which has been developed in Helsinki and seeks to facilitate, promote and accelerate expansive learning in the workplace. An important feature of this work is the emphasis on engaging with the historically accumulated contradictions which are embedded in the practices of the workplace.

Taken together these three chapters provide a concise view of recent work which engages with the very important but often neglected learning that takes place as practitioners learn to cross boundaries. This kind of learning is, of course, central to the kind of transformative activity that innovation requires. Ignoring a consideration of these issues could result in stagnation and the ossification of processes of teaching and learning.

2.1 Transfer of knowledge between education and workplace settings

Michael Eraut

Introduction

The first half of this chapter examines the different knowledge cultures of higher education and the workplace. In particular, it contrasts the different discourses for describing knowledge, the different criteria used to value knowledge and the different ways in which knowledge may be acquired and used. Specifically, performance in the workplace typically involves the integration of several different forms of knowledge and skill, under conditions that allow little time for the analytic/deliberative approach favoured in higher education. One consequence is a greater reliance on tacit knowledge (Eraut, 2000, 2004a); and one significant area of this tacit knowledge relates to the transfer of knowledge from higher education settings to workplace settings. I argue that transfer between different settings is a complex learning process, whose very existence is underrated, if not denied. To draw attention to the types of learning involved, I have conceptualised transfer in terms of five stages and draw attention to their distinctive characteristics and learning challenges. The neglect of transfer is attributed both to the cultural gap between formal education and the workplace and to profound ignorance of the nature and amount of the learning involved.

Cultural knowledge and personal knowledge

Both knowledge and learning can be examined from two perspectives, the individual and the social. An individual perspective on knowledge and learning enables us to explore differences both in what and how people learn and in how they interpret what they learn. A social perspective draws attention to the social construction of knowledge and of contexts for learning, and to the wide range of cultural practices and products that provide knowledge resources for learning. In formal higher education, the most prominent of these resources is the academic knowledge embedded in texts and databases and the cultural practices of teaching, studentship, scholarship and research. However, not all such knowledge is both codified and accessible; that depends on it passing the scrutiny of editors, publishers and referees, then being distributed or being purchased and organised by the libraries of educational institutions. Codified academic knowledge is constructed through social processes and builds on the work of countless others, but still carries one or more names, whose contribution is treated as the achievement of a small number of individuals.

My starting assumption is that learning is significantly influenced by the context and setting in which it occurs. Contexts and settings are socially constructed. Even when only one person is present, cultural influence is strongly asserted through the physical environment for learning and cultural artefacts. From that perspective one can argue that all knowledge is cultural knowledge and is socially situated. Understanding the significance of this cultural perspective involves locating knowledge in space and time and determining its distribution, and possibly differential interpretation, across a range of cultural groups. Who has this knowledge? Who was involved in its construction over time? How has it developed from and how is it now positioned in relation to other cultural knowledge? What different forms does it take? How is it evolving? These questions apply equally to education and workplace settings and especially to the interactions and disconnections between the settings. Current approaches to professional and vocational learning are impossible to understand without knowledge of their various traditions, histories and cultures.

Cultural knowledge that has not been codified also plays a key role in most work-based practices and activities. There is considerable debate about the extent to which such knowledge can be made explicit or represented in any textual form, and the evidence gathered so far suggests that its amenability to codification has been greatly exaggerated (Eraut, 2000). What does appear to be generally acknowledged is that much uncodified cultural knowledge is acquired informally through participation in social practices, and much is often so 'taken for granted' that people are unaware of its influence on their behaviour. This phenomenon is much broader in scope than the implicit learning normally associated with the concept of socialisation. In addition to the cultural practices and discourses of different occupations, one has to consider the cultural knowledge of other social groups that permeate their working beliefs and behaviours.

Whereas codified cultural knowledge is frequently discussed in terms of its truth and validity, uncodified knowledge is discussed in terms of its ownership, location and history: who uses this knowledge, where and when? Both types of knowledge may be investigated for their range of meanings, and this is where the interaction of social and individual perspectives is particularly enlightening. The theory of *situated learning* postulates that the personal meaning of a concept, principle or value is significantly influenced by the situations in which it was encountered and the situations in which it was used. Hence the personal meaning of a concept or theory is shaped by the series of contexts in which it has been used. In these days of rapid mobility, the sequence of such contexts is likely to be unique for each individual practitioner, and this may lead to them giving slightly or widely different meanings. Even codified knowledge is personalised to some extent.

I chose the terms *personal knowledge* and *capability* for the individual-centred counterpart to cultural knowledge and defined it as 'what individual persons bring to situations that enables them to think, interact and perform' (Eraut, 1997, 1998). This enabled me to investigate the effects of personal knowledge without necessarily having to represent that knowledge in codified form. The rationale for this definition is that its defining feature is the *use* of the knowledge, not its *truth*. Thus I argue that personal knowledge incorporates all of the following:

- codified knowledge in the form(s) in which the person uses it
- know-how in the form of skills and practices
- personal understandings of people and situations
- accumulated memories of cases and episodic events (Eraut, 2000)
- other aspects of personal expertise, practical wisdom and tacit knowledge
- self-knowledge, attitudes, values and emotions.

The evidence for personal knowledge comes mainly from observations of performance, and this implies a *holistic* rather than *fragmented* approach to knowledge, because unless one stops to deliberate, the knowledge one uses is already available in an *integrated form* and ready for action.

While remaining a strong supporter of the concept of situated learning, I strongly dissent from those theorists, such as Lave and Wenger (1991), who attempt to eradicate the individual perspective on knowledge and learning. Their research, based mainly on fieldwork in stable communities, focuses selectively on common rather than differentiated features of people's knowledge and fails to recognise the need for an individually situated (as well as a socially situated) concept of knowledge in the complex, rapidly changing, post-modern world. Individuals belong to several social groups in which they both acquire and contribute knowledge, and their experiences of multiple group membership cannot be ring-fenced. Many of these groups have changing memberships and relatively short lifetimes. Thus members of a group acquire only part of the knowledge present in that group and interpret it within a personal context and history that has been shaped by their experiences in other groups, both prior and contemporary.

There will also be aspects of a person's knowledge that have been constructed through lifelong learning and have become unique to them, i.e. outside the circle of shared cultural knowledge, because of the unique set of situations in which they have participated. For example, a single idea will acquire a distinct web of meaning for each individual user according to the sequence of situations in which they used it. The greater the range of usage, the more distinctive its personal meaning is likely to be (Eraut, 2000).

Finally, I draw attention to the advantage of using the term 'capability' in that it can refer not only to an individual, but also to a group or an organisation, thus bringing the concepts of 'use' and 'action', and possibly also the concept of 'understanding', to social as well as individual agents.

Types of knowledge acquired in education contexts

Teachers in secondary and post-compulsory education are organised according to the subjects they teach, each of which forms a distinctive sub-culture and provides a major part of their professional identity (Goodson, 1983; Becher, 1989). Most learning pathways that precede full-time employment comprise mainly subjects which have potential vocational relevance but are taught primarily under the auspices of general education. When subjects are claiming territory on the timetable, arguments based on vocational relevance are used with vigour, if not rigour. But, once their territory has been established, historical traditions, the prevailing assumptions of the subject culture and the expertise of the current teaching staff dominate the selection and treatment of academic content. The prime objective becomes progression within the discipline and increasing participation in its culture to first-degree level and beyond, even though only a small minority of students follow that particular path. In many subjects applied aspects are given just a 'walk-on part' and an occasional mention.

Professional and vocational education programmes typically include three kinds of content: these derive from (1) disciplines which feature prominently in general education and form major components of honours degrees, e.g. mathematics, sciences, social sciences, languages; (2) the applied field which sponsors the programme e.g. business, engineering, education, health professions; and (3) occupational practice itself. According to their background and orientation, individual teachers have a primary allegiance to one of these three types of content but are sometimes also required to teach a second. In every case the treatment of the content and its relationship to practice are significantly influenced by the academic and vocational experience of those who teach it.

Most teaching within an applied field is also strongly influenced by an often quite recently constructed body of knowledge about that field, which thus becomes either a quasi-discipline like education or nursing or a constellation of quasi-disciplines like business studies or engineering. Over time, teachers in the applied field are drawn from its own graduates, and a cultural succession becomes possible whereby new teachers are recruited with little or no work experience in the relevant occupation. These may remain a minority, but the codified academic knowledge of the field, as represented in publications, begins to dominate knowledge derived from personal experience of occupational practice, both culturally and experientially, as the impact of early occupational experience recedes. Some of this theory of the applied field is concerned with the application of theories and concepts from scientific disciplines; some is based on empirical research and conceptual frameworks peculiar to the applied field; some is based on the elaboration of practitioner maxims and practical principles; some is based on what can best be described as a preferred view or ideology of the occupation, a theoretical justification of its purposes and practices in terms of moral principles, views of society and occupational beliefs about the effectiveness of various practices.

This last aspect of 'applied field' theory is strongest in occupations based on personal interaction with clients, where there is a strong tendency to construct theories of practice which are ideologically attractive but almost impossible to implement. The main problem is that the professionals concerned are urged to adopt practices that involve much greater levels of time and effort than service users and/or the public purse can possibly finance. Hence, there is a significant gap between the theories of practice taught by former practitioners, based on how they would have liked to have practised, and the activities performed by current practitioners. This contrasts with the common workplace stance, in which current practice is uncritically accepted as an inevitable reality, and any impetus towards improving the service provided by an occupation is lost. Neither provides an adequate basis for a professional career. There are so many variants of problem-based learning (PBL) curricula and staffing strategies that it is impossible to discern the extent to which PBL even attempts to bridge this cultural gap between education and workplace settings.

The third type of course found in education settings involves teaching occupational practice through skill workshops or simulations, or, if there is concurrent work experience, seminars linked to discussions that interpret that experience and introduce relevant theory in order to facilitate learning in the workplace. This last is commonly described as the 'reflective practitioner' model. To be successful these skills sessions or reflective seminars require small student groups, good facilities and hyperactive staff who sustain close working links with practitioners. Recruiting and retaining such staff is often difficult; and in higher education the demands of such bicultural work tend to conflict with activities more likely to lead to promotion.

To conclude this section, I shall briefly summarise the kinds of knowledge which vocational and professional education programmes claim to provide.

1   *Theoretical knowledge* constructed in the context of either a subject discipline or an applied field. This introduces concepts and theories to help students to explain, understand and critique occupational practices and arguments used to justify them, and to appreciate new thinking about the role of the occupation and proposed new forms of practice.
2   *Methodological knowledge* about how evidence is collected, analysed and interpreted in academic contexts and in occupational contexts, and the procedural principles and theoretical justifications for skills and techniques used in the occupational field.

3 *Practical skills and techniques* acquired through skills workshops, laboratory work, studio work, project work, etc.

4 *Generic skills* claimed to be acquired during further and/or higher education, either through direct teaching or, more often, as a side-effect of academic work. These include:

- basic skills in number, language and information technology
- modes of interpersonal communication
- skills associated with learning and thinking in an academic context
- self-management skills.

5 *General knowledge about the occupation*, its structure, modes of working, cultural values and career opportunities.

Although most of these types of knowledge are described as transferable, there is little evidence about the extent to which 2, 4 and 5 are acquired by students and about the chances of 1 and 3 being subsequently transferred (or not) into the workplace. There is even some doubt as to whether the phenomena described as 'transferable skills' have sufficient affinity with workplace activities for the term 'transfer' to be a valid description of any suggested connection.

Types of knowledge used in the workplace

Two research projects studying mid-career learning (Eraut *et al.*, 2001) and early career learning (Eraut *et al.*, 2005a; Eraut, 2007a,b) in the business, engineering and healthcare sectors led to a typology of what was being learned that was applicable across sectors and levels of experience. This involved a combination of (1) urgent, occupation-specific tasks required for meeting the immediate demands of one's allocated work, and (2) longer-term progress along those learning trajectories for which learning opportunities were either explicitly available or embedded in work activities and contexts. Figure 2.1.1 below shows how we have mapped a range of these potential trajectories under eight main headings: task performance; awareness and understanding; personal development; academic knowledge and skills; role performance; teamwork; decision making and problem solving; and judgement. Although our system for coding data used only these eight main headings, most of our final interviews used prompt cards for each heading that included all the sub-categories. These confirmed that the sub-categories were readily understood by all our participants; and we found that every sub-category was recognised as an area of learning progress by at least one participant and usually by several participants. The examples described below come from the first three years of learning at work by accountants, engineers and nurses.

Task performance is a requirement of all jobs. Important issues were the interaction between technical and interpersonal aspects of many tasks and the distinction between tasks that one was quickly able to routinise and tasks in which there were usually some aspects that were slightly, if not totally, novel. Often tasks described in the same words had a long gradient of complexity, along which one learned one's way over long periods of time. For example accountants' audits covered a huge range of complexity, which was reflected in the time taken and the size of the audit team, and nurses often progress from more general to more specialist wards, and within those wards from less complex and risky patients to those that were more challenging. The nature of a professional's tasks also varies with level of responsibility. Even the most senior professional has tasks to perform, and some of them, such as allocation of work or hiring temporary staff, are extremely important.

Task performance
Speed and fluency
Complexity of tasks and problems
Range of skills required
Communication with a wide range of
    people
Collaborative work

Awareness and understanding
Other people: colleagues, customers,
    managers, etc.
Contexts and situations
One's own organization
Problems and risks
Priorities and strategic issues
Value issues

Personal development
Self-evaluation
Self-management
Handling emotions
Building and sustaining relationships
Disposition to attend to other perspectives
Disposition to consult and work with
    others
Disposition to learn and improve one's
    practice
Accessing relevant knowledge and
    expertise
Ability to learn from experience

Academic knowledge and skills
Use of evidence and argument
Accessing formal knowledge
Research-based practice
Theoretical thinking
Knowing what you might need to know
Using knowledge resources (human,
    paper-based, electronic)
Learning how to use relevant theory in a
    range of practical situations

Role performance
Prioritisation
Range of responsibility
Supporting other people's learning
Leadership
Accountability
Supervisory role
Delegation
Handling ethical issues
Coping with unexpected problems
Crisis management
Keeping up-to-date

Teamwork
Collaborative work
Facilitating social relations
Joint planning and problem solving
Ability to engage in and promote mutual
    learning

Decision making and problem solving
When to seek expert help
Dealing with complexity
Group decision making
Problem analysis
Formulating and evaluating options
Managing the process within an
    appropriate timescale
Decision making under pressure

Judgement
Quality of performance, output and
    outcomes
Priorities
Value issues
Levels of risk

Figure 2.1.1   A typology of learning trajectories

Awareness and understanding normally include a considerable amount of tacit knowledge, because people learn a lot in this area without being aware of it. Much of this contributes to what they call 'intuition', but might be better described as experience that has not been subjected to reflection (Eraut, 2000, 2004a,b). One form of this found in all professions is pattern recognition, which plays an important part in recognising when a patient is deteriorating or a set of accounts is inconsistent. Understanding of people and situations is also a cumulative process, as accountants recognised when returning to the same client a year later. Engineers tended to be engaged with much longer-term projects:

Technically I probably don't need to learn too much more … It will be the same skills that are used over and over on our projects … Until I see a project through from beginning to end, I won't have a proper grasp of what goes on at the project with different stages … so, until I've done that, I can't get a proper appreciation of what the programme requires us to do … I need to have a better understanding of what I'm doing which will come with time.

Personal development was very visible to our interviewers, who had the opportunity to visit the same person up to four times in three years. It was also something they frequently referred to, often in passing. Self-management, especially self-organisation and time management, was most prominent in their overt conversation, but they also indirectly informed us about their self-evaluation. Accountants were able to come to terms with multi-tasking, because they had a clear learning trajectory:

The most difficult thing to learn is how to organise yourself around other people … You need to … try and get an understanding of what everyone is going to be doing. … That's something that's … new. Before it was always, went on the job … went off and did it, and if you needed help from someone you got it. Whereas now I'm on the other side … and if someone needs help they come to me … And the chances are you're going to be juggling a few jobs, and finishing off one job while you're doing another, and cope with the needs of both.

Nurses, on the other hand, found that their ongoing duties always exceeded the time available to perform them, and those who lacked support were particularly vulnerable to emotional stress. This threatened both their personal development and their commitment to their profession:

I feel completely overwhelmed by the emotions that I have for this job and completely overwhelmed by the things that I have to deal with on a day-to-day basis which really do affect people's lives, and yet I feel like I am completely underachieving. I've got so many abilities that I don't feel are tapped and so much potential which isn't being looked at, and it frustrates me.

Academic knowledge and skills were used and occasionally extended by engineers and nurses, but it often took some time to recognise when they were relevant and how best to use them (see later sections). Surprisingly, several were given short specialist knowledge courses in some areas without getting any subsequent opportunity to use them; this was yet another source of frustration.

Role performance, on the other hand, was probably the most reported aspect of learning, because most participants were expanding their roles throughout our research. Indeed, just summarising their responsibilities at the end of the three-year period provides an excellent overview of what they had to learn in order to properly perform the roles they were assigned. For nurses this entailed:

- Being in charge of the ward (and all that entails), e.g. always being the one that people ask; patient allocation; efficient running of the ward; ensuring staff have breaks; acting as a 'filter' for information both down to nurses working in the bays and up to senior nurses on shift and also laterally to other professionals such as doctors and physiothera-pists; as well as to the public.

- Dealing with clinical and managerial issues, as opposed to just clinical issues.
- Being responsible for other members of staff as well as patients.
- Taking on extra duties such as giving formal teaching sessions, off-duty planning, dealing with complaints, venepuncture and cannulation skills and attending to the budget.

Another aspect of leadership mentioned by a few participants was challenging other people or policies, which required personal skills and timing as well as good arguments.

Teamwork is found to varying degrees in all three professions, but does not appear to be on their learning agendas. What was noticeable was the role of shared artefacts jn team communications. The accountants had audit files, past and current, as jointly held records of progress; the nurses shared protocols and made daily use of handover notes; the engineers shared diagrams, software packages and files. The tight deadlines in accounting help to strengthen team behaviours, but these teams rarely stayed together for very long. Shift allocations and high proportions of agency staff often reduced attempts to develop teams in hospital wards. Short-term construction projects put a high premium on teamwork, because the workers are highly interdependent, but other engineering projects are so large and long that co-ordination roles take precedence over teamwork.

Decision making and problem solving and *judgement* frequently arose in conversations with workers who felt challenged, but were usually missing from the others. Lack of this respon-sibility was usually the major cause of dissatisfaction for those who experienced it. I return to this in a later section.

In the opening section of this chapter we noted that most occupational activities require that several types of knowledge are integrated into a holistic performance. How then can we reconcile the use of learning trajectories depicting changes in aspects of performance over time with recognition of the holistic nature of most kinds of performance? We decided that points on our learning trajectories should be treated as windows on episodes of practice, in which (1) the aspect of learning portrayed by the trajectory had played a significant part, and (2) the current use of the trajectory had been sustained or enhanced. This could be achieved only if each window included the following information about the performance:

- the setting in which it took place, and features of that setting that affected or might have affected the performance;
- the conditions under which the performance took place, e.g. degree of supervision, pressure of time, crowdedness, conflicting priorities, availability of resources;
- the antecedents to the performance and the situation that gave rise to the performance;
- the other categories of expertise involved;
- any differences from previously recorded episodes;
- indicators of expertise in the domain of the trajectory having been maintained, widened or enhanced.

This gives considerable emphasis to working contexts and conditions. Not only is situational understanding context-specific, but it requires knowledge acquired through experience, and the capability to decide and act requires both experience of working in the context and adapta-tion to a range of local conditions. Moreover, it is unusual for a performance to use knowledge from only one trajectory. Hence it is important to discover the interactions within a cluster

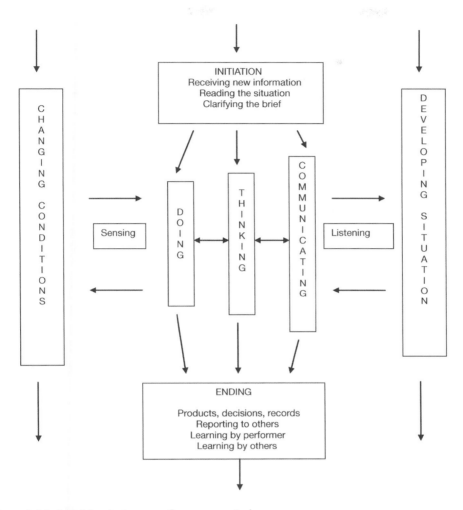

Figure 2.1.2 Activities during a performance period

of relevant trajectories. One possible response to this is to consider the interactions between different types of activity during a performance period, as shown in Figure 2.1.2 above.

The period chosen for analysis will vary according to the focus and the occupation; for example one could consider a lesson, a clinic, a shift or a day. A major aspect of professional experience is that many tasks do not get completed during a performance period, so there is the constant problem of 'picking up the threads' at the beginning or receiving new information that will cause a change of plan; then a need to record progress at the end and/or to hand clients over to a colleague. This is reflected in the separate boxes for 'initiation' to indicate the initial briefing and reading of the situation when the period starts, and for 'ending' to indicate what has been achieved, or left undone, by the time the period ends.

One advantage of using a performance period is that situations often develop over time. So, instead of a static model in which all decisions and plans are made at the beginning of a period, one has a dynamic model in which a constantly changing environment provides a changing input that leads to the constant modification of plans. The input side is shown by placing the activities within a context characterised by changing conditions and a developing situation, with the opportunity for inputs prompted by sensing and listening. A great deal of competent behaviour depends not just on being able to do certain things (output) but also on the correct reading of the ongoing situation (input) so that the appropriate action can be taken. Nor is it only the external environment that changes of its own accord. The performer is an actor who affects that environment, not always in totally predictable ways. So another role of input is to provide feedback on the effect of one's own performance. This applies whether one is making something and sensing it change, or talking to people while listening to their reply and observing their reaction.

The interpretation of this input is just one aspect of the cognitive element, indicated by a central column labelled 'thinking'. Other aspects of thinking include planning and monitoring one's activities and solving problems. People are constantly thinking and making decisions as they go along, even though they could probably tell you very little about it afterwards. Hence 'thinking' is shown in constant interaction with 'doing' and 'communicating'. These activities overlap to some extent, the main distinction being that between acting on inanimate objects and interacting with other human beings.

Another aspect of complexity arising from this model of a performance period is that interaction and integration can occur both across learning trajectories and within any particular learning trajectory. Complex knowledge cannot often be described by using only one mode of representation.

Factors affecting modes of cognition in workplace performance

The performance-period approach introduces issues pertaining to the pace and pressure of the workplace, and, through emphasising the importance of cognition, raises the question of when and how workers find the time to think. This led to a model linking four types of professional activity to different amounts of thinking time and, hence, to examining the *modes of cognition* employed in professional work (Figure 2.1.3). The four types of activity were:

1   Assessing clients and situations (sometimes briefly, sometimes involving a long process of investigation) and continuing to monitor their condition.
2   Deciding what, if any, action to take, both immediately and over a longer period (either on one's own or as a leader or member of a team).
3   Pursuing an agreed course of action, modifying, consulting and reassessing as and when necessary.
4   Managing oneself, one's job and one's continuing learning in a context of constrained time and resources, conflicting priorities and complex inter- and intra-professional relationships.

These activities can take many different forms according to the speed and context and the types of technical and personal expertise being deployed. Although analytically distinct, they may be combined into an integrated performance that does not follow a simple sequence of assessment, decision and then action. For example a health professional will often have to decide whether to take action and then reassess whether to continue with a further assessment of their client or whether to simply wait and see. There may be several assessments,

Type of process	Mode of cognition		
	Instant/reflex	**Rapid/intuitive**	**Deliberative/ analytic**
Reading of the situation	Pattern recognition	Rapid interpretation	Review involving discussions and/or analysis
Decision-making	Instant response	Intuitive	Deliberative with some analysis or discussion
Overt activity	Routinised action	Routines punctuated by rapid decisions	Planned actions with periodic progress reviews
Metacognitive	Situational awareness	Implicit monitoring. Short, reactive reflections	Conscious monitoring of thought and activity. Self-management. Evaluation

Figure 2.1.3 Interactions between time, mode of cognition and type of process (Eraut, 2000)

decisions and actions within a single period of consultation and treatment. Indeed recording both the nature of these activities and the ways in which they are sequenced and combined is another very useful approach to describing professional practice.

In order to understand the nature of workplace performance, one has to examine the thinking entailed in carrying out these activities, which depends on both (1) the conditions and constraints on the performer, and (2) what the performer has learned to do, with or without stopping to think. Sometimes the situation itself demands a rapid response; sometimes rapid fluent action is the hallmark of the performer's proficiency; sometimes the number of activities proceeding simultaneously limits the attention that can be given to any of them, i.e. the workload is so heavy that there is little time to think. Thus the model assumes that *time* is the variable that most affects *mode of cognition* and divides the time-continuum into three sections, headed 'instant', 'rapid' and 'deliberative'. These terms attempt to describe how the timescale is perceived by the performer and are interpreted differently according to the orientations of performers and the nature of their work. For example, in one context *rapid* might refer to any period less than a minute, while in another context it might include periods of up to ten minutes or even half an hour. The critical feature is that the performer has little time to think in an analytic mode.

The *instant/reflex* column describes routinised behaviour that, at most, is semi-conscious. The *rapid/intuitive* column indicates greater awareness of what one is doing and is often characterised by rapid decision making within a period of continuous, semi-routinised action. Typically it involves recognition of situations by comparison with similar situations previously encountered, then responding to them with already learned procedures.

The time available affects the degree of mismatch that is tolerated, because rejection of action based on precedent leads to a deliberative, problem-solving and hence more time-consuming approach. The *deliberative/analytic* column is characterised by explicit thinking about one's actions in the past, present or future, possibly accompanied by consultation with others. It involves the conscious use of prior knowledge, sometimes in accustomed ways, sometimes in novel ways or in a more critical manner.

The interesting question arises as to whether performers are aware of the knowledge embedded in their practice when it is not explicitly used at the time. Four very different circumstances may pertain:

1   The practice was modelled on that of other professionals without understanding the reason for it or being aware of any underpinning knowledge.
2   The practice was developed with awareness of its rationale and underpinning theory, but that awareness dissipated over time and with it the ability to explain or justify it.
3   The practice can still be justified by citing underpinning theory but cannot withstand any challenge because there has been no critical evaluation of the practice since it was first adopted.
4   The practice not only can be justified but remains under the professional's critical control because it has been periodically re-evaluated.

The need for knowledge transfer during initial training and the period of workplace learning that follows it will largely be determined by whether the desired option is (1) or (4) above.

Two problems are likely when the use of underpinning knowledge is not under critical control. First, conflicts may arise in problematic cases between competing responses based on different practical principles – these cannot be resolved unless the underlying reasons for these principles are understood. Second, there is a danger that 'scientific' knowledge will be replaced by unscientific knowledge – that which falls within the domain of a discipline but is regarded by leading professionals as either incorrect or alarmingly incomplete. The normal assumption is that being a competent professional implies keeping one's practice under critical control and therefore keeping up to date with relevant areas of theory and research. Reviews of practice may arise from individual reflection and consultation or, more officially, from the work of an appointed group that reviews the rationale for the practice, the evidence for its effectiveness, alternative approaches and recent research, and may lead to a decision to retain the practice unchanged, modify it or adopt an alternative But, in spite of the growing emphasis on audit and on evidence-based practice, such reviews are far from frequent and are restricted by the limited, and often exaggerated, scope of research-based evidence.

Transfer as a learning process

My own definition of transfer is 'the learning process involved when a person learns to use previously acquired knowledge/skills/competence/expertise in a new situation'. This may be short and easy if the new situation is similar to some of those previously encountered, or long and very challenging if the new situation is complex and unfamiliar. At least four variables are important influences:

1   the nature of what is being transferred
2   differences between the contexts

3   the disposition of the transferee
4   the time and effort devoted to facilitating the transfer process.

In the complex situations encountered by most professional workers, the transfer process typically involves five inter-related stages:

1   extracting potentially relevant knowledge from the context(s) of its acquisition and previous use;
2   understanding the new situation, a process that often depends on informal social learning;
3   recognising what knowledge and skills are relevant;
4   transforming them to fit the new situation;
5   integrating them with other knowledge and skills in order to think/act/communicate in the new situation.

Transferring a specific concept or idea from an education setting to a workplace setting is particularly difficult, because of the considerable differences in context, culture and modes of learning. One major justification for teaching theory in an education setting is its transfer-ability and generalisability, but to what extent is this true in practice and for whom is it true? Within higher education settings, the prevalent but not universal view of an ideal student is a person who has taken ownership of a repertoire of theoretical ideas and used them in essays and projects in novel ways. This is reflected in degree classification schemes that use criteria which include a student's use of ideas in a manner that goes beyond one specific knowledge source. My own experience is that significantly independent use of ideas, which transcends reasonable comprehension and good organisation of material, is associated with an Upper Second class of degree, a level reached by about half the candidates. For sub-degree awards, the proportion of students demonstrating, or even getting an opportunity to demonstrate, independent ownership of ideas is significantly lower. Not surprisingly, there is a contrast between the 'preferred view' of lecturers and research into students' learning orientations.

The distinction between deep and surface approaches to learning derives from research by Marton *et al.* (1984). They defined a deep approach to learning in terms of trying to understand the underlying purpose and meaning of the information encountered, to make a critical assessment of it and to reach a personal viewpoint; whereas a surface approach is demonstrating acquaintance with and comprehension of information without actively seeking to restructure it or develop any personal perspective. Most authors assume, not always explicitly, that a deep approach is desirable, but its accomplishment is treated in different ways. For example Perry (1968) regards it as a result of intellectual and ethical development in the higher education context, while others have treated it more like a sophis-ticated skill or threshold competence. Yet others interpret it as being dependent on interest in the subject, an indicator of intrinsic motivation. Ideologically, the notion of deep learning is well attuned to the academic psyche, but those who see the purpose of undergraduate education as getting qualified and acquiring useful competence will tend to regard it as a luxury.

While Marton's work was based on research into how students learn from texts, more sociologically orientated research has focused on the effect of the academic context on students' levels and direction of effort. Becker *et al.* (1968), Snyder (1971) and Miller and Parlett (1974) present accounts of students seeking to survive and succeed by maximising the return on their academic effort. They learn to recognise what the system rewards, set their own goals and try to achieve them economically at minimum risk. Thus students' approaches to learning are determined primarily by the teaching and assessment regime and students' strategies for negotiating it. They observe what teachers reward, not what goals they espouse. Academics, with only limited control over their teaching and assessment regimes, do not find this line of research attractive and are generally reluctant to see themselves as task masters rather than role models and students as pursuing grades rather than learning for its own sake.

There is substantial evidence from psychologists (Entwistle, 1992) to suggest that most teaching and assessment regimes encourage surface approaches to learning, so the two research themes are intimately connected. Moreover, research into professional education, in particular, suggests that one effect of occupational socialisation is that most aspiring professionals come to value practical experience more highly than academic courses. For most students, codified academic knowledge has not been liberated from its original academic source and is unlikely to be *ready for transfer* unless there is special provision through problem-based learning or seminars whose prime purpose is to link prior theoretical knowledge with reflections on personal experience in the workplace.

Situational understanding in the workplace is highly dependent on experience. Dreyfus and Dreyfus (1986) describe *advanced beginners* as having limited situational perception and using guidelines for action based on the perceived attributes or aspects of each situation. Aspects are global characteristics of situations, recognisable only after some prior experience; and, at this stage, all attributes are treated separately and given equal importance. In contrast, *proficient workers* see situations holistically rather than in terms of aspects and see what is most important in a situation. They perceive deviations from the normal pattern and use maxims for guidance, whose meaning varies according to the situation. Related learning often entails a combination of the unconscious aggregation in memory of experiences with cases and episodes of activity, incidental learning from other people about the salient aspects of situations and reflection on one's more memorable experiences.

Such processes, however, are not theory-free, and the Dreyfus brothers give little attention to the role of theory in situational understanding. Knowledge of theories taught in education settings may alert workers to the implications of particular aspects of situations, e.g. fluid balance in a hospital patient, electrical hazards or theories of motivation, provided their relevance is recognised. But personal theories are also constructed out of experience as part of the natural human process of looking for patterns and meanings and trying to make sense of one's experience. These ways of construing and thinking about the world have been called 'schemes of experience' (Schutz, 1967), 'personal constructs' (Kelly, 1955) or 'schemas' (Bartlett, 1932). The use of scientific theories is discussed further below, while the problem of making personal theories explicit and bringing them under critical control is discussed by Argyris and Schon (1974) and Eraut (2000).

Recognising what knowledge and skills are relevant is not as simple as it seems. When teachers in education settings spend time discussing how their theoretical contributions relate to practice, a large collection of potentially relevant theory is quickly assembled. But who uses which parts of it, why and when? The earlier section on modes of cognition noted that time to consider theory is at a premium in the workplace and suggested that most theory was more likely to be embedded in practice than explicitly used in daily decision making. There is a marked contrast between the very large number of knowledge areas deemed relevant by those who teach them and the very limited number of knowledge areas that can be taken into account at any one time by a busy practitioner with a high caseload. The practitioner has to assess the priority to be accorded to each particular area of knowledge

Status of knowledge	Emergency	Short-term action	Medium to long-term future	Review of practice
Embedded in Assessment Decisions Behaviour				
Explicit influence on Assessment Decisions Behaviour				

Figure 2.1.4 Framework for deciding priority areas of knowledge

in each particular situation, but in practice patterns of attention will soon be developed and only some knowledge areas will even be considered.

Recognising what theory you need in any particular situation is mainly learned through participation in practice and getting feedback on your actions; most components of a practitioner's theoretical repertoire remain dormant until triggered by a very specific aspect of the situation. In healthcare contexts the nature of the client(s) is the main factor determining what knowledge and skills are relevant; but timescale is also important. Figure 2.1.4 presents a useful framework for discussing and deciding not just which areas of theory are relevant to a particular case but also their respective priority. It can be supported by an appropriate checklist of areas of theory.

The two rows allow a distinction to be made between (1) knowledge embedded in practice through routines or protocols but which remains essential for the justification of that practice and (2) knowledge which needs to be explicitly considered at the time. Such knowledge may influence how the client is assessed, what decisions are made and/or how the practitioner interacts with the client.

The column headings reflect the assumption that priorities will vary according to the timescale. For example, the knowledge used to treat a patient in hospital with a stable condition will not necessarily be given priority in an emergency, and yet other kinds of knowledge may become important when longer-term issues are being considered.

The fourth column, headed 'review of practice', has been added for two reasons. First to ensure that embedded knowledge is reviewed at some time and, second, to enable contextual factors constraining practice to be identified and addressed in a way which would not normally be possible when an individual client is the focus of attention. Such reviews of practice might occur in the context of audit, continuing professional development, a formal evaluation or funded research.

The framework presented in Figure 2.1.4 can be used both to find out what practitioners currently do, in which case embedded knowledge may be difficult to elicit without using special methods of inquiry (Eraut, 2000; Fessey, 2002), and to discuss what they ought to do. Repeated use on a case-by-case basis would reveal common patterns of practice, differentiation between clients and concerns about the efficacy of practice, including the cumulative effect of neglecting longer-term issues. Using this framework to broaden the scope of cases used in problem-based learning could also play an important role in orienting students towards the significance of a wider range of theory without inducing cognitive overload.

In order to consider the problems entailed in *transforming and resituating theoretical knowledge*, I shall focus attention on the use of scientific knowledge by healthcare professionals, using a broad definition of scientific knowledge to include the social sciences as well as the natural science disciplines and theoretical knowledge from the practice-orientated literature of individual professions. The knowledge maps I use as heuristics for eliciting and discussing practitioner knowledge were developed during research into the use of scientific knowledge by nurses and midwives (Eraut *et al.*, 1995, 1996). Our approach was to interview experienced practitioners, engaged in mentoring students, about recent cases involving the use of particular areas of scientific knowledge and to use a matrix to summarise the information we gathered.

Figure 2.1.5 is the first half of a map depicting aspects of knowledge about acute pain used by surgical nurses and when and how they are used. The rows cover relevant topics of codified knowledge within the area of acute pain, while the column headings describe the range of activities that constitute the practice of surgical nurses. The missing half contains a further 14 columns under the headings 'alternative methods', 'drugs' and 'assess response'. The use of knowledge from a particular topic (row) during a particular activity (column) is indicated by making an entry in the appropriate box. Our research found significant differences in the headings of the matrix between specialisms, and some variation according to the type of clinical setting. Relatively few differences were noted between respondents from similar settings, but samples were not large enough for that to be a definitive finding.

The entries in the boxes indicate different kinds of knowledge use, codified for brevity. The 'R' coding indicates that 'recognition' is all that is required, very little further interpretation is needed and the transfer problem is mainly that of spotting when it is relevant; whereas the 'U' coding indicates that significant 'understanding' of the knowledge is required and probably some transformation. The knowledge has to be reinterpreted in order to be resituated. The numerical headings relate to the mode of cognition and correspond to the 'instant', 'rapid' and 'deliberative' modes of response portrayed in Figure 2.1.3:

1   *simple application*, for which recognising that some specific piece of knowledge was relevant, was virtually all that was needed in order to take appropriate action;
2   *situational adaptation*, where the appropriate response from an established repertoire was selected according to how the situation was understood, usually by matching one's model of the situation with situations previously encountered (described by Klein (1989) as Recognition Primed Decision Making); and
3   *problem solving*, where the appropriate course of action had to be worked out from first principles.

Only with this third category was scientific knowledge explicitly used during the relevant episode of practice. In categories (1) and (2) any scientific knowledge used was embedded in already familiar understandings and actions. Since category (2) depends on the knowledge user having sufficient prior experience of similar situations, those lacking such experience have either to consult more experienced colleagues or engage in a slower, problem-solving approach that makes more explicit use of scientific knowledge. Resorting to consultation is quicker but usually leads to new practices being acquired without any theoretical justification.

Areas of knowledge	ASSESS PATIENT			ASSESS PAIN			ASSERTAIN CAUSE					
	Person-ality	Know-ledge	History	Vital signs	Ability to cope	Inten-sity	Unrelated to surgery	Signs of infection	Haema-toma	Retention of urine	Constip-ation	Wound assessment
1 Nerve pathways				U3			R2					
2 Transmission/ perception of pain	U2	U2				U2	U2		U2	U3	U3	U3
3 Causes of pain	U2	U2	U2	U3	U2	U2	U2	U2	U2	U3	U3	U3
4 Effects of pain	U2	U2		U3	U2	U2				U2	U2	
5 Bacteriology			U2	U2			R2	U3		R2		R2
6 Pharmac-ology			U2									
7 Anaesthesia			U2	U2			R2					
8 Wound healing				U3				U3	U2			U3
9 Barriers to expression of pain	U2	U2	U2		U2	U2						
10 Pre and post operative care			U2	U3	U2	U2		U3	U3	U3	U3	U3
11 Alternative methods	U3	U3			U3	U3						

KNOWLEDGE USE CODE

R Appreciating the relevance of the knowledge
U_Understanding and interpreting the knowledge

1 Simple application
2 Situational adaptation
3 Problem solving

Figure 2.1.5 Part 1: Knowledge of acute pain used by surgical nurses

Parboteeah (2001) found that the use of knowledge maps is best taught to student nurses in practice settings and in 'real time' as and when relevant events occur. But, after an initiation period of 'on-the-spot' tutoring, students become able to use knowledge maps on their own with consultative access to 'experts' and even to create new maps as part of a group project. Newly qualified practitioners will need a similar induction before they can begin to use knowledge maps as a guide to the kinds of knowledge that need to be fed into their decision-making processes, for the identification of their learning needs and for the debriefing of experts who find it hard to explain their apparently intuitive decisions. We have found them to be especially useful in initiating discussions about knowledge use and the more hidden aspects of practice during Continuing Professional Development.

The final stage in transfer involves combining the various relevant aspects of knowledge and skill into an *integrated, holistic, performance*. It will probably interact with those aspects of the previous stage that are relatively new, and will cease to be distinguishable as a separate stage when sufficient practice has created a rapid response. In practice reviews, prior attention should be given to the selection of the most relevant aspects of knowledge (see Figure 2.1.3), before using knowledge maps as aids to probe more deeply.

Conclusion

To discuss the implications of this analysis of transfer, let me introduce the metaphor of an iceberg. The learning of codified knowledge for assessment in an examination can be represented by that part of the iceberg that appears above the surface. This learning is explicit and well supported by textbooks and formal teaching. The further learning required to convert that codified knowledge into personal knowledge that is ready for use in a range of possible situations can be represented by that part of the iceberg which is hidden below the surface. Some books shed a little light in some areas, but the terrain is mainly obscure. Knowing how to use theoretical knowledge is largely tacit knowledge. Support for such learning is minimal and little time is set aside for it. The very existence of ice below the surface is symbolically denied. So when students find such learning difficult (which it usually is) they are likely either to blame themselves for being inadequate or to reject the theoretical knowledge as irrelevant. This raises the important further question of how much further learning is required in order to transfer theoretical knowledge from an academic setting into occupational practice. The analysis in this chapter suggests, in accordance with the metaphor of the iceberg, most of which lies below the surface, that the transfer process may entail considerably more learning than the original acquisition of the academic knowledge, i.e. that traditional thinking about transfer underestimates the learning involved by an order of magnitude.

Although professional preparation programmes include both theory and practice, few of them give serious attention to the issues discussed above, and in some professions the separation of theory and practice components over time and space militates against their integration. In vocational programmes we now have qualification frameworks that separately specify knowledge and competence, without giving any attention to the linkage between them or to how knowledge use might be assessed. These are areas where the intelligent development of more integrated programmes and more appropriate staffing could make a real difference. In particular, the introduction of a practice development role that incorporates responsibility for both students and new staff, and the facilitation of continuing learning in the workplace by experienced staff, should be considered. Until the nature and importance of transfer is recognised and supported in this way, the impact of education on the workplace will continue to be lower than expected, and the quality of work will suffer from the limited use of relevant knowledge. Surely it is time that government policies for qualifications and lifelong learning began to address this problem?

Acknowledgements

Reproduced from *Workplace Learning in Context*, edited by Helen Rainbird, Alison Fuller and Anne Munro, © 2004 Routledge. Reproduced by permission of Taylor & Francis Books UK.

References

Argyris, C. and Schon, D.A. (1974) *Theory in Practice: Increasing Professional Effectiveness*, San Francisco, Jossey Bass.

Bartlett, F.C. (1932) *Remembering: A Study in Experimental and Social Psychology*, Cambridge University Press.

Becher, T. (1989) *Academic Tribes and Territories*, Buckingham, Open University Press.

Becker, H., Geer, B. and Hughes, E.C. (1968) *Making the Grade: The Academic Side of College Life*, New York, Wiley.

Dreyfus, H.L. and Dreyfus, S.E. (1986) *Mind over Machine: The Power of Human Intuition and Expertise in the Era of the Computer*, Oxford, Blackwell.

Entwistle, N. (1992) *The Impact of Teaching on Learning Outcomes in Higher Education*, Sheffield, CVCP Staff Development Unit.

Eraut, M. (1997) 'Perspectives on defining "the learning society"', *Journal of Education Policy*, 12(6), pp. 551–8.

—— (1998) 'Concepts of competence', *Journal of Interprofessional Care*, 12(2), pp. 127–39.

—— (2000) 'Non-formal learning and tacit knowledge in professional work', *British Journal of Educational Psychology*, 70, pp. 113–36.

—— (2004a) 'Informal learning in the workplace', *Studies in Continuing Education*, 26(2), pp. 247–73.

—— (2004b) 'The practice of reflection', *Learning in Health and Social Care*, 3(2), pp. 47–52.

—— (2007a) 'Feedback and formative assessment in the workplace'. Presentation to TLRP seminar series on Assessment of Significant Learning Outcomes, University of London Institute of Education, 1 May.

—— (2007b) 'Learning from other people in the workplace', *Oxford Review of Education*, 33(4), pp. 403–22.

Eraut, M., Alderton, J., Boylan, A. and Wraight, A. (1995) *Learning to Use Scientific Knowledge in Education and Practice Settings*, London, English National Board for Nursing, Midwifery and Health Visiting.

—— (1996) 'Mediating Scientific knowledge into health care practice: evidence from pre-registration programmes in nursing and midwifery education'. Paper presented to the AERA Conference, New York, April.

Eraut, M., Alderton, J., Cole, G., and Senker, P. (2001) 'Development of knowledge and skills at work'. in Coffield, F. (ed.), *Differing Visions of a Learning Society*, Bristol, Policy Press, vol. 1, pp. 1231–62.

Eraut, M., Maillardet, F., Miller, C., Steadman, S., Ali, A., Blackman, C. and Furner, J. (2005a) 'What is learned in the workplace and how? typologies and results from a cross-professional longitudinal study'. Paper presented at the EARLI biannual conference, Nicosia.

Fessey, C. (2002) 'Capturing expertise in the development of practice: methodology and approaches', *Learning in Health and Social Care*, 1(1), pp. 47–58.

Goodson, I. (1983) *School Subjects and Curriculum Change*, Beckenham, Croom Helm.

Kelly, G. A. (1955) *The Psychology of Personal Constructs*, New York, Norton.

Klein, G. A. (1989) 'Recognition-primed decisions', in Rouse, W. B. (ed.), *Advances in Man-Machine Systems Research*, Greenwich CT, JAI Press, pp. 47–92.

Lave, J. and Wenger, E. (1991) *Situated Learning: Legitimate Peripheral Participation*, Cambridge University Press.

Marton, F., Hounsell, D. and Entwistle, N. (eds) (1984) *The Experience of Learning*, Edinburgh, Scottish Academic Press.

Miller, C.M.L. and Parlett, M. (1974) *Up to the Mark: A Study of the Examinations Game*, Guildford, SRHE.

Parboteeah, S. (2001) 'The effect of using knowledge maps as a mediating artefact in pre-registration nurse education'. DPhil thesis, University of Sussex.

Perry, W.G. (1968) *Forms of Intellectual and Ethical Development in the College Years: A Scheme*, New York, Holt, Rinehart & Winston.

Schutz, A. (1967) *The Phenomenology of the Social World* (trans. G. Walsh and F. Lehnert from 1932 original), Evanston, IL, Northwestern University Press.

Snyder, B.R. (1971) *The Hidden Curriculum*, New York, Knopf.

Reflective questions

1   One key issue running through this chapter is the complexity and partly tacit nature of work. Try to analyse a complex activity in which you have acquired some skill and unpick its various components and/or aspects by using in turn:
   • the bullet points on page 66
   • Figure 2.1.1, the typology of learning trajectories
   • Figure 2.1.2, the performance period diagram
   • Figure 2.1.3, on modes of cognition.
2   Can you locate one or two pieces of academic knowledge which you have used in a work or community setting? If so, can you remember how long it took you to recognise its relevance and how you learned to adjust it to fit the new context?

Further reading

Tuomi-Gröhn, T. and Engeström, Y. (eds) (2003) *Between School and Work: New Perspectives on Transfer and Boundary-crossing*, Amsterdam, Boston, Pergamon.

2.2 Learning in and for multiagency working

Paul Warmington

Introduction

The notion of 'multiagency' working pervades contemporary UK social policy. This is particularly the case in children's services, where since 2003 local authority provision has been framed by the *Every Child Matters* agenda. Ushered in by the New Labour government, the *Every Child Matters* Green Paper emphasised the need to begin 'integrating professionals through multi-disciplinary teams responsible for identifying children at risk, and working with the child and family to ensure services are tailored to their needs' (Department for Education and Skills, 2003, p. 51). Multiagency working has thus been characterised as a driver of social inclusion. Effective collaboration across education, social care, health services, mental health services and criminal justice has been depicted as essential to supporting young people and families who are 'at risk' of social exclusion. However, relatively little attention has been paid to how professionals might learn to 'do' multiagency working or 'become' multiagency workers. Arguably, this is because much of the UK literature has underestimated the qualitative changes in professional practice that shifts towards multiagency working entail; much policy and strategic literature implies models of working that no longer match the landscape of emerging practice. As service providers increasingly work across traditional service and team boundaries, professionals find themselves located in complex, vertiginous settings in which individual and collective practices are undergoing radical transformation that necessitates new learning and knowledge creation.

This chapter outlines some of the key concepts necessary to understand and develop professional learning in multiagency settings. It draws upon findings emerging from the Learning in and for Interagency Working project (LIW), a four-year study funded by the Economic and Social Research Council, in which researchers conducted intensive studies of multiagency work practices in a set of UK local authorities (see Acknowledgements at the end of this chapter). In each authority researchers worked with children's services practitioners, principally in workshop settings, to analyse the development of current professional knowledge and practices, identify existing contradictions in practice and thereby encourage new professional learning, rooted in reflective, systemic analysis of multiagency working. The LIW research was informed, in part, by an interest in the challenges of what Victor and Boynton (1998) describe as 'co-configuration' work. In the context of multiagency working for social inclusion, co-configuration can be thought of in terms of ongoing partnerships between professionals, young people and families to support young people's pathways out of social exclusion. This co-configuration work demands a capacity to recognise and access expertise distributed across local systems and to negotiate the rules of responsible professional action with other professionals and clients.

In this chapter, therefore, discussion of learning in and for multiagency working focuses upon the concept of distributed expertise, the ways in which practitioners carve trails to access the expertise of others and the kinds of boundary-crossing that this necessitates. It considers the tools and rules that can enable or constrain multiagency working and the prevalence of creative rule-bending among professionals who work across traditional organisational and sector boundaries. Also emphasised is the necessary intersection between the 'horizontal learning' that develops as practitioners negotiate residual boundaries between professions or agencies and the 'vertical learning' that results from new flows of knowledge between those working at operational and strategic levels. Exploration of these concepts is framed by the innovations in *activity theory*-derived research developed by Engeström (1987, 2001, 2004, 2007). These are concerned with 'expansive learning': a conceptual framework for understanding forms of learning that do not adhere to standard models of competence (in which stable, defined bodies of knowledge and skills are acquired over time by individuals or organisations). Instead, Engeström argues (1987, 2001), expansive learning develops in settings, such as multiagency working, in which existing knowledge and practices do not suffice and workers are developing new, inchoate professional practices.

Multiagency learning

In the wake of *Every Child Matters* UK children's services professionals have found themselves responding to demands for new, qualitatively different forms of multiagency practice, in which providers operate across traditional service and team boundaries. Portmanteau terms such as 'interagency', 'interprofessional' and 'multiagency' may be used to imply a range of structures, approaches and rationales (Atkinson *et al.*, 2002; Warmington *et al.*, 2004). However, the LIW project was not principally concerned with bureaucratic variants but with the learning of professionals engaged in the creation of new forms of practice. The research was informed by three particular concerns:

- the identification of new professional practices emerging within multiagency settings;
- the creation of new knowledge rooted in reflective, systemic analysis, which might be levered into more effective multiagency working;
- the location of emergent multiagency practice within an understanding of the changing character of service provision and user engagement.

The main fieldwork phases of the LIW project comprised intensive studies of multiagency groupings in a total of five English local authorities; these were organised around series of workshop interventions adapted from Engeström's 'developmental work research' approach. These research interventions included work with a youth offending team, a children in public care team, extended services operating around a school and a multiprofessional team comprising education and social care professionals.

Activity theory

The LIW project's analytical framework was derived from recent innovations in activity theory, particularly the work of Engeström (1987, 2001, 2004, 2007), who has extensively studied the creation of new professional practices in Finnish public services. Like Engeström, the LIW project defined learning as an ability to interpret our worlds in increasingly complex ways and to respond effectively to those interpretations. The 'expansive learning' described by Engeström (1987, 2001) is a driver of both individual and organisational change. Expansive learning produces culturally new patterns of activity; it expands understanding and changes practice. Standard theories of learning (those which concern themselves with the mastery of tightly defined competencies) fail to explain how new forms of practice are created and organisations transformed. How professionals respond to changes in the organisation of work very much depends on what the workplace (and the tools, rules and divisions of labour that define it) allows. Therefore, the standpoint of the LIW project was that understandings of individual learning cannot be separated from understandings of organisational learning (Daniels *et al.*, 2007). The project built on this view in two ways. First, it examined learning across traditional organisational and professional boundaries and not simply within one organisation or team. Second, the project examined professional learning by following the 'object' of professional actions.

Activity theory provided a framework in which to analyse these dimensions of professional learning. It is rooted in the work of the Russian social psychologist L. S. Vygotsky and his successors in the field (Vygotsky, 1978, 1986; Leont'ev, 1978). In essence, Vygotsky was concerned to understand human activity in terms of the dynamics between human actors (*subjects*) and the conceptual and/or material artefacts (*tools*) that they developed in order to impact upon aspects of the world around them (the *object* of their activities). This is an object-orientated analysis of human activity; that is, its starting point is understanding what it is that individuals or organisations are seeking to change or to shift. In the course of the LIW project's work in local authorities, therefore, researchers asked different groups of professionals to explain what it is that they were 'working on'. When we asked this kind of question we were not just concerned with the broad outcomes that professionals wanted to achieve, such as, for instance, improving client referral systems; we wanted to encourage professionals to explain the exact practices that they believed they would have to transform in order to improve referral processes. It might be, for example, that they were trying to find a way to ensure that a child and family had to complete only one assessment form, rather than a series of forms. In this case the transformation of the assessment form process became the *object* of the activity; the various children's services professionals carrying out the activity were the *subjects*; their *tools* were the artefacts that they created to work on improving assessment forms (this could be anything from a new electronic information system to the appointment of a case co-coordinator to a new diary system).

In developing activity theory Engeström (2001, 2004) has focused on examining systems of activity at the level of the collective and the community, in preference to concentrating only on the individual actor. This 'second generation' of activity theory aims to represent the collective nature of activity through the consideration of elements such as *community*, *rules* and *division of labour*, alongside the triad of subject–tool–object. An important aspect of Engeström's version of activity theory is an understanding that object-orientated activity is always characterised by ambiguity, surprise, interpretation, sense making and potential for change. When we asked participants in the LIW study what they were 'working on' the answers we received were complex, diverse and often contradictory. Engeström (1987, 2001) emphasises the importance of contradictions within activity systems as the driving force of change and development. By referring to 'contradictions' in work practices, Engeström (2001, p. 137) is alluding to 'historically accumulating structural tensions' that emerge over time in organisational practices. These contradictions may constrain professional practice at certain points but they may also become a source of new practices. For instance, in the LIW study we identified numerous instances in which the efforts of different professional groups (such as teachers, educational psychologists, health workers, social care staff) to work on a shared object (such as the well-being of at-risk young people) were shaped by the contradictions that emerge from having to work to conflicting, contradictory sets of rules, such as different professional targets, referral thresholds and assessment procedures.

Developmental work research

The LIW project worked with children's services practitioners in five local authorities. In each site the study was organised around a series of research workshops mainly involving operational staff. These were adapted from the workshop format used by Engeström (2001, 2007) in what he has termed *developmental work research* (DWR). This is a methodology for applying activity theory in order to develop expansive learning in workplace settings. Its value to the LIW project was that DWR does not assume that practitioners are always learning to master stable, defined bodies of knowledge and skills; instead it focuses on the kind of 'process' learning required in many contemporary settings, wherein work practices and organisational configurations are undergoing rapid change and workers are creating new knowledge and new ways of working. DWR-style workshops were apposite to our research sites, where professionals were responding to the demands of the broad agenda of *Every Child Matters* and, in some instances, to local reorganisations of divisions of labour.

DWR workshops begin with professionals and researchers jointly questioning embedded workplace practices, then progressing through stepwise transformations that envisage new forms of practice. The LIW researchers worked jointly with practitioners to interrogate the deep-seated rules underpinning past and current work practices and surface their inherent structural tensions. This cycle offered opportunities for reconceptualising the objects that professionals were working on, the tools that they used in their multiagency work and the rules in which their professional practices were embedded. In the most effective instances the workshops became spaces for actively and collectively developing new patterns of professional activity. Prior to the workshops the research team collected interview and observational data that was later jointly scrutinised in workshop settings by researchers and professionals. Analysis focused upon:

- *present practice:* identifying structural tensions (or 'contradictions') in current working practices;
- *past practice:* encouraging professionals to consider the historical development of their working practices;
- *future practice:* working with professionals to suggest new forms of practice that might effectively support innovations in multiagency working.

Using activity theory as a shared analytical framework, the workshops were designed to support reflective systemic analysis by confronting professionals' 'everyday' understandings of their work activity with critical analyses of the ways in which current working patterns either enabled or constrained the development of multiagency practice.

However, Engeström's (2007) recent work on professional identity and organisational change has drawn attention to the risks and anxieties that make expansive learning cycles unstable. In the LIW workshops there were clear instances in which participants acknowledged, as a result of reflective analysis, that changes were required in organisational practices, but this recognition did not ensure that practitioners were able to imagine themselves leading these changes (Daniels *et al.*, 2007). This directs attention to the affective dimensions of change which are too often under-theorised in studies of the development of new forms of professional practice.

Distributed expertise

One of the pervasive features of the multiagency settings in which the LIW project worked was the emergence of forms of distributed expertise. Multiagency service provision means that the case of an 'at-risk' child is rarely the province of one 'team' but entails diverse professionals from education, social care, health and other agencies coalescing around the child's case trajectory. Therefore, issues of how expertise and specialist knowledge are claimed, owned and shared are important and often problematic. It is not only how expertise is distributed between professionals and around cases that is important; the emergence of patterns of distributed expertise has also prompted examination of professional values and beliefs about learning to work with other professionals whose values, priorities, targets and systems might be different (Leadbetter *et al.*, 2007). Accessing distributed expertise is strongly dependent on professionals understanding the rules, both formal and informal, within which other professionals' practices are embedded. Contradictions emerge in multiagency activities because of contrasting professional values and because different professionals may work to divergent targets, statutory guidelines and thresholds of concern. Frequently, in the settings examined in the LIW project, there were contradictions between, for instance, 'whole-child' initiatives in schools and the pressures upon teachers to meet academic targets. These contradictions stemmed from the different statutory requirements under which, say, teachers and social care staff operate but also from different informal assumptions about children's well-being and the purpose of schooling.

In order to understand patterns of distributed expertise, it is important to explore the dynamic, relational ways in which professional learning and professional practice unfold. One challenge presented by distributed expertise is the need to develop tools to support joint, holistic readings of young people's cases, wherein different professionals try to address young people's cases through simultaneous, 'parallel' collaboration rather than producing atomised, 'sequential' analyses of clients' needs. The shift from sequential to parallel collaboration has been explored by Puonti (2004), who describes shifts in the handling of fraud cases by multiple agencies. While there is a lengthy history of courts, police and tax officers collaborating to counter fraud, there are distinctions between the forms that multiagency case work has taken. In sequential modes cases are passed from one agency to another in linear fashion, without any more interaction between agencies than is necessary to transfer the caseload; by contrast, in the parallel model, joint action is undertaken in real time, simultaneously, and the understanding of the case is subject to continual, nuanced negotiation between the participating agencies. This complex depiction of the case object as a trajectory bears comparison with the holistic approach to assessing and managing clients' cases now favoured (in theory, at least) in multiagency working in UK children's services (cf. Lloyd *et al.*, 2001; Atkinson *et al.*, 2002).

The LIW project surfaced several examples of tensions between sequential and parallel collaboration being generated by local authorities' different approaches to orchestrating distributed expertise. In reflecting on recent cases, groups of diverse professionals were disconcerted when they realised that they had a tendency to talk about young people's cases in terms of passing on 'bits' of the case from one agency to another. They acknowledged the challenges of drawing together distributed expertise in ways that would support a 'whole-child' approach. Across the course of each series of workshops, participants repeatedly emphasised processes of coming to know potential networks or 'trails' of colleagues and resources. These 'cognitive trails' (cf. Cussins, 1992) were more fluid and dynamic than formal teams or networks and suggested potential ways for practitioners to navigate their way around the distributed expertise existing in their local authorities. Such trails might prefigure effective multiagency working.

Boundaries and trails

The notion of *boundary-crossing* offers a means of conceptualising the ways in which collaboration between workers from different professional backgrounds might generate new professional practices (Kerosuo and Engeström, 2003). As such, boundary-crossing connotes the risks and cultural tensions generated by multiprofessional or multiagency working, as well as the knowledge creation generated when practitioners operate outside of traditional silos. Standard notions of professional expertise imply a vertical model, in which practitioners develop competence over time as they acquire new levels of professional knowledge, graduating 'upwards' level by level in their own specialisms. By contrast, boundary-crossing suggests that expertise is also developed when practitioners collaborate *horizontally* across sectors. Among the multiagency children's services groups involved the LIW project boundary-crossing enabled the development of 'knowing who' trails: the building of knowledge about the kinds of skills and expertise other professionals could offer and a confident understanding of how to access others' expertise. These trails often unfolded informally; they were described in terms 'corridor conversations' or instances when a practitioner had supplemented or circumvented formal referral procedures by telephoning or emailing an acquaintance. However, such trails could also be supported by formalised tools, such as case meetings, referral processes and information-sharing databases.

Insofar as boundary-crossing represents a movement across professional silos, across expertise and specialisation, it is predicated not only on knowledge of what other professionals do but *why* they operate as they do. There is a need to focus on the ways in which professional knowledge, relationships and identities incorporate learning 'who', 'how', 'what', 'why' and 'when'; that is, *who* should be contacted in a particular case, *when* to call upon the expertise of other professionals, *how* other professionals might be accessed. Moreover, it is important to explore the dynamic, relational ways in which professional learning and professional practice unfold. This means asking *with* whom practices are developed, *where* current practices lead *to*, where practices have emerged *from* and *around* what activities and processes new practices emerge. These are questions that acknowledge professional learning in multiagency settings as being embedded in fluid social and cultural contexts.

Tools, resources and systemic change

Activity theory's conceptual framework can facilitate analysis of the tools that professionals draw upon and develop (or, in some cases, create anew) in order to work upon the objects of their practice. In the LIW study these tools were sometimes described by practitioners simply as 'resources'; they might be concrete tools, such as case meetings or assessment forms, or conceptual tools. In our workshops professionals were asked to present summaries of cases in which they had been involved. As well as asking questions about who was involved in the case and how different professionals coalesced around the case, questions about tool or resource creation were also explored. Workshop participants were asked:

- what tools/resources do you already have?
- how are you using them?
- can they be built into the system?

The question of whether practitioners' tools could be used more systemically than they sometimes were at present was central to our concern with knowledge creation. A scenario that emerged in a number of instances suggested that professionals sometimes developed isolated innovations in practice that left wider systems of activity untouched. For example, in one multiprofessional team an educational psychologist and an education welfare officer worked beyond the call of duty with a child who had experienced severe bullying in her secondary school and was now refusing to attend. The two professionals' informal contacts with each other suggested that, over time, they had laid effective trails that had enabled them to access each other's expertise when necessary. They also felt able, within reason, to bend referral rules where necessary, in order to secure the well-being of the child. However, what was absent was a real sense that their practices made a systemic impact on the school with which they were working, since the school's processes for identifying bullying, dealing with it and making referrals to extended services remained largely unchanged. As such, the multi-professional team members remained hero-innovators but isolates. Their practice was driven by expanding the object of their practice in an 'ideological' sense, so that the 'whole child' became their object, rather than just attendance issues. The well-being of the child, rather than the process rules of the school, was the key driver. The flexible, innovative practice produced addressed the immediate problem but there was no 'systemic' expansion of the object. In short, there was an unproductive contradiction between new multiagency practice and old system rules, which suggested that, were a similar case to arise, its solution would again be dependent on the goodwill and heroic practice of individual professionals.

Nuanced understandings of tool creation have been developed by Wartofsky (1979) and Engeström (1990). New tools are embodiments of new knowledge and may be much more complex than they first seem. Engeström (1990) elaborated Wartofsky's (1979) three-level hierarchy of artefacts according to their use:

- 'what' tools point to the evident connection between the tool and its use;
- 'how' tools explain how something is done and diagnostic 'why' artefacts explain why particular practices are employed;
- 'where to' tools are 'future orientated', in that they point towards potential developments in practice.

In the LIW research sites the challenge of developing 'where to' tools was a pervasive feature of the workshops. In one local authority site the creation of new tools and rules was driven by a major reconfiguration of labour, in which a multiprofessional team that had previously comprised professionals from education backgrounds, such as educational psychologists, counsellors and education welfare officers, was reorganised to incorporate social care staff, too. In this case there were clear examples of work taking place around all three levels of tool creation. When the multiprofessional team was reconfigured to incorporate social care professionals it became apparent that 'what', 'why' and 'where to' knowledge began to be renegotiated within the new team because the common experiences and backgrounds that had bound together the education staff were disrupted by the entry of another professional culture. The creation of 'where to' tools was also a key issue in the multiprofessional team's work with schools. Multiprofessional staff indicated that it was much easier to initiate systemic work in schools if the school had already begun some systemic reform of its own. In such cases the multiprofessional team and the school met midway because both were driven by a desire to expand existing school systems. In a sense, this kind of shared 'ideological' basis was a 'where to' tool in itself, in that it assisted the multiprofessional team in progressing beyond making marginal heroic innovations and impacting instead on the school's systemic learning.

Rule-bending

As was evident in the case in which members of a multiprofessional team loosened standard referral rules in order to meet the needs of a bullied pupil, the LIW study suggested that responsive, multiagency service provision often called for a degree of 'rule-bending' on the part of staff. 'Rule-bending' occurred in cases where staff had identified the need for exceptional, partially improvised decision-making in order to meet highly personalised client needs and/or rapidly changing situations. In such cases professionals sought to ensure that local authority processes and routines did not unduly constrain their responses to clients' needs. Constructive forms of rule-bending relied upon the creation of organisational climates that supported flexible, responsive action by professionals and promoted learning for future practice from the ways in which staff negotiated structural tensions between rules, tools, objects and professional identity. Glisson and Hemmelgarn's (1998) study of the effects of organisational climate and interorganisational co-ordination on the quality and outcomes of US children's services systems offers noteworthy findings in respect to rule-bending. They conclude that efforts to improve children's services provision should focus on developing positive organisational climates that are conducive to practitioner improvisation. While high-quality services are characterised, in part, by forms of process-orientation that ensure availability, comprehensiveness and continuity, 'process-related requirements for quality service are not necessarily related to outcome criteria' (Glisson and Hemmelgarn, 1998, p. 416). In short, approaches that are overly process-orientated risk limiting 'employee discretion and responsiveness to unexpected problems and opportunities'. Their analysis indicates that improved outcomes for young people are strongly related to practitioners' 'tenacity in navigating … bureaucratic hurdles … to achieve the most needed services for each child' (Glisson and Hemmelgarn, 1998, p. 416).

Co-configuration

Organisational climates that allow for rule-bending have something in common with Victor and Boynton's (1998) concept of *co-configuration*, which they define as the production of intelligent, flexible services with a high degree of client participation. This definition resembles innovations evident in some current children's services provision, where a range of agencies and otherwise loosely connected professionals coalesce to work with young people and their families. Co-configuration is, therefore, characterised by shifts away from compact teams or professional networks. Children's services professionals working with particular families may not share a common professional background or values, or even a common physical location; they may meet quite fleetingly in a variety of configurations. Arguably, children's services professionals increasingly operate on the cusp between new co-configuration-type work and longer-established professional practices. Rule-bending climates are predicated upon highly responsive, highly personalised case work and customised relationships between professionals and young people that emphasise the need for client participation in planning and decision-making. Moreover, these climates are driven by results in relation to whole-child well-being, rather than rigid adherence to process. Discussion in the LIW workshops surfaced the role that rule-bending (negotiating and challenging the structural tensions that exist in professional systems) can play in expanding professional learning in multiagency children's services settings.

Conclusion

Multiagency working has acquired totemic status within current UK social policy, yet demands for 'joined up' social provision are rarely informed by conceptualisation of the professional learning necessary to effect new forms of practice. Moreover, because much literature on multiagency working stems either from strategic visions of 'ideal' service delivery or neat good practice modelling, the extent to which lived experience of multiagency developments is marked by contradictions, ambiguity, anxieties and sense-making is often under-emphasised. Participatory research concerned with developing transformative models of professional learning in and for multiagency work must be predicated upon substantive understanding of the changing character of organisational work and user engagement. Activity theory offers analyses of individual and organisational learning that extend beyond the description of bureaucratic formations, procedures, conventions and strategies. The professional learning challenges identified in this chapter demand a capacity to access distributed expertise, to negotiate the boundaries of responsible professional action with other professionals and, in certain instances, to push those boundaries by bending existing rules. Multiagency expertise is created when practitioners collaborate horizontally across sectors. However, it is likely that spaces in which practitioners are able to learn in and for multiagency working are only effectively created where there is also vertical learning, developed within boundary zones between strategic and operational levels of practice. Intersections between vertical and horizontal learning are what support flexible, responsive action by professionals and promote learning for future multiagency practice by creating work climates in which professionals can creatively negotiate structural tensions between rules, tools, objects and divisions of labour. Understanding of the different ways in which professionals are learning to negotiate such contradictions should continue to inform research into learning in and for multiagency working.

Acknowledgements

This paper draws on conceptual and methodological developments emerging from the Economic and Social Research Council-funded Teaching and Learning Research Programme study, 'Learning in and for Interagency Working'. The project was directed by Professor Harry Daniels (University of Bath) and Professor Anne Edwards (University of Oxford) between January 2004 and December 2007.

References

Atkinson, M., Wilkin, A., Stott, A., Doherty, P. and Kinder, K. (2002) *Multi-agency Working: A Detailed Study,* Slough, National Foundation for Education Research.

Cussins, A. (1992) 'Content, embodiment and objectivity: the theory of cognitive trails', *Mind*, 101, pp. 651–88.

Daniels, H., Leadbetter, J. and Warmington, P., with Edwards, A., Martin, D., Middleton, D., Popova, A., Apostolov, A. and Brown, S. (2007) 'Learning in and for multiagency working', *Oxford Review of Education*, 33(4), pp. 521–38.

Department for Education and Skills (2003) *Every Child Matters*, London, DfES.

Engeström, Y. (1987) *Learning by Expanding: An Activity-theoretical Approach to Developmental Research,* Helsinki, Orienta-Konsultit.

—— (1990) *Learning, Working and Imagining: Twelve Studies in Activity Theory,* Helsinki, Orienta-Konsultit.

Engeström, Y. (2001) 'Expansive learning at work: toward an activity theoretical reconceptualisation', *Journal of Education and Work*, 14(1), pp. 133–56.

—— (2004) 'New forms of learning in co-configuration work', paper presented to the Department of Information Systems 'ICTs in the contemporary world' seminar, LSE, January 2004.

—— (2007) 'Putting activity theory to work: the change laboratory as an application of double stimulation', in H. Daniels, M. Cole and J.V. Wertsch (eds), *The Cambridge Companion to Vygotsky*, New York, Cambridge University Press, pp. 363–82.

Glisson, C. and Hemmelgarn, A. (1998) 'The effects of organizational climate and interorganisational coordination on the quality and outcomes of children's service system', *Child Abuse and Neglect*, 22(5), pp. 401–21.

Kerosuo, H. and Engeström, Y. (2003) 'Boundary crossing and learning in creation of new work practice', *Journal of Workplace Learning*, 15(7–8), pp. 345–51.

Leadbetter, J., Daniels, H., Edwards, A., Martin, D., Middleton, D., Popova, A., Warmington, P., Apostolov, A. and Brown, S. (2007) 'Professional learning within multi-agency children's services: researching into practice', *Educational Research*, 49(1), pp. 83–98.

Leont'ev A.N. (1978) *Activity, Consciousness, and Personality*, Englewood Cliffs, Prentice Hall.

Lloyd, G., Stead, J. and Kendrick, A. (2001) *Hanging On in There: A Study of Interagency Work to Prevent School Exclusion*, London, National Children's Bureau/Joseph Rowntree Foundation.

Puonti, A. (2004) *Learning to Work Together: Collaboration between Authorities in Economic-crime Investigation*, Helsinki, University of Helsinki.

Victor, B. and Boynton, A. (1998) *Invented Here: Maximizing Your Organization's Internal Growth and Profitability*, Boston, Harvard Business School Press.

Vygotsky, L. (1978) *Mind in Society*, Cambridge, MA, Harvard University Press.

—— (1986) *Thought and Language*, Cambridge, MA, Massachusetts Institute of Technology Press.

Warmington, P., Daniels, H., Edwards, A., Leadbetter, J., Martin, D., Brown, S. and Middleton, D. (2005) *Interagency Collaboration: A Review of the Literature*, University of Bath, Learning in and for Interagency Working Project.

Wartofsky, M. (1979) *Models, Representations and the Scientific Understanding*, Dordrecht, Reidel.

Reflective questions

1   I have argued that the notion of boundary-crossing suggests professional expertise is developed when practitioners collaborate horizontally across sectors. Identify instances in which your own work has entailed interprofessional or interorganisational boundary-crossing. What new learning was produced? What tensions were generated?

2   I have suggested that responsive, multiagency service provision often calls for a degree of 'rule-bending' on the part of staff. Think of settings in which you have worked. To what extent has the organisational climate either facilitated or constrained constructive rule-bending? What have been the effects on professional practice and the ability to meet clients' needs?

Further reading

Daniels, H. and Warmington, P. (2007) 'Analysing third generation activity systems: power, contradictions and personal transformation', *Journal of Workplace Learning*, 19(6), pp. 377–91.

Engeström, Y. (2001) 'Expansive learning at work: toward an activity theoretical reconceptualisation', *Journal of Education and Work*, 14(1), pp. 133–56.

Glisson, C. and Hemmelgarn, A. (1998) 'The effects of organizational climate and interorganisational coordination on the quality and outcomes of children's service system', *Child Abuse and Neglect*, 22(5), pp. 401–21.

2.3 Expansive learning in and for work

Hanna Toiviainen and Yrjö Engeström

Introduction

This chapter addresses the challenges of expansive learning in and for work.[1] In today's society and working life, expertise activities involve complex boundary-crossings and a readiness to integrate multiple fields of professional work into the production of goods and services. The customers and end-users are actively contributing to production activity, which calls for new ways of societal interaction and new media of communication. By adopting the cultural-historical activity theory approach, we claim that the object of work in expertise work is radically expanding socially in collaborative networks; materially by integrating complex knowledge; and temporally by involving long-term partnerships and products that learn over time. The key points made in this chapter are:

1   Expansive learning in and for work means working on the changing and expanding object of activity and taking mastery over the future challenges of collaborative production.
2   Co-configuration is one way of conceptualizing the future mode of production that may answer the challenges.
3   The hypothesis of co-configuration needs to be analyzed in concrete, historical work activity. The empirical case presented emphasizes the fact that the creation and implementation of new tools are crucial in the transformation to more advanced modes of collaboration and production activity.
4   The major transformations and expansive learning in and for work do not take place spontaneously. They need to be carefully analyzed and supported by deliberate learning interventions in close collaboration with the workers. The Change Laboratory is a method designed to support such development of work activity.
5   To put the important points to work, we present as a case study the Change Laboratory that was carried out with a group of investment managers providing services to exclusively rich customers while facing major changes in wealth-management activity.

Expansive learning in and for work: the roots and current development

The idea of expansive learning differs considerably from what we traditionally may conceive as learning. It is customary to think that learning has taken place when an individual acquires some knowledge or skill that a competent teacher transfers to him or her through instruction and scaffolding. This learning mechanism has also been recognized at the level of organizations as knowledge is created and stored in the organization's knowledge repositories.

Collective-level models are often rather metaphorical adaptations of the individual-level cognitivist concepts, as has been pointed out in some studies of organizational learning (Araujo, 1998; Casey, 2005). Expansive learning, on the contrary, is based on a form of socio-cultural thinking according to which learning does not primarily deal with individual minds and well-bounded stocks of knowledge. Learning is culturally mediated in the society which opens up perspectives to analyze the learning of communities as well as its individual members (Engeström, 1987).

The notion of mediation, or artifact-mediated human action, was first articulated in psychology by Vygotsky (1978) during the 1920s and 1930s, later identified as the start of the approach known as cultural-historical activity theory. Engeström (2001, p. 134) has summarized the significance of this beginning:

> The insertion of cultural artifacts into human actions was revolutionary in that the basic unit of analysis now overcame the split between the Cartesian individual and the untouchable societal structure. The individual could no longer be understood without his or her cultural means; and the society could no longer be understood without the agency of individuals who use and produce artifacts. This meant that objects ceased to be just raw material for the formation of logical operations in the subject as they were for Piaget. Objects became cultural entities and the object-orientedness of action became the key to understanding human psyche.

Vygotsky's research, which concentrated on individual action, was developed into the theory of collective activity by his contemporaries (Leont'ev, 1978) and later on by researchers in the West since the 1970s (Chaiklin *et al.*, 1999; Engelsted *et al.*, 1993; Engeström *et al.*, 1999; Nardi, 1996). The theory of expansive learning (Engeström, 1987) and the Change Laboratory method (Engeström, 2007) aimed at enhancing expansive learning in and for work belong to the current developments of activity theory.

Since Vygotsky, cultural-historical activity theory has evolved through several generations of research. Engeström (2001) argues that the most recent one addresses networks of multiple activity systems, which means that the unit of analysis should include two activity systems, at minimum, orienting towards at least partially shared objects of activity. However, what we face more and more when studying learning in various work settings are rapidly organizing and ever-changing collaborative knots and 'mycorrhizae' activities (Engeström, 2006), where the identification of whole systems may be problematic. In addition, the novel technologies change and challenge the modes of mediation of human activity, which calls for new approaches (Bødker and Andersen, 2005). These are theoretical tensions to be dealt with and solved in future research. Today's activity-theoretical concepts and methodological tools will obviously need to be further elaborated and enriched.

One of the principles informing the current activity theory studies is the possibility of expansive transformation in activity systems. As Engeström (2001, p. 137) puts it:

> An expansive transformation is accomplished when the object and motive of the activity are reconceptualized to embrace a radically wider horizon of possibilities than in the previous mode of the activity. A full cycle of expansive transformation may be understood as a collective journey through the *zone of proximal development* of the activity. (Italics in the original text.)

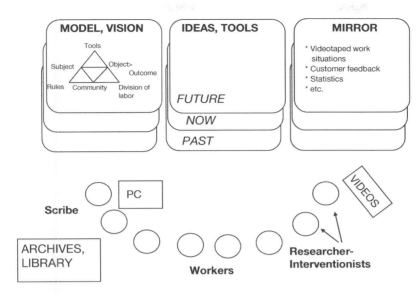

Figure 2.3.1 The prototypical layout of the Change Laboratory

The concept of the zone of proximal development, for Vygotsky (1978) a tool for analyzing a child's developmental potential, is in the theory of expansive learning elaborated to mean the distance between the present everyday actions of individuals and the historically new form of the societal activity that can be collectively generated as a solution to the contradictions of the activity (Engeström, 1987, p. 174). Expansive learning may thus be seen as a process whereby the learners are searching for solutions to the contradictions and moving in the direction of the zone of proximal development. It proceeds through subsequent steps, the learning actions, which are: questioning, analyzing, modeling, implementing, and reflecting and consolidating. It is noteworthy that the knowledge to be learned is not given but actually collaboratively constructed during and through the process. What is given are the cultural means and resources available for the actors. This kind of learning process towards a more advanced activity is far from being harmonious; rather it is characterized by a multi-voicedness and tension-laden encounters.

The Change Laboratory method, then, may be seen as a practical implementation of the cycle of expansive learning, working on the zone of proximal development of the participants' collective activity, such as the work activity in a working unit or across organizational boundaries. Figure 2.3.1 shows the prototypical layout of the Change Laboratory, a space organized near the work location to enhance both a closeness to and reflective distance from the everyday activity (Engeström, 2007). The role of the tools is most central in the setting. On the one hand, the Change Laboratory provides the participants with representational tools to analyze the disturbances and to construct new models of the work activity. On the other, when modeling the activity, the design and implementation of new tools for work is crucial for expanding the object of work. In the case presented here we carried out a process of 12 Change Laboratory sessions with the wealth-management unit in which we followed the phases of expansive learning from questioning of the present activity to the implementation of the new model of activity and finally towards reflection on its workability.

To summarize, we focus here particularly on the analysis of the zone of proximal development of the work done by the investment managers in a wealth-management unit. We take the notion of co-configuration as a historically derived hypothesis of a more advanced way of working and collaborating and analyze to what extent the implementation of a new tool by the participants contributes to the expansion of the object of work and, thereby, enhances learning in and for work. The reader may reflect upon three questions while following our analysis:

1   What kind of tool is the new investment plan in relation to the work of the investment managers and to the potential of co-configuration?
2   How was the investment plan implemented in the wealth-management unit during the Change Laboratory intervention?
3   What does the implementation of the investment plan tell us about the potential of co-configuration and expansive learning in and for work?

Historical analysis: co-configuration in the zone of proximal development of investment management

Our working hypothesis is that co-configuration as a mode of organizing production represents a historically new way of working. Victor and Boynton (1998) argue that co-configuration is following the previously predominant forms of work: craft, mass production, process enhancement, and mass customization. Work is done today in collaborative networks. The customer, the producer, and the product will be committed to a long-term partnership which will not end at the delivery of the ready-made product. The partnership is living and changing throughout the product's life-span, during which the parties, the product included, learn from each other and from the transformation process. In co-configuration the product mediates the customer relationship and maintains the dialogue between the partners. Thus the knowledge produced and used in the process will change; co-configuration is based on dialogic knowledge. The products and services typically produce and document customer-specific knowledge which becomes an essential part of the product.

What would co-configuration mean for the work of the investment managers who produce immaterial wealth-management services rather than material products? 'The product' has traditionally been embodied in an individual investment manager, which has made the service production vulnerable and formed a barrier to knowledge sharing. The knowledge is to a great extent tacit in nature, which Victor and Boynton associate with craft-like expertise. Following co-configuration, the product should carry an inbuilt feature of creating and storing customer-specific knowledge. This requires material instruments, tools for wealth management, mediating the changing needs of the customer as well as supporting learning in the producer, user, and the service interaction.

The zone of proximal development of the investment managers is defined in terms of the expanding object of work and the long-term orientation required from more profitable investment management services (Figure 2.3.2). We may analyze four historically specific types of work, in which the object of work and the expertise needed differ markedly from each other. One of the types has been broker work (Field 1) which partly explains the strong orientation to stock trading even in current investment management activity.

The phase following broker activity was the work of investment managers in Field 2. During the 1980s, customers became more and more aware of their needs, requiring resource-

Expanding object of work

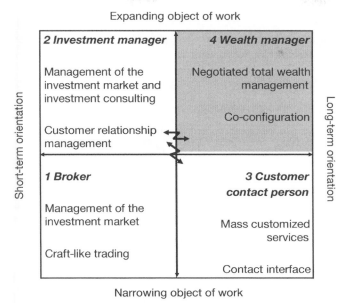

Figure 2.3.2 Co-configuration in the zone of proximal development of the investment managers' work (gray field)

intensive services. People got wealthy, new customer types emerged, and the financing units decided to group their clientele according to their needs and the amount of their wealth.

The lightning-shaped arrows show the contradictory directions in the zone of proximal development. The transition from the present investment manager's work to wealth management and co-configuration (Field 4) is anything but self-evident. Co-configuration would expand the work to a more collaborative practice among the service-providing experts and customers. The investment manager's role would change to have a responsibility for the realization and justification of the overall strategy. The crucial issue is under which conditions this kind of activity is profitable and productive. The solution in many wealth-management companies has been a model where the customer is contacted individually, but the offering consists of standardized sets of mass products. This means that the customer interface and the specialist expertise have been differentiated (Field 3). For our investment managers this was a scenario in which their work would be reduced to the maintenance of the contact interface.

In a favorable market situation at the turn of the millennium there was not much need to break out of the relatively narrow broker–investment manager work and the stock trading orientation. The object of work was the investment portfolios. In 2003 the need for change was expressed by several agents. First, the management of the wealth-management unit started to worry about weakened profitability. Second, the customers that we interviewed wished to get more holistic wealth-management services. Third, the investment managers themselves reflected on their work as being mainly stock trading and following the market, whereas they felt they should be starting to develop broader and more comprehensive services for their customers.

New investment plan as a tool of co-configuration

The implementation of a new wealth-management tool, the investment plan, coincided with our Change Laboratory project and investigation of co-configuration work. The investment plan was a digital form of several items to be filled in with the customer. The items included the description and analysis of the total wealth of the investor and the property to be invested, the goals of investing, the risk level adopted, evaluation of the present investments in relation to the goals, taxation aspects, and the description of the selected investment strategy.

From the company's perspective, the investment plan was meant to improve the quality of services, find new earning possibilities and improve risk management. Without a written plan there was a risk of not specifying the customer's goals or documenting the selected investment strategy explicitly enough. The service producer had to be able to show that these issues had been addressed and then followed accordingly. In addition, officials such as the Financial Supervision Authority and the Committee of European Securities Regulators (CESR) had set new guidelines on up-to-date information on the customer's wealth management which clearly called for new tools for managing investment services.

We as researchers saw that the investment plan included elements that might support the shift to the co-configuration work of wealth managers – to working with a network of service providers and having a more long-term and holistic orientation than was possible in the broker–investment manager work. We interviewed the investment managers, who talked about their present ways of planning the customers' investment strategies. Instead of drawing heavily on written plans, they based their consulting on the risk profile that they made with the customer and recorded in the service contract. They also put emphasis on personal, long-term contacts with the customers, including discussions sometimes even on a daily basis. Throughout the interviews we were able to observe the dilemma that these workers faced when trying to conceal the requirements of long-term planning, on the one hand, and reacting to the daily market on the other. In practice, the investment managers told us, planning mainly took place 'in one's head', the object being that of reacting to the shifts in the market. Trading was based on the customer's risk profile, on memorizing what had been planned, and consulting with the customer. Written plans were often seen as time-consuming extra work and bureaucracy, which implies that the motivation to take the new tool into use was not necessarily strong, at least for the time being.

Implementation of a collaborative tool during Change Laboratory

The implementation of the new investment plan in the company could be supported by the simultaneous process of analyzing the potentials of co-configuration in the Change Laboratory. Following the episodes during the process reveals the dilemmas faced and the novel perspectives adopted by the participants in relation to the new tool and its meaning at work. Characteristically, they are critical points that open up possibilities towards expansion – or contraction – of the object of work. From the point of view of expansive learning, it is crucial to understand how the investment managers saw the potential and problems of the tool in each phase and what course of action they undertook respectively. Did the investment plan expand the perspectives of work or was it experienced as a constraint as some of our interviewees had suggested?

The following analysis is based on data gathered during the eight-month period when the Change Laboratory sessions were run and the subsequent implementation phase. Implementation not only concerned the investment plan but the overall model of activity created collaboratively for the wealth-management unit. We take up six episodes out of this collection of data.

1 Contradiction between the ideal model and the real actions for planning investment services: 'This does not fit the model really'

In the starting phase of Change Laboratory, the investment managers were asked to describe and model their present customer processes. They were further asked to make observations on actual practices during one working week and to compare their findings with the model. The outcomes from these tasks reproduced the contradiction between the holistic approach and the narrow orientation of the customer process. The models depicted the customer services process as a wide range of services to be offered to the customer on the basis of the investment plan.

> Excerpt 1
> We started roughly [from the present situation], how it takes place today. A new customer enters in, we make a need analysis and an offer, after that a contract in which we include the investment plan and analyze all the services that have come out of here, taxation and legal services ... bank services, all that the customer and the customer's family needs.
> (Working group 2, Change Laboratory 1)

The investment managers were ready to admit that the descriptions of the process and the investment planning embedded in the process were to some degree ideal. During the follow-up to the real work process, one of the interventionist-researchers went to visit the investment managers on site. How was the model working?

> Excerpt 2
> Investment manager 5: At least [it has come out] that this does not fit the model really, because that model is actually based on lifecycle thinking. In a normal situation we just take care of customers and, kind of, concentrate on portfolio management, on the existing portfolio, what we can do, and we discuss it with the customer.
> Researcher: What are you doing right now?
> Investment manager 5: Well, here we are following the stock market a little bit. I have discussed with the customer what we are going to do if the stock prices are moving in the direction we expect or wish them to move. Then I'll call the customer to make sure if the deal will be done. Part of the deal was already done, a part remained open. Just waiting where we are going to.
> (Change Laboratory, intermediate task 1)

Thus the contradiction between the ideal model and real actions for planning the investment services appeared as the most concrete issue with practical implications. This contradiction was used in Change Laboratory to motivate the participants to start developing a new way of working along the lines of providing holistic investment services.

2   Investment plan in relation to contract-making: 'It shows the significance of investment planning'

This episode also dates to the group work at the start of the Change Laboratory. One of the groups pointed out that according to the present practice the individual investment plan was made after making the contract with the customer. Now that we make special investment plans, shouldn't we integrate the risk profile and the investment strategy into it and complete the plan before the final contract? the presenters asked. Which comes first, the contract or the investment plan?

> Excerpt 3
> Investment manager 12: This is interesting what came out that in some cases we have to make changes to the contract after having made the investment plan. In some sense it shows the significance of investment planning. ...
>
> Manager 2 of the unit: The point is that we wouldn't need to include these issues in the contract if we had such a strict investment planning process that we would really always make [the plan]. Now that it is not systematically implemented we need to include issues that specify the clauses in the contract. If this investment plan will be made systematically, we will not need to include these in the contract.
>
> (Change Laboratory 1)

It is obvious that once the participants were asked to model their customer service process they started to see the significance of investment planning and its relation to contract making at the beginning of the process. It was perceived that the new investment plan included elements that in the present practices were connected to the contract. Should the plan therefore be made before the actual contract? was the question. If not, the investment plan that came after the contract could even lead to changes in or adjustments to the clauses of the contract. This emphasized the importance of the investment plan as a part of the process.

3   Investment plan as a solution to customer relations management: 'I think the wealth-management plan could do the trick here'

In the middle of the Change Laboratory process the investment managers had the task of analyzing their clientele by sorting it into different types of customers. Some of the types were considered to be especially interesting and challenging for, but also suited to, the negotiated total wealth management (Figure 2.3.2). Typically this type of customers used a variety of specialists in the management of their property. The customer cases were discussed and analyzed in the Change Laboratory.

> Excerpt 4
> Investment manager 7: ... as I was thinking about this I could find quite similar features in different customers, and I think that this can be structured, we can offer total solutions answering to a great deal of our customers' needs. [Lists the needs.] I think that we should definitely get a better grip of our customers and I think the wealth-management plan could do the trick here.
>
> (Change Laboratory 7)

This episode shows that the participants now started to consider the investment plan as a beneficial and concrete tool for managing customer relations. In the preceding episode, the meaning given to the tool was more formal and legal. It is noteworthy that the speaker above calls the tool 'a wealth-management plan', which the interventionist-researchers – as well as those who launched the tool in the company – had suggested to emphasize the scope of the work. As yet, this term had not generally been adopted by the workers.

It was realized that many of the customers expressed a need for supplementary services but the coordination of different service providers and the pricing basis was not easy to carry out. The next 'homework' for the participants was to formulate an investment plan for a real customer case – 'Lady' – discussed in the Change Laboratory. The steering group, whose task was to implement and develop the work of the Change Laboratory within the wealth-management unit, was assigned to list potential service-product ideas while the investment managers themselves went on charting the service needs of their own customers.

4 Investment plan as a support of present activity: 'We shouldn't start too complicated systems to do this'

Another shift of perspective was observable when dealing with the homework. This time the change involved a more extensive turning point, which had some effect on the learning outcomes of the Change Laboratory. A number of the investment managers questioned the concept of negotiated total wealth management and – as they saw it – the introduction of novel services to the present concept of activity. The debate on the need for extra services was ongoing. Voices were simultaneously heard that claimed the need for support to the present duties and investment services rather than radically expanding the scope of work. The intensification of the present services gained support regardless of the fact that the fragility, even non-profitability, of the present earning logic had been demonstrated by the management at the beginning of the Change Laboratory. This episode was crystallized in this comment by a participant:

> Excerpt 5
> Investment manager 1: ... sure I would be much more interested in this project if we concentrated on these issues and searched for a way to get the present elements to work in the best possible way. Whether portfolio management or extra services that we already have on offer, rather than thinking that we should invent new things out of the blue. ... Rather make the present [activity] more effective than look for new. We already have the basic elements, [we are doing] right things that we could just do better and better.
> (Change Laboratory 8)

Participants in the Change Laboratory started to develop an idea of support and collegial 'sparring' in order to intensify and improve their ways of working. This finally led to the development of 'the sparring way of working' as an intermediate step towards the negotiated total wealth management initially suggested by the interventionist-researchers (Engeström *et al.*, 2005). The formulation of investment plans for the 'Lady' and analyzing these together in the Change Laboratory made the participants realize the benefits of sharing the investment planning with colleagues.

Even though the idea of mutual sparring and collaborative learning was apparently an innovative one, the concentration on the present practice jeopardized the deliberate shift towards more holistic investment services. Comments such as 'We shouldn't start too complicated systems to do this, just come to terms with how we manage the thing' can be interpreted as a sign of unwillingness on the part of some participants to implement the new investment plan.

5   *Investment plan as the object and tool of sparring: 'One good plan is better than ten bad ones'*

In the Change Laboratory session that followed a week later, the leading interventionist-researcher started a discussion and invited the participants to model the sparring way of working and to plan how it could be implemented in the working unit. The leader then summarized the discussion and asked whether the new investment plan introduced in the unit was, after all, the best possible tool to enhance holistic working. The investment managers admitted that the form was laborious to fill in but the reasons for not using it resided elsewhere:

Excerpt 6
Investment manager 15: It's because there is no stick and carrot, no control. If we had clear objectives, let's say that Mika has got to do ten [investment plans] by the end of the year or else he won't get his salary at the end of December. In that case Mika would do ten of them. Or if Mika did twenty, he would get some more salary in April.

(Change Laboratory 9)

'Stick and carrot' were debated and some of the speakers emphasized the qualitative criteria instead of aiming at quantitative outcomes. The leader summarized, 'It's better to do one good plan than ten bad ones.' A participating representative from the support services unit remarked, 'If I worked in the customer interface I would make plans for those I have the most to lose with and for those with the most to win.' Another participant linked this to the case of the 'Lady', which he/she saw as representing the 'most to win' option, and another customer type was also discussed as an example of the 'most to lose' case. In the end, the idea of sparring was further elaborated. The person who had made the stick-and-carrot comment specified:

Excerpt 7
Investment manager 15: What might work well is that for instance Mika makes two [investment plans] per month and they are presented and discussed together in a group meeting … and there they get critique and sparring. Because if he prepares them alone in a dark corner it will not lead anywhere.

(Change Laboratory 9)

As a result of this Change Laboratory session the executive steering group figured out a way of working in weekly team meetings. Each investment manager in turn would prepare a real investment plan for the team, to be discussed through sparring, in other words by collaboratively commenting on it and drawing from the collegial expertise. Experts from the internal support services unit would be invited when needed. The quantitative goal was also present even when the focus was on this qualitative change of work.

Excerpt 9
Manager 3 of the unit: It was pointed out that without goal-setting this will not start effectively enough. It was agreed that from this week on we are going to set quantitative

goals, and of course the team leaders will follow the realization of the goals. And, at the same time, we will organize a follow-up model for the entire unit level.

(Change Laboratory 11)

Regardless of the promising new model of work, this episode shows signs of the narrowing scope of the implementation of investment plans. The persistent emphasis on the quantitative goal as the criterion of development seemed to contradict our hypothesis of the investment plan as a potential tool of co-configuration.

6   *Contradiction between the use value and the exchange value of investment planning: 'Let's say five plans, and deadline at the end of the year'*

The first 'sparring' meeting among the investment managers took place a few weeks after the last Change Laboratory session. Two investment managers presented their investment plan case studies. Both had brought the plan with them and they explained how they had been working on them. Other participants raised questions, and best practice for interviewing a customer and filling in the plan formula was discussed. The interventionist-researchers considered the sparring way of working to have made a good start and supported the preparation of investment plans.

Three weeks later another sparring meeting took place. This time no plans were prepared and presented in the meeting. The participants started to question the relevance of doing investment plans. Why spend time and energy on them?

Excerpt 9
Investment manager 2: One must find the meaning somewhere. I can't see it, frankly, I confess it. I am a kind of opponent in this sense, I don't see the benefit. That's why I don't find it meaningful. I will prioritize other things, because that's what gives something directly below the line. Maybe the benefit comes sometime in the future.

(Sparring meeting 2)

Positive voices were also heard in the meeting. The use of the investment plan might both broaden (new property) and deepen (the concentration on an individual customer) the scope of work.

Excerpt 10
Investment manager 5: About the investment plan, what I think might be the benefit of planning it is that new property may be found that we haven't known anything about. They may tell us ...

(Sparring meeting 2)

Excerpt 11
Investment manager 4: I would say – having made just a few [plans] but started to look at them – here you concentrate on an individual customer. Because during the day, you do, like Mika is also doing, [work that is about] whether we should buy UPM or sell Nokia – that's what we are doing quite a lot in any case. How often do we concentrate on the whole?

(Sparring meeting 2)

The discussion ended with a reminder of the quantitative goal. We may say that the strongest motivation for doing the investment plans came from the exchange value in terms of bonuses given to an individual investment manager.

Excerpt 12
Investment manager 1: Everybody knows, let's say it's five [plans], and the deadline is at the end of the year. At New Year we will check whether there are five [plans]. If not, one bears the consequences, less salary or something else.

(Sparring meeting 2)

As no concrete investment plans were addressed, the sparring way of working was not realized in this meeting, neither could we observe any signs of co-configuration. What the participants did was discuss their individual relationships to the new tool and its implementation.

Conclusion: the potential and fragility of expansive learning in and for work

We have analyzed the implementation of a new investment plan in a wealth-management unit during a Change Laboratory process. The Change Laboratory was a special context of work development, which allowed us to look into the potential for expansive learning in and for work. It could be seen that the implementation as such was not a smooth and linear process but advanced through multiple and tension-laden events. Our special interest was in the historical transformation towards the co-configuration type of work that researchers have suggested as one of the prominent trends of contemporary business life. We will summarize the findings according to the three questions addressed in this chapter.

1   *What kind of a tool is the new investment plan?*

Activity-theoretical studies have pointed out that rather than looking at the changes in individuals' thinking and action or the changes in communities' routines, we should focus on the creation and implementation of new tools when trying to understand the preconditions of learning in and for work (Miettinen and Virkkunen 2005a,b). The introduction of a new tool for work activity always includes the potential for change to present ways of working. Correspondingly, the shift to co-configuration and other more advanced modes of collaboration requires the adoption of new tools and instruments.

The investment plan looked like a promising tool in the transition towards co-configuration work. First, it was a means of mediating between the investment manager and the customer, a visible artifact to work with when planning wealth management according to the goals and preferences of the customer. Second, the investment plan could help coordinate the activity of an investment manager and other service-producing agents of the organization and act as a shared knowledge repository. Thus it was an instrument possibly enhancing the transition from traditional craft-type broker–customer interaction towards negotiated total wealth management. By taking the investment plan into use the investment managers were expected to invite their customers and other service providers in the unit to participate in the creation of wealth-management planning, which implied a transformation of the entire object of work. Rather than addressing the investment portfolio and stock trading, the work was meant to orient itself to the customers' needs related to total wealth management in the different phases of their life.

2   How was the investment plan implemented in the wealth-management unit?

We analyzed the implementation of the investment plan in six episodes. Each opened up a new perspective on the tool, either expanding or narrowing the orientation to tool use and work in general. The episodes were produced collaboratively by the interventionist-researchers and participants when working on the learning tasks designed in the Change Laboratory. These tasks dealt with present and future ways of working, such as modeling the present activity, analyzing the customer types, and charting the pool of services.

On the other hand, the identification and naming of these learning episodes were an outcome of the researchers' analysis and interpretation. We were interested in the possibilities of co-configuration in such a specialized service provider as wealth management. The first episode demonstrated the need for work development in terms of the contradiction between the ideal model and the reality of work. Episodes 2 and 3 opened up visions and expansions of work which supported our co-configuration hypothesis. The redefinitions and turning to the development of internal collaboration in episodes 4 and 5, and finally the emphasis on quantitative goals in episode 6 show, on the contrary, some narrowing of the scope of development. In sum, the careful analysis of the episodes revealed the varied, partly unanticipated and even vulnerable pathways of learning in and for work.

3   What does the implementation of the investment plan tell about the potential of co-configuration and expansive learning in and for work?

According to Victor and Boynton (1998), the transition from one phase of work organization to another proceeds stepwise as the 'right path', which means that to achieve a new phase an organization has to go through and learn all the preceding steps in turn. What we see in work practices is nothing as linear as the authors claim it to be. We described the learning challenges of the investment managers by means of a four-field matrix, in which the historically emerging modes of production exist today, paralleled and in tension with each other (Figure 2.3.2). Even the object of work underwent contradictory interpretations, mainly defined as daily market-oriented trading with the investment portfolio, but also as a more holistic total wealth management based on the customer's goals and financial strategies.

The implementation of the investment plan had the potential for expansive learning because it included a new and broader concept of the object of work. The plan may look like a tool given hierarchically 'from the top down' that has to be adopted according to the official norms or the quality improvement efforts of the company. Nevertheless, when using the tool the investment managers inevitably start to form a new object of work in collaboration with the customers and, therefore, expand the scope of wealth-management services 'from the bottom up'. The users transform the tool locally by giving it a meaning and characteristics regardless of how narrow or broad it was when it entered the work community. The users of the new tool take a step towards their zone of proximal development and direct the future development through their learning actions.

Note

1   We gratefully acknowledge the work of Auli Pasanen and Vaula Haavisto, the co-authors of the empirical analysis reported in the Finnish publication (Pasanen *et al.*, 2006).

References

Araujo, L. (1998) 'Knowing and learning as networking', *Management Learning*, 29(3), pp. 317–36.

Bødker, S. and Andersen, P.B. (2005) 'Complex mediation', *Human-Computer Interaction*, 20(4), pp. 353–402.

Casey, A. (2005) 'Enhancing individual and organizational learning: a sociological model', *Management Learning*, 36(2), pp. 131–47.

Chaiklin, S., Hedegaard, M. and Juul Jensen, U. (eds) (1999) *Activity Theory and Social Practice: Cultural-Historical Approaches*, Aarhus University Press.

Engelsted, N., Hedegaard, M., Karpatschof, B. and Mortensen, A. (eds) (1993) *The Societal Subject*, Aarhus University Press.

Engeström, Y. (1987) *Learning by Expanding: An Activity-Theoretical Approach to Developmental Research*, Helsinki, Orienta-konsultit Oy, available online at http://lchc.ucsd.edu/MCA/Paper/Engestrom/expanding/toc.htm

—— (2001) 'Expansive learning at work: toward an activity-theoretical reconceptualization', *Journal of Education and Work*, 14(1), pp. 133–56.

—— (2006) 'Development, movement and agency: breaking away into Mycorrhizae activities', in K. Yamazumi (ed.), *Building Activity Theory in Practice: Toward the Next Generation*, Osaka, Center for Human Activity Theory, Kansai University, pp. 1–43.

—— (2007) 'Putting Vygotsky to work: the change laboratory as an application of double stimulation', in H. Daniels, M. Cole and J.V. Wertsch (eds), *The Cambridge Companion to Vygotsky*, New York, Cambridge University Press, pp. 363–82.

Engeström, Y., Miettinen R. and Punamäki, R.-L. (eds) (1999) *Perspectives on Activity Theory*, Cambridge University Press.

Engeström, Y., Pasanen, A., Toiviainen, H. and Haavisto, V. (2005) 'Expansive learning as collaborative concept formation at work', in K. Yamazumi, Y. Engeström and H. Daniels (eds), *New Learning Challenges: Going beyond the Industrial Age System of School and Work*, Osaka, Kansai University Press, pp. 47–77.

Leont'ev, A. N. (1978) *Activity, Consciousness, and Personality*, Englewood Cliffs, Prentice-Hall.

Miettinen, R. and Virkkunen, J. (2005a) 'Epistemic objects, artefacts and organizational change', *Organization*, 12(3), pp. 437–56.

Miettinen, R. and Virkkunen, J. (2005b) 'Learning in and for work, and the joint construction of mediational artifacts: an activity-theoretical view', in E. Antonacopoulou, P. Jarvis, V. Andersen, B. Elkjaer and S. Høyrup (eds), *Learning, Working and Living. Mapping the Terrain of Working Life Learning*, Houndmills, Palgrave Macmillan, pp. 154–69.

Nardi, B.A. (ed.) (1996) *Context and Consciousness: Activity Theory and Human-computer Interaction*, Cambridge, MA, The MIT Press.

Pasanen, A., Haavisto, V., Toiviainen, H. and Engeström, Y. (2006) 'Kohti yhteiskehittelyä? Sijoitussuunnitelman käyttöönotto työyhteisön oppimisprosessina' (Towards co-configuration? The implementation of investment plan as a learning process of a work community), in H. Toiviainen and H. Hänninen (eds), *Rajanylitykset työssä: Yhteistoiminnan ja oppimisen uudet mahdollisuudet*, Juva, PS-Kustannus, pp. 165–200.

Victor, B. and Boynton, A. C. (1998) *Invented Here: Maximizing Your Organization's Internal Growth and Profitability*, Boston, MA, Harvard Business School Press.

Vygotsky, L. S. (1978) *Mind in Society: The Development of Higher Psychological Processes*, Cambridge, MA, Harvard University Press.

Reflective questions

1 Analyze a work activity you know and have possibly participated in. What is the product and outcome of work? What kind of historical transformations has it gone through and can you identify any signs of co-configuration in the present state of work?

2 Expansive learning is characterized as a process in which developmental contradictions and multi-voicedness are encountered and worked. When reflecting on your own learning experiences, can you recognize expansive learning?

3 We argue that collaborative creation, analysis, and implementation of new tools are important in the development of activity. Can you explain to your fellow student how this is connected to learning in and for work?

Further reading

Engeström, Y. (2005) *Developmental Work Research: Expanding Activity Theory in Practice*, ICHS International Cultural-historical Human Sciences, vol. 12, Berlin, Lehmanns Media.

Engeström, Y., Lompscher, J. and Rückriem, G. (eds) (2005) *Putting Activity Theory to Work: Contributions from Developmental Work Research*, ICHS International Cultural-historical Human Sciences, vol. 13, Berlin, Lehmanns Media.

Section 3

Diversity and equity
Introduction

Jill Porter

(Cartoon by Ros Asquith)

This section asks the overall question of how we account for difference. What is the role of education with respect to issues of equity and diversity? The six chapters in this section reveal the dangers of adopting a single stance to provide accounts of difference that inform teaching and educational research. Taken in turn they provide a set of alternative lenses through which to consider issues of culture, gender, difficulties in learning and disability. The section starts with a chapter by Kris Gutiérrez and Barbara Rogoff, who ask the important question 'how do we go about understanding the role of culture in learning?' They argue that too often culture is seen wholly with respect to ethnicity or race, resulting in the creation of a sense of homogeneity, over-emphasizing static characteristics of a group without looking at the history of changes and the embedded nature of practices within activities. As a result there has been a tendency to use norms based on American and European middle-class measures of learning, adopting a single approach to intervention and ascribing one style of learning to entire groups. Adopting a socio-cultural historical understanding, the study of culture is presented as a dynamic study of patterns, looking closely at people's participation in activities that are part of their cultural community, reflecting on traditions as well as changes across generations. These authors provide an example of the ways in which changes in one element of societal practice have a myriad of interrelated changes in other aspects of daily life.

Embedding education in the framework of a global economy Rassool, in the next chapter, looks at the way we understand issues of diversity and equity given ongoing economic, political and technological change and the 'maelstrom of contemporary people flows'. She reminds us that worldwide, systems are marked by interconnectedness in part as a result of the role of key agencies (the World Bank, UNESCO and the World Trade Organization) in defining transnational policy frameworks, which in turn shapes educational policies, structures and provisions. As she argues, education has an enhanced place and significance in determining national economies and is seen as a way of reducing poverty. However, the potency of these transnational frameworks is reduced by the lack of resources and access to teacher training in many developing countries. She draws on the concept of a learning ecology rather than that of multicultural education, to analyse and interpret the changes taking place and to provide a sense of the complex, dynamic, multi-layered nature of understanding the impact of the educational experiences on children from transmigratory groups. How do we best accommodate children who may not have experienced school before, who may have had classes under the trees and who have experienced psychological trauma and uncertain identity in their migration to find a country that can and will accommodate them? She charts the situation of Somali children, some of who will have moved across countries without parents or relatives in the belief that their life chances, especially in terms of education, will be improved.

In the following chapter we turn to issues of gender, the term referring to a social construction rather than a biological state. Dillabough sets out to examine the theoretical stances adopted in the study of gender and the implications this has had for research. She outlines the early research into the ways in which education served to reproduce stratifications seen elsewhere in society, ways in which masculine 'rationality and female subservience' were maintained through schooling. Research then diversified, with a growing emphasis on gender identity and a recognition of its shifting nature and as a consequence the possibility of multiple positions. She explores four themes in her chapter: the complexity of identity given competing and contradictory experiences in school that suggest we need to view gender as more 'permeable and changing' than we have before; the importance of culture and family as revealed through studies of gender and ethnicity research; the role of market forces in contributing to social inequalities; and theories of social change that have directed research to looking at the often contradictory messages and the transformations in gender relations. In short this chapter highlights some of the ways in which our understanding of gender and gender identity has developed from simple constructions around issues of discrimination to recognition of the shifting and complex nature of gender identity and the contributions of schooling to these changes.

In contrast to the previous chapters, which have illustrated the need for a multi-layered understanding of issues of difference, Säljö and Hjörne illustrate the ways in which professionals within a particular institution can give rise to particular accounts of difference that lead to a narrowing and almost deterministic account. This chapter illustrates a circular relationship in the way difficulties are described and categorised and used to access resources. These socially constructed categories are seen by the authors to enable a shared understanding and underpin the process of decision-making in schools. Historically, Sweden, like other countries, has seen in turn an emergence of different categories reflecting societal concerns about the religious and moral, the social and familial and the biomedical. The focus of this chapter is how these categories are introduced and talked about amongst different professional team members using case studies of children who are assigned a label of 'attention deficit disorder' or 'minimal brain dysfunction'. An analysis of the meetings over the course of a year illustrates the speed with which consensus is reached as to the cause of the child's difficulty in the face of quite contradictory descriptions of behaviour taken without reference to context or teacher intervention. This illustrates the need for professionals to recognise the possibility of other explanations to account for difference.

In a chapter with a focus on difficulties in learning, Florian and Kershner take a rather different approach from others in this section by arguing for commonalities rather than difference with the adoption of inclusive pedagogies. Instead of adopting specialist pedagogies they advocate the need to build on approaches that are generally available with a recognition that (all) students have 'an open-ended potential for learning'. They argue for multimodal responses using combined strategies that promote participation in shared (rather than different) purposeful learning where activities are meaningful and relevant to all students. They contrast this with the recipe-like approach that can be advocated in response to particular types of need. Instead teachers are called on to become explicit in their strategic responses when students encounter difficulties gaining knowledge through 'reflective practice and tinkering'. For the novice teacher this may be demanding and the authors cite research to suggest that such practice is best sustained where organisational aspects of the school together with resourcing are supportive of inclusive practices.

While Kershner and Florian might be described as adopting a social model in which disability is seen to result from the barriers that schools and society present, Shakespeare argues against the narrowness of rigidly adopting a single view or model and in particular the inappropriateness of reducing impairment to a socially constructed state. He recognises from his own perspective as a disabled activist that there is an 'experiential reality' that should not be denied. Instead he argues for a holistic understanding of the interaction between the individual, including their personality, qualities and abilities as well as the impairment and the external context in which they find themselves, which in turn reflects a wider set of cultural and societal values. He accuses others of not recognising the continuum of impairment or of differences that arise from a condition that is static compared to one which is variable. In contrast to the chapter by Kershner and Florian he uses the term 'integration' to reflect an argument of *shared* responsibilities between the individual and society – it takes 'two to tango'. For him disability is more complex than issues of equity arising from gender or race, because, in his words, it is intrinsically 'connected to disadvantage'. This is a strong chapter on which to end this section and to lead us to ask again: How do we account for difference? How are these accounts reflected in our practices, both as an individual and as an institution?

3.1 Cultural ways of learning

Kris D. Gutiérrez and Barbara Rogoff

Introduction

Today, communities in nations across the industrialized world are experiencing an unprecedented flow of new communities of people into existing communities. The consequences of the resulting transculturalism and intercultural exchange between the old and familiar and the new and unfamiliar make relevant the importance of understanding what is actually cultural about people's ways of doing and being. This is particularly important as national communities are grappling with how to address the effects of increased immigration. How communities and their members conceive of and respond to difference, educationally, economically, and sociopolitically influences the school and workplace. This chapter argues that culture is not a single variable or something that can be identified directly by a person's appearance, race/ethnicity, or national origin. Nor can culture be reduced to familiar practices that are often associated, in everyday notions, with particular ethnic, racial, and national groups.

Our article addresses the theoretical issue of how to characterize commonalities of learning approaches of individuals who are members of ethnic groups that historically have been underserved in US schools (e.g., African-American, Latino, and Native American students). We believe that a cultural-historical approach offers a way to get beyond a widespread assumption that characteristics of cultural groups are located within individuals as 'carriers' of culture – an assumption that creates problems, especially as research on cultural styles of ethnic (or racial) is applied in schools.[1] In this article, after a brief discussion about how cultural styles research has helped the field think of differences rather than deficits, we use cultural-historical theory to revise the default assumption. Our chapter also presses cultural-historical research to make progress in characterizing commonalities in the variations across individuals and groups.

Cultural styles: a way of talking about differences rather than deficits

Research on cultural learning styles first appeared in the United States at the end of the 1960s, in Lyndon Johnson's 'War on Poverty' and research efforts to understand 'cultural deprivation'. Much of this work grew out of the critical need to ameliorate the inequitable and deplorable schooling experiences of poor and working-class students in US public schools – predominantly students of color, many of whom were English-language learners.

The cultural styles approach arose from these efforts, as researchers attempted to leave behind deficit-model thinking, in which cultural ways that differ from the practices of dominant groups are judged to be less adequate without examining them from the perspective of the community's participants (Cole and Bruner, 1971; Hilliard and Vaughn-Scott, 1982; Howard and Scott, 1981; McLoyd and Randolph, 1985; McShane and Berry, 1986). An alternative to the cultural styles approach is to deny cultural difference; however, ruling out discussions of cultural variation has often meant that the cultural practices of the dominant group are taken as the norm. Although deficit-model thinking is still with us, the cultural styles approach offered an alternative by characterizing cultural ways of different groups in terms that are respectful, attempting to describe them without making value judgments that suggest value hierarchies in cultural practices.

Work on cultural learning styles, however, is sometimes used in ways that are overly static and categorical – in schools, in cross-cultural comparisons, and in some of the cultural styles work that tries to avoid or that challenges the deficit model. Treating cultural differences as traits, in our view, makes it harder to understand the relation of individual learning and the practices of cultural communities, and this in turn sometimes hinders effective assistance to student learning.

Helping students learn: having styles or participating in practices

A common objective across the various approaches we discuss is the desire to increase student learning. However, treating cultural difference as a trait leads to a strategy of locating characteristics separately in the person and in the 'context', and 'crossing' style and context as in the aptitude × treatment approach. In educational settings, work on learning styles has often attempted to take context into account by seeking style matches between student and schooling experiences or between student and teacher (Banks, 1995). However, some applications of this approach are based on an assumption that an individual's 'style' is a trait that is independent of tasks and contexts, and that is constant over time. Such a matching strategy does not account for change – in the individual, the activity setting, or the community – and it assumes one style per person according to the individual's group categorization. We are particularly concerned with implications of such applications for students from non-dominant groups.

Learning styles constructs have been used to distinguish the learning styles of 'minority' group members and to explain 'minority' student failure (see Foley, 1997; Kavale and Forness, 1987; Irvine and York, 1995 for reviews). For example, individuals from one group may be characterized as learning holistically whereas individuals from another group may be characterized as learning analytically, or individuals may be divided into cooperative versus individualist learners on the basis of membership in a particular cultural group.

Addressing learning styles as traits also seems to be a common way to prepare teachers to make the link to diversity (Guild, 1994; Matthews, 1991). Clearly, teaching to a difference that one can be labeled (e.g., learning modalities) sounds appealing to teachers who have limited resources, support, or training to meet the challenges of new student populations. An observation by one high-school English as a second language teacher illustrates the application of a common perception reported in our studies of English-language learners:

> I think it's also very important to include … multimedia techniques because we have a group now in school that is very diverse in their learning strategies. You know most are visual language learners, so if you give them something they can see or touch, they are tactile. That gets to them; they can understand that.
>
> (Gutiérrez, Crosland, and Berlin, 2001)

Of course, there is value in utilizing multiple forms of assistance, including media. Our focus, however, is on the importance and benefit of knowing about the histories and valued practices of cultural groups rather than trying to teach prescriptively according to broad, underexamined generalities about groups. In cultural-historical approaches, learning is conceived of as a process occurring within ongoing activity, and not separated into separate characteristics of individuals and contexts (Cole and Engeström, 1993; Lave, 1996). Including consideration of the history of a person's or a group's related engagements can account for 'dispositions' they may have in new circumstances. However, the crucial distinction we are making is between *understanding processes* and *locating characteristics*. Without situating social practices and the histories of participants in particular communities, approaches that attribute style to membership in a group make it difficult to account for variation and change in individuals or their practices.

Treating cultural differences as individual traits encourages overgeneralization

The trait approach assumes that there is a built-in relationship between learning style and minority group membership. For example, approaches that accommodate instructional practice to group styles treat what is 'known' about a group as applying to all individuals in the group. This makes it more likely that groups will be treated as homogeneous, with fixed characteristics carried by the collection of individuals that constitute the group.

Scholars from a wide range of disciplines have called attention to the problems of 'essentializing' people on the basis of a group label and have underlined the variability that exists within groups and their practices. Scholars examining cultural styles have argued for a more situated and dynamic view of the cultural practices of ethnic and racial groups (Banks, 1995; Gay, 1995, 2000; Irvine and York, 1995; Nieto, 1999).

Yet, the problem of overgeneralization persists, especially in attempts by schools to design learning experiences that complement the learning-style differences of particular ethnic groups (e.g., Dunn and Dunn, 1992; Dunn, Griggs, and Price, 1993). Although the work on learning styles often cautions against stereotyping and generalizing about the cognitive styles of various groups, matching individual learning style to a particular ethnic group may encourage the idea that patterns of performance derive from the essence of an individual or a group. For example, some studies that contrast the learning styles of students from several ethnic groups make prescriptions for creating learning environments that complement the learning-style differences of the various ethnic groups such as the time of day individuals of particular groups are receptive to instruction or instructional seating arrangement most conducive to particular ethnic groups (Dunn, Griggs, and Price, 1993; Dunn, Gemake, Jalali, Zenhausern, Quinn, and Spiridakis, 1990; Hickson, Land, and Aikman, 1994).

Unfortunately, categorization of individuals in groups has been treated causally, yielding explanations and expectations of individual skills and behaviors on the basis of category membership, assuming that all group members share the same set of experiences, skills, and interests. This has led to a kind of tracking in which instruction is adjusted merely on the basis of a group categorization.[2]

Within a styles approach, a single way of teaching and learning may be used with a particular group without accounting for individuals' past experiences with certain practices or without providing instruction that both extends those experiences and introduces new and even unfamiliar ways of doing things. This stands in stark contrast to the strategic forms of assistance that we have observed in robust learning communities where the co-construction of a community's various practices and individual development support the changing nature of participation and the forms of assistance provided in joint activity. In these classroom communities, students receive multiple forms of assistance and participate in rigorous learning activities that extend their initial approaches to learning and participation (Gutiérrez, Baquedano-Lopez, and Tejeda, 1999; Moll, Saez, and Dworin, 2001; Rogoff, Goodman Turkanis, and Bartlett, 2001). As a result, students have ongoing opportunities to assume new roles and learn new approaches.

There are several explanations for the sustained currency of trait approaches as plausible explanations of individual performance. Notions of individual learning styles are common-place in both public and educational discourse. Descriptions and subsequent methods of identification of learning styles can be easy to understand and to identify within the taxonomies in inventories that provide measures of individual differences and resultant profiles (Price and Dunn, 1997). Furthermore, reductive notions of culture and cultural groups may reinforce the broad application of trait approaches.

Beyond reductive approaches

Often, normative views of culture are employed in ways that appear benign, especially when they purport to focus on individual differences rather than on deficits in the individual or in the social group. This is an exceedingly important issue as there continues to be a reductive tendency in the social sciences to seek and accept singular effects to explain social and cognitive phenomena. Supported by static or normative understandings of culture, the application of trait approaches to individual school performance sometimes leads to what Rose (1998) calls a kind of 'cognitive reductionism'.[3] As Rose argues:

> A further problem – sometimes inherent in the theories themselves, sometimes a result of reductive application – is the tendency to diminish cognitive complexity and rely on simplified cognitive oppositions: independent vs. dependent, literate vs. oral, verbal vs. spatial, concrete vs. logical. These oppositions are textbook-neat, but … are narrow and misleading. (p. 268)

In some cases, the learning or cognitive styles typologies have a basis in observations of average differences in some populations. In some cases, however, the typologies are offered simply as categories without research substantiating their relationship to the groups so characterized or their utility for practice. As Tiedeman (1989) suggested, 'To date, research evidence is inadequate to judge [cognitive styles'] validity or usefulness in adapting instruction to individuals; some have been called seriously into question' (p. 599).

A cultural-historical approach can help researchers and practitioners characterize the commonalities of experience of people who share cultural background, without 'locating' the commonalities within individuals. However, within cultural-historical approaches, there has not yet been sufficient attention to figuring out how to talk and think about regularities across individuals' or cultural communities' ways of doing things. To move beyond the idea of traits located in individual members of ethnic groups, we need to make progress in understanding regularities in how engagement in shared and dynamic practices of different communities contributes to individual learning and development.

Conceiving of style as an individual trait can lead to a strategy of matching characterizations of individuals (or collections of them), on the one hand, and characterizations of contexts on the other. This approach treats contexts as if they exist independently of the people active in creating and maintaining them, and views individuals as though their characteristics are unrelated to the contexts in which they and their families have participated in recent generations. We argue that people *live* culture in a mutually constitutive manner in which it is not fruitful to tote up their characteristics as if they occur independently of culture, and that it is not fruitful to think of culture as if it occurs independently of people.

A shift to experience participating in cultural practices

We are concerned with how researchers and practitioners can conceive of regularities in approaches to learning among people of similar cultural background experiences without reifying those cultural patterns and practices as located in individuals. We propose a shift from the assumption that regularities in groups are carried by the traits of a collection of individuals to a focus on people's history of engagement in practices of cultural communities. In cultural-historical approaches, cultural differences are attributed to variations in people's involvement in common practices of particular cultural communities (Moll, 2000; Rogoff, Mistry, Göncü, and Mosier, 1993). A central and distinguishing thesis in this approach is that the structure and development of human psychological processes emerge through participation in culturally mediated, historically developing, practical activity involving cultural practices and tools (Cole, 1996).

People's varied *participation* in the practices of dynamic cultural communities can be distinguished from *membership* in ethnic groups, which is often treated in all-or-none, static fashion (Rogoff, 2003). Individuals participate in varying and overlapping ways that change over their lifetimes and over historical change in a community's organization and relationships with other communities (Cole, 1998; Lave, 1996; Rogoff and Angelillo, 2002). As Cole and Engeström (1993) argue, culture 'is experienced in local, face-to-face interactions that are locally constrained and heterogeneous with respect to both "culture as a whole" and the parts of the entire toolkit experienced by a given individual' (p. 15).

Of course, there are regularities in the ways cultural groups participate in the everyday practices of their respective communities. However, the relatively stable characteristics of these environments are in constant tension with the emergent goals and practices participants construct, which stretch and change over time and with other constraints. This conflict and tension contribute to the variation and ongoing change in an individual's and a community's practices (Engeström, 1993; Gutiérrez, 2002).

We believe that looking for cultural regularities will be more fruitful – both for research and practice – if we focus our examination of differences on cultural processes in which individuals engage with other people in dynamic cultural communities, some of which involve ethnic or racial group membership in important ways. By cultural community we mean a coordinated group of people with some traditions and understandings in common, extending across several generations, with varied roles and practices and continual change among participants as well as transformation in the community's practices (see Rogoff, 2003). For example, people draw on intergenerationally conveyed concepts, ways of talking, and belief systems that may be utilized and negotiated locally in communities that are often identified internally and by their neighbors in terms of ethnicity and race.

By focusing on the varied ways people participate in their community's activities, we can move away from the tendency to conflate ethnicity with culture, with assignment to ethnic groups made on the basis of immutable and often stable characteristics, such as Spanish surname or country of birth. Equating culture with race, ethnicity, language preference, or national origin results in overly deterministic, static, weak, and uncomplicated understandings of both individuals and the community practices in which they participate (Gutiérrez, Asato, Santos, and Gotanda, 2002).

We are not arguing that group membership defined by ethnicity, race, and language use is irrelevant. These categories have long-standing influences on the cultural practices in which people have the opportunity to participate, often yielding shared circumstances, practices, and beliefs that play important and varied roles for group members. People do not just *choose* to move in and out of different practices, taking on new and equal participation in cultural communities.

Toward a cultural-historical way to describe cultural regularities

From a cultural-historical perspective, we can examine people's usual ways of doing things, trying to understand individuals' history of involvement in the practices of varied communities, including ethnic or national communities as well as others such as academic or religious communities (Rogoff, 2003). Consider the finding that children who immigrated recently to the United States from rural Mexican communities more often studiously observed ongoing events without pushing adults to explain them than did children whose families immigrated from Europe generations before (Mejía Arauz, Rogoff, and Paradise, 2003). To make sense of this difference, we may gain some understanding by examining the dynamic structure of the sending and receiving communities' traditions. For example, the rural Mexican communities' frequent inclusion of children in a range of adult activities may relate to the attentiveness of children who may have been encouraged to observe and take part in their families' work and social lives (Rogoff, Paradise, Mejía-Arauz, Correa-Chávez, and Angelillo, 2003). The European-American communities' tradition of excluding children from adult activities – where they could observe what they are supposed to be learning – may also help us understand the proclivity of some of these students to request adult explanation even in a situation that calls for observation.

Examining cultural variation in terms of familiarity with different practices in dynamic communities organized in distinct manners is a very different approach than attributing a 'visual' style to Mexican children or a 'verbal' style to European-American middle-class children. We argue that it is more useful to consider differences in the children's, their families', and their communities' histories of engaging in particular endeavors organized in contrasting manners. This avoids the implication that the characteristic is 'built in' to the individual (or a group) in a stable manner that extends across time and across situations, and it recognizes the circumstances relevant to an individual's likelihood of acting in certain ways.

Cultural-historical theory leads us to expect regularities in the ways cultural communities organize their lives, as well as variations in the ways individual members of groups participate and conceptualize the means and ends of their communities' activities. For example, Tejeda and Espinoza (2002) observed that high-school students from migrant farmworker backgrounds often used hybrid language practices in sense-making activities designed to promote critical reflection about their course subject-matter as well as about their life experiences as migrants. We noted similar linguistic practices in the learning repertoires of elementary-school children in computer-mediated learning clubs (Gutiérrez, Baquedano-Lopez, and Alvarez, 2001). As with the research of Mejía-Arauz *et al.* (2003), intent observation and minimal question asking seemed to characterize the participation patterns of both the elementary-school children and the high-school students.

These descriptions of regularities are useful in understanding literacy development. However, our references to 'migrants' and 'English-language learners' and their practices are used as descriptors rather than as a categorical classification of individuals or groups. We attribute the regularities to the students' participation in familiar cultural practices as well as to their public schooling experiences that restrict engagement and limit the use of the cultural resources that are part of their repertoires. We must also understand such regularities in light of the colonizing practices of which they have been a part (Tejeda, Espinoza, and Gutiérrez, 2003).[4] A cultural-historical approach assumes that individual development and dispositions must be understood in (not separate from) cultural and historical context. In other words, we talk about patterns of people's approaches to given situations without reducing the explanation to a claim that they do what they do because they are migrant farmworkers or English-language learners. We attend to individuals' linguistic and cultural-historical repertoires as well as their contributions to practices that connect with other activities in which they commonly engage.

Repertoires for participating in practices

By 'linguistic and cultural-historical repertoires' we mean the ways of engaging in activities stemming from observing and otherwise participating in cultural practices. Individuals' background experiences, together with their interests, may prepare them for knowing how to engage in particular forms of language and literacy activities, play their part in testing formats, resolve interpersonal problems according to specific community-organized approaches, and so forth. An important feature of focusing on repertoires is encouraging people to develop dexterity in determining which approach from their repertoire is appropriate under which circumstances (Rogoff, 2003).

Characterizing children's repertoires or proclivities would involve characterizing their experience and initiative in prior cultural activities (Rogoff, 1997). We would characterize their repertoires in terms of their familiarity with engaging in particular practices on the basis of what is known about their own and their community's history. For example, students who have participated in varying cultural traditions would differ in repertoires for engaging in discussions with authority figures, answering known-answer questions, analyzing word problems on the basis of counterfactual premises, seeking or avoiding being singled out for praise, spontaneously helping classmates, observing ongoing events without adult management, responding quickly or pondering ideas before volunteering their contributions, and many other approaches that are sometimes treated as characteristics of individuals.

It is relevant to take into account the development of the cultural activities as well. To understand both individual and community learning it is necessary to examine the nature and forms of cultural artifacts and tools used; the social relations, rules, and division of labor; and the historical development of individuals and communities. We would then be able to characterize a child's repertoires and dexterity in moving between approaches appropriate to varying activity settings. In the process, we would have a historical developmental account of that child's or that community's familiar, value-laden experience, and we would be able to speak about the usual, customary, or even the habitual approaches taken by individuals (and communities) in known circumstances. The circumstances would have to be taken into account as aspects of the regularities described and not just 'crossed with' the independent characteristics of individuals.

A few suggestions for proceeding with the idea of repertoires of practice

For both researchers and teachers, the trait approach has the attraction of apparent simplicity. In research and practice, we often have to proceed on the basis of partial information. We need to consider the implications for research and educational practice when only a little cultural information is available.

For example, how can a teacher proceed with minimal cultural background information on which to base action? The teacher would look for students' familiarity of experience with cultural practices by seeking to understand the students' short- or long-term history. For example, a new teacher in an African-American low-income neighborhood, inspired by Carol Lee's (1993, 2001) research, may wonder if he or she can extend the students' out-of-school skills in analysis of metaphor and figurative language to the analysis of literature, making use of familiarity with the practice of 'signifying' (ritualized language play involving clever insults). To do so, the teacher would need some understanding of this practice and would need to check his or her assumption that these students are familiar with it, to confirm or disconfirm his or her hypothesis that these students have similar background experience to Lee's students. Rather than pigeonholing individuals into categories and teaching to the students' 'traits' or attempting to replace those traits, the emphasis would be placed on helping students develop dexterity in using both familiar and new approaches.

The researcher's work, from a cultural-historical approach, is similar: Focus on understanding developing individuals and changing communities, making first guesses about patterns and seeking confirmation or disconfirmation to extend what is known. Researchers thus need understanding of the practices under study, including an understanding of the relationship between a community's practices and the routine practices in which an individual participates. They would check their assumptions about an individual's familiarity with the focal practice, as well as seek further information about whether and how an individual might participate in the practice.

The work ahead of us is to characterize the dynamic patterns of individuals' participation in building on historical constellations of community practices, continuing and transforming across generations. In this concluding section, we offer some specific suggestions that we have found useful in moving into this approach in our research.

1 To avoid making overly general statements based on research, it helps to speak of the findings in the past tense – 'the children did such and such' – rather than the continuing present – 'children do such and such' (Rogoff, 2003). Using the past tense marks the findings as statements of what was observed rather than too quickly assuming a timeless truth to what is always a situated observation. Summary statements that refer to the activities or situations in which observations were made are likely to help avoid generalizing too quickly about populations. Only when there is a sufficient body of research with different people under varying circumstances would more general statements be justified.

2 To ground cultural observations in the historical, dynamic processes of communities, labels that are often used to refer to research participants can be treated not as categories but as narrative descriptors of the participants' backgrounds (e.g., middle class, Catholic, farming, of Armenian heritage, in California, immigrated to escape massacre, two generations ago). In other words, ethnic and other cultural descriptors may fruitfully help researchers examine cultural practices if they are not assumed to imply essences of the individuals or groups involved and are not treated as causal entities.

3   To examine how aspects of participants' community background cluster and how they change, it helps to treat them as a constellation of factors (Rogoff and Angelillo, 2002). This contrasts with trying to isolate or 'control' independent categories to determine the active ingredient causing an outcome or a trait. Rather than trying to hold all 'factors' but one or a few constant, cultural research requires focus on the dynamically changing configuration of relevant aspects of people's lives.

4   To avoid overgeneralizing, statements based on single observations should be made very cautiously, limiting generalization of simple observations of test performance or behavior under restricted circumstances beyond the situations observed. The aim is to ground observations across multiple settings and communities and to assume various vantage points to understand the complexity of human activity. The intent, especially in regard to poor children and children of color, would be to identify a course of action or assistance that would help insure student learning, rather than to define who a child is or that child's future potential (Berlin, 2002).

We propose these suggestions to advance the conversation about how to account for both cultural regularities and variations, with a cultural-historical emphasis on understanding individuals as participants in cultural communities. We believe that attending to these issues will help move us away from oversimplified approaches to the learning, achievement, and potential of individuals and cultural groups.

Acknowledgements

We are grateful to Carol Lee for engaging us together for this project, for her insightful questions and comments that prompted our further thinking, and for her patience and wit. We also appreciate the discussions with and comments of Frederick Erickson, Geneva Gay, Michael Cole, and Alfredo Artiles on earlier drafts of this work and Jolynn Asato for her research assistance. This work was supported by UC ACCORD, the UC Latino Policy Institute, and by the UC Santa Cruz Foundation chair in psychology.

Notes

1   The custom of trying to locate cultural difference within individuals leads to commonplace but ludicrous statements such as referring to individuals as diverse, 'The class has a large proportion of diverse students' – referring to students from educationally underserved populations as diverse with the implication that the others are the standard – normalizing the dominant group. Difference cannot be attributed to a single side of a contrast.

2   Or, even more insidious, the presumed characteristic may be used to justify restricting opportunities, as with teachers who refer to a group's presumed cooperativeness to justify placing some students in activities that they have not chosen (while others' preferences are granted), or requiring some children to share textbooks or other materials: 'Well, you see, Hispanics are cooperative children. They don't mind sharing things. These other students like to work alone and independently. With Hispanics it is all right to have students work together' (Ortiz, 1988, p. 79).

3   Another colleague credits what she calls 'main effects junkies' in part for this tendency in the social sciences.

4   For example, Spanish is the first language of many of the students we observe – an artifact of their interactions/participation in their communities' activities; it is also an artifact of the colonization of Central

America and the US Southwest. A similar analysis can be developed, in part, for the students' code switching from Spanish to English (i.e., their participation in multiple communities and institutions, as well as their language status, English-only policies, etc.). These are not neutral cultural practices. Cultural tools must be understood in terms of the current and historical intent.

References

Banks, J.A. (ed.) (1995) *Handbook of Research on Multicultural Education*, New York, Macmillan.

Berlin, D. (2002) 'The social construction of deviance: affects of labeling on students with learning difficulties', unpublished doctoral dissertation, University of California, Los Angeles.

Cole, M. (1996) *Cultural Psychology: A Once and Future Discipline*, Cambridge, MA, Harvard University Press.

—— (1998) 'Can cultural psychology help us think about diversity?', *Mind, Culture, and Activity*, 5(4), pp. 291–304.

Cole, M., and Bruner, J.S. (1971) 'Cultural differences and inferences about psychological processes', *American Psychologist*, 26, pp. 867–76.

Cole, M., and Engeström, Y. (1993) 'A cultural-historical approach to distributed cognition', in G. Salomon (ed.), *Distributed Cognitions: Psychological and Educational Considerations*, New York, Cambridge University Press, pp. 1–46.

Dunn, R., and Dunn, K. (1992) *Teaching Elementary Students through their Individual Learning Styles*, Boston, Allyn and Bacon.

Dunn, R., Gemake, J., Jalali, F., Zenhausern, R., Quinn, P., and Spiridakis, J. (1990) 'Cross-cultural differences in learning styles of elementary-age students from four ethnic backgrounds', *Journal of Multicultural Counseling and Development*, 18, pp. 68–93.

Dunn, R., Griggs, S.A., and Price, G.E. (1993) 'Learning styles of Mexican-American and Anglo-American elementary school students', *Journal of Multicultural Counseling and Development*, 21, pp. 237–47.

Engeström, Y. (1993) 'Developmental studies of work as a testbench of activity theory: the case of primary care medical practice', in S. Chaiklin and J. Lave (eds), *Understanding Practice: Perspective on Activity and Context*, Cambridge University Press, pp. 64–103.

Foley, D. (1997) 'Deficit thinking models based on culture: the anthropological protest', in R. Valencia (ed.), *The Evolution of Deficit Thinking: Educational Thought and Practice*, Washington, DC, Falmer Press, pp. 113–31.

Gay, G. (1995) 'Curriculum theory and multicultural education', in J.A. Banks (ed.), *Handbook of Research on Multicultural Education*, New York, Macmillan, pp. 25–43

—— (2000) *Culturally Responsive Teaching*, New York, Teachers College Press.

Guild, P. (1994) 'The culture/learning style connection', *Educational Leadership*, 51(8), pp. 16–21.

Gutiérrez, K. (2002) 'Studying cultural practices in urban learning communities', *Human Development*, 45(4), pp. 312–21.

Gutiérrez, K., Asato, J., Santos, M., and Gotanda, N. (2002) 'Backlash pedagogy: language and culture and the politics of reform', *The Review of Education, Pedagogy, and Cultural Studies*, 24(4), pp. 335–51.

Gutiérrez, K., Baquedano-Lopez, P., and Alvarez, H. (2001) 'Literacy as hybridity: moving beyond bilingualism in urban classrooms', in M. de la Luz Reyes and J. Halcón (eds), *The Best for Our Children: Critical Perspectives on Literacy for Latino Students*, New York, Teachers College Press, pp. 122–41.

Gutiérrez, K., Baquedano-Lopez, P., and Tejeda, C. (1999) 'Rethinking diversity: hybridity and hybrid language practices in the third space', *Mind, Culture, and Activity*, 6, pp. 286–303.

Gutiérrez, K., Crosland, K., and Berlin, D. (2001) 'Reconsidering coaching: assisting teachers' literacy practices in the zone of proximal development', paper presented at the meeting of the American Educational Research Association, Seattle, WA.

Hickson, J., Land, A. J., and Aikman, G. (1994) 'Learning style differences in middle school pupils from four ethnic backgrounds', *School Psychology International*, 15, pp. 349–59.

Hilliard, A.G., III, and Vaughn-Scott, M. (1982) 'The quest for the "minority" child', in S.G. Moore and C.R. Cooper (eds), *The Young Child: Reviews of Research*, vol. 3, Washington, DC, National Association for the Education of Young Children, pp. 175–89.

Howard, A., and Scott, R.A. (1981) 'The study of minority groups in complex societies', in R.H. Munroe, R.L. Munroe, and B.B. Whiting (eds), *Handbook of Cross-cultural Human Development*, New York, Garland, pp. 113–52.

Irvine, J., and York, D. (1995) 'Learning styles and culturally diverse students', in J.A. Banks (ed.), *Handbook of Research on Multicultural Education*, New York, Macmillan, pp. 484–97.

Kavale, K.A., and Forness, S.R. (1987) 'Substance over style: assessing the efficacy of modality testing and teaching', *Exceptional Children*, 56(3), pp. 228–39.

Lave, J. (1996) 'Teaching, as learning in practice', *Mind, Culture, and Activity*, 3, pp. 149–64.

Lee, C. (2001) 'Is October Brown Chinese? A cultural modeling activity system for underachieving students', *American Educational Research Journal*, 38(1), pp. 97–41.

Lee, C.D. (1993) *Signifying as a Scaffold for Literary Interpretation*, Urbana, IL, National Council of Teachers of English.

Matthews, D.B. (1991) 'Learning styles research: implications for increasing students in teacher education programs', *Journal of Instructional Psychology*, 18, pp. 228–36.

McLoyd, V.C., and Randolph, S.M. (1985) 'Secular trends in the study of Afro-American children: a review of *Child Development*, 1936–1980', in A.B. Smuts and J.W. Hagen (eds), *History and Research in Child Development*, Monographs of the Society for Research in Child Development, vol. 50(4–5), Ann Arbor, MI, Society for Research in Child Development, pp. 78–92.

McShane, D., and Berry, J.W. (1986) 'Native North Americans: Indian and Inuit abilities', in J.H. Irvine and J.W. Berry (eds), *Human Abilities in Cultural Context*, Cambridge University Press, pp. 385–426.

Mejía-Arauz, R., Rogoff, B., and Paradise, R. (2003) 'Cultural variation in children's observation of a demonstration', *International Journal of Behavioral Development*, 29(4), pp. 282–91.

Moll, L.C. (2000) 'Inspired by Vygotsky: ethnographic experiments in education', in C. Lee and P. Smagorinsky (eds), *Vygotskian Perspectives on Literacy Research: Constructing Meaning through Collaborative Inquiry*, New York, Cambridge University Press, pp. 256–68.

Moll, L., Saez, R., and Dworin, J. (2001) 'Exploring biliteracy: two student case examples of writing as a social practice', *Elementary School Journal*, 101(4), pp. 435–49.

Nieto, S. (1999) *The Light in their Eyes: Creating Multicultural Learning Communities*, New York, Teachers College Press.

Ortiz, F.I. (1988) 'Hispanic-American children's experiences in classrooms', in L. Weis (ed.), *Class, Race, and Gender in American Education*, Albany, NY, SUNY Press, pp. 63–86.

Price, G.E., and Dunn, R. (1997) *LSI Manual*, Lawrence, KS, Price Systems, Inc.

Rogoff, B. (1997) 'Evaluating development in the process of participation: theory, methods, and practice building on each other', in E. Amsel and A. Renninger (eds), *Change and Development: Issues of Theory, Application, and Method*, Hillsdale, NJ, Erlbaum, pp. 265–85.

—— (2003) *The Cultural Nature of Human Development*, New York, Oxford University Press.

Rogoff, B., and Angelillo, C. (2002) 'Investigating the coordinated functioning of multifaceted cultural practices in human development', *Human Development*, 45, pp. 211–25.

Rogoff, B., Goodman Turkanis, C., and Bartlett, L. (2001) *Learning Together: Children and Adults in a School Community*, New York, Oxford University Press.

Rogoff, B., Mistry, J., Göncü, A., and Mosier, C. (1993) *Guided Participation in Cultural Activity by Toddlers and Caregivers*, monographs for the Society for Research and Child Development, vol. 58(8), Ann Arbor, MI, Society for Research in Child Development.

Rogoff, B., Paradise, R., Mejía-Arauz, R., Correa-Chávez, M., and Angelillo, C. (2003) 'Firsthand learning through intent participation', *Annual Review of Psychology*, 54, pp. 175–203.

Rose, M. (1988) 'Narrowing the mind and page: remedial writers and cognitive reductionism', *College Composition and Communication*, 39(3), pp. 267–301.

Tejeda, C., and Espinoza, M. (2002) 'Reconceptualizing the role of dialogue in transformative learning', paper presented at meetings of the American Educational Research Association, New Orleans.

Tejeda, C., Espinoza, M., and Gutiérrez, K. (2003) 'Toward a decolonizing pedagogy: social justice reconsidered', in P. Trifonas (ed.), *Pedagogy of Difference: Rethinking Education for Social Change*, New York, Routledge, pp. 10–40.

Tiedeman, J. (1989) 'Measures of cognitive style', *Educational Psychologist*, 24(3), pp. 261–75.

Reflective questions

It would be useful to ask yourself the following questions to help make visible cultural assumptions you might hold:

1 How would you define culture?
2 How would you identify a cultural practice?
3 What are some consequences of equating culture with race or ethnicity?
4 Why do people's conceptions of culture matter in the context of intercultural exchange or interaction?

Further reading

Cole, M. (1996) *Cultural Psychology: A Once and Future Discipline*, Cambridge, MA, Belknap Press of Harvard University Press, chapter 5.

Erickson, F. (2005) 'Culture in society and in educational practices', revised chapter in J. Banks and C. M. Banks (eds), *Multicultural Education: Issues and Perspectives*, 5th edition, New York, John Wiley, pp. 31–59.

Human Development (2002) Special issue on culture, vol. 45(4).

Rogoff, B. (2003) *The Cultural Nature of Human Development*, New York, Oxford University Press.

3.2 Equity and social justice discourses in education

Naz Rassool

Introduction

Schools and classrooms play a pivotal role in mediating sociocultural, economic and political change; they also reflect geopolitical power relations and demographic shifts. The impact of colonialism/imperialism on educational policy and practice provides a historical example of this. During the colonial period education played a major role in mediating the power of the colonial state through both the hidden and overt curriculum in order to secure the social relations of domination and control. The ideology of colonialism, grounded in unequal power relations between rulers and ruled, permeated the educational system. Colonial power relations were implicated in the social construction of knowledge and in demarcating differential levels of access to education for colonized groups in different parts of the world, resulting in the unequal distribution of life chances. Much of this was achieved through, *inter alia*, the choice of language for teaching and learning, curriculum form and content, the availability of teaching and learning resources – and by regulating who could have access to different forms and levels of education.

By the end of the nineteenth century education also played a significant role in mediating sociocultural, political and economic changes taking place within Western European nation states. It played an important role in securing the hegemonic consciousness and social relations as well as the necessary skills and knowledge base to sustain the transition from primarily agrarian and trade-based economies to industry-driven modern capitalist economies. Education and knowledge represented a potent form of cultural capital to be exchanged within the burgeoning capitalist labour market. This was reflected in the development of mass schooling, which also had significant symbolic value in relation to building the knowledge infrastructure to support the development of liberal democratic citizenship.

At the start of the third millennium, we again are experiencing a period of sustained economic, cultural, technological and political change giving rise to new imperatives in educational policy and practice. Of concern to me in this chapter is the complex arena within which education operates in the modern world, how geopolitical changes impact on the formal schooling of young learners who are caught up in the maelstrom of contemporary people flows, and the implications that this has for how we conceptualize issues of equity and diversity in relation to the distribution of knowledge and, ultimately, opportunities within the labour market. I ask the question: within an ever-shifting global geopolitical and cultural terrain, as well as evolving economic imperatives, how do we theorize social exclusion discourses in educational frameworks?

Overall, this chapter focuses on the social relations emerging in the changing global cultural economy. It examines some of the ways in which discursive power relations operating within the global terrain have impacted on concepts of equity, inclusion/exclusion and social justice as these relate to the distribution of cultural capital and the social capital of learners in schools and classrooms. The last two concepts refer to changing forms of knowledge, networks of support, learning communities, contexts of learning and, more importantly, the shaping of the 'lifeworld' of diverse groups of learners within the changing sociocultural, economic and political milieu. The concept of the 'lifeworld' here derives from Habermas (1997) and refers simply to the lived domain constituting informal, culturally grounded sensibilities, individual and group competences, expectations, aspirations, beliefs and values that influence choices for individual, group and social action. As will be shown later, there is a synergy between the concept of the 'lifeworld' as explicated here and Bourdieu's notion of 'habitus'. The argument that these two concepts are significant for reinterpreting and redefining concepts and issues related to diversity and inclusion/exclusion within the interactive global cultural economy – and their relationship with empowerment/disempowerment of both individuals and groups – is an underlying theme in the discussion.

This analysis draws on the sociohistorical narratives of learners who are contemporary refugees from Somalia. The reason for this emphasis is that the educational terrain to be negotiated by transmigratory groups is complex and not entirely understood and appreciated. There is a growing awareness that Somali children 'previously resident in the Netherlands and Sweden are finding it difficult to settle in English schools and are underachieving' (QCA, 2003). As a social group they are also regarded as being invisible in research, that is to say, there are very few studies that focus on the specific factors that contribute to their underachievement, compared with other minority groups (Diriye, 2005). My premise is that the debate on equity, social justice and diversity in education needs to be located within the broader context of geopolitical and demographic changes globally.

The changing global cultural economy

It is now taken for granted that the current phase of globalization has generated fundamental demographic, economic, cultural and political shifts within countries across the world. These developments have impacted in a major way on sociocultural, economic and political practices and processes, altering ways of life and living, concepts of knowledge and ways of knowing. Continuous interconnectedness between countries and continents, at different levels, is a defining element of the current phase of globalization. Dynamic flows of people, trade and capital as well as the diffusion of global culture through mass communication practices and processes, lie at the centre of the global cultural economy. Supported by symbolic (e.g. world languages) and physical infrastructure (e.g. transport, information, financial and banking systems) facilitated by microelectronics technology, states and societies are becoming 'increasingly enmeshed in worldwide systems and networks of interaction' (Held and McGrew, 2003, p. 3). Geopolitical changes have been effected through political/economic/cultural power ensembles such as the World Bank, the World Trade Organization (WTO) and UNESCO operating as key policy-defining agencies within the global arena. As will be argued later, the interactions between these agencies and national educational policy frameworks have had major impacts on educational systems, educational opportunities and experiences as well as the shaping of learner and learning identities in different parts of the world.

The point that I want to make here is that the notion of a highly competitive knowledge-based international economy has enhanced the place and significance of education for national economies. The concept of the 'knowledge economy' relates to the centrality of knowledge, communication and technological capability to new technological production regimes and work practices, business and finance exchange and management as well as networks of information flows globally (Castells, 1996, 1997; Rassool, 1999). These include knowledge sharing, and knowledge transfer, within and across educational institutions and industry, placing emphasis on developing human capital as the foundation of future success in the international knowledge economy. As such, policy drives for widening participation of a diverse range of groups, of 'education for all' and increased emphasis on quality assurance frameworks are reflected in educational discourse frameworks nationally and internationally. How these initiatives are supported, challenged or undermined is discussed in the next section.

Transnational policy frameworks

Global power ensembles such as UNESCO's 'Education for All' initiative, the World Bank/ IMF through structural adjustment policies (SAPs) and the controls that inhere in trade regulatory frameworks such as the WTO have a significant impact on educational policy frameworks nationally. Together they exercise influence over the provision, maintenance and development of national educational infrastructure, levels of access to education and thus possibilities for the development of knowledge and skills capability amongst learners within both developed and developing countries. Sometimes their impacts have been contradictory in relation to equity possibilities and outcomes.

World Bank

In particular, the conditionalities of the World Bank's structural adjustment policies have created many dilemmas for national governments in developing countries to meet UNESCO's drive for 'Education for All' within the broader framework of the UN Millennium Development Goals (MDGs). Most countries have prioritized education as a means toward reducing poverty and hunger by providing universal primary education and reducing gender inequalities in primary and secondary education. However, much of this has had to take place within the constraints of national education budgets. These in turn have been limited by the conditionalities of the SAPs, underscored by neoliberal ideology centred on decreasing the role of the state in the public sector. This has led to budget cuts in social expenditure, the introduction of user fees and privatization in educational provision. Here then we are looking at barriers to education being integral to national educational policy (and imposed externally), increasing reliance on funding of provision by non-government organizations and multilateral agencies.

Within these contexts, the concept of inclusive education develops a complexity that extends beyond the usual concerns about constraints within the broad spectrum of special educational needs circumscribed by educational policy frameworks such as the principles adopted in the *Salamanca Statement and Framework for Action on Special Educational Needs* (UNESCO, 1999). The Salamanca Statement supports the principle of inclusion in ordinary schools of all children, regardless of their physical, intellectual, emotional, social, linguistic or other conditions. Article 2 states that:

> Regular schools with this inclusive orientation are the most effective means of combating discriminatory attitudes, creating welcoming communities, building an inclusive society and achieving education for all.

As stated earlier, although highly laudable, many of these meanings and intentions have been undermined by the pressures placed on schools to accommodate budgetary cuts through the SAPs.

At the level of the individual learner, neoliberal ideology emphasizes notions of knowledge competence, skills transferability, continuous professional development and thus self-management/self-regulation, that is, personal efficacy in relation to market demands. With the onus for employability transferred to individual learners, imperatives have been created for them to adapt to an increasingly complex sociocultural, political and economic terrain. How learners who do not have the requisite social, economic and cultural capital are enabled to participate (or prevented from participating) equitably in the educational context – and ultimately compete within the international labour market – is therefore an important issue to be examined. This is particularly important if we consider the fact that, amongst other exclusionary factors, many developing countries are chronically under-resourced with regard to well-trained teachers, teaching and learning resources, including materials, as well as having an under-developed teacher education and in-service training infrastructure.

WTO and GATS

These constraints run the risk of intensifying as a result of trade agreements within the framework of the WTO. The WTO underscores liberalization of trade and investment, the deregulation of markets leading to greater competition and market efficiency. The General Agreement in Trade in Services (GATS) represents one of the major agreements of the WTO and advocates the deregulation, the liberalization, of trade in services. The notion of 'freedom of trade' is grounded in the neoliberal concept of the 'free market' and is orientated towards 'the opening up of public services to corporate capital … it aims to create a "level" playing field so that there is no discrimination against foreign corporations entering the services market' (Rikowski, 2002). In practice, GATS, underscored by the neoliberal principles of competition, cost–benefit analysis and demand/supply issues, is geared towards maximizing corporate profits. Education services within the context of GATS include primary education, secondary education, technical and vocational education, higher education (tertiary), adult education (literacy) and also educational support services. Developing countries would be greatly disadvantaged in the event that GATS succeeds. Removing the limitations on trade would run 'the risk of converting education from a subjective public right into a process of simple commercialisation of educational packages' including the distribution of textbooks, maps, evaluation and certification systems and uniforms (de Siqueira, 2005, p. 1). This would create further problems in societies where there is already a shortage of textbooks *per se*. Moreover, the courses, textbooks, literature, curricula, teaching programmes, tests and so forth exported would more likely be in the languages of countries that have the capacity to produce and export them on a large scale. These resources are therefore likely to be published in the medium of ex-colonial and/or regional languages. In this regard globalization through the processes and practices of the WTO represents a powerful constraint in relation to the ability of countries to sustain cultural and linguistic diversity as well as having curriculum materials with content, languages and images that are relevant to the sociocultural experiences of learners using them. In effect, cost-effectiveness drives would lead to countries importing texts with a regional or international focus. Thus, ironically, the free market in education, in this instance, would be orientated towards homogenization and the standardization of knowledge to externally established quality and social norms.

The involvement of organizations such as the World Bank and the WTO in circumscribing national development possibilities has meant that national governments are no longer the sole determinants of their educational (and societal) development trajectories. In this regard 'the state is no longer the only site of sovereignty and the normativity that accompanies it' (Sassen, 1998, p. 81). Instead, international educational frameworks operating through the regulatory processes of global policy definers such as the World Bank and WTO have contributed to the fact that national policies of education, and institutional performance, are being referenced increasingly to the requirements and measures of global standards (Scholte, 2000). This contrasts with common views on the fluidity of cultural and knowledge exchanges within the global arena.

With inequalities permeating social and educational policy frameworks, as is evident in the discussion thus far, it is clear that barriers to educational access as well as the quality of teaching and learning experiences have been seriously compromised, especially within developing countries. Further complexities have been inserted into this broad terrain by the continuing trend of mass transmigration of people across countries and continents.

Transmigration

Whilst there are intertextual links with the previous period of transition from one sociopolitical, economic and cultural milieu to another, there also are significant changes. Whereas previous political shifts emphasized the development of the modern nation state, the current phase of globalization contests the notions of territoriality and the idea of a politically and economically stable and culturally homogeneous nation which, together, provide the organizing principles of the modern nation state. Much of this relates to the fact that the current epoch is defined in an unprecedented way by multiple risk factors that have changed geopolitical dynamics globally. Beck (1997) argues that risk in the form of natural and human-made disasters is intrinsic to late modernity, thus inserting uncertainty and ambivalence into everyday life. Of significance are the changing cultural landscapes created by the continuing trend of mass transmigration of people within and across countries and continents. Transmigration has intensified in recent years as a result of a variety of push factors including, for example, poverty, high rates of unemployment as well as underemployment in particular sectors, lack of job opportunities, natural disasters and sustained political instability, violence and systemic corruption within developing countries. For some, transmigration is a short-term phenomenon. In the case of Iran and Pakistan, for example, at least 2 million Afghan refugees had returned home by the end of 2002 (UNHCR, 2003). Other situations have remained unresolved for long periods of time, in some instances up to 20 or 30 years. This has been the case with Ethiopian refugees in Sudan as well as the Palestinian diasporic peoples. The Palestinian diaspora represents the world's biggest refugee population spread across the world, the largest number (3.6 million) residing in Jordan, Syria and Lebanon (UNHCR, 2000).

Displaced identities: the case of Somali refugee children

The anarchy that followed the collapse of the national government in Somalia in 1991 resulted in a sustained mass exodus of people, creating a diaspora in cross-border refugee camps and in North America, Europe, South Africa and the Arab states. Nomadism within the framework of the extended family, moving across national borders and ethnic boundaries, has been integral to Somali culture through the ages, this has become distorted in the post-1991 exodus, which has resulted in children being sent, unaccompanied and with new identities, to cultures having different beliefs systems and sets of values. Protracted refugee situations in which people remain in a long-term and intractable state of limbo mean that people live in situations where their 'basic rights and essential economic, social and psychological needs remain unfulfilled after years of exile' (UNHCR, 2004, p. 1). Having fled war, violence and poverty, many continue to live alienated, displaced personal lives in refugee camps and later also in their destination/receiving country. These transmigratory groups often remain trapped in a vicious cycle of dependency.

Transmigration has exerted immense pressure on the economic base of receiving countries, especially in the developing world, many of which have under-developed social infrastructures. The long-term settlement of large groups of displaced peoples presents complex problems to be solved by social policy within host societies, often with support from the UNHCR and other non-government organizations (NGOs). Provision for refugees, and scope for their social and economic integration in protracted situations, varies amongst different countries. According to the UNHCR (2004, p. 2):

> In some cases, prospects for local integration are minimal, requiring the international community to continue to provide assistance on a daily basis; in others, refugees have become economically self-sufficient, largely because the host society has provided access to land or the labour market.

How successful countries are in their ability to absorb diverse people flows and accommodate them in their educational systems depends largely on the strength of their economic capability and social infrastructure. These dynamic people flows have generated major adjustments in national educational delivery systems in order to accommodate ever-changing demographies as well as the complex sociocultural, emotional, psychological and educational needs of school and classroom populations. Within a world increasingly defined by global labour migration and immigration flows, classrooms across the world also reflect a range of cultural and linguistic needs and capabilities as well as social, political and cultural experiences. Consequently there are ever-growing pressures on schools and classrooms globally to adapt to ever-shifting cultural and linguistic landscapes whilst, at the same time, being able to respond to the evolving skills demands of the global labour market. How schools and classrooms are socially constructed, how they construct learners and learning, how schools name these experiences, needs and attributes – and how they engage with them – are significant. Not all people flows are free and unbounded; not all knowledge exchange/knowledge transfer takes place in an equal relationship. In some instances, barriers to accessing knowledge and learning have intensified, raising new sets of questions about notions of social justice and equity with regard to transmigratory groups. Attempting to address some of these issues, the next section focuses on learners and highlights the diversity of needs and demands in contemporary schools and classrooms, especially as these relate to transmigratory groups – and, particularly, Somali refugee children in British schools.

Classroom and learner subjectivities

Classrooms comprise different subjectivities with a range of life experiences, abilities, aptitudes, expectations, dreams, aspirations and desires. Research since at least the 1960s has provided evidence that starting points in school-life are not equal (see Coleman, 1960; Plowden, 1967; Halsey *et al.*, 1980). Children come to school endowed with different levels of social and cultural capital. For example, language represents potent linguistic capital;

those who are fluent in the language of teaching and learning have an advantage over those who are not. Moreover, whilst some are already literate upon entry, and have knowledge and experience of the everyday practices of school life, others might not have had a systematic formative pre-school experience. Diriye (2005, p. 6) argues that this is an important aspect of Somali children in UK schools, as children who

> may never have been to school arrive in [the] UK during the school term and are usually placed according to their age. Their classmates are obviously in a favourable position as they have been studying for several years and have laid their educational foundations firmly.

I was made aware of this in my experience in an inner-city London school during the 1980s, then receiving children from rural Bangladesh who had never attended school. One of the main tasks of teachers initially was to socialize the pupils into the routines and mores of school life, introducing them to the discipline of the school day and keeping them inside the school environment.

The lack of schooling in countries of origin for refugees from developing countries in many instances is related to sustained under-investment in education. This, compounded by the impact of the World Bank SAPs on social policy, has contributed to under-developed educational infrastructure. It is commonplace, for example, in many developing countries, especially those throughout the sub-Saharan region and in rural areas in India, Pakistan and Thailand, for teaching and learning to take place in classrooms that are located outside – under trees. According to recent UNHCR information on refugee education in developing countries, during the 2002/3 period:

> more than one-third of all classes were classified as temporary or open-air structures ... The highest proportion of temporary or open-air classrooms is found in Thailand (100% of the 1,530 reported classrooms), Nepal (88% of the 775 classrooms) and Tanzania (14% of 1,010 classrooms) (UNHCR, 2003, p. 3).

Nearly half (45 per cent) of the temporary or open-air classrooms were in UNHCR-provided schools (UNHCR, 2003). In most instances, pupils from refugee groups living in camps, in effect, exist outside formal educational policy provision within receiving countries. Needless to say, these gaps in provision fail to maximize the potential of refugee groups to acquire appropriate forms and levels of cultural capital to exchange in the formal labour market of the receiving country and thus to contribute to its GDP. As stated earlier, in some instances, refugees are prevented from being productively employed. Ideally, presented with a coherent and relevant curriculum and teaching resources, they would be enabled to accumulate skills and knowledges in exile, which could ultimately facilitate their social and economic integration into their countries of origin and thus contribute to their home economies. I return to this point again later.

Children also have distinctive life experiences as a result of their social position; they are influenced by the historical narrative that has shaped and influenced their cultural, familial and individual habitus (Bourdieu, 1990); their individual and collective lifeworlds (Habermas, 1997 – see above), the unconscious ways by which they know, understand, experience and live their lives. In the case of Somali pupils, IRIN (2003) data report high aspirations amongst parents for their children's education, to the extent that they pay sometimes unscrupulous agents to transport their children unaccompanied by a relative to countries in Europe and

North America. In these instances, networks of communities exist to facilitate this process, although 'sometimes the children end up being left for long periods of time in "middle countries" before arriving at the intended destination' (IRIN, 2003, p. 23). The key point to make here is that given that the historical narrative of these children comprises multiple displacements it is reasonable to assume that individually their 'lifeworld' or 'habitus' would reflect the uncertainties inserted into their lives by their social and political experiences. They would have internalized the fact that risk is intrinsic to their lives. Facilitating access to education for this group of learners would therefore involve much more than a relevant curriculum and the availability of adequate teaching and learning resources.

What is significant about the experience of Somali learners discussed here is the enforced adoption of new, invented, identities and the confusion that this potentially generates for some. Upon leaving their country with the help of paid agents, they have scripts given to them renarrativizing their lives, and deviation from it could have dire consequences which may include being sent to a detention centre and, finally, deported back to their home country. What it also highlights is the fact that they are, as a result, engaged in a continuing reflexive dialogue with the self in relation to their evolving identities and redefined personal narratives. For many this is a complex and painful process. The IRIN Report (2003, p. 32) cites a psychologist in Sweden working with displaced children who had been separated from their families who states:

> These children have deep psychological problems, but it is difficult sometimes to know the origins: from before the journey, or during the journey, because of separation from their families. Some cry uncontrollably when they do talk … It's difficult to get sense out of them. I would say every unaccompanied child experiences problems of some sort, it's just the degree of severity – inability to sleep, nightmares, and anxiety about parents, loneliness, self-preoccupation. Some suffer posttraumatic disorder and depression. Among the boys, we see many of the boys 'acting out' their problems – getting violent at school … There is one word really that describes the feeling they have: loneliness. I would say they don't really live inside society, but on the edge of it … it's not a good prognosis.

In addition to pupils from Somalia, there are those also from Senegal, Sudan and the Democratic Republic of Congo, to name a few. The implications of the complex experiences of transmigratory groups for how we analyse and understand issues related to social justice, equity and diversity in schools and classrooms is therefore profound. It necessitates a broadening of the scope of inclusion/exclusion discourses to focus also on identity formation, the psychological and emotional needs of transmigratory groups and their histories, including the political and cultural experiences of learners who have transmigrated across different countries, for whom displacement and uncertainty have become an integral part of their habitus. The effect of these factors on the cognitive and emotional development of children in these situations, in turn, has implications for how pedagogy is formulated. This is the case if we take into account Bruner's (2006: 175) view that [neither] 'the study of development nor its application in pedagogy can be divorced from the pervasive political, social and economic forces that shape the society and thereby shape the conditions of growth'.

At the same time, whilst it is accepted that barriers to learning are constructed externally and internally, they do not *ipso facto* determine outcomes unproblematically. Rather, they are also challenged, negotiated, reworked and redefined in complex ways. The emphasis therefore is on how learners construct themselves, as well as how they strategize, adapt and redefine themselves in relation to their own personal, cultural and politicohistorical narratives to overcome political, institutional, curricular and cultural barriers to progress in education. How psychologically and socially displaced learners in our schools engage with themselves in relation the above, and how they manage to forge a productive life for themselves, is an important area for research into social justice and empowerment in and through education.

Conclusion: towards a redefined analytical framework

Together the issues discussed in this chapter call into question arguments centred on standardized views of inclusion/exclusion in education within the contemporary world. As stated earlier, it also calls into question existing analytical frameworks that are linear in their focus and have a primarily economistic or static cultural orientation. The latter refers to the uncritical, and implicitly separatist, perspective of multiculturalism. I want to argue that addressing the discursive changes and interactions that have been raised throughout this chapter, and their impact on schools and classrooms, requires a language repertoire, a textured discourse borrowing terms and concepts across the disciplines. It needs to incorporate complexities, changing realities, shifting cultural and linguistic landscapes, encompassing not only the maintenance of cultural values but also engaging with the redefinition of cultures, of adaptation, rights, entitlements, and also of obligations.

My theoretical task here, therefore, is to expand the analytical framework within which we seek to understand the impact of multiple change processes within the global arena on educational access for diverse displaced population groups within and across countries and continents. In an attempt to begin the process of providing an integrated analytical framework that caters for discursive meanings and interactions, this section draws on a concept within the life sciences and uses the idea of schools and classrooms as representing learning ecologies. Although this concept has gained in popularity in recent educational discourse, its meaning has been reduced largely to the process of learning and factors that facilitate learning efficiency within the fields of cybernetics (Dimitrov, 2000) and applied language studies (Mühlhäusler, 1999). In order to explain its particular use here, the next section locates the concept within the social sciences.

Defining ecologies of learning

The concept of ecology, in a literal sense, refers to the interactions between living creatures and their environment, the structures that sustain them and which they in turn adapt to in order to survive. By that fact, it also includes the changes that take place within the structures and processes of that ecology itself. In the case of humans, the concept obtains a second-order meaning; it is also an environment within which discursive networks of meaning are produced. With regard to education, this refers not only to the production of different forms of knowledge, information and skills but also the shaping of individual and group subjectivities; their self- (or tacit) knowledges, dispositions, aspirations, expectations, attainments and achievements. Furthermore, learners are positioned not only in relation to their teachers and their peers but also the content and process of the curriculum, including, for example, learning practices, knowledge production and assessment frameworks. Meanings then are produced within and through the structures, systems and processes in which formal education is constituted. These in turn interact with, and impact on, learners' experiences in culture and society. In relation to groups and individuals, meanings are produced in the interaction between persons as well as the reflexive inner dialogue which is integral to the learning process and also part of the process of self-definition. At the meta-level meanings are produced also in the interaction between learners and their sociopolitical, cultural, economic and pedagogic environment. Thus although meaning production is relational, it takes place within a discursive and interactive context.

Of further significance is the fact that learners are not regarded as docile subjects, for they actively make strategic choices in relation to developments/expectations/opportunities within their sociopolitical, cultural and economic environment as an intrinsic part of their quest for survival. In an anthropological sense, adaptation is an active, dialectical process through which people change their environment whilst in the process of changing themselves and their social arrangements. This is central to the analysis of the experience and educational needs of transmigratory groups. Clearly then, rather than a restrictive, rigid and deterministic analytical framework, the concepts of interaction and reflexive self-definition are central to the idea of a learning ecology. It represents an environment that is adaptive, within which learners contest, incorporate, reinterpret and redefine meanings and themselves as learners and as individuals. Thus they develop tacit knowledges and strategic planning. Instead of a static rights-based focus on multicultural education, the learning ecology approach seeks to engage with communities and to create space and opportunity for self-reflection and dialogue with displaced peoples, hopefully to become communities having a stake in their adopted countries. This represents a more positive approach than the quest of multiculturalism to replicate 'home', the 'Heimat' culture of looking back to an idealized simple, rural way of life, of religious intransigence and intolerance.

To summarize, the notion of a learning ecology therefore is grounded in organic and complex internal relations that, in turn, exist in an ongoing dialogue with external networks of power. It is within these interactions that possibilities are shaped, presented, curtailed, accepted or contested – and either rejected or redefined. Together these factors highlight the fact that the concept of a learning ecology, as an analytical approach, represents a multi-level and dynamic process of meaning-making. As such, it offers a means of analysing and interpreting the complex changes taking place within the global cultural economy and how they impact on the educational experiences of transmigratory groups caught up in this dynamic.

Key points

- Dynamic sociocultural, geopolitical and economic changes taking place within the global arena have impacted on everyday classroom life on a very practical level.
- Classrooms have become culturally more diverse.
- Classrooms reflect different types and levels of need that are dialogically related to historical experiences as well as to changes taking place in the world today.
- Together these have undermined static and linear concepts of equity, social justice and inclusion/exclusion in education.
- A redefined analytical framework is needed that allows for the analysis of complexities, changing realities and shifting cultural and linguistic landscapes, of reflexive self-definition as an intrinsic part of the teaching and learning process.

References

Beck, U. (1997) *Risk Society: Towards a New Modernity*, London, Sage Publications.

Bruner, J.S. (2006) *In Search of Pedagogy: The Selected Works of Jerome S. Bruner*, London, Routledge.

Castells, M. (1996) *The Information Age: Economy, Society and Culture*, vol. I, *The Rise of the Network Society*, Oxford, Blackwell Publishing.

—— (1997) *The Information Age: Economy, Society and Culture*, vol. II, *The Power of Identity*, Oxford, Basil Blackwell Publishing.

de Sigueira, A.C. (2005) 'The regulation of education through the WTO/GATS', *Journal for Critical Education Policy Studies*, 3, available online at http://www.jceps.com/?pageID=articlean darticleID=41, accessed 28 June 2007.

Dimitrov, V. (2000) 'Learning ecology for human and machine intelligence', ZULENET, available online at http://www.zulenet.com/see/LearnEcologyHuman.html, accessed 2 May 2007.

Diriye, A. (2005) 'Somalis in the UK', unpublished discussion paper.

Habermas, J. (1997) *The Theory of Communicative Action: Reason and the Rationalization of Society*, vol. 1, Cambridge, Polity Press.

Held, D. and McGrew, A. (2003) 'The great globalization debate', in *The Global Transformations Reader*, ed. D. Held and A. McGrew, Cambridge, Polity Press, pp. 1–50.

Integrated Regional Information Networks (IRIN), (2003) *Gaps in Their Hearts: The Experience of Separated Somali Children*, Nairobi, Kenya, UN Office for the Coordination of Human Affairs.

Mühlhäusler, P. (1996) *Linguistic Ecology: Language Change and Linguistic Imperialism in the Pacific Region*, London, Routledge.

Rassool, N. (1999) *Literacy for Sustainable Development in the Age of Information*, The Language and Education Library, 14, Clevedon and Philadelphia, Multilingual Matters.

Rikowski, G. (2002) *Globalisation and Education*, London, House of Lords Select Committee on Economic Affairs Inquiry into the Global Economy.

Sassen, S. (1998) *Globalization and its Discontents*, New York, The New Press.

Scholte, J.A. (2000) *Globalization: A Critical Introduction*, London, Palgrave.

UNESCO, (1999) *Salamanca Five Years On. A Review of UNESCO Activities in the Light of the Salamanca Statement and Framework for Action Adopted at the World Conference on Special Needs Education: Access and Quality*, Paris, UNESCO, Special Needs Education, Division of Basic Needs Education.

United Nations High Commissioner for Refugees (UNHCR) (2000) *The State of the World's Refugees: Fifty Years of Humanitarian Action*, Oxford, Oxford University Press.

—— (2003) *Refugee Education in 2002/3: Indicators and Standards for 66 Camp Locations*, Geneva, Population Data Unit/PGDS, with the assistance of the Education Unit/HCDS, Division of Operational Support, UNHCR.

—— (2004) *Protracted Refugee Situations*, Geneva, Executive Committee of the High Commissioner's Programme, UNHCR.

Reflective questions

1   Dynamic sociocultural, geopolitical and economic changes taking place within the global arena have impacted on everyday classroom life in a very practical way so that classrooms have become culturally more diverse. Drawing on your own recent experience, how is this reflected in different types and levels of need in the classroom?

2   How are these dialogically related to historical experiences as well as changes taking place in the world today? What are the implications for school-level policy for promoting a greater understanding of these needs?

Further reading

de Sigueira, A.C. (2005) 'The regulation of education through the WTO/GATS', *Journal for Critical Education Policy Studies*, 3, available online at http://www.jceps.com/?pageID=articlean darticleID=41, accessed 28 June 2007.

Held, D. and McGrew, A. (2003) 'The great globalization debate', in *The Global Transformations Reader*, ed. D. Held and A. McGrew, Cambridge, Polity Press, pp. 1–50.

Integrated Regional Information Networks (IRIN), (2003) *Gaps in their Hearts: The Experience of Separated Somali Children*, Nairobi, Kenya, UN Office for the Coordination of Human Affairs.

3.3 Gender theory and research in education

Jo-Anne Dillabough

Introduction

This chapter addresses current debates in the study and theoretical analysis of gender and gender equity in education. Both gender and equity have been linked as I view them as deeply intertwined in relation to current theoretical debates in education. However, the main thrust of the chapter is concerned with an overview of the field across the last two decades with an emphasis upon the part played by theory in the making of the field. A secondary aim is to describe and assess cutting-edge debates about gender (as operating conceptually in education) in the field in the United Kingdom, North America and continental Europe. In summary, then, the goal of the chapter is to provide a broad overview of the field and both elaborate and speculate on its future directions in relation to larger theoretical trends, broad educational changes and debates in the social sciences and humanities.

The development of gender in education as a field of study

Some may argue that the field of gender in education has its origins in the theoretical work of Ann Oakley (1972) and education feminists investigating links between gender, school structures and broader social arrangements. Oakley's key argument, for example, was that the social category 'gender' in the study of inequality was preferable to a focus on sex differences, since it perceived gender as a social construction rather than as a fixed biological entity. To put this another way, if gender, as opposed to sex, was ultimately a social construct, then its links to socialization could be understood primarily as an aspect of gender identity formation.

In keeping with this shift, education feminism in the late 1970s and early 1980s moved beyond the distinctive concerns of liberal and radical feminists to an analysis of education's role in gender socialization patterns and the reproductive functions of education in shaping gender relations (Dillabough and Arnot, 2002). It was in these respects that Oakley's (1972) work provided feminists with the conceptual tools for expanding the boundaries of gender research.

Second-wave feminist concerns influenced the direction in which this kind of gendered analysis of education might go. For example, research documenting the manifestation of sexual discrimination in schools began to emerge (see Wolpe, 1976; Byrne, 1978; Deem, 1978, 1980; Stanworth, 1981) alongside studies highlighting the links between the form of girls' education and capitalism (Barrett, 1980; MacDonald, 1980). In such studies, gender and class differentiation and patriarchal school structures were major concerns, as were the consequent equity issues for education. In following the work of radical feminists, early gender analyses examined the patriarchal language of school subjects and school structures (Mahony, 1983, 1985) and exposed what Spender (1980) dubbed the 'patriarchal paradigm of education'. Influenced by a strong Marxist inflection, many education feminists sought to expose the gender and class inequities emerging from sex-segregated schooling, while others identified important links between the aims of educational policy, male domination and a capitalist economy (David, 1980; Walker and Barton, 1983). By the early 1980s, the most significant motifs were a notion of gender as a theoretical construct, education as a site for the cultivation of gender inequalities (Delamont, 1980) and a concentration on the relationship between the state, national policy and the economy in shaping girls' education.

As we will see, the theoretical premises – whether Marxist, structuralist or functionalist – associated with this work emphasized schools as sites for the *potential* democratization of gender relations even though gender socialization was understood to be shaped, above all, by residual patriarchal relations rather than by a dynamic of social *change*. This meant that earlier liberal preoccupations with sex differences and roles began to give ground to deeper concerns about the relation between gender and social structure. Critical forms of gender equity research sought, in part, to challenge those early liberal positions focusing on the psychological characteristics seen as 'intrinsic' to girls and women. In their place came new emphases upon the gendered nature of social structures and the particularity of gender identity formation.

Such concerns contributed to the building of a new theoretical agenda for studying gender in education from a broad social and political perspective to which many education feminists from the late 1970s have remained committed. This was an agenda dedicated to the project of uncovering the gendered nature of school knowledge/curriculum (Bernstein, 1978), and revealing its role in shaping girls' and boys' identities and aspirations. It was also an attempt to address the pragmatic problems of gender inequity and feminist pedagogy in schools, drawing upon wider social concerns for, and about, women (Weiner and Arnot, 1987; Weiner, 1994). In each of these respects, much of the early equity research work represented a sustained attempt to expose sexist school practices, engage in school reform and to challenge what Dale Spender (1980), Bob Connell (1987) and others had identified as patriarchal school structures.

While this early phase of education feminism undoubtedly contributed substantially to the field, its initiatives were not without their difficulties. Indeed, many feminists began to disassociate from mainstream 'equity research' that focused too narrowly on girls' education and issues of discrimination, access and attainment. Such work, it was argued, was entrenched in middle-class values and narrowly defined visions of the category 'female'. As such, it was ill-equipped to address questions about issues of identity, culture and women's differences (Carby, 1982; Brah and Minhas, 1985). For this reason, the study of identity began to emerge as central to a reconfiguration of the field.

Gender, educational structures and social reproduction

In this early stage of change, education, as a mediating structure of the economy, was still seen as a major site for the reproduction of class culture rather than as a site for the construction of broader social identities associated with, for example, race and sexuality. Innovative gender research within this tradition was principally concerned with the part played by education in *reproducing* dominant class structures, codes and corresponding classed identities. A theoretical interest in the notion of schools as sites for the cultural reproduction and development of social identities (chiefly relating to class and gender), while distanced from earlier functionalist traditions, therefore continued to emphasize the importance of mapping economic structures onto school structures (Dillabough and Arnot, 2002).

Within this framework, significant attention was given to issues of gender politics/inequity in schools (Arnot and Weiner, 1987) and to women's education as training a 'hierarchically stratified workforce' for the 'reserve army of labour'. Such work highlighted the role of education in constructing women teachers and female pupils as servants to the state (Steedman, 1985). It also revealed the gender hierarchies of educational management and the masculine expectations by which they were framed. In sum, the achievement of such work was to expose the reproductive role of education in maintaining symbolic representations of male rationality and female subservience.

Emphasis on the reproduction of the social and economic order through education led towards a feminist version of *reproduction theory*:

> In 'hard' versions of social reproduction theory (Bowles and Gintis 1976), education was conceptualized as an instrument of capitalism through which the subordination of women and working class girls was reproduced. As might be expected, class culture appeared with great regularity as the social formation which not only pre-figured, but determined, girls' educational experiences, identities and forms of consciousness.
>
> (Dillabough and Arnot, 2002, p. 12)

Later versions of reproduction theory took on somewhat different theoretical inflections, and mark a shift in our understanding of social theory generally, and feminist thinking more specifically. Such accounts of reproduction theory drew widely upon theories of class hegemony (Gramsci, 1971), cultural capital (Bourdieu and Passeron, 1977) and educational codes (Bernstein, 1977, 1978). Of particular significance was the attention which these approaches gave to the role of masculinity and femininity in shaping class relations and gender inequality in schools, with disaffection expressed as a celebration of resistant masculinities (Willis, 1977) or a 'cult of femininity' (McRobbie, 1978). Here, the cultural reproduction of class and gender positioning in the state emerged as a kind of 'parallelism' (Willis, 1977) between young people's resistance to élitist school norms and an apparent class commitment to the construction of traditional gender positions.

As expressed in the now seminal works of Willis (1977) and McRobbie (1978), the emergence of gender inequality in school cultures was not as straightforward as social reproduction theorists such as Bowles and Gintis (1976) had suggested. Male and female youth were also involved in the active construction of their own complex identity positions. Such work revealed the critical importance of diverse school experiences and the cultural identities and social positioning which prefigured them. Cultural identity therefore began to emerge as a much more complex element in the study of male and female youth's lived experiences of schooling.

Cultural reproduction theorists were not without their critics. Their approach tended to devalue women's political agency and the part played by both education and women's movements in the recontextualization of gender and class relations. Nor did they address issues of difference – beyond class – broadly or seriously enough. In particular, the category 'gender' was under reconstruction in some feminist research in this period. Yet cultural reproduction theorists had started gender research on a course which began to resist narrow and overly deterministic understandings of educational processes and school cultures and their role in shaping diverse and resistant identities. Such shifts in educational research were indicative of a larger interest within cultural and social theory of moving beyond 'the charge of essentialism' and challenging what was seen as a conceptually impoverished and reductive way of thinking about identity formation. In the place of cultural reproduction came a broader understanding of gender as a more permeable social construct held together through elements of discourse.

Transformations in gender theory and educational research

In the light of these broad theoretical shifts, new questions could now be raised about modern feminist theory and its application to the study of gender in education. In looking to these shifts – in effect, the movement from modernist to postmodernist/poststructuralist analyses, or what Francis (1999) has described as a move from a realist to a relativist feminist framework – a number of important theoretical questions have emerged. While still concerned to a degree with gender equity, curriculum and gender reform policies, these newer questions settle their key problematic upon a philosophical concern about the nature of gender identity and the ways in which educational discourses shape the modern individual.

Some of the most salient questions which have arisen about gender in education concern the 'meaning and significance of identity', and 'relationships between identity and difference' (Weir, 1996, p. 1). As a key representative of one side of the debate regarding the formative place of identity in social theory, Judith Butler (1990, p. 39) writes that the 'heterosexual imperative enables certain sexual identifications and forecloses and/or disavows other identifications'. Butler's words reveal a concern with social difference and notions of female identity 'in which sexuality is the main axis of operation and normative heterosexuality as the main obsession' (Anderson, 1998, p. 8). If we do not wish to repress difference, how, as education feminists, might we theorize it in relation to gender and other social formations 'without making false claims to authority and authorship' (Weir, 1996). These questions have played a substantial role in recasting the debates about gender equity in 'education feminism', though more traditional sociological and pedagogical questions have also maintained much of their force. Gender research has, moreover, continued to shed light on the shifting and constructed nature of curricular knowledge in relation to educational practices over time (Measor and Sikes, 1992; Murphy and Gipps, 1996; Paechter and Head, 1996), as well as on sociological, cultural and historical analyses of women teachers' and teacher educators' working lives (Acker and Feurverger, 1997).

Despite the range of topics spanning the field, the argument I now wish to pursue suggests that an emphasis on gender identity rather than equity *per se* has emerged, in part as a response to larger transformations in social theory and the evolution of education within the humanities and social sciences. Some of the key issues which have emerged as a result of these transformations include the viability of the modem democratic education project, the 'death of the female subject' (i.e. a uniform notion of female identity), and the question of whether social and cultural theory can serve as grounds for struggle over values inherent in education feminism, such as the goal of gender equity.

At the same time, it is important to remember that there remain education feminists who argue that there is a continuing need to examine the relationship between gender identity both as a *category of analysis* and as a coherent narrative which is shaped, in part, through educational forces. By contrast, those who are more formally entrenched in assessing the shifting nature of gender identity in schools (e.g. poststructuralists) argue that we need to get beyond viewing gender as a core element of selfhood and instead examine the equity implications for education policy of *understanding multiple positions on identity*. Still others argue that equity itself is framed within a liberal humanist or liberal democratic project that honours some female groupings (i.e. the middle class) and marginalizes others. There are, then, many diverse positions from which to engage the significance of gender identity for education.

Emerging themes/theoretical orientations in gender and education

Four major themes mark contemporary theory in *gender in education*. ... It is to a considera- tion of each of these themes, their related research and theory, and their impact on education that I now turn.

Gender, poststructuralism and the 'sexed identity' in education

The mid- to late 1980s represented a transformative period in the study of gender and education, when it could be suggested, for example, that the category 'woman' or 'girl' was either illusory or could no longer speak for all women in the name of a straightforward or simplistic notion of social and cultural reproduction. Modernist feminist perspectives in education could therefore be 'seen as rationalistic explanations and master narratives' – which not only identified the causes of gender inequality but had uniformly described the core premises of gender identity formation in modernity (Dillabough and Arnot, 2002). Such explanations, as the work of Willis (1977) and McRobbie (1978) had suggested, bore little relation to the complexity of gender identities and experiences in schools.

In the struggle against essentialism in 'education feminism', a more explicit research interest in the *multiple forms of gender identity* and their manifestations in education began to emerge. Such analyses took a variety of forms, including studies of the part played by the 'sexed identity' (Butler, 1990) in school performance (Epstein *et al.*, 1998), the role of identity formation in influencing the effectiveness of gender equity policies (Kenway, 1997) or definitions of teacher professionalism and accounts of the lives and experiences of female teachers and teacher educators (Acker, 1994).

Within this emergent tradition, one strand of identity research has proliferated in recent years and has addressed the ways in which educational discourses lead to multiple forms of masculinity and femininity in schools. In this section, I highlight how the study of femininity and masculinity – perhaps more than other domains of educational research – is an example of how 'education feminism' has attempted to grapple with changes in social/cultural theory stimulated by poststructural thinking, particularly in relation to shifting gender identities. This shift could be charted as a move away from the 'sociology of women's education' and political and pedagogical concerns with gender equity (as pragmatic issues) towards a broader theoretical concern with the formation of gender identities and novel *gender theories* of education.

One of the most prominent theories drawn upon in recent years to problematize uniform understandings of 'gender' has been feminist poststructuralism. ... In short, that which distin- guishes poststructuralism from *rational* forms of structuralism or other modernist feminisms is its link to deconstruction as a conceptual tool for critiquing language, and its insistence that gender identity is not a coherent or stable narrative to be known in any ultimate sense.

Several terms favoured by poststructuralists, such as 'discourse', 'deconstruction', 'subjec- tivity' and 'regimes of truth' have been much drawn upon by education feminists to examine the gendered nature of educational language. The aim here has been to reveal the cultural elements of educational life (e.g. peer culture, teachers' talk, school text) as discourses (i.e.

as embedded in language) rather than rigid social forces, shaping masculinity and femininity. One of the earliest illustrations of this theoretical shift in education was the work of Bronwyn Davies. Davies (1989, pp. 1–2, 13) writes: 'In learning the discursive practices of their society, children learn that they must be socially identifiable as [either male of female]. Positioning oneself as male or female is done through discursive practices and through the subject positionings which are available within those (linguistic) practices.'

While Davies' work was principally concerned with educational life in Australia, it drew upon earlier projects on the construction of femininity in the UK. For example, Valerie Walkerdine (1981) and Walkerdine and Lucey (1989), drawing upon both psychoanalytic and poststructural approaches, championed the idea that historical images of women which mirror the private sphere are mobilized within education *discourses* to propagate the subordination of women and girls. Following Foucault, they argued that a 'regime of truth' about gender identity which people understand to be historically continuous and unitary is thus always present in classrooms. In this sense, femininity and masculinity are merely performed in honour of the discourses that construct them. For Walkerdine, dominant understandings of gender identity represent fictional accounts of an old and rather unimaginative reincarnated story about men and women across time and space.

As a further development of this earlier work, the study of masculinity has emerged as central to identity research in education. Often drawing upon aspects of poststructural theory, this research suggests that there is no one form of masculinity in schools; rather, there are many competing and contradictory forms, each of which is contingent on the conditions of gender *regulation* in schools. Examples of this work include studies of the gendered language which is drawn upon by male youth to legitimize various positions on masculinity, a practice which ultimately privileges some dominant 'identity' forms over others – for example, the difference between being a 'swot' or 'wimp' (Mac an Ghaill, 1994; Haywood and Mac an Ghaill, 1996; Davies, 1997; Kehily and Nayak, 1997; Skelton, 1997). Other studies address how, for example, homophobia is constructed through the heterosexist language of boys' everyday practices in school cultures (Epstein, 1997). Recent work drawing on poststructuralism has also examined the language forms of educational policy and the media, such as the 'underachieving boy', and the implications such language has for reproducing gender inequity in reactive policy measures such as 'saving' the 'underachieving boy' through educational support offered up by famous footballers (Raphael Reed, 1999).

Why has such a sustained focus on masculinity in education taken place in recent years? Even though feminists have explored the lives of girls and women, and described a 'cult of femininity' (McRobbie, 1978), they have not until recently fully explored what it meant to study gender (as opposed to sex) in the broadest social sense; to study girls alone cannot address the issue of gender relations. While Willis (1977) entered this territory over 20 years ago, he remained committed to masculinist theories of reproduction to explain masculinity (grounded in notions of class conflict). The contemporary trends in tackling issues of masculinity have attempted to challenge such positions by drawing upon theoretical work which offers new understandings of competing gender discourses and their role in shaping diverse gender identities.

Masculinity research in education also relates directly to the broader preoccupation with identity debates in social and cultural theory. It has exposed novel equity issues associated with a range of masculinities emerging in schools and paved the way for viewing gender as more permeable and changing than in previous periods of educational research. A special concern with the gendered elements of educational discourse has also meant that key issues such as 'failing boys' and 'boys' underachievement' have been examined from a poststructural perspective. Ironically, most poststructuralists were hoping to do away with identity as a category of analysis, but it seems to loom large in most of this work. ... Yet it is clear that this work has been extremely effective in charting the everyday language regulating the lives of male and female pupils and teachers. And in conducting micro-feminist analyses of gender in education and moving beyond liberal, maternal and Marxist accounts, it has achieved much that had seemed beyond the reach of mainstream education feminists.

Gender, ethnicity and social exclusion: the transformative power of black, post-colonial and standpoint feminisms

Another example of alternative feminist theorizing which has gained greater prominence over the last decade is 'black feminism' and variants on 'stand-point feminism' (Hill-Collins, 1990), some of which are aligned to a greater or lesser extent with 'feminist critical realism' or 'post-colonial feminism' (Brah and Minhas, 1985; hooks, 1989; Mirza, 1993). Key educational ideas which have been central to such analysis can be summarized as follows: (1) women and girls' education is formulated within a colonial narrative where the 'other' emerges as the marginal identity to be gazed upon; (2) colonial models of education reproduce the cross-cultural domination of women and girls through conformity to values and ideals embedded in white narratives of educational success; and (3) educational research fails to recognize the key question of difference – that black and minority ethnic girls' experiences and family life are distinct from the white cultural narrative and therefore cannot be measured in relation to it (Mirza, 1992). Much of this research analyses the relationship of black families (Phoenix, 1987), communities (Mirza and Reay, 2000) and black women and girls to capitalism and imperialism (Hill-Collins, 1990). In so doing, the Eurocentric and racist elements of a good deal of earlier feminist theorizing have been exposed (Wright *et al.*, 1998).

From its inception, black feminist analysis has revealed the ways in which the liberal democratic education project has constructed stereotypes of the 'black girl and boy' (Phoenix, 1987; Blair, 1995; Blair and Holland, 1995). It also went beyond the school context to explore black family life and its impact on the formation of black students' identities. It therefore challenged traditional and stereotypical notions that black girls suffered from problems of self-esteem against an image of the confident, white, middle-class girl. Instead, it highlighted the positive and subversive power of families in shaping young girls' identities (Mirza, 1992). It also castigated liberal and Marxist feminist research for focusing too narrowly on a stereotypical view of black youth that often projected 'black failure'.

Mirza's (1992) work was perhaps the most influential in moving mainstream education accounts of 'black female youth and achievement' studies beyond the schooling context. Her purpose was to critique the liberal emphasis on black female achievement and instead highlight the significance of other contextual, cultural and political issues more broadly linked to identity. Her work therefore exposed the importance of school culture and family as important mediators of girls' racialized identities. Black femininity and masculinity could no longer be solely understood on the basis of what many education feminists had referred to as the 'gender binary' – colonial and class distinctions between male and female or the public and private spheres. Alongside the work of others (e.g. Blair, 1995; Wright *et al.*, 1998), Mirza also exposed the racialized and gendered elements of upward social mobility and illustrated how rationalized strategies of school success served only to reinstate the various educational and labour market constraints that black men and women encountered in the workforce.

In recent years, black feminists have been instrumental in defining a new category of educational research on the 'social exclusion' of black and minority ethnic youth. For example, recent gender/race research conducted by Callander and Wright (2000) has moved beyond a concern with 'girls' and 'women' to an engagement with the ways in which working-class black boys and girls are constructed by exclusionary school processes within 'cycles of confrontation and underachievement' (Wright *et al.*, 1998, p. 85). Such processes include the cultural politics of school sanctions and teacher discipline, and the interactive place of race and gender in the formation of exclusionary school hierarchies.

Perhaps the greatest significance of this important body of work lies neither in the image of black girls resisting power structures nor their compliance in conforming to the achievement standards of an educational system. It rests instead on black feminist emphases on the potentially coercive role of external constructions (the colonial narrative, racism) and exclusions in shaping the gendered and racialized pupil. Gender identity within black feminist perspectives thus emerges as a product of social and cultural experience. It is invoked to highlight the communicative and interactive elements of collective, cultural self-understandings. It is understood as culturally contingent yet indispensable for moving beyond the masculine gaze of an education system premised on colonial practices. In highlighting difference, the question of who benefits from gender equity policies moves to the forefront. As Mirza (1992) suggests, this work should not therefore be viewed as an attempt to accommodate the mainstream. It is an attempt to define what Mirza and Reay (2000) have called the 'third space' – not one which is necessarily embedded in the colonialist tension between the public and private spheres, but one which identifies 'other' worlds. These 'other worlds' represent the value of knowledge claims which emerge from a different cultural standpoint. In charting 'other worlds', both the potential and the limits of purportedly liberating gender school reform policies come sharply into focus.

Gender, markets and educational processes

Another recent contemporary theme in gender theory and educational research is feminist analyses of 'marketization', or what is sometimes referred to as post-Fordist analysis. A renewed emphasis on the study of educational markets has been ignited by a return to 'class' issues in ways which move beyond locating class within the individual (e.g. 'working-class girls') or viewing class solely as divisive (such as class conflict, social stratification). This return to class is instead concerned with the role of market forces in *regulating* education. While some of this research is grounded in poststructuralist theory (regulation, governance), it also serves as a critique of market theory and its influence over the field of education (Ball *et al.*, 1992).

In this model of research, there is a shift away from the study of exclusion as an issue of identity towards a concern with *social inequality* in relation to instituted market policies such as examination performance, school choice, achievement and standards in 'an ostensibly open market' (Brown, 1997, p. 394). Much of this work appears to be concerned with a very particular notion of social inequality that unfolds as an interaction between class positioning and market forces, largely at the expense of a study of race and gender (Carter, 1997). The impact of marketization on the formation and regulation of identities positioned differently by race, class and gender is therefore an element of this research that deserves greater attention.

The principal actors in analyses of school markets are consumers (students) and workers (teachers, administrators, policy discourse). It is argued that the interactions between these groups reflect the social and global relations (or language) of production. Key questions therefore arise around notions of identity in market school cultures. Recent work by Ball and Gewirtz (1997), for example, has highlighted the importance of seeing school markets as elements of entrepreneurship which view girls not as students with needs but as commodified 'objects and consumers of the market' (Ball and Gewirtz, 1997, p. 208). In the past, women were constructed as symbolic of the private sphere or objectified as sexualized service providers. In this new school context, governed by market policies, girls and women teachers are presented as consumers and rationalized as a commodity.

Post-Fordist theories have also stimulated feminist research which charts the relationship between family life, education and the market. For example, David *et al.*'s (1994) recent work on mothers and school choice and Reay's (1998) research on mothers' involvement in school markets have exposed the gendered nature of 'school choice' as an element of marketization. They have also highlighted the reproduction of traditional ideals and expectations attached to labels such as 'femininity' and 'motherhood' in schools. Other studies examining the marketization of education focus more directly on educational policy as a form of *regulating* women and girls (see Kenway and Epstein, 1996). This work has raised important questions about the regulative role of market discourse (rationality, expediency) and the 'new managerialism' in reconfiguring gender hierarchies in diverse educational contexts (Kenway and Epstein, 1996; Blackmore, 1997; Mahony and Hextall, 1997). Education feminism is also beginning to examine the forces of globalization, and their impact on the way gender is viewed in educational policy under the influence of market cultures (Unterhalter, 2000).

In summary, this assembly of work has exposed the gendered nature of market forces in the radical restructuring of schools and their impact on girls and women. It examines how 'education markets' and new right politics undermine gender reforms and create novel forms of gender inequality (Ball and Gewirtz, 1997; David, 2001). At the same time, such research has exposed the novel forms of male rationality found at the basis of new reform policies, school choice and the like (see Dillabough, 1999). As a result, the asymmetry between markets, school cultures and gender equity has come more clearly into view. Feminist post-Fordist critiques of education have effectively demonstrated how neo-liberal educational policies mediate both the economy and gender relations in the interests of the global state.

In analyses of this sort, it can be difficult to discern whether the category of identity sustains any conceptual and theoretical relevance. It is worth noting that researchers such as Ball and Gewirtz (1997) might argue that gender inequality – as one element of social inequality – emerges as more significant in post-Fordist approaches, particularly because market policies, rather than identity, loom large. By contrast, it might also be argued that this work precisely exposes the interaction between school policy and identity (Dillabough, 1999). It is, in other words, torn between fixed and more permeable understandings of gender identity in the critique of market ideology.

New gender identifications and theories of social change

Feminist youth studies and the study of social change – what Madeleine Arnot and I have called '*critical modernization* studies' (Dillabough and Arnot, 2001) – are two related and ongoing areas of study in gender education research. This work is firmly rooted in more traditional sociological emphases, since its main concerns are with tracking social change and its impact on male and female youth identities. Broadly speaking, this work is concerned with representing, through the study of youth themselves, both the continuities and transformations in gender identity over time.

Beck's (1992) examination of the 'the risk society' and the 'hidden pressures it places on individuals to engage in a process of "reflexive individualization"' (Dillabough and Arnot,

2001, p. 44) appears to be the point of departure for many gender researchers. In such analyses, feminism is seen as only one of many elements of modernity which have transformed male and female identities. Proponents of this view argue that modernity (as a historical period of social change) has provided a more flexible social context for the construction of gender identity, particularly for girls. However, in a fractured moral society where the benefits of modernity (e.g. equal opportunity policies) are only accorded to the privileged few, social theorists such as Beck argue that only particular groups of women and men will benefit from such changes. In the 'risk society', the social world becomes increasingly fractured and gaps between the middle and working classes widen.

Much of the research which falls under the category 'youth, gender and social change' suggests that young girls stand at the intersection of a range of highly contradictory messages deriving, in part, from broad economic and social changes and modem transformations in gender relations (Chisholm and Du Bois Reymond, 1993). Such messages highlight, on the one hand, the significance of new patterns of educational attainment, a more flexible and open workforce (Arnot *et al.*, 1999), transformations in gender relations and state commitments to the education of women. On the other hand, such messages coexist alongside reductions in social and educational support for particular groups of female youth, the rise in new right social policies and the escalation in national levels of female poverty. Such tensions are seen as key factors contributing to the increasing levels of school/social exclusion experienced by impoverished female youth and the reconfiguration of youth identities in schools (Hey, 1997; Dillabough, 2001). Research of this kind therefore tracks the contradictory social changes in education and their *differential* impact on female youth identities (Wilkinson, 1996).

At the same time, such research also alludes to changes in class structures and their positive impact on the achievement of girls. For example, Chris Mann's (1996, 1998) work on class and educational attainment highlights the key role of shifting family structures in enhancing working-class girls' chances of educational success. These studies point to the movement of working families into higher level income categories through the educational mobility of parents – what could be identified as the social transformation of, or 'intra-class' changes in, the culture of poverty itself. In these studies, families (largely mothers) who ultimately transcend their own class boundaries are seen to place greater pressure upon schools and teachers to encourage working-class girls to persist with education despite the barriers of class positioning.

Another aspect of this work is the study of gender and performance in schools (Arnot *et al.*, 1998, 1999; Francis, 2000). This work is also concerned with broader debates about gender identity theorizing in social theory, although not explicitly so. Largely through social analyses of changing patterns of male and female achievement, it has brought to centre stage the novel ways in which young people identify with and respond to changes in social, political and educational cultures across time. For example, Arnot *et al.*'s (1999) explanatory account of performance patterns tracks the movement from a Victorian model of women's education to the contemporary moment, revealing key forces of social change in the achievement patterns of girls. It highlights the symbolic power of the feminist movement in shaping female identities, exposes intra-class changes in working-class families, reveals subsequent influences on girls' achievement patterns and highlights the restructuring of equal opportunity policies.

Education feminists have also recently concentrated on clarifying the changing nature of gender hierarchies in schools and higher education, and the changing patterns of women teachers' careers and their experiences of exploitation in the workplace (Acker and Feurverger, 1997). Such work has therefore revealed both continuities and changes in the social order, and exposed the enduring stability of the gender order in girls' and women's working lives, despite transformations in contemporary gender relations. Education feminists concerned with social change have thus embraced both the old and the new traditions in gender research in education, viewing them in dialectical relation. No exploration of identity, no analysis of social change can be done without an awareness of the other.

In short, what emerges from this work is new gender knowledge about young people's transitions and the gendered processes of identification at work in social change. Simultaneously, however, it has identified the ways in which girls' identities are still mediated by the continuing effects of social reproduction (particularly social class inequalities) (Dillabough and Arnot, 2001, p. 45). At the level of social analysis, the historicity of women and girls' oppression comes clearly into view as an ongoing force in the processes of social change. As Calhoun (1995, p. 155) suggests, it also addresses precisely those problems identified in social critiques of postmodernist perspectives on identity:

> They [postmodernists] address various changes in media ... the shift from production oriented consumerism to ... seduction oriented consumerism but they do not address the empirical question of whether in fact social relations, most basically relations of power, are undergoing fundamental transformations – and whether those transformations affect more the systematic character of indirect [social] relations.

Conclusion

Despite the diversity of thinking in the early stages of education feminism, most feminists remained concerned with women's education, the reproduction of gender inequality in schools, women teachers' work and gender equity policies. Since the mid-1980s, however, education feminism has become more explicitly concerned with issues of gender identity, even though 'gender' has been viewed as a social category since the development of the concept by Ann Oakley (1972). My own argument has focused, in part, on the use by education feminists of 'identity' as a conceptual device for transforming the practice of educational research. I have argued that shifts over time in social theory have influenced the ways in which identity has been taken up as both a critique of education in modernity and as a category of analysis. As a result, identity has been deployed in diverse and contesting ways across the different domains of emerging research traditions over the last two decades. It has also been called upon both to sustain traditional theoretical positions and to establish new ones.

At the same time, research traditions in the study of gender and education continue to reflect modernist goals such as class and race analyses. The dual properties of much of this research highlight the importance of understanding that while the development of alternative research approaches represented by poststructuralism may involve a paradigmatic shift, they do not necessarily jettison all aspects of the preceding paradigm. Hence, modernist ideals in education feminism (such as gender equity) will persist to the extent that they drive a relevant research agenda, and are likely to be contested when they undermine shifts in other domains of social theory. The process of change in the progress of education feminism is, like change in other domains, a dialectical one producing a synthesis which is not an abrupt break with the past but moves categorically beyond it.

What then can we make of the diversity of trends in the study of gender in education over the last two decades? How, as feminists and scholars who remain concerned with the positioning of women, should we respond to such trends at the level of theory and practice? These are difficult questions to answer in the short term. However, research which embraces the best of both theoretical worlds – modernist and postmodernist/poststructural theories – will be, in my judgement, the most useful in moving forward. But in so doing, we should avoid consumer-orientated and trendy 'pick and choose' approaches that ultimately possess limited theoretical integrity and analytical cohesion. Educational research needs to wrestle with the tensions in feminist theory and attempt to resolve them. ... In my view, we ought to come to terms with the impasses that are presented to us in social theory in the name of the political issues still at stake in education feminism. It is time now to get beyond gender 'identity' – both the fluid and the stable – not to repress particularity, but in the true spirit of social analysis in education feminism. We need new terms of reference through which to explore the broad range of exciting research topics which have arisen in recent years. Clearly, identity, as a conceptual tool (if we wish to call it that) cannot be used to situate the range of issues which need exploring, particularly if we wish to sustain an emphasis on gender equity in education.

In light of the collapse of recent gender equity school reforms in Australia and the UK (Arnot *et al.*, 1999), a sustained focus on the social and political elements of schooling is important. We need to broaden our theoretical vocabulary in the study of gender and education. In so doing, we may explore unknown territory while remaining committed to the role that feminist educational theory ought to play in our work. Without it, we will be ill-equipped to deal with the challenges which lie ahead and deprived of a clear vision of precisely where we hope to go.

Acknowledgements

Reproduced with kind permission of Open University Press from *Investigating Gender: Modernist Traditions and Emerging Contemporary Themes*, edited by B. Francis and C. Skelton (Milton Keynes: Open University Press, 2001, pp. 11–26).

References

Acker, S. (1994) *Gendered Education*, Buckingham, Open University Press.
Acker, S. and Feurverger, G. (1997) 'Doing good and feeling bad: the work of women university teachers', *Cambridge Journal of Education*, 26(3), pp. 401–22.
Anderson, A. (1998) 'Debatable performances: restaging contentious feminisms', *Social Text*, 54, 16(1), pp. 1–24.
Arnot, M. and Weiner, G. (eds) (1987) *Gender and the Politics of Schooling*, London, Hutchinson.
Arnot, M., Gray, J., James, M. and Rudduck, J. (1998) *A Review of Recent Research on Gender and Educational Performance*, Ofsted Research Series, London, HMSO.
Arnot, M., David, M. and Weiner, G. (1999) *Closing the Gender Gap*, Cambridge, Polity Press.
Ball, S. and Gewirtz, S. (1997) 'Girls in the education market: choice, competition and complexity', *Gender and Education*, 9(2), pp. 207–23.
Ball, S., Bowe, R. and Gold, A. (1992) *Reforming Education and Changing Schools: Case Studies in Policy Sociology*, London, Routledge.
Barrett, M. (1980) *Women's Oppression Today: Problems in Marxist Feminist Analysis*, London, Verso.
Beck, U. (1992) *Risk Society: Towards a New Modernity*, London, Sage.
Bernstein, B. (1977) *Class Codes and Control*, 3rd edn, London, Routledge & Kegan Paul.
Bernstein, B. (1978) 'Class and pedagogies: visible and invisible', in J. Karabel and A. Halsey (eds) *Power and Ideology in Education*, Oxford, Oxford University Press.
Blackmore, J. (1997) 'The gendering of skill and vocationalism in twentieth-century Australian education', in A. Halsey, H. Lauder, P. Brown and A. Wells (eds) *Education: Culture, Economy, Society*, New York, Oxford University Press.

Blair, M. (1995) 'Race, class and gender in school research', in J. Holland, M. Blair and S. Sheldon (eds), *Debates and Issues in Feminist Research and Pedagogy*, Clevedon, Multilingual Matters.

Blair, M. and Holland, J. (eds) (1995) *Identity and Diversity*, Clevedon, Multilingual Matters.

Bourdieu, P. and Passeron, J.C. (1977) *Reproduction in Education, Society and Culture*, London, Sage.

Bowles, S. and Gintis, H. (1976) *Schooling and Capitalist America*, London, Routledge & Kegan Paul.

Brah, A. and Minhas, R. (1985) 'Structural racism or cultural difference: schooling for Asian girls', in G. Weiner (ed.), *Just a Bunch of Girls: Feminist Approaches to Schooling*, Buckingham, Open University Press.

Brown, P. (1997) 'The "third wave": education and the ideology of parentocracy', in A. Halsey, H. Lauder, P. Brown, and A. Wells (eds), *Education: Culture, Economy, Society*, New York, Oxford University Press.

Butler, J. (1990) *Gender Trouble*, New York, Routledge.

Byrne, E. (1978) *Women and Education*, London, Tavistock.

Calhoun, C. (1995) *Critical Social Theory*, Oxford, Blackwell.

Callander, C. and Wright, C. (2000) 'Discipline and democracy: race, gender, school sanctions and control', in M. Arnot and J. Dillabough (eds), *Challenging Democracy: International Perspectives on Gender, Education and Citizenship*, London, Routledge.

Carby, H. (1982) 'Schooling in Babylon', in Centre for Contemporary Cultural Studies (eds), *The Empire Strikes Back*. London, Hutchinson.

Carter, J. (1997) 'Post-Fordism and the theorisation of educational change: what's in a name?', *British Journal of Sociology of Education*, 18(1), pp. 45–62.

Chisholm, L. and Du Bois Reymond, M. (1993) 'Youth transitions, gender and social change', *Sociology*, 27(2), pp. 259–79.

Connell, R. W. (1987) *Gender and Power*, London, Routledge.

David, M. (1980) *Women, Family and Education*, London, Routeldge.

—— (2001) 'Gender equity issues in educational effectiveness in the context of global, social and family life changes', plenary paper presented to the 14th International Congress for School Effectiveness and Improvement, Toronto, Canada, 5–9 January.

David, M., West, A. and Ribbens, J. (1994) *Mother's Intuition? Choosing Secondary Schools*, London, Falmer.

Davies, B. (1989) *Frogs and Snails and Feminist Tales*, London, Allen & Unwin.

—— (1997) 'Constructing and deconstructing masculinities through critical literacy', *Gender and Education*, 9(1), pp. 9–30.

Deem, R. (1978) 'Women and schooling', in R. Deem (ed.), *Schooling for Women's Work*, London, Routledge & Kegan Paul.

—— (ed.) (1980) *Schooling for Women's Work*, London, Routledge & Kegan Paul.

Delamont, S. (1980) *Sex Roles and the School*, London, Methuen.

Dillabough, J. (1999) 'Gender politics and conceptions of the modern teacher: women, identity and professionalism', *British Journal of Sociology of Education*, 20(3), pp. 373–94.

—— (2001) 'Gender, social change and the study of impoverished youth in Ontario schools', Social Sciences and Humanities Research Council Grant Proposal, under review, Ottawa, Canada.

Dillabough, J. and Arnot, M. (2001) 'Feminist sociology of education: dynamics, debates, directions', in J. Demaine (ed.), *Sociology of Education Today*, London, Macmillan.

—— (2002) 'Feminist perspectives continuity and contestation in the field', in D. Levinson, A. Sadovnik and P. Cookson (eds) *Encyclopaedia: Sociology of Education*, New York, Garland.

Epstein, D. (1997) 'Boyz' own story: masculinities and sexualities in schools', *Gender and Education*, 9(1), pp. 105–16.

Epstein, D., Elwood, J., Hey, V. and Maw, J. (eds) (1998) *Failing Boys? Issues in Gender and Achievement*, Buckingham, Open University Press.

Francis, B. (1999) 'Modernist reductionism or poststructuralist relativism: can we move on? An evaluation of the arguments in relation to feminist educational research', *Gender and Education*, 11(4), pp. 381–94.

Francis, B. (2000) *Boys, Girls and Achievement: Addressing the Classroom Issues*, London, RoutledgeFalmer.

Gramsci, A. (1971) *Selections from the Prison Notebooks of Antonio Gramsci*, London, Lawrence & Wishart.

Haywood, C. and Mac an Ghaill, M. (1996) 'Schooling masculinities', in M. Mac an Ghaill (ed.), *Understanding Masculinities*, Buckingham, Open University Press.

Hey, V. (1997) *The Company She Keeps: An Ethnography of Girls' Friendship*, Buckingham, Open University Press.

Hill-Collins, P. (1990) *Black Feminist Thought: Knowledge, Consciousness, and the Politics of Empowerment*, Boston, MA, Unwin Hyman.

hooks, b. (1989) *Talking Back: Thinking Feminist, Thinking Black*, Boston, MA, South End Press.

Kehily, M.J. and Nayak, A. (1997) 'Lads and laughter: humour and the production of heterosexual hierarchies', *Gender and Education*, 9(1), pp. 69–87.

Kenway, J. (1997) 'Taking stock of gender reform policies for Australian schools: past, present, future', *British Educational Research Journal*, 23(3), pp. 329–44.

Kenway, J. and Epstein, D. (eds) (1996) 'Introduction: the marketisation of school education: feminist studies and perspectives', *Discourse*, 17(3), pp. 301–14.

Mac an Ghaill, M. (1994) *The Making of Men*, Buckingham, Open University Press.

MacDonald, M. (1980) 'Schooling and the reproduction of class and gender relations', in L. Barton, R. Meighan and S. Walker (eds), *Schooling, Ideology and the Curriculum*, Lewes, Falmer.

McRobbie, A. (1978) 'Working class girls and the culture of femininity', in Women's Studies Group Centre for Contemporary Cultural Studies, University of Birmingham (eds), *Women Take Issue: Aspects of Women's Subordination*, London, Hutchinson.

Mahony, P. (1983) 'How Alice's chin really came to be pressed against her foot: sexist processes of interaction in mixed sexed classrooms', *Women's Studies International Forum*, 16(1), pp. 107–15.

—— (1985) *Schools for the Boys: Coeducation Reassessed*, London, Hutchinson.

Mahony, P. and Hextall, I. (1997) 'Sounds of silence: the social justice agenda of the Teacher Training Agency', *International Studies in Sociology of Education*, 7(2), pp. 137–57.

Mann, C. (1996) 'Finding a favourable front: the contribution of the family to working-class girls' achievement', unpublished PhD dissertation, University of Cambridge.

—— (1998) 'The impact of working class mothers on the educational success of their adolescent daughters at a time of social change', *British Journal of Sociology of Education*, 19(2), pp. 211–26.

Measor, L. and Sikes, P. (1992) *Gender and Schooling*, London, Cassell.

Mirza, H. (1992) *Young, Female, and Black*, Buckingham, Open University Press.

—— (1993) 'The social construction of black womanhood in British educational research: towards a new understanding', in M. Arnot and K. Weiler (eds) *Feminism and Social Justice in Education: International Perspectives*, London, Falmer.

Mirza, H. and Reay, D. (2000) 'Redefining citizenship: Black women educators and the "third space"', in M. Arnot and J. Dillabough (eds), *Challenging Democracy: International Perspectives on Gender, Education and Citizenship*, London, Routledge.

Murphy, P. and Gipps, C. (eds) (1996) *Equity in the Classroom: Towards an Effective Pedagogy for Girls and Boys*, London, Falmer.

Oakley, A. (1972) *Sex, Gender and Society*, London, Temple Smith.

Paechter, C. and Head, J. (1996) 'Power in the staffroom', *British Educational Research Journal*, 22(1), pp. 57–69.

Phoenix, A. (1987) 'Theories of gender and black families', in G. Weiner and M. Arnot (eds), *Gender Under Scrutiny: New Inquiries in Education*, London, Hutchinson.

Raphael Reed, L. (1999) 'Troubling boys and disturbing discourses on masculinity and schooling: a feminist exploration of current debates and interventions concerning boys in school', *Gender and Education*, 11(1), pp. 93–110.

Reay, D. (1998) *Class Work: Mothers' Involvement in their Children's Schooling*, London, UCL Press.

Skelton, C. (1997) 'Primary boys and hegemonic masculinities', *British Journal of Sociology of Education*, 18(3), pp. 349–70.

Spender, D. (1980) *Man Made Language*, London, Routledge & Kegan Paul.

Stanworth, M. (1981) *Gender and Schooling: A Study of Sexual Divisions in the Classroom*, London, Women's Research and Resources Centre Publications Collective.

Steedman, C. (1985) '"The mother made conscious": the historical development of primary school pedagogy', *History Workshop Journal*, 20, pp. 149–63.

Unterhalter, E. (2000) 'Transnational visions of the 1990s: contrasting views of women, education and citizenship', in M. Arnot and J. Dillabough (eds), *Challenging Democracy: International Perspectives on Gender, Education and Citizenship*, London, Routledge Falmer.

Walker, S. and Barton, L. (eds) (1983) *Gender, Class and Education*, Lewes, Falmer.

Walkerdine, V. (1981) 'Sex, power and pedagogy', *Screen Education*, 38, pp. 14–24.

Walkerdine, V. and Lucey, H. (1989) *Democracy in the Kitchen: Regulating Mothers and Socialising Daughters*, London, Virago.

Weiner, G. (1994) *Feminisms in Education: An Introduction*, Buckingham, Open University Press.

Weiner, G. and Arnot, M. (eds) (1987) *Gender under Scrutiny*, London, Hutchinson.

Weir, A. (1996) *Sacrificial Logics: Feminist Theory and the Critique of Identity*, New York, Routledge.

Willis, P. (1977) *Learning to Labour*, Aldershot, Saxon House.

Wolpe, A. (1976) 'The official ideology of education for girls', in M. Flude and J. Ahier (eds), *Educability, Schools and Ideology*, London, Croom Helm.

Wright, C., Weekes, D., McGlaughlin, A. and Webb, D. (1998) 'Masculinised discourses within education and the construction of black male identities amongst African Caribbean youth', *British Journal of Sociology of Education*, 19(1), pp. 75–87.

Reflective questions

1   What have been some of the key trends in the field of gender and education over the last 20 years?

2   Why have gender and education researchers focused so much on the concept of identity and what part might the history of gender research play in this focus?

3   How has the field moved from a focus on gender roles and socialization toward the study of culture and the changing nature of gender relations? Provide some examples of research reviewed in the chapter.

4   What is the difference between gender as a category and gender as a social relation? Why are these distinctions important in understanding the changing nature of educational research on gender in schools?

5   How have the wider fields of feminism and the sociology of education shaped debates on gender and education?

6   How are schools (as social institutions) and gender linked to the state?

Further reading

Weiner, G. (1994) *Feminisms in Education: An Introduction*, Buckingham, Open University Press.

Weiner, G. and Arnot, M. (eds) (1987) *Gender under Scrutiny*, London, Hutchinson.

Weir, A. (1996) *Sacrificial Logics: Feminist Theory and the Critique of Identity*, New York, Routledge.

3.4 Symptoms, categories, and the process of invoking labels

Roger Säljö and Eva Hjörne

Introduction

Categorization is fundamental to human existence. It penetrates every context of collective social action and individual reasoning. We simply cannot describe, reflect on, or deal with reality without invoking categories and, thus indirectly, systems and traditions of categorization by means of which we render events and objects intelligible. Categories are codified in language and largely invisible to us. We treat them as transparent and rarely run into situations where we have to doubt their relevance. Many categories undergo naturalization (Bowker and Star, 1999, p. 294), and appear as self-evident, even though they may in fact have been problematic in the past. But there is also the opposite process. Categories referring to race, ethnicity or gender have passed unnoticed as indicative of a natural state of affairs in the past, but later they emerged as cultural constructions contingent on a certain social order and/or world view. And as such, they can be contested.

In a sociocultural perspective (Wertsch, 1991, 1998), categories serve as mediational means, as cultural tools that are fundamental to our making sense of what we encounter. They exist in the reasoning of individuals as well as between people in social interaction. Categories are not just names for things and relationships, they do a real job by signifying and informing us about how to classify and act in specific contexts. Social action is contingent on classifications, they are essential in the 'doing' of social life, to use ethnomethodological parlance (Heritage, 1984). 'We hang murderers, we lock up the insane man, we free the victim of circumstances, we pin a medal on the hero', as Hayakawa (1965, p. 217) puts it. And we argue by means of such tools. Are the actions committed by a political and military elite in a region in a state of war to be construed as a 'heroic defence' of the country against enemies, or as 'genocide' and instances of 'crimes against humanity?' At the time of writing, this is exactly what is being argued about at the International Court in The Hague.

In institutional settings, categories and classifications are central as they mediate between individuals and collectives. The social worker or the officer at the employment agency uses classifications of people and their situation in order to determine whether they are entitled to specific kinds of support. The issue of the interplay between categories and institutional action is classical in social science (cf. Mäkitalo and Säljö, 2002). In the present study, this problem will be addressed within the context of how schools categorize and deal with children, who, for some reason, find it difficult to adapt to the norms and expectations of the institutional activities that by tradition are offered in such settings. The main focus of this article is on analyzing how categories are introduced in institutional practices as resources for making decisions and talking about life at school, and what implications they have for the children and for the school.

At present, biomedical, psychiatric, and neuropsychological categories offering neuropsychiatric diagnoses play an important role in schools in many countries, including Sweden, where this line of research has been very active. Labels such as MBD (minimal brain dysfunction), DAMP (deficit in attention, motor control and perception), ADHD (attention deficit hyperactivity disorder),[1] Asperger's, dyslexia, dyscalculia, etc. are used widely in schools as categories for classifying children, for organizing teaching and learning opportunities, and for the distribution of economic and other kinds of resources. This practice has resulted in a rapid increase in the number of children in Sweden who are categorized as in some sense handicapped. Kadesjö (2000; Kadesjö and Gillberg, 1998), a specialist with a medical background, claims that 21 per cent of all school children have some kind of neuropsychiatric problem (Kadesjö and Gillberg, 1998, p. 799). Considering that the number of people who have 'classical' handicaps (physical handicaps, blindness, deafness, etc.) is but a fraction of this (about or slightly below 2 per cent[2]), these claims regarding the relative frequency of neuropsychiatric disorders are dramatic. If correct, there will be profound effects on school policy and school practices, as we will return to.

The aim of this article is to analyse the *in situ* use of diagnoses of this kind within the Swedish school. This implies that we are not taking a stand on the controversial issues of the nature and aetiology of these conditions, or whether these diagnoses can be seen as valid and reliable indicators of identifiable medical and/or psychological conditions. In this article, we will focus on how the neuropsychiatric classifications are used in the school setting, and in particular how they are introduced as categories relevant for understanding what are perceived as problems in the daily practices. The latter is our primary research question. We base our analyses on audio-recorded data from institutionalized meetings where professionals in a school discuss and make decisions on how to handle situations when children are reported as having difficulties accommodating to school practices. In our empirical work, we have followed the regular meetings of the pupil welfare team (PWT) in a Swedish comprehensive school during one year.

Classification systems as institutional artifacts

> The question, 'What is it really?' 'What is its right name?' is a nonsense question ... one that is not capable of being answered. ... When we name something, then, we are classifying. The individual object or event we are naming, of course, has no name and belongs to no class until we put it in one ... What we call things and where we draw the line between one class of things and another depend upon the interest we have and the purposes of the classification. ... Most intellectual problems are, ultimately, problems of classification and nomenclature.
>
> (Hayakawa, 1965, pp. 215–20)

Categories emerge as outcomes of the activity that the philosopher Nelson Goodman (1978) refers to as 'kind-making'. Categories and classifications are relative to human practices, they are embedded in various discourses, and they *re*-present the world in manners that are relevant for a certain activity. They enable shared understandings among people operating in social practices, who can communicate efficiently by identifying objects and events in standard terms (cf. Goodwin and Opper, 1992). Animals, for example, are classified in one way by the meat industry, in another way by the leather industry, in a third manner by a zoologist, in a fourth manner by a conservationist, and in still a different way by an economist. Categories are the basic working tools of institutional actors in their mundane and undramatic daily activities. As Douglas (1986) points out, institutions 'think' in terms of categories. Thus, the social worker, the bank manager, the physician and many others, rely on categories when analyzing a situation and when making a decision.

In school, which is one of society's oldest institutions catering to the needs of the entire population, categories referring to entities such as age, abilities, handicaps, academic subjects and many other dimensions have played, and continue to play, an important role at many levels. They are used when discussing the practices pursued in such settings as well as in our argumentation about the objectives and responsibilities of schooling (Mehan, 1992). Calhoun (1973), for instance, gives an interesting illustration of how the shift from one category ('teaching problems') to a different one ('learning problems') in the United States during the nineteenth century was a critical element in what was to be a radical change in how schools defined their responsibilities. Thus, during the eighteenth century and well into the nineteenth, 'schoolmasters' had 'teaching problems, but children seemed not to have what the twentieth century would call "learning problems"'. Thus, and as a concrete illustration, 'whatever blocks arose in the way of transmitting simple reading and arithmetic to children, the people who reported these blocks almost never blamed them on stupidity or dullness' (p. 72). As soon as the ideas of early intelligence testing began to penetrate institutionalized schooling, 'learning problems' entered the stage as the preferred category in terms of which responses by groups of children to the activities characteristic of schools were understood. By and large, the problems came to be localized in the child and seen as indicative of a lack of (usually innate) intellectual resources. The subsequent development of the intelligence test naturalized this assumption and made it almost invisible in many school systems (cf. Stevenson and Stigler, 1992, p. 97, who discuss the differences between American and Japanese schools (and parents) when it comes to using assumed intellectual capacities among children as explanatory factors of school success).

The critical factor we point to is, thus, the circularity between the categories we use and how we perceive the world. This circularity implies that 'discourses do not simply describe the social world', rather 'they bring phenomena into sight' (Parker, 1990, p. 191). Or, even more strongly, discourses and categories are best conceived as 'practices that systematically form the objects of which they speak' (Foucault, 1972, p. 49). Attending to categories, and the manner in which they constitute phenomena in institutional settings, thus, is an important research task in modern society.

Naming diversity in school: ideologies in action

In the context of schooling, the categories used for describing various groups have changed over the years. In Sweden, the compulsory school attendance law appeared in the middle of the nineteenth century. As a consequence, a large number of pupils, many from families with little or no prior exposure to schooling as an institutional activity, entered the classroom. Not surprisingly, a range of new problems arose. Reports from frustrated teachers fuelled the debate about how to bring order to classrooms through various strategies that would imply segregating pupils into those who fit in and those who were to be given special treatment or even excluded (Trent, 1994; Sundqvist, 1994). To manage this task, classifications that could serve as instruments for making distinctions between pupils were urgently needed. The categories produced during this period to a large extent reflect what Hacking (1986) refers to as the 'analyse moral'. Children were described by means of terms grounded in religious and moral assumptions of what constituted normality and deviance. Thus, and as has been described by Sundqvist (1994) and Börjesson (1997), one finds categories such as vicious, lazy, slow, nailbiters, sons/daughters of vagrants, and so on for describing children who did not fit into the system.

Categories generated from the psychological discourse of ability testing subsequently replaced these terms. Schools for 'idiots' and 'feeble children' were launched, and psychometric tests such as the famous Stanford-Binet and Terman-Merrill tests were widely used as tools for sorting pupils. The categories that emerged from this psychometric breakthrough were diverse and included a fine-grained set of concepts, especially for describing the lower end of the scale. Terms such as feeble-minded, mentally deficient, ill-balanced, idiot, imbecile, moron, moral imbecile, subnormal, mentally retarded were among those suggested and used in practice. Since some of these terms soon after their introduction became pejorative, new ones were introduced. Each new classification was supposed to improve on the previous one used for, more or less, the same type of characteristic. The point of this discursive technology, some authors argue, 'was to control difficult children, divert them away from schools" and send them 'into institutions or regimens of treatment' (Hacking, 1999, p. 111). As a consequence, various kinds of remedial classes and special schools increased dramatically during the first 50 years of the twentieth century (Ohlander, 1956; Trent, 1994).

In our opinion, the use of categories such as ADHD (or, in Sweden, the equivalent DAMP) must be related to the changes in public schooling in Sweden. The nine-year comprehensive school was introduced in the decades following the Second World War. The ideological premise was that it was supposed to be a school catering to the needs of the entire population and it should operate without streaming.[3] All pupils should fit in, even those who were previously separated into various types of remedial classes and special clinics. Another important feature of this transformation was that drop-outs were not tolerated. Considering that previously only a minority of children would proceed beyond Grade 6 (38 per cent of an age cohort at the end of 1940s, cf. Lindensjö and Lundgren, 2000), this was a radical change in expectations regarding schools. This implies that a broad variation of abilities and interests on the part of children was represented in the same classroom. This heterogeneity, of course, was a pedagogical challenge, and inevitably once again introduces the issue of how to handle differences in academic performance, motivation, social background and so on among the children.

So, the interesting question arises, where does one look for the categories that will be used to debate, analyze, and work with diversity? The immediate predecessor of ADHD/ DAMP was MBD (minimal brain dysfunction) (see Gillberg, 1991, for an in-depth account of the transition from MBD to ADHD/DAMP). The use of MBD, a brain injury so small it could not be detected when examining the brain, represents a return to biomedical categories and explanations as the more dominant voice in a living tradition of argumentation oscillating between biological, social and moral/religious positions (Billig, 1987; Shotter, 1993; Mäkitalo, 2002). During the 1960s and 1970s, family relationships and psychological explanatory models had been widely used to account for symptoms such as hyperactivity, concentration difficulties, and school failure. But in the 1970s, the concept of MBD entered the stage and quickly established itself as a diagnosis relevant for explaining children's difficulties in Swedish schools (Hagberg, 1975; Rydelius, 1999). During the 1980s this concept fell into disrepute in many parts of the world. This process followed a massive critique from researchers arguing that there was no homogeneity in terms of symptoms among the children classified in this manner (Schmidt *et al.*, 1987). New terms were introduced, and these varied somewhat across countries. In Sweden (and some other

Scandinavian countries) the term DAMP came to be widely used. In the US, the same syndrome was referred to as ADHD, and in the UK the acronym HKD (hyperkinetic disorder) was adopted.

An important general point to keep in mind is that categories (like all linguistic expressions) can never be absolutely neutral. Communication always implies contextualizing, and in this process perspectivizing is necessary and inevitable. Thus, issues that relate to the 'politics of representation' (Mehan, 1993) can always be raised. In our opinion, categorization in the school context should be studied as a practice; it is something that people *do* in order to manage their daily chores. As categories are part of institutional practices, they are also material in their consequences. It matters whether we describe people in one way or the other. The material consequences of categories implies that it is meaningful and relevant to study the use of categories, even if their ontological status may be questioned. Thus, even if many would argue that concepts such as ADHD and DAMP have no reliable or uniform definition (cf. Kärfve, 2000, who very explicitly makes this claim), their use in school practices and in the rhetoric about school failure must be attended to. It is a social fact that ADHD/DAMP is part of a living tradition of argumentation and that this syndrome serves as a widely accepted explanation of children's learning disabilities and school performance. ADHD/DAMP as a category, thus, has established itself within schooling, and in this sense it is both a social fact and a resource that is actively used for dealing with problems. It has implications for the manner in which teaching is organized and for the use of limited resources. It will also have consequences for the students' educational career, and obviously, a neuropsychiatric diagnosis, indicative of a brain injury, will play a critical role in identity formation of young people.

Empirical setting and method

In our opinion, it is important to highlight the process through which children are diagnosed with ADHD/DAMP. And, as we will show, this is a process. A critical, early phase in the process towards being diagnosed in the Swedish context can be found in the discussions and decisions made in so-called pupil/student welfare team meetings (PWTM).[4] This is an institutional arena where, amongst other things, various problems are discussed. The participants in these meetings vary somewhat between schools, but generally the principal, the vice-principal, teachers, special teachers, the school psychologist, school nurse and/or a social worker will be present. In the school we have studied, there was also a speech therapist, who would often participate in these meetings.

The institutional procedure for conducting PWTMs implies that one of the participants, for instance a teacher or the school psychologist, decides that problems experienced by a child should be discussed at an upcoming meeting. In the session, the child's situation is presented and decisions are made on how to proceed. This setting, thus, is critical in the sense that it is here that institutional categories and accounting practices will play a decisive role in interpreting what happens in school, and in initiating the kind of process that eventually may result in a child being diagnosed as ADHD/DAMP.

The findings reported derive from a field study. The empirical setting in which the study has been carried out is a school – West Valley Comprehensive School – situated in a village close to a city. The village is in an agricultural area. Most inhabitants live in single-family houses. West Valley has 800 children from preschool to grade nine. About 2 per cent of the children are immigrants (which is substantially below the national average).[5] The study is limited to children in grades one to five. There are about 475 pupils in these grades, and 76 of these children were discussed in the PWTMs during the school year of 2000–1, i.e. the period we have followed.

The school has a pupil/student welfare team (PWT), consisting of the principal (PR),[6] the assistant principal (AP), the school psychologist (SP), the school nurse (SN), the speech therapist (SE), and the special needs teacher (ST). There are three assistant principals, each of whom is responsible for about six classes. This team meets twice a month for discussions and decision-making about how to handle various kinds of problems. The data used for the present study were generated during these meetings, which we have followed through participant observation over one year. During this year, there were a total of 14 meetings. These have been audio-recorded and later transcribed. In total, there are 35 hours of recorded material. In addition, some of the conferences involving the parents have been recorded. Field notes were taken throughout the year, and we also have access to the relevant documentation including protocols from PWTMs. Transcription conventions are given in the Appendix. The study reported here was preceded by a pilot in the same school carried out by one of the authors (E. H.). During this pilot study, the contacts with the school and the staff were established. The purpose of the research, i.e., studying how the staff handled children with various problems, was explained. This implies that when the data reported here were collected, the researcher was well-known to the staff and the children.

It should also be pointed out that this study follows a process longitudinally. This implies that we did not know at the start which children would be discussed at the PWTMs, nor when the category of ADHD/DAMP would be invoked by members of the team.

Results

Among the 76 children (50 boys and 26 girls) who were discussed during the PWTMs during this period, 19 already had an ADHD/DAMP diagnosis or were thought to have this problem. These children were (the figures in brackets indicate the number of times that each of these children was discussed during the 14 meetings): Julia (10), Axel (9), James (9), Lukas (7), Kenny (6), Robert (5), Peter (5), Karl (4), Patrick (3), Melvin (3), Noa (3), Sandy (3), Tony (3), Jonas (3), Tom (2), Penny (1), Gloria (1), Leo (1), and Frederic (1). The remaining pupils were defined as having various kinds of problems, for example, other medical diagnoses such as Asperger's (3 pupils) or dyslexia (12) or, alternatively, they were defined as having social/relational problems or more general learning disabilities.

The focus of our study is on scrutinizing how the category of ADHD/DAMP is used and in what situations it is introduced as a resource for understanding and managing the problems experienced in school.

Table 3.4.1 Overview of pupils discussed in the PWTMs

Pupils	*Categories used for describing school difficulties*		
	ADHD/DAMP	Other problems	Total
Boys	15	35	50
Girls	4	22	26
Total	19	57	76

The process of invoking ADHD/DAMP

The first step in the process of categorizing pupils is taken in the classroom. The teacher has to report a pupil to the assistant principal, and thus bring the perceived problem to public attention. The next step is that the pupil and his/her problems are discussed in the context of the PWTM. Here, a further decision on how to proceed is made. Various options are available (see Figure 3.4.1). One frequent solution is that it is decided that the regular teacher should try to resolve the problem within the normal classroom context. Other options are that it is decided that a special needs teacher should attend to the matter, or that the social authorities should be contacted. But it is also in the context of the PWTM that the suggestion that the problem might be of a neuropsychiatric nature will be voiced publicly and discussed. Following such a suggestion, a decision to go ahead with a full assessment may be taken. Before starting a psychological assessment, however, the parents have to be informed and give their consent (see Figure 3.4.2). After the child has been tested, the psychologist informs the parents of the results before reporting back to the PWTM. Here, the team has to decide how to take the matter further. Usually the assistant principal informs the teacher, and the result will sometimes be to have a personal assistant assigned to the student or, alternatively, extra educational staff in the classroom. Another solution, though less frequent, is to transfer the child to a special group in another school. Yet another outcome of this process is that nothing at all happens. The problems disappear from view as far as the PWTM process is concerned.

Figure 3.4.1 gives an overview of the complexities involved in this process of handling difficulties, which are discussed in the PWTMs. At various stages, the process can go in different directions depending on the problem experienced by the teacher or the child, but also on the traditions and experiences within a particular school. For instance, already at the first and second stages a teacher might define the problem very differently. Similar behaviors in the classroom may be dealt with differently, and they may or may not be reported to the assistant principal.

When it has been decided that the child should preferably be assessed for ADHD/DAMP, additional steps are taken, as shown in Figure 3.4.2. The first step in this second phase (Step

Step 1	Classroom	a pupil is perceived to have difficulties
Step 2	Teacher	reports the problem to his/her superior for discussion in PWTM
Step 3	Assistant principal	reports the teacher's observations
Step 4	PWTM	discussions of how to proceed
Step 5	Measures suggested	a) testing for ADHD/DAMP b) testing for dyslexia/Asperger's c) an extra school-year d) skip a school-year e) learning disability group f) special teaching group g) personal assistant h) social services i) child guidance clinic j) back to teacher's concern

Figure 3.4.1 The institutional process of decision-making in West Valley Comprehensive School

6) is to gain the parents' consent to test the child, as we have already mentioned. After the child has been assessed and maybe thought to have ADHD/DAMP different solutions, mostly connected to financial resources, are discussed during the PWTM. The proposed measure could be, for instance, to send the child to a special teaching group or to send the child back to the classroom for the teacher to deal with. The latter option implies that the problems are handled as part of the regular school practices.

For our purposes, the critical point is when, and in what circumstances, the ADHD/DAMP concept is invoked in this process by the participants and publicly discussed. What are the problems and behaviors that are considered indicative of this diagnosis? In order to understand this, we turn to the discussion in the PWTM.

'What about the DAMP, then?': ADHD/DAMP as a discursive category in school

The general purpose of the PWTM is to come to a decision about what to do when children have difficulties and do not fit into the regular system. From an analytical point of view, the discussion can be seen as a series of attempts to classify what is reported in a manner that will resolve the matter by suggesting a solution. In the following excerpt, the team members are discussing Julia, eight years of age, who reportedly has had problems in accommodating to life in school (and who is the pupil most frequently discussed during this year, in 10 meetings of the 14, but she did not at the time of discussion have a confirmed diagnosis). The excerpt illustrates the dramaturgy of the most typical manner of arguing in the sense that a series of behaviors and/or events are presented. This is followed by a suggestion that there must be 'something about Julia' or some similar conclusion.

Excerpt 1: Julia, 8 years old, first meeting
1.   AP: she finds it difficult to break off a task, she has difficulties in
2.   starting working, and when she's working she finds it difficult to
3.   stop, she has difficulties with [changes]
4.   ST: [mmm]
5.   (...)[7]

Step 6	Parents' conference	reporting to the parent with the intention of gaining consent to test the child for suspected disorder
Step 7	Psychological assessment	testing
Step 8	Medical expert	motor-test, confirmation of diagnosis
Step 9	Parents' conference	psychologist reports the results of the tests
Step 10	PWTM	psychologist reports the tests to the team and a decision about how to proceed is made
Step 11	Outcome of process	personal assistant special teaching group medical treatment back to teacher's concern

Figure 3.4.2 Steps in the second phase of the institutional process of decision-making in West Valley Comprehensive School: conducting an ADHD/DAMP-assessment.

6. SP: is she able to co-operate [at all now] [?]
7. AP: [no she has dif]ficulties co-operating
8. as well
9. ST: she has almost no friends ... and she can't [subordinate] herself
10. SP: [mmm]
11. ST: ... and then there was this business of the mother who is very worried
12. that this could be some kind ehhh ... of letter[8] or something
13. (...)
14. ST: Julia has no learning disabilities and that's usually a part of
15. this thing ... and there is something about Julia, but what [?]

According to this analysis, Julia 'has difficulties with changes'. She reportedly finds it difficult to start working but she is also unwilling to interrupt what she is doing and start on something new (1, 2), and she is unwilling to subordinate herself (9). She also has problems with her peer relations (9), and she reportedly finds it difficult to co-operate (7). It is reported that the mother has explicitly mentioned her worry about her daughter suffering from a neuropsychiatric disorder (11). Through this mode of reasoning, and the contributions of the various parties who provide direct and indirect information, the suspicion of ADHD/DAMP is implicitly confirmed as the relevant categorization.

In this excerpt, the special needs teacher argues that she has no learning disabilities (which should be expected, given the diagnosis suggested in (12) by the special needs teacher, i.e., the special needs teacher includes learning disabilities in the ADHD concept). This is one of the few occasions in our material where a counterargument, or some kind of disconfirming information, to the suspicion of an ADHD/DAMP diagnosis is given. Yet the special needs teacher implicitly confirms the potential relevance of the category by arguing that still 'there is something about Julia' (15).

In another case, the team again describes a child's problem through a series of categories and they end up by suggesting that it could be DAMP.

Excerpt 2: Robert, 7 years old
1. SN: (...) at the slightest problem he needs extra time ... and you have to
2. explain very carefully ... and prepare him for what will happen ...
3. PR: He needs planning in advance all the time [!]
4. (...)
5. AP: his mother has been wondering if it could be DAMP or something ... she
6. has also said that there is something wrong with him ... that [something]
7. is the matter
8. Many: [mmm]
9. SP: but here I guess we should start an [assessment] ... of this
10. Many: [mmm]

Robert reportedly, according to the school nurse, needs extra time 'at the slightest problem' (1). He also needs explanations (2) and extensive preparations (2) to handle changes. In addition, the principal establishes that he needs planning in advance (3). In this case, the conclusion again is that 'there is something wrong with him' (6), and that this 'something' is causing his problematic behavior. Again, the suggestion that it might be ADHD/DAMP is reported as coming from the mother. From this description, the psychologist establishes that the boy ought to be assessed for ADHD/DAMP (9).

In the third case, Axel, the team members also talk about 'something' that has been disturbing the boy for quite some time. Again, the presupposition is that there is something inside the boy that is disturbing him. In this case, the psychologist, indirectly and without using the term, introduces the category ADHD/DAMP.

Excerpt 3: Axel, 7 years old
1.   SP: it seems like this business of the concentration problems, that what we
2.   have is a boy who should be assessed
3.   (…)
4.   SP: this is a boy who has been considered for an assessment at … his day-
5.   care center … that's an indication that there has been something wrong
6.   for a long time

Some interesting features of these discussions are obvious, and one can argue that they represent a particular accounting practice. The child and his/her behaviors are targeted fairly quickly as objects of discussion. A central feature of the accounts is that the child has difficulties with 'changes'. There is an implicit commitment to the assumption that there is a cause that can be found within the child. The disturbing overt behaviors are generally not contextualized in relation to concrete events in the classroom that might be relevant to understanding them. Even in cases where one points to relatively concrete factors such as that children need extra time or careful explanations of what to do, these problems are generally contextualized as symptoms of something that resides within the child. Within this framing, the categories for understanding child behavior offered by biomedical discourse seem to come to mind easily, and they are obviously considered practically useful within the school context. The team continues during another meeting to discuss Julia's behaviors in a rather open manner. The professionals negotiate about the explanations of her conduct, and the ADHD/DAMP category seems to be the answer, which everybody finds relevant to pursue.

Excerpt 4: Julia, 8 years old, second meeting
 1.   AP: (…) as soon as things change or something well, … she's very
 2.   sensitive to that … it must always be on Julia's terms … if you
 3.   sort of keep things calm, nothing happens … if you don't provoke her in
 4.   any way then everything is quiet and all right but you have to
 5.   like … something can very very easily [happen] …
 6.   Many: [mmm]
 7.   AP: the problem is with the peer relations and to do what the others are
 8.   doing … like when you say 'now we're going to do maths' and she insists
 9.   on writing ehh … a story or something then that's what she wants to do
10.   [and then you can't] …
11.   PR: [(inaudible) everything is on her terms] [?]
12.   AP: yes, [yes]
13.   PR: [deep sigh]
14.   [Pause, 11s])
15.   AP: but … but there's so much more to it … now she's doing a lot of
16.   schoolwork but sometimes she refuses to show things she has done or she
17.   doesn't always do …[laughter]
18.   PR: the right things [?]

19. AP: no … she can easily get stuck on doing something she wants to do … she
20. works on page 8 or 37 way ahead in the book although they
21. should be on page two or something like that
22. PR: what about the DAMP then [?]
23. AP: yes that's just the thing … like the mother ehh … had felt that there
24. were some things she had seen on a TV program that fitted into this …
25. like difficulties in following rules and things [like that]
26. SP: [mmm] the mother was
27. supposed to phone me …
28. AP: yes [?]
29. SP: but she has[n't]
30. AP: [no] [?]
31. PR: but if a DAMP-assessment is to be carried out, it's high time to start
32. on it now when she is in, in … second grade

The assistant principal here points to a range of different, sometimes rather contradictory, behaviors on the part of Julia; refusing to do things (16), insisting on an activity (8, 19), having problems with peer-relations (7). She also suggests a tendency towards aggressive behavior (3, 5). Different characteristics of the girl also become important in the discussion. The assistant principal mentions that the girl is obstinate (2, 11), dominant (2, 11, 19), that she has difficulties in following rules and instructions (16, 19, 25), and that she is very sensitive to changes (2). These different kinds of problems in Julia's conduct are connected to her inner characteristics, and the principal suggests that Julia should be assessed for ADHD/ DAMP (22, 31). The assistant principal supports this by referring to the mother's opinion (23). It can be observed that the language is both sociological and social when the assistant principal speaks about Julia's problems with peers and working in school. However, the principal refers to the biomedical category and the suspicion from the previous meeting by saying 'What about the DAMP then?' (22). Here, the biomedical language enters the stage, and it is obviously seen as a relevant category for understanding Julia. From a rhetorical perspective, this is the nature of the transformation that is occasioned by the introduction of the category of ADHD/DAMP. When the assistant principal re-enters into the discussion (23), she confirms the potential relevance of this category by referring to the mother's reactions to a television program she has seen, where behaviors of the kind ascribed to Julia ('difficulties in following rules') were described as indicative of a neuropsychiatric disorder. The psychologist closes the discussion by saying that the mother has not called her as yet. Through this move, she supports the principal's suggestion and implicitly confirms that the next step in the procedure is to talk to the parents and get their permission for the child to be assessed for a suspected neuropsychiatric disorder.

Again, and as we will return to in the final discussion, the discussions of the problems experienced to a large extent have the character of enumerations of observations that have been made concerning Julia's behaviors. Julia is described as 'doing a lot of schoolwork', but still not following the expected work patterns by changing tasks when she is supposed to, and she is also described as 'sensitive.' There are few systematic attempts to contextualize Julia's activities and problems in the pedagogical setting or to view them as relative to some concrete circumstance or some identifiable type of challenge. Instead, generalized and ambiguous descriptions of the girl's behavior dominate the discussion. A key part of this accounting practice, apparent in most cases when ADHD/DAMP is considered, is the claim that these children have difficulties with 'changes' and/or with changing from one activity to another in the manner expected. Viewing these discussions in terms of their discursive properties, it seems as if the category ADHD/DAMP is easily available and is perceived as creating closure in the discussion by somehow pointing in the right direction.

In the next excerpt, the assistant principal presents Peter's difficulties by explicitly referring to them as a relational problem. However, the initial account is transformed during the discussion, and it soon becomes a problem of Peter himself. Also in this case, the team express a concern that there is 'something else' disturbing the boy (18).

Excerpt 5: Peter, 9 years old
 1. AP: then let's see ... Peter in the third grade ... he has worked a lot with
 2. the special needs teacher and there are some problems between them
 3. [between the special needs teacher and Peter, our comment] they find
 4. that ... or, yes I've been talking to the special needs teacher as well,
 5. and she says that the chemistry between them isn't [very good]
 6. SP: [between] the
 7. special needs teacher and Peter [?]
 8. AP: the special needs teacher and Peter yes ... so it's... not only that Peter
 9. says so but the special needs teacher feels the same
10. (...)
11. ST: wasn't he all over the place last year and... fell over a lot and bustled
12. [about] ...
13. AP: [mmm]
14. ST: and walked on crutches and ehh ... all those [kinds of thi–]
15. AP: [yes, that's] him
16. ST: yes I think ... clumsy even though he doesn't look clumsy [and then]
17. AP: [mmm]
18. ST: you may sort of start thinking whether there's something else that's
19. disturbing [him]
20. Many: [mmm]
21. ST: ... when he's kind of generally diffi[cult]
22. AP: [mmm]
23. ST: well ... he seems like that ... should a DAMP assessment be underta– [?]
24. (...)
25. Many: [inaudible]
26. SP: [WE TALKED] probably about this a year ago... in these terms too ... with
27. lack of concentration and [such things]
28. ST: [yes exactly]

In this excerpt the problem of the boy is first described as relational (2) between the special needs teacher and Peter, (the special needs teacher talked about is not the one attending the meeting). However, the discussion does not continue along these lines but, rather, recontextualizes the problem by focusing on Peter (11 and onwards). His conduct and the alleged motor function problems are discussed as problematic in general terms. Thus, he was 'all over the place' last year, he 'fell over' (11), he 'walked on crutches' (14), is 'clumsy' (16), 'generally difficult' (21), and shows a 'lack of concentration' (27). Also in this case it is reported that there is 'something else that's disturbing him' (18), and this seems to be the decisive factor for suggesting a biomedical diagnosis as ADHD/DAMP. Thus, from this rather general description of the boy's conduct, the team members decide to initialize an

ADHD/DAMP-assessment (23). In this case, it is the special needs teacher who initiates the suggestion of a suspected ADHD/DAMP and leads the discussion towards a solution, which in this case is a diagnosis of the child.

The accounting practice used here again illustrates the de- and recontextualizing elements that seem to be an underlying premise in the PWTMs. The team does not see it as relevant to include in its analyses the role and actions of teachers and other relevant actors. The assumption somehow seems to be that teachers are fulfilling their duties in the manner that can be expected, and the analyses in this sense do not have to embrace the system in which the various actors operate. Learning problems of individual pupils are legitimate targets of discussion while teaching problems are not. The very design of the PWTM, in which the staff meets to discuss 'problems', seems to induce such a perspective of the matters to be talked about.

In the case of Axel, the school nurse presents the problems experienced in class, and she strongly emphasizes a series of difficult behaviors.

Excerpt 6: Axel, 7 years old
1. SN: I met Axel this morning and right now it's a dis[aster] [!]
2. SP: [mmm]
3. SN: he stands out in all kinds of ways … lack of concentration, anxious …
4. has difficulties with peer [relations]
5. SP: [mmm]
6. SN: … he can't sit still won't listen to instructions goes out and
7. screams, slams the [doors]
8. SP: [mmm]
9. SN: … very [!] provocative …
10. (…)
11. SP: what's the reason [?] … should we consider a diagnosis, or [?]

In this case, the biomedical diagnosis is immediately suggested as a next step. By introducing a diagnosis, closure seems to be created and the team members obviously consider this a relevant solution. So, when Axel some time later finally, and in the local jargon, 'gets' a diagnosis, the news is greeted with relief.

Excerpt 7: Axel, 7 years old, some meetings later
1. AP: The psychologist talked about him being in line for the small
2. group[9]
3. SN: yes [!]
4. AP: … but if he gets a place I don't know … so as the situation is right
5. now we need … there's got to be an [assistant]
6. SN: [mmm] … what kind of diagnosis was
7. it [?]
8. AP: ADHD
9. SN: I see, that was just as [well]
10. AP: [mmm]
11. SN: … I mean that it [finally] happened
12. AP: [mmm]

The comment made by the school nurse that 'it finally happened' (11) testifies to the manner in which the diagnosis is construed as the end point of an institutional process. The diagnosis provides a platform on which the demands for additional resources (normally a personal assistant) can be successfully claimed.

Discussion and conclusions

The process of categorizing is a practice of engaging in sense-making within the context of a particular institutional practice and its accounting practices. From an analytical perspective, it is, we argue, legitimate to ask what these accounting practices are like, how they operate, and why they are used as resources for mediating between the interests of collectives and individuals. The problem for the team we have studied is to continuously solve institutional dilemmas by means of closing the gap between a problem and possible solutions through categories available to the members. The accounts of the problems provided by the staff indicate that there are many different kinds of problems. In spite of the diversity in behaviors and problems observed, it is fascinating to see that the discussion of these children leads to one specific biomedical category, ADHD/DAMP. This category – as an inference-rich member's category in Sacks' (1992) sense – seems to close the gap between the descriptions of children's behaviors and the probable causes in a satisfactory manner for the team members.

There is a high degree of consensus in the meetings, which indicates that the accounting practices employed are well established and accepted. Expressed differently, the neuropsychiatric category of ADHD/DAMP is reflexively used in the constitution of normality and deviance in the meetings. As a member's category it 'can be seen to presume that the features of the object … being categorized are pre-given, i. e. they are presumed to exist independently of the activity of categorization itself' (Hester, 1991). The communicative strategy utilized implies enumerating a number of problems that have occurred and that are associated with a particular child. The participants contribute by adding illustrations that confirm and extend the account that is evolving. This is followed by implying that there is a cause within the child itself that is likely to produce inappropriate behaviors. This is a very clear, and powerful, rhetorical figure in the reasoning employed. The logic and some of the central categories used in the discussion are illustrated in Figure 3.4.3.

The transformation of the various observations into a claim that there is some clearly definable problem inside the child, which is captured in the category ADHD/DAMP, testi-

The child 'has'	The child 'is'	The child 'behaves'
concentration problems	provocative	is shutting her/himself out
problems with peer relations	anxious	refuses to do things
difficulties to follow rules	obstinate	insists on doing things
relational problems	stubborn, alone and sullen	falls over
difficulties with changes	sensitive	is all over the place
something	generally difficult	bustles about
introvert DAMP	introvert	

Figure 3.4.3 Terms used as descriptions of child behavior by staff

fies to the appeal of the biomedical model of diagnostic reasoning in this discourse community, and the 'things ontology' (Shotter, 1993) it builds on. This model localizes the cause of the problems in the child's brain as an organic structure, and posits problems in behavior as a direct outflow of biological dysfunctions. No further analysis of the relationship between the alleged brain injury and the broad range of behaviors described is made at the meetings. The correlation is presumed rather than challenged. Expressed differently, the basic metaphor underlying the discussion is not a developmental and contextual one, where children's actions are seen as contingent on previous experiences and local practices. The analyses preferred effectively make the role of the teachers and a broad range of contextual elements invisible as ingredients in the problems observed.

One of the most salient features of the discussions is the lack of argumentation and critical analysis. Consent within the team is easily produced and maintained. The general comments and claims made by the participants regarding the behaviors of students are never challenged in a concrete sense by asking when and where the events took place, or by clarifying details of the circumstances. No contributor is held accountable for the claims they make regarding the children's problems. Counterarguments offering alternative interpretations of events are almost completely absent. Invoking parents' suspicions of a neuropsychiatric disorder, a strategy employed in several cases, adds to this picture of consent regarding the nature of the problem. In this context, it is interesting to note that even though the team is multi-disciplinary, and the members represent different competencies, this does not result in any apparent variations in the manner in which the problems experienced are presented and discussed.

The accounts of children are ambiguous, at times even contradictory. A child can be described as too focused on what he/she is doing, while another child is unable to concentrate and 'all over the place'. A child may be disruptive but show no problems in her learning capacities, even though this should be expected. Other children are introverted and passive. Even when accounting for the behaviors of the same child, and sometimes even during the same PWTM, the categories used may be incompatible. Figure 3.4.4 gives a presentation of some of the contradictory terms used by team members to back up their suggestion that a particular pupil should be tested for ADHD/DAMP (the items on the same row in the two columns refer to the same child).

The pupil	
is provocative	is sensitive
can't concentrate	is shutting himself out
is all over the place	is difficult to get through to
is clumsy	doesn't look clumsy
shows signs of LD	does not show signs of LD

Figure 3.4.4 Contradictory categories of children's behaviors/problems used in discussions that precede the decision to initiate an ADHD/DAMP assessment (all terms are used in our corpus)

If one looks at these terms, and the manners in which they are used in the discussion, they are not only contradictory but also quite vague. But even though they may appear vague and general, they operate, we argue, with a high level of precision in the institutional context. When children are accounted for in this vague manner at the meetings, the outcome is that a process to instigate an assessment into a possible neuropsychiatric disorder will be considered and, in most cases, also decided on. The vagueness, thus, is only apparent. When the discussion reaches a stage where the child is described as suffering from 'something', or, alternatively, when it is claimed that there is something 'disturbing" him or her, these comments are read in a fairly specific way. In the context of institutional reasoning, the kinds of terms listed in Figure 3.4.4, contradictory as they may seem, are inference-rich and move the discussion in a specific direction.

In passing, let us comment briefly on two observations that conflict with what has been reported in the literature. In contrast to what has been argued in other studies (cf. Mehan, 1993), the neuropsychiatric categories seem to resonate with parents' views. As we have already pointed out, in several instances in our material, the parents are quoted by staff as having suggested to teachers and other representatives of the school that they suspect that ADHD/DAMP (or some other similar 'letter' symptom) is the problem that their child is suffering from. The category thus serves as a meeting ground for the various parties involved and as a bridge between professional, semi-professional, and lay discourse. There is very little resistance on the part of parents in our material to having their children diagnosed for a neuropsychiatric disorder, which *per se* is an interesting observation.

Also, when invoking ADHD/DAMP in the meetings, the social background and the immediate family conditions seem to be effectively bracketed. This is at odds with what is often claimed with respect to how school failures are accounted for. For instance, Lubeck and Garrett (1990), in their study of the social construction of the 'at risk' child, argue that the 'concept of children at risk defines the nature of the social problem: certain children are unable ... to avail themselves of the opportunities that schools present'. Thus, the 'problem of poor school performance resides not in social, political, economic, and educational institutions, but rather in the child, and, by extension, in the family' (p. 327). In our material, and specifically in relation to this group, the interest in pursuing issues of the relationship between family, socializing practices and schooling seems almost non-existent. This contrasts with how the team members reason in the context of other problems that children may have (for instance, dyslexia and emotional problems). In our interpretation, this decontextualization of the child from her/his life circumstances is produced by this category through the adoption of a biomedical voice, which points to factors held to be of a different nature. And perhaps this is also why the category of ADHD/DAMP serves as an attractive meeting ground for school staff and parents in the discussion of children's problems.

But on yet another level, the meetings are very interesting because of the kinds of analyses and discussions not present. Thus, there is almost no professional pedagogical discussion involved in the meetings we have recorded. For instance, there are few, if any, analyses of the kinds of situations that elicit the problematic behaviors reported, and that would be conducive to producing an understanding of what is common to or characteristic of the contexts where the child reacts in a disruptive or unpredictable manner. In other words, there are no attempts to understand the child and his/her problems as they surface in the attempts to adapt to the role of being a pupil and acting in an educational setting. Also, there are no discussions of the kinds of measures that have been taken to deal with the problems, and what the effects have been. This is also confirmed by the abstract nature of the written documentation, which does not document in any detail the analyses made or the progress of the work with the child. In this sense, there is no systematic and cumulative problem-solving process that focuses on the child and his/her problems in school.

At a general level, our results illustrate how a specific accounting practice is employed within a particular institutional system. And, to use Wittgenstein's (1953, §106) groundbreaking insight, the findings also demonstrate the profound manner in which we 'predicate of the thing what lies in the method of representing it'. In this tradition, behavioral problems are understood in terms of brain dysfunctions rather than as responses to concrete events in the school situation. This testifies to a basic assumption of medicalization: brain injuries are real while other kinds of explanations referring to the child's biography or contextual factors are seen as vague. In fact, the participants in the meetings are forced to be quite flexible when connecting the broad range of contradictory behaviors and attitudes to this particular syndrome. In spite of this, the idea of the appropriateness of ADHD/DAMP as a solution to the problems experienced seems to be shared by all the parties in our material. The category does a concrete job on many levels; it is a link in the process of attracting resources by classifying the child as handicapped, it relieves all the parties, including parents, of responsibility, and it creates closure in the situation by offering a reasonable explanation of problematic behaviors, thus avoiding going into issues that have to do with the child's biography. And it allows the institutional process to go on; the decision to initiate an assessment of a suspected neuropsychiatric disorder is seen by the team members as a concrete outcome and a step forward towards resolving the problem. But, as Mehan, Hertweck and Meihls (1986, p. 164) in a study of a similar problem have pointed out, disability 'exists neither in the head of educators nor in the behaviors of students'. Instead, it is 'a function of the interaction between educators' categories, institutional machinery, and students' conduct'. The ADHD/DAMP diagnosis is symptomatic but our results indicate that it is read as pointing to a clear and definite cause that is indisputable, and that in a deterministic manner limits the possibilities of children to participate in, and profit from, school practices. Considering the growing number of children who are claimed to suffer from such handicaps, the acceptance by educators of medical categories of this kind is indirectly a powerful statement with regard to who fits into mainstream schooling in late-modern society. In this manner, the medical categories do a concrete job by placing this particular discussion outside political and ideological considerations.

Acknowledgements

Reproduced with permission of Taylor & Francis (www.informaworld.com) from *Journal of Language, Identity and Education*, 2004, 3(1), pp. 1–24.

Notes

1   A note on classification of classifications. In Sweden, the acronym DAMP has been frequently used as a neuropsychiatric diagnosis. DAMP to a large extent replaced the previous term MBD (the English acronym was used in Swedish as well). Today, there is a tendency to use DAMP and ADHD as more or less identical in terms of their symptomatic features (Socialstyrelsen, 2002). Sometimes, the combined expression ADHD/DAMP is used, and this is another indication that the categories have in fact been collapsed. In order to facilitate the reading of this text, we will use the expression ADHD/DAMP, except in quotations, where the transcript reproduces the category used by the speaker.

2   It is very difficult to estimate the number of children who are handicapped, since handicaps do not appear in public records. Also, and relating to our topic, the definitions of what exactly constitutes a handicap are not clear. The figure of 2 per cent of a cohort as handicapped (in the classical sense) is taken from a government report, where it is claimed that 0.5 per cent of a cohort have vision or hearing impairments (including those who are deaf) or have physical disabilities. Slightly more than 1 per cent have severe

learning disabilities and attend special schools, and another small number of children have other medical problems (SOU 2000, p. 188).

3   This was (and still is) the political ambition, but there were exceptions and special arrangements for various groups. Special schools were kept for children with some types of handicaps, for instance those with severe learning difficulties.

4   The Swedish term is either EVK (short for elevvårdskonferens) or EVT (short for elevvårdsteamsmöte). The latter acronym is used in this school.

5   This is an estimate of the proportion of children who are first- and second-generation immigrants. The criterion used is that they are entitled to mother-tongue teaching. The difficulty in establishing who is an immigrant is in itself an illustration of the problem of using categories in a uniform manner, which we are addressing in this article.

6   These abbreviations are used in the excerpts.

7   Some dialogue not relevant to this analysis has been left out.

8   The term 'letter' refers to an expression in Swedish, bokstavsbarn, which literally translates into 'letter children'. This term is frequently used in schools (and elsewhere) for this group of children who have a diagnosis expressed in the form of an acronym (DAMP, ADHD, MBD, etc.).

9   A special teaching group with few students.

Appendix

Transcript symbols

[ ]	simultaneous talk
..	interruption, the speaker interrupts himself at the end of a word
...	untimed pause
(...)	indicates that some talk is left out
[?]	marks intonation of a question
[!]	indicates an animated tone
,	continuing intonation
UPPER CASE	loud talk

References

Billig, M. (1987) *Arguing and Thinking: A Rhetorical Approach to Social Psychology*, Cambridge University Press.

Börjesson, M. (1997) *Om skolbarns olikheter: diskurser kring 'särskilda behov' i skolan – med historiska jämförelsepunkter* (On differences between children: discourses about 'special needs' in the school – with historical comparisons), Stockholm, Liber.

Bowker, G.C., and Star, S.L. (1999) *Sorting Things Out: Classification and its Consequences*, Cambridge, MA, MIT Press.

Calhoun, D. (1973) *The Intelligence of a People*, Princeton, NJ, Princeton University Press.

Douglas, M. (1986) *How Institutions Think*, London, Routledge and Kegan Paul.

Foucault, M. (1972) *The Archaeology of Knowledge*, London, Tavistock/Routledge.

Gillberg, C. (1991) 'Nordisk enighet om MBD-bedömning: termen otidsenlig och olämplig' (Nordic consensus on MBD-assessment: the term is out of date and inappropriate), *Läkartidningen*, 88(9), pp. 713–17.

Goodman, N. (1978) *Ways of Worldmaking*, Indianapolis, IN, Hackett Publishing Company Inc.

Goodwin, C., and Opper, S. (1992) 'Rethinking context: an introduction', in A. Duranti and C. Goodwin (eds), *Rethinking Context: Language as an Interactive Phenomenon*, Cambridge University Press, pp. 1–42.

Hacking, I. (1986) 'Making up people', in T.C. Heller, M. Sosna and D. Wellbury (eds), *Reconstructing Individualism: Autonomy, Individuality, and the Self in Western Thought*, Stanford, CA, Stanford University Press, pp. 222–36.

—— (1999) *The Social Construction of What?*, Cambridge, MA, Harvard University Press.
Hagberg, B. (1975) 'Minimal brain dysfunction: vad innebär det för barnets utveckling och anpassning' (Minimal brain dysfunction: what does it mean for the child's development and adaptation), *Läkartidningen*, 72(36), pp. 3296–300.
Hayakawa, S.I. (1965) *Language in Thought and Action*, London, George Allen and Unwin.
Heritage, J. (1984) *Garfinkel and Ethnomethodology*, Cambridge, Polity Press.
Hester, S. (1991) 'The social facts of deviance in school: a study of mundane reason', *British Journal of Sociology of Education*, 42, pp. 443–63.
Kadesjö, B. (2000) 'Neuropsychiatric and neurodevelopmental disorders in a young school-age population: epidemiology and comorbidity in a school health perspective', unpublished dissertation, Göteborg University.
Kadesjö, B., and Gillberg, C. (1998) 'Attention deficits and clumsiness in Swedish 7-year-old children', *Developmental Medicine and Child Neurology*, 40, pp. 796–804.
Kärfve, E. (2000) *Hjärnspöken: DAMP och hotet mot folkhälsan* (Figments of imagination: DAMP and the threat to popular health), Stockholm, Brutus Östling.
Lindensjö, B., and Lundgren, U.P. (2000) *Utbildningsreformer och politisk styrning* (Educational reforms and political steering), Stockholm, HLS Förlag.
Lubeck, S., and Garrett, P. (1990) 'The social construction of the "at-risk" child, *British Journal of Sociology of Education*, 11(3), pp. 327–41.
Mäkitalo, Å. (2002) *Categorizing Work: Knowing, Arguing, and Social Dilemmas in Vocational Guidance*, Göteborg Studies in Educational Sciences, 177, Göteborg, Acta Universitatis Gothoburgensis.
Mäkitalo, Å., and Säljö, R. (2002) 'Talk in institutional context and institutional context in talk: categories as situated practices', *Text*, 22(1), pp. 57–82.
Mehan, H. (1992) 'Understanding inequality in schools: the contribution of interpretive studies', *Sociology of Education*, 65(1), pp. 1–20.
—— (1993) 'Beneath the skin and between the ears: a case study in the politics of representation', in S. Chaiklin and J. Lave (eds), *Understanding Practice: Perspectives on Activity and Context*, Cambridge, MA, Cambridge University Press, pp. 241–69.
Mehan, H., Hertweck, A., and Meihls, J.L. (1986) *Handicapping the Handicapped: Decision Making in Students' Educational Careers*, Stanford, CA, Stanford University Press.
Ohlander, M. (1956) *Hjälpskolan i Göteborg 1906–1956* (Remedial school in Göteborg 1906–1956), Borås, Aktiebolaget J F Björsell.
Parker, I. (1990) 'Discourse: definitions and contradictions', *Philosophical Psychology*, 3(2), pp. 189–204.
Rydelius, P-A. (1999) 'Bokstavsbarn: gengångare från förr med ny beteckning' (Letter children: ghosts from earlier times in a new terminology), *Läkartidningen*, 96(30/31), pp. 3332–8.
Sacks, H. (1992) *Lectures on Conversation*, vol. 1, Oxford, Blackwell.
Schmidt, M., Esser, G., Allehoff, W., Geisel, B., Laucht, M., and Woerner, W. (1987) 'Evaluating the significance of minimal brain dysfunction: results of an epidemiologic study', *Journal of Child Psychology and Psychiatry*, 28, pp. 803–21.
Shotter, J. (1993) *Conversational Realities*, London, Sage.
SOU (2000) *Från dubbla spår till elevhälsa i en skola som främjar lust att lära, hälsa och utveckling* (From double tracks to pupils' health in a school promoting the will to learn, health and development), SOU 2000:19, Stockholm, Liber.
Socialstyrelsen (2002) *ADHD hos barn och vuxna* (ADHD among children and adults), Stockholm, Modin-Tryck.
Stevenson, H.W., and Stigler, J. (1992) *The Learning Gap. Why our Schools are Failing and What We Can Learn from Japanese and Chinese Education*, New York, Summit Books.
Sundkvist, M. (1994) *De vanartade barnen: Mötet mellan barn, föräldrar och Norrköpings barnavårdsnämnd 1903–1925* (The degenerate children: The encounter between children, parents and the child welfare board of Norrköping), Södertälje, Hjelm Förlag.
Trent, J.W. (1994) *Inventing the Feeble Mind: A History of Mental Retardation in the United States*, Berkeley, CA, University of California Press.

Wertsch, J.V. (1991) *Voices of the Mind: A Sociocultural Approach to Mediated Action,* Cambridge, MA, Harvard University Press.

—— (1998) *Mind as Action,* New York, Oxford University Press.

Wittgenstein, L. (1953) *Philosophical Investigations,* Oxford, Blackwell.

Reflective questions

1   What kinds of explanation of learners' difficulties have currency in your organization?
2   What kinds of evidence are used to support these explanations and who contributes to it? Does this involve discussion of pedagogy?

Further reading

Bowker, G.C., and Star, S.L. (1999) *Sorting Things Out: Classification and its Consequences,* Cambridge, MA, MIT Press.

Mäkitalo, A. and Säljö, R. (2002) 'Talk in institutional context and institutional context in talk: categories as situated practices', *Text,* 22(1), pp. 57–82.

Mehan, H. (1979) *Learning Lessons: Social Organization in the Classroom,* Cambridge, MA, Harvard University Press.

And perhaps:

Daniels, H. (2006) 'The dangers of corruption in special needs education', *British Journal of Special Education,* 33(1), pp. 4–10.

3.5 Inclusive pedagogy

Lani Florian and Ruth Kershner

Pedagogy is the act of teaching together with its attendant discourse.

Alexander, 2004, p. 11

Introduction

Increasingly teachers are expected to cater for a wide range of students in each class, including students identified as having 'special' or 'additional' educational needs compared to others of similar age (DfES, 2001). The tendency to liken students to their peers is unsurprising given the common expectations in western culture about children's typical developmental progress from birth. Furthermore, schools in the UK tend to be organised in year groups with external pressures to achieve certain standards of student performance at the end of each key stage in primary and secondary education. These structural features of the school system help to set the point at which certain students' educational needs come to be defined as 'special'. This is when the forms of provision and approaches to teaching that are generally available and effective for most students do not appear to work in particular cases.

Traditionally such students were thought to need something 'different from' or 'additional to' that which is ordinarily available, and this thinking defined special educational needs provision throughout the twentieth century. It was often assumed that separate special educational provision would inevitably be needed for children identified with an impairment, condition or pattern of behaviour commonly associated with educational difficulties. Today, however, more consideration is given to the concept of inclusive education for all children. Here the focus is less on what is 'different from' or 'additional to' that which is more generally available, and more on challenging complacency about what is 'generally available' (Florian, 2007). Thus, we would argue that inclusive education offers a more just and equitable approach to responding to student diversity than traditional special needs approaches focusing on individual differences. Inclusive education is distinguished by an *acceptance* of differences between students as an ordinary aspect of human development.

What are the implications of such a view for teaching? In attempting to map these out we need to ask a number of questions about educational goals, priorities and circumstances, such as: teaching what? by whom? to which students? in what context? under what constraints? Unfortunately, there is a tendency in the education literature to fragment knowledge about effective teaching and/or reduce it to generic recipes. The intuitive appeal of approaches to teaching where interventions are matched to the apparently unique characteristics of an individual or particular set of students (e.g. those identified with autism or Down syndrome) is an example. And yet when one looks carefully at this literature the recommendations about 'what works' are often indistinguishable from each other and not very helpful to teachers in mainstream classrooms. All children have much in common, including the fact that their individual characteristics and preferences are uniquely interrelated rather than neatly categorisable.

Moreover, because such interventions are based on a traditional special needs approach to student diversity that focuses on difference as a problem, attempts to match them to certain special types or patterns of learning do not help to expand or enhance the educational provision, approaches and teaching strategies that are already generally available. There is need for new ways of understanding the nature of effective teaching strategies for students who experience difficulties in learning that both capitalise on and extend teachers' professional knowledge about 'what works' for all students in different contexts. One way to do this is to consider the ways in which we perceive all children as learners, innovators, future citizens and so on, bearing in mind what we know about the processes and trajectories of human development over time (Kershner and Florian, 2006). To have most educational effect, this means connecting the discourses of 'special educational needs' and 'inclusion' with the ways of knowing children that are embedded more generally in current UK government initiatives and guidelines, such as 'personalised learning' (http://www.standards.dfes.gov.uk/personalisedlearning/), while continuing to reflect on the meaning and function of these ways of thinking about children and education.

The aim of this chapter is to explore how what Alexander (2004, p. 11) calls 'the act of teaching together with its attendant discourse', or pedagogy, applies to the education of diverse groups of students, including those who experience difficulties in learning in school. In Alexander's words, pedagogy involves 'what one needs to know, and the skills one needs to command, in order to make and justify the many different kinds of decisions of which teaching is constituted' (ibid.). He remarks further on the several domains of ideas and values which not only describe key considerations in teaching but also inform each other in practice. At a basic level these include the understandings of children, learning, teaching and curriculum which enable teaching to happen, and the school and policy contexts which formalise and legitimise it. However, as Alexander also says, attention needs to be given to the more fundamental elements of 'culture', 'self' and 'history'. These, he argues, locate teaching and ' anchor it firmly to the questions of human identity and social purpose without which teaching makes little sense' (p. 12). As we will show, this 'sociocultural' view of education is central to the development of inclusive pedagogy.

Those interested in the education and inclusion of students identified with special educational needs will find Alexander's different elements of pedagogy very familiar, because students' special needs tend to be identified when pedagogical mismatches and clashes become visible and discomforting. For instance, if an individual child does not make the learning progress that is expected of the age group and required for school accountability then the pedagogical framework is stretched and skewed out of its usual workings. The common response is to argue that it is the child who needs something 'different', often necessitating his or her removal from the classroom. In this way, the general pedagogical framework is protected by the exclusion of the child.

Inclusion requires not only a different way of thinking about causality and blame but also a more flexible understanding of the relationship between the various pedagogical elements involved. Our central argument is that a conceptualisation of teaching that is inclusive of all learners, in other words, inclusive pedagogy, does not deny individual differences among students but suggests that such differences do not have to be construed as problems inherent within learners that are outside of the expertise of classroom teachers.

The elements of inclusive pedagogy clearly spread beyond individual classrooms to include the beliefs, values and decision-making processes evident in the wider contexts of school and society. In this chapter we focus primarily on what is asked of teachers when students encounter difficulties in classroom learning. Drawing on sociocultural views of learning, we explore the argument that knowledge develops through shared activity in social contexts. As teachers engage and reflect on what constitutes 'acts of teaching' when students experience difficulty they create the conditions for inclusive education to flourish. This is brought to fruition by ways of working that are collaborative and strategic.

A sociocultural perspective on inclusive pedagogy

Sociocultural theory offers a productive way of thinking about how to understand and respond to the complexities inherent in educating diverse groups of students in different contexts. This approach has developed from the work of Vygotsky, his collaborators and followers, and it has been discussed extensively, in its different forms, by authors such as Bruner (1996), Daniels (2001), Edwards (2005), Tharp and Gallimore (1988) and Wertsch (1991) to name a few. A sociocultural framework has also been applied specifically to the education of students who experience difficulties in learning, including those who are designated as having special educational needs (e.g. Daniels and Cole, 2002; de Valenzuela, 2007; Gindis, 2003).

One of the main principles of sociocultural analysis is to take account of what happens in different contexts when people participate in activities, develop knowledge together and generally contribute to the development of the cultural beliefs, practices and artefacts which are valued in the immediate and wider contexts of social life. Individuals learn and change through their contacts with other people and they, in turn, become capable of changing what is understood and valued in the other social and cultural settings where they participate. At one level these processes are evident in the familiar experiences identified by Tharp and Gallimore (1988, p. 72) as the 'who, what, when, where, and why, the small recurrent dramas of everyday life, played on the stages of home, school, community, and workplace'.

In these settings people use what have been described as sociocultural 'tools' in order to achieve certain ends. Most of these tools are so thoroughly embedded in social life that they have become taken for granted and almost invisible. They range from artefacts such as measuring devices and writing materials to symbolic concepts, such as ways of thinking about learning, and general uses of language, images, game rules, routines, social roles, etc. The 'object' of tool use, i.e. what is being worked on, can take a number of forms in the school setting, ranging from a formal mathematical problem being tackled by a student, to a collective staff decision that needs to be made about timetabling, curriculum planning, or the provision of language support for bilingual families, for instance.

Edwards (2005) gives an example of how tool use can reveal thinking, as when a student decides whether to use fingers, pencil and paper, calculator or previously learned multiplication tables to perform a calculation and completes the task more or less successfully. Yet even if the student interprets the mathematical problem correctly, the successful completion of this task might be hindered more by lack of time in the lesson than by the student's choice of the most effective calculation tool. In this case, Edwards remarks that this produces a contradiction between the chosen calculation tool and the problem at hand (the 'object'), which could lead the teacher to question whether there is an unhelpful school emphasis on curriculum coverage over learning. In this case more is revealed about the workings of the system than about the child's mathematical thinking, and intervention would therefore be targeted at this 'school' level too.

With regard to inclusive pedagogy, one of the key points is that it is these sociocultural tools, both material and symbolic, which make everyday activities possible for all learners in school and which inevitably influence the teacher's understanding of individual students' capabilities. The presence (or absence) of relevant tools in the classroom environment and discourse helps to define or obscure what may be otherwise seen as individual students' preferences, capabilities and impairments. This is not just to do with the familiar equipment that helps certain students to see, walk or write more easily. The tools in question can be the very language and ways of thinking that inform discussion of students' apparent individual differences, learning difficulties and educational needs. For example, congenital impairments (such as microcephalus) are often portrayed negatively in language (imbecile), in literature (the hunchback of Notre Dame), in IQ testing (below average/subnormal), and so on. We see here that the language, literature and educational practices in a given society may all contribute to the socially constructed representation of disability as a tragic loss of functioning that would otherwise render the person normal.

A concept of disability can serve an important function in society by associating its infrequency (congenital impairments are unusual, most children are born without impairments) with the idea that the impairment is a bad thing. This privileges what people have in common, denigrating difference, often tacitly, in ways that are taken for granted and unquestioned. The value judgement of 'bad', then permits those without impairments to be seen as 'good', and by a similar process of association, the concept of normal as average can also be constructed as 'good' (Nussbaum, 2004). This understanding of normality then permeates the ways in which relationships are formed, decisions are made and resources allocated in the educational system. Yet, in the case of impairments, it has to be pointed out that anyone can become disabled at any time. In fact most people acquire disabilities of some kind if they live long enough.

In schools and classrooms, many specific ways of thinking, communicating and acting are based on assumptions of what is normal. Impairment is viewed at least tacitly as an unusual and negative human difference which is disruptive or outside of the 'normal' education process and, therefore, something that is best dealt with by specialists elsewhere. Yet even by talking about 'children who experience difficulties in learning', rather than 'children with learning difficulties', we immediately open up the possibility that a child does not possess a learning difficulty but may encounter one as he or she moves through the curriculum. This alternative way of thinking about learning and learning difficulty is central to the work of researchers like Hart, Dixon, Drummond and McIntyre (2004) working with the relatively unusual teachers who explicitly reject concepts of fixed ability and predetermined educational outcomes in favour of an approach of 'learning without limits' which assumes that all children's capacity to learn is transformable.

Yet how is it possible to gain the commitment and confidence of *all* teachers in developing an inclusive pedagogy for all children? As Skidmore (2004) demonstrates in his research in English secondary schools, alternative ways of thinking about students' learning may persist within different staff constituencies, notably contrasting a 'discourse of deviance' which highlights 'within-child' notions of fixed ability, with a 'discourse of inclusion' which assumes that every student has an open-ended potential for learning. Skidmore notes that while there can be a working compromise and theoretical overlap between these different ways of thinking about students, long-term school development towards inclusion will be helped or hindered by the degree to which alternative discourses are taken up by staff members in a position to set the agenda and implement significant changes in areas like staff appointments and budget allocation.

Open-ended views of all children's potential for learning present challenges to the deeply held convictions about the intrinsic value and necessity of basing specialist educational intervention on specialist knowledge of human differences. While some have argued that making special or additional support for some students is discriminatory because it excludes them from the opportunities that are generally available to their peers, others point out that it is difficult for mainstream classroom teachers to understand and cope with the full range of human differences, especially given limited resources and competing political agendas. Progress in resolving this dilemma requires more attention to be paid to the classroom learning that actually lies at the heart of different students' success or failure in the educational system.

What is involved in classroom learning and teaching?

There are different ways of understanding students' learning in the complex and demanding classroom environment. Constructivist views of learning and information-processing models support the uses of dialogue, other forms of interaction and practical activity to enhance students' memory, reasoning, problem-solving, factual knowledge, self-regulation and metacognition (i.e. the awareness and control of one's thinking and learning). Social constructivism places emphasis on shared purposeful activity as the basis of learning, focusing therefore on the facilitation of students' participation and communication in relevant and meaningful activities. Behaviourism emphasises the observable demonstration of successful learning, and the targets, prompts and reinforcements that guide students in that direction. Ecological models draw attention to the 'fit' and the transactions between the learner and his or her environment.

These approaches to understanding learning are theoretically distinct and their metaphorical power has been extensively discussed (Sfard, 1998), but in the practice of teaching and the learner's experience, there are likely connections between them. For example, a discussion of purely behavioural targets for a child to count from 1 to 10 is likely to increase his or her metacognitive awareness of the teacher's learning aims in this area. The classroom uses of behavioural target-setting and individual education plans for students identified with special educational needs became common practice in 1970s special education in the UK, but they are unlikely to reflect the teacher's commitment to the behaviourist psychological theory on which it is based. Such programmes are more representative of the teacher's positive effort to 'concentrate on factors over which we have some influence' in helping students to succeed (Ainscow and Tweddle, 1988, p. 15). In Edwards's (2005) terms therefore, behavioural target-setting can be seen socioculturally as one of a set of classroom practices which provide 'possibilities for action' (p. 58) to which individual learners adapt and contribute as they move between activities and situations in and out of school. The teacher's central role is to orchestrate these classroom practices drawing on the basic understandings of children, learning, teaching and curriculum which make teaching possible.

Typical classroom activities may include writing stories, carrying out science experiments or having a class discussion. Yet these superficially similar classroom activities do not result in similar experiences of learning and teaching from day to day or between schools. This is because, as Tharp and Gallimore (1988) remark, '(w)e must understand especially the meaning attached to the activity by participants, which in turn determines important matters such as strategies applied or the manner in which participants interact' (p. 73). This view of how the people involved may interpret their experiences, interact with each other and apply different strategies adds to our understanding of why packaged 'cook book' approaches to teaching students identified with special or additional needs, or indeed to inclusive practice, can be so unsatisfying and ineffective for teachers and students. The main focus of the next section relates to the teacher's immediate, strategic decision-making in classroom practice as informed by inclusive principles and values.

Inclusive pedagogical knowledge and decision-making

One of the implications of sociocultural thinking is to acknowledge teaching as a complex activity that is situated in the collective experience of classroom learning in particular contexts. Pedagogy, by definition, cannot be taken out of context and transferred between different educational settings. Yet there are some well-known aspects of learning and teaching which appear to be intrinsically inclusive, in that they incorporate approaches which take account both of the collective experience of learning and the individuality of learners' needs and experiences. For instance, the importance of dialogue between teachers and pupils has been thoroughly established by researchers like Alexander (2005), Mercer (2000) and Wells (1999). This principle of learning, which applies to all children, suggests the need explicitly to support some individuals in expressing their views and listening to others so that they can co-operate and contribute fully. Work on multimodal communication (Kress, Jewitt, Ogborn and Tsatsarelis, 2001), taking in language, image, gesture and action, offers further ways of understanding and responding to some students' apparent difficulties in grasping the less obvious ways in which most students come to understand what is expected and conveyed about knowledge and routines in the classroom setting.

From a sociocultural perspective inclusive pedagogy is best seen as a strategic process which centrally focuses on supporting the processes of children's learning, motivation and social interaction, rather than primarily on identifying special needs, differentiating work and providing additional resources and support. One of the key elements of this process relates to the teacher's role in deploying the available tools and resources to support learning, with an appropriate combination of teaching strategies for different purposes. Such 'tools and resources' inevitably will include school staff and others who provide support for learning.

Combining teaching strategies in inclusive pedagogy

A teaching strategy might best be defined as the skilful, purposeful and responsive use of several different classroom resources and types of interaction to assist students' efforts to learn. For one student this might involve detailed, personal guidance and encouragement to write a poem, while for another the strategy would be to provide a quiet space and time for the child to concentrate undisturbed. Each of these approaches might be used for different purposes on other occasions, and indeed other teaching strategies are likely to be required to teach the same children at other times. In practice it is the teacher's interrelated use of such approaches which comprises the chosen strategy in particular lessons and over time. The goals for individual students will vary at any one time between supporting them in developing active learning strategies, participating in educationally worthwhile activities and demonstrating their achievements to themselves and others. The full identification and analysis of teaching strategies in conducting a lesson for a group of students requires constantly shifting perspectives, depending on the purpose, and is often undertaken so rapidly that it is difficult to observe. It is only when students experience difficulties in learning that the teaching act becomes explicit as the teacher analyses what has gone wrong and what, strategically, to do about it. These strategic decisions are influenced by a number of factors in pedagogy which exist within and beyond the classroom, including the goals for learning, the students' apparent educational needs, the development of practice over time and the multi-professional teamwork involved.

We can see how the goals of teaching specifically affect the combination of teaching strategies in inclusive pedagogy. For example, in the teaching of reading there is a need to attend explicitly to the phonological, syntactic, semantic and metacognitive aspects, and to the connections with spelling and writing. Lower order and higher order reading skills interact to influence reading outcomes and longer-term literacy development. Current debates in the UK about teaching early reading with 'synthetic phonics' reflect the ongoing fierce differences of opinion in the field, but there is substantial research evidence of the value of integrating phonics teaching with work on reading comprehension with 'highly engaging texts' (Wyse and Styles, 2007, p. 38, citing Berninger *et al.*, 2003). The most effective interventions for pupils who experience difficulty in learning to read are those which employ a comprehensive model of reading to build a combined instructional approach. It is the explicit and complex understanding of what is involved in reading that allows a clear understanding of the rationale for combining teaching strategies. Evidence from research and professional experience then provides guidance about the actual teaching strategies likely to be required for different pupils. Similarly, research in the United States has shown that clear goals for the transfer and generalisation of learning in subjects like mathematics and science call for the combination of explicit instruction with guided problem-solving and discussion for pupils identified as having learning disabilities (or 'specific learning difficulties' in the UK) (Gersten, Baker and Pugach, with Scanlon and Chard, 2001).

Beliefs about students' complex learning and individual needs add to the factors involved in teachers' strategic decision-making. There are different aspects to consider here. For instance, a combination of teaching strategies can be a response to the identification of students' multiple needs – e.g. hearing impairment *and* attentional difficulties. The approach then might be to target combinations of teaching strategies in response to observations of a student's different areas of difficulty. This approach also applies in teaching children with complex syndromes, such as those identified as having autistic spectrum disorders or dyslexia and to those whose difficulties may have several different causes – such as chronic school refusers. Several intervention programmes and teaching packages have been developed for children identified in this way, but research reviews and professional experience suggest the need to draw on this growing evidence base to develop combined, multidimensional, individualised and often unconventional teaching approaches (Davis and Florian, 2004).

The combination of teaching strategies in inclusive pedagogy can be seen as something that evolves over time, especially when the context is expanded beyond the classroom. For example, Doyle (2003) describes the way in which nurture group principles for supporting young children with social, emotional and behavioural needs can spread from a small group to the whole school – with attention to such factors as the social development curriculum, the physical environment, the enhancement of play opportunities, classroom management strategies, playtime routines, school assemblies, etc. In this case strategy combination grows as the intervention becomes embedded in school, allowing the extension of useful teaching strategies to a larger group of pupils, involving more staff, and with a broader understanding of how specific strategies may be understood in relation to what else is happening in school.

Finally there is the question of who is involved in orchestrating teaching strategies in inclusive pedagogy. Previous points about multiple learning goals, multiple needs, and changes over time, draw attention to the essential division of labour between adults working to develop inclusive pedagogy. Most classrooms involve teamwork between teachers and other adults in helping students to participate in classroom activities, engage in active learning and communicate their ideas. These principles of supporting children are embedded in UK national policies such as the Every Child Matters agenda in England (http://www.every-childmatters.gov.uk/), and Scotland's Getting It Right for Every Child (http://www.scot-tishexecutive.org.uk). Many students identified with complex special educational needs will already be supported by a multiprofessional collaboration (e.g. teachers, speech therapist and occupational therapist). This division of labour, often involving many different people with their own purposes and goals in mind, calls for consideration not only of alternative professional and parental understandings, but also of each student's actual experience over time with the combined and multilevel strategies central to inclusive pedagogy.

Conclusion

The development of inclusive pedagogy involves complex day-to-day decisions in school and other learning contexts, using the many resources which are to hand. This inevitably involves more than one type of activity, with a combination of teaching strategies. The idea of combining teaching strategies and multimethod responses to students who experience difficulties in learning is not new but there is a growing literature documenting the effectiveness of combined strategies. Recognition of the need for teaching which takes account of context as well as learner differences is a key consideration in any reflection on what 'combining teaching strategies', and therefore inclusive pedagogy, may mean to the different people involved. The teaching challenge is to develop multiple, complementary strategies for accommodating pupils in all their diversity and responding to individual differences.

At the very least this implies that responding to students identified with special educational needs is a collaborative responsibility extending beyond individual class teachers to include all the sociocultural resources of the school, community and wider knowledge from other teachers and researchers. More fundamentally, we might recognise, with a sociocultural perspective, that the knowledge required by teachers builds in part from the act of teaching diverse groups of students not the abstract preparation for it. The interplay between teachers and learners, and the strategic collaboration with others involved allows new knowledge about learning to emerge, so the experience of bringing diverse students to learn together is itself the basis for what may become quite radical changes in society as language, beliefs and values alter over time.

Sociocultural theory suggests that the knowledge that teachers need develops partly through practice. Reflective practice and 'tinkering' (Hargreaves, 1997) has been found to be central to expert teaching. Teachers are particularly concerned with applying their, often tacit, knowledge in day-to-day practice in the light of their understanding of how children develop in the contexts of home, school and community and the multiple aims existing for individuals and groups of students (Kershner, 2007). Yet it is clear that knowledge of students' individual differences, for example an impairment (such as a cognitive memory difficulty), a medical condition (such as asthma) or a cultural difference (such as home language) does not obviously give rise to specialist pedagogies associated with those differences. Knowledge of children is, rather, an aspect of pedagogy in different educational contexts, with evident interrelationships with relevant learning, teaching and curriculum factors. Thinking of inclusive pedagogy as broadly as Alexander (2004) suggests, requires teachers to understand that differences are part of the human condition not something that distinguishes or separates one group of learners from another. From such a starting point, teachers can develop inclusive practices, focusing on learning, that are responsive to individual differences without the necessity of excluding some students by sending them out for additional support.

One of the challenges in developing inclusive pedagogy in this way is to understand how knowledge about the difficulties students experience in learning emerges from the ongoing investigation of their learning in school. This dynamic process depends on having in place what Florian (1998) has called the necessary but not sufficient conditions to support inclusion. These conditions involve various elements of support, leadership, commitment, collaboration, staff development, partnership with students, knowledge and skill (Ainscow, 1997; Florian, 1998). They are necessary in that meaningful inclusion cannot occur without them but they are not sufficient in and of themselves to bring about inclusion. There is some evidence that teachers' practice may be constrained by the availability of resources and by organisational factors within schools (Florian and Rouse, 2001). All of the conditions must be met in order to create the synergy required to sustain the practice.

The educational rights-based argument that all children should learn together regardless of type or degree of learning difficulty presents a particular challenge to those who teach in twenty-first-century schools. In this chapter we have tried to show how an acceptance of a philosophy of inclusion does not depend on a rejection of individual differences. Rather it depends on understanding how learners differ and how the different aspects of human development interact with experience to produce individual differences that is the starting point for inclusive practice. The broad implications are for establishing the conditions which allow inclusive practice in all phases of education so that knowledge about what it means to include all learners can develop fully. The use of sociocultural theory to understand inclusive pedagogy complements the growing body of empirical evidence in drawing attention to particular elements, interactions and levels of analysis that might otherwise be neglected in research and practice.

References

Ainscow, M. (1997) 'Towards inclusive schooling', *British Journal of Special Education*, 24(1), pp. 3–6.

Ainscow, M. and Tweddle, D. (1988) *Encouraging Classroom Success*, London, Fulton.

Alexander, R. (2004) 'Still no pedagogy? Principle, pragmatism and compliance in primary education', *Cambridge Journal of Education*, 34(1), pp. 7–33.

—— (2005) *Towards Dialogic Teaching: Rethinking Classroom Talk*, 2nd edn, York, Dialogos UK.

Berninger, V.W., Vermeulen, K., Abott, R.D., McCutchen, D., Cotton, S., Cude, J., *et al.* (2003) 'Comparison of three approaches to supplementary reading instruction for low-achieving second-grade readers', *Language, Speech, and Hearing Services in Schools*, 34, pp. 101–16.

Bruner, J. (1996) *The Culture of Education*, Cambridge, MA, Harvard University Press.

Daniels, H. (2001) *Vygotsky and Pedagogy*, London, RoutledgeFalmer.

Daniels, H. and Cole, T. (2002) 'The development of provision for young people with emotional and behavioural difficulties: an activity theory analysis', *Oxford Review of Education*, 28(2/3), pp. 311–29.

Davis, P. and Florian, L. (2004) *Teaching Strategies and Approaches for Pupils with Special Educational Needs: A Scoping Study*, Research Report 516, London, DfES, available online at http://www.dfes.gov.uk/research.

DfES (Department for Education and Skills) (2001) *Special Educational Needs Code of Practice*, London, DfES.

Doyle, R. (2003) 'Developing the nurturing school', *Emotional and Behavioural Difficulties*, 8(4), pp. 252–66

Edwards, A. (2005) 'Let's get beyond community and practice: the many meanings of learning by participating', *The Curriculum Journal*, 16(1), pp. 49–65.

Florian, L. (1998) 'Inclusive practice: what? why? and how?', in C. Tilstone, L. Florian and R. Rose (eds), *Promoting Inclusive Practice*, London, RoutledgeFalmer, pp. 13–26.

—— (2007) 'Reimagining special education', in L. Florian (ed.), *The SAGE Handbook of Special Education*, London, Sage, pp. 7–20.

Florian, L. and Rouse, M. (2001) 'Inclusive practice in English secondary schools: lessons learned', *Cambridge Journal of Education*, 31(3), pp. 399–412.

Gersten, R., Baker, S. and Pugach, M., with Scanlon, D. and Chard, D. (2001) 'Contemporary research on special education teaching', in V. Richardson (ed.), *Handbook of Research on Teaching*, 4th edn, Washington, DC, AERA, pp. 695–722.

Gindis, B. (2003) 'Remediation through education: sociocultural theory and children with special needs', in A. Kozulin, B. Gindis, V.S. Ageyev and S.M. Miller (eds), *Vygotsky's Educational Theory in Cultural Context*, Cambridge University Press, chapter 10.

Hargreaves. D. (1997) 'In defence of research for evidenced-based teaching: a rejoinder to Martyn Hammersley', *British Educational Research Journal*, 24(4), pp. 405–19.

Hart, S., Dixon, A., Drummond, M.J., and McIntyre, D. (2004) *Learning Without Limits*, Maidenhead, Open University Press.

Kershner, R. (2007) 'What do teachers need to know about meeting special educational needs?', in L. Florian (ed.), *The SAGE Handbook of Special Education*, London, Sage, pp. 486–98.

Kershner, R. and Florian, L. (2006) 'Teaching strategies for pupils with SEN: specialist or inclusive pedagogy?', in R. Webb (ed.), *Changing Teaching and Learning in the Primary School*, Maidenhead, Open University Press, pp. 115–27.

Kress, G., Jewitt, C., Ogbord, J., and Tsatsarelis, C. (2001) *Multimodal Teaching and Learning: The Rhetorics of the Science Classroom*, London, Continuum.

Mercer, N. (2000) *Words and Minds*, London, Routledge.

Nussbaum, M.C. (2004) *Hiding from Humanity: Disgust, Shame and the Law*, Princeton, NJ, Princeton University Press.

Sfard, A. (1998) 'On two metaphors for learning and the dangers of choosing just one', *Educational Researcher*, 27(2), pp. 4–13.

Skidmore, D. (2004) *Inclusion: The Dynamic of School Improvement*, Maidenhead, Open University Press.

Tharp, R.G. and Gallimore, R. (1988) *Rousing Minds to Life: Teaching, Learning and Schooling in Social Context*, Cambridge University Press.

de Valenzuela, J.S. (2007) 'Sociocultural view of learning', in L. Florian (ed.), *The SAGE Handbook of Special Education*, London, Sage, pp. 280–9.

Wells, G. (1999) *Dialogic Inquiry: Toward a Sociocultural Practice and Theory of Education*, Cambridge University Press.

Wertsch, J.V. (1991) *Voices of the Mind: A Sociocultural Approach to Mediated Action*, Cambridge, MA, Harvard University Press.

Wyse, D., and Styles, M. (2007) 'Synthetic phonics and the teaching of reading: the debate surrounding England's 'Rose Report', *Literacy*, 47(1), pp. 35–42.

Reflective questions

1   Explain how a sociocultural approach to learning can help to promote a form of pedagogy that is inclusive of all learners. What does this approach offer that is different from other theoretical approaches to learning?

2   What material and symbolic 'tools' have you seen in use in formal and informal educational settings? To what extent does the availability of such tools effect the identification of particular individuals as having 'special educational needs'?

3   In this chapter, we argued that the development of inclusive pedagogy involves complex day-to-day decisions in schools using a combination of teaching strategies and other resources. What is the role and responsiblity of the teacher in understanding and coping with the 'full range of human differences'?

Further reading

Hart, S., Dixon, A., Drummond, M.J., and McIntyre, D. (2004) *Learning without Limits*, Maidenhead, Open University Press.

Tharp, R. G. and Gallimore, R. (1988) *Rousing Minds to Life: Teaching, Learning and Schooling in Social Context*, Cambridge University Press.

de Valenzuela, J.S. (2007) 'Sociocultural view of learning', in L. Florian (ed.), *The SAGE Handbook of Special Education*, London, Sage, pp. 280–9.

3.6 Disability

A complex interaction

Tom Shakespeare

Introduction

In this chapter, I begin to construct an alternative account of disability, one which is based on an interactional or relational understanding. Disability results from an interplay of individual and contextual factors. In other words, people are disabled by society *and* by their bodies. This approach bridges the political gulf between the medical and social models of disability.

First, I should state my theoretical allegiance. In my work, I have found a plurality of approaches beneficial in the analysis of disability. For example feminism offers the concept of the personal being political; Foucault highlights the medical gaze, and the genealogical method; poststructuralism deconstructs notions of identity; postmodernism challenges binary dichotomies and opens up space for complexity; Ian Hacking critiques social constructionism and explores how different ways of conceptualising categories change people's possibilities for self-understanding (Hacking, 2000). The work of Nancy Fraser (1995, 2000) and Axel Honneth (1995) has proved powerful in explaining the demands of radical social movements and the different dimensions of oppression. Rather than tie myself to one view or model, I have tried to take useful elements from different theorists. This selectivity may lead to inconsistency, but avoids the danger of trying to fit the complexities and the nuances of life into an over-rigid structure or system. In order to put my ontological cards on the theoretical table, I should state now that I find the critical realist perspective to be the most helpful and straightforward way of understanding the social world, because it allows for this complexity.

Critical realism means acceptance of an external reality: rather than resorting to relativism or extreme constructionism, critical realism attends to the independent existence of bodies which sometimes hurt, regardless of what we may think or say about those bodies. Critical realists distinguish between ontology (what exists) and epistemology (our ideas about what exists). They believe that there are objects independent of knowledge: labels describe, rather than constitute, disease. In other words, while different cultures have different views or beliefs or attitudes to disability, impairment has always existed and has its own experiential reality. Within disability research, strong statements from the critical realist perspective have been made by Simon Williams (1999) and Danermark and Gellerstedt (2004). Both seek to avoid arguments over medical-model versus social-model perspectives by demanding an approach that gives weight to different causal levels in the complex disability experience. For example, Williams concludes:

> Disability ... is an emergent property, located, temporally speaking, in terms of the interplay

between the biological reality of physiological impairment, structural conditioning (i.e. enablements/constraints) and socio-cultural interaction/elaboration.

(Williams, 1999, p. 810)

whereas Danermark and Gellerstedt suggest:

This implies that injustices to disabled people can be understood neither as generated by solely cultural mechanisms (cultural reductionism) nor by socio-economic mechanisms (economic reductionism) nor by biological mechanisms (biological reductionism). In sum, only by taking different levels, mechanisms and contexts into account, can disability as a phenomenon be analytically approached.

(Danermark and Gellerstedt, 2004, p. 350)

The critical realist perspective appears to offer a good basis on which to elaborate a workable understanding of disability, which combines the best aspects of both the traditional and the radical accounts.

Disability as an interaction

According to those who follow the social model (Oliver, 1990; Barnes, 1998), traditional accounts of disability have been individual and medical in their focus. The alternative social model of disability is a structural and social approach, emphasising barriers and oppression. While the UK disability movement has endorsed the social-model perspective, academic dissenting voices have been raised both within (Morris, 1991; Crow, 1996; French, 1993) and outside (Williams, 1999) the disability studies community. These criticisms have centred on the failure of the social model to recognise the role of impairment, as well as the inability of the social model to encompass the range of different impairment/disability experiences.

The approach to disability which I propose to adopt suggests that disability is always an interaction between individual and structural factors. Rather than getting fixated on defining disability either as a deficit or a structural disadvantage, a holistic understanding is required. The experience of a disabled person results from the relationship between factors intrinsic to the individual, and extrinsic factors arising from the wider context in which she finds herself. Among the intrinsic factors are: the nature and severity of her impairment, her own attitudes to it, her personal qualities and abilities, and her personality. Among the contextual factors are: the attitudes and reactions of others, the extent to which the environment is enabling or disabling, and wider cultural, social and economic issues relevant to disability in that society.

The difference between my interactional approach and the social model is that while I acknowledge the importance of environments and contexts, including discrimination and prejudice, I do not simply define disability as the external disabling barriers or oppression. I thus avoid what Mårten Söder calls 'contextual essentialism'. The problems associated with disability cannot be entirely eliminated by any imaginable form of social arrangements. The priority for a progressive disability politics is to engage with impairment, not to ignore it.

The difference between my approach and what social modelists would describe as the medical model is that I do not explain disability solely in terms of impairment. My approach is non-reductionist, because I accept that limitations are always experienced as an interplay of impairment with particular contexts and environments. Impairment is a necessary but not sufficient factor in the complex interplay of issues which results in disability. Social modelists would claim that 'medical modelists' assume that 'people are disabled by their bodies', whereas they say instead that 'people are disabled by society, not by their bodies'. I would argue that 'people are disabled by society and by their bodies'.

There are similarities between my interactional approach and the relational model adopted by Carol Thomas (1999). She developed her amended version of the social model as a result of the qualitative research she carried out with disabled women. This led her to add the concept of 'impairment effects' to the dualistic conception of impairment and disability which Oliver had outlined. This concept allows Thomas to account for individual limitations which arise from impairment, rather than from social oppression. Thomas has also made two other innovations. First, she argued that disability (by which she means social oppression) has psycho-emotional effects. This I agree with, although I would add that impairment also has psycho-emotional effects. Second, she argued that the original UPIAS (Union of the Physically Impaired Against Segregation) approach should be understood relationally, and that disability should be defined in terms of oppression rather than barriers. She distinguishes (2004a,b) between what she sees as the original UPIAS social relational understanding and the subsequent social model of disability. Thomas equates the social model with a stress on barriers to activity and believes that it is this which has caused the confusion over impairment.

However, in my opinion Thomas has falsely made a distinction between a social oppression and a social barriers version of the social model. Both aspects co-exist in both the UPIAS formulation and the subsequent development of the social model.

Thomas appears to be trying to refine, develop and tweak the social model to deal with the absences, limitations and confusions to which it leads. While she now suggests that the social model should be set to one side (2004b, p. 3), she does not want to abandon it. Although for her it is not a 'credible social interpretation of disability', she believes it is of symbolic importance both because it differentiates disability studies from medical sociology, and orients disability studies to the disability movement.

Thomas and I both agree that a relational approach to understanding disability is needed. By relational, I mean that the disability is a relationship between intrinsic factors (impairment, etc.) and extrinsic factors (environments, support systems, oppression, etc.). However, Thomas uses the term 'social relational' to refer to the relationship of 'those socially constructed as problematically different because of a significant bodily and/or cognitive variation from the norm and those who meet the cultural criteria of embodied normality' (Thomas, 2004b, p. 28).

While recognition of the role of power is important for any theory of disability, Thomas' approach is fatally flawed because it defines disability (and hence disabled people) in terms of oppression – 'Disability is a form of social oppression involving the social imposition of restrictions of activity on people with impairments and the socially engendered undermining of their psycho-emotional wellbeing' (Thomas, 1999, p. 60).

There are a number of problems with this claim:

1   Thomas reproduces the circularity within the traditional social model. If disability is defined in terms of oppression, then this puts social researchers into a difficult position. When researching disability, they are committed to finding that disabled people are oppressed, by definition. The only question is the extent to which disabled people are oppressed. Anders Gustavsson (2004, p. 67) quotes Mårten Söder arguing that this circular reasoning is a particular danger of either clinical or contextual essentialism.

2   It seems that Thomas is further committed to separating two categories: the set of people with impairment (who may experience impairment effects) and within that the subset of disabled people (meaning people with impairment who experience oppres-

sive social reactions in addition to their impairment effects). For example, I may not consider myself to be oppressed much of the time: I certainly have an impairment, and sometimes environments, policies or social reactions are oppressive and damaging to my psycho-emotional wellbeing. Often, however, they are not. In other words, in some situations I am a person with impairment, and in other situations I am a disabled person, according to Thomas' definitions. This seems impractical and confusing.

3   Many disabled people, much of the time, actually experience positive responses from non-disabled people. For example, they may receive support from non-disabled relatives, friends, or strangers who assist them in daily activities. Or they may experience positive benefit from statutory or voluntary services. To define disability entirely in terms of oppression risks obscuring the positive dimension of social relations which enable people with impairment.

Note the difference between the impairment/disability distinction, and the sex/gender distinction with which it is often compared. Feminists (for example Oakley, 1972) distinguished between biological sex (male/female) and socio-cultural gender (masculine/feminine). They argued that to be a man or woman in a particular historical and cultural context was a social, not a biological, experience. Yet they did not claim that gender equalled oppression, even though they provided evidence that women had historically been oppressed in different ways. Gender was socio-cultural, and often associated with oppression. Compare Thomas' view of disability: impairment is defined, in the social model, as an individual biological attribute (corresponding to sex for the feminists). But the social model does not define disability as the socio-cultural experience of impairment. Instead, disability is defined as oppression – or in Thomas' phrase 'forms of oppressive social reaction visited upon people with impairments' (2004b, p. 579).

Thomas argues (2004b) that I am committed to a commonplace meaning of disability as 'not being able to do things' and as 'restricted activity'. I deny her interpretation of the position outlined in Shakespeare and Watson (2001). Then, as now, I define disability as the outcome of the interaction between individual and contextual factors – which includes impairment, personality, individual attitudes, environment, policy and culture. Rather than reserving the word disability for 'impairment effects' or 'oppression' or 'barriers', I would rather use the term broadly to describe the whole interplay of different factors which make up the experience of people with impairments. Impairment is a necessary but not sufficient element in the disability relationship. It is always the combination of a certain set of physical or mental attributes, in a particular physical environment, within a specified social relationship, played out within a broader cultural and political context, which combines to create the experience of disability for any individual or group of individuals (Sim *et al.*, 1998). I am happy to accept that both social barriers and oppression play a part in generating disability for many disabled people in many contexts. But I cannot accept that disability should be defined as either social barriers or oppression.

I would not claim to have a wholly new and original understanding of disability. The obviousness of my conception is one of its merits, and others have argued very similar things (Williams, 1999; Danermark and Gellerstedt, 2004; Gabel and Peters, 2004). For example, the Nordic relational approach corresponds closely to my understanding of disability: Anders Gustavsson talks about the relative interactionist perspective as an alternative to essentialism, 'a theoretical perspective that rejects assumptions about any primordial analytical level and rather takes a programmatic position in favor of studying disability on several different analytical levels' (Gustavsson, 2004, p. 62).

A recent paper by van den Ven and a Dutch team (van den Ven *et al.*, 2005) came to a similar conclusion based on qualitative research. They concluded:

> Both the individual with a disability and others in society have a shared responsibility with respect to the integration of people with disabilities into society. Each must play their part for integration to occur: it takes two to tango. An individual with a disability should be willing to function in society and adopt an attitude towards others in society in such a way that they can join in with activities and people in society. On the other hand society should take actions to make functioning in society possible for people with disabilities. In other words, society should be inclusive with respect to people with disabilities by passing laws on anti-discrimination, ensuring accessibility of buildings and arranging appropriate care facilities for people with disabilities.
>
> (van den Ven *et al.*, 2005, p. 324)

These authors, like myself, balance medical and social aspects. They refer to three issues which influence integration: individual factors, which include personality and skills as well as impairment; societal factors, referring to accessibility, attitudes, etc.; and factors within the system of support, by which they mean social support, professional care and assistive devices. The interrelation of these three sets of factors determines or produces disability. This research team adopt a conception of integration which I also find helpful. They highlight five elements:

1   functioning in an ordinary way without getting special attention or being singled out as a result of disability;
2   mixing with others and not being ignored in friendship and networks;
3   taking part in and contributing to society whether through paid work or volunteering;
4   trying to realise one's potential – which may need help from others;
5   being director of one's life.

This approach seems adequate to the complexity and diversity of disabled people and their aspirations, and a helpful basis for future research.

Thomas (2004a) is right to suggest that there are no contradictions between my own understanding and that of Williams or Bury, or indeed of the WHO's International Classification of Functioning, Disability and Health (ICF). The medico-psycho-social model which lies at the heart of the ICF does seem to me a sensible and practical way of understanding the complexity of disability. Some disability rights commentators have rejected the new WHO framework as being no more than a rebadging of the discredited International Classification of Impairments, Disabilities and Handicaps (Pfeiffer, 1998, 2000; Hurst, 2000). Yet the new approach does recognise the role of the environment in causing restriction (Imrie, 2004). It does not use the term 'disability' to refer to either impairment, functional limitation or indeed environmental barriers, but uses it to describe the entire process:

> the locus of the problem and the focus of intervention are situated not solely within the individuals, but also within their physical, social and attitudinal environments. The label of disability becomes a description of the outcome of the interaction of the individual and the environment and not merely a label applied to a person.
>
> (Bornman, 2004, p. 186)

Following Zola (1989), the ICF framers recognise that the entire population is at risk of impairment and its consequences (Bickenbach *et al.*, 1999). While Rob Imrie (2004) is correct to note that the ICF is theoretically underdeveloped, for all these reasons I believe that it offers a way forward for defining and researching disability, and should be endorsed by disability studies.

An interactional model is able to account for the range and diversity of disability experiences. For example, there can be variation depending on the nature and extent of the impairment. Simo Verdant (2008) has written about Steve, a man with profound intellectual impairments. Steve cannot communicate or live independently, let alone work. However, he can respond to certain stimuli and can express pleasure and pain. Verdant argues that Steve will not be helped by initiatives such as independent living, civil rights or barrier removal: they will not make a difference to his life, because his impairment is so limiting. Any social theory of disability has to avoid the error of conflating the variety of disabled people's experience. Impairment is scalar and multi-dimensional, and differences in impairment contribute to the level of social disadvantage which individuals face.

Failure to appreciate the impairment continuum contributes to some of the sterile arguments about the nature of disability. It appears to me that some of those who see disability as a tragedy which should be prevented at all costs are seeing only the most severe end of the continuum. And some of those who deny that impairment can be problematic, and see disability as just another difference, are seeing only the milder end of the continuum. In other words, the two camps are talking at cross-purposes: because they think of different cases when they discuss disability, they are unable to come to agreement about how disability should be understood or defined.

A related phenomenon is the distinction which disability studies theorists have attempted to draw between chronic illness and impairment. This appears to be an attempt to reject the critique of medical sociologists such as Michael Bury, Gareth Williams and Michael Kelly (Barnes and Mercer, 1996). It also shores up the social model by emphasising disabled people who have static conditions which do not degenerate or need medical care. But in practice it is hard to say that people with multiple sclerosis, HIV/AIDS or cystic fibrosis are not disabled people, and it has been important to include such conditions in disability discrimination legislation. For some individuals impairment is a major limiting factor, which renders any social manipulation or barrier removal almost irrelevant. For others, impairment itself causes little restriction: it is the reaction of others which causes problems of exclusion and disadvantage. The interactional model can allow for this variation.

One of the reasons why disability rights activists and disability studies have been unwilling to look too closely at the issue of impairment differences is perhaps the fear of reinforcing a hierarchy of disability. There is a reluctance to imply that some disabled people are better or more worthy than others. Yet it seems to me inescapable that some forms of impairments are more limiting than others. Some disabled people are very restricted by their impairments, and others are not.

A precise ranking of impairment is of course very difficult, because it depends on subjective or cultural judgements as to how different factors are weighted: presence of pain, reduced life expectancy, visibility, mobility and other aspects would presumably be viewed differently by different people. It seems likely that, in general, disabled people come to terms with their own personal circumstances, while often thinking of other impairments as harder to deal with: the human capacity for accommodation and adaptation to adverse circumstances is extraordinary (Albrecht and Devlieger, 1999). Despite the reluctance to admit it, there are many instances of disabled people themselves adopting a hierarchy of impairment (Deal, 2003).

None of these claims contradict two important points which disability studies has asserted strongly. First, non-disabled people generally perceive impairment to be far more negative and limiting than those who experience it directly (Young, 1997). Second, social barriers and social oppression are major factors in the lives of people with impairment, and for many disabled people cause more problems than their impairment. A key dimension of disability is the extent to which a society removes barriers and enables people to participate, regardless of their individual differences. The value of the social-model tradition is in highlighting oppression and exclusion, issues which have been neglected in all previous research on disability. Yet impairment almost always plays some role in the lives of disabled people, even if social arrangements or cultural context minimises the exclusion or disadvantage.

As the Dutch research highlights, the interactional approach also makes space for an often neglected aspect of disablement: personal attitudes and motivation. It is not just the extent or nature of impairment, or the extent of the barriers and oppression which dictate the extent of disadvantage. For example, people with very similar impairments in the same society have different experiences, depending on their attitudes and reactions to their situation. Enabling disabled people to take a more positive approach and enhancing their self-esteem and self-confidence may sometimes transform their lives as much as providing better facilities or access to medical treatments. Joining a self-advocacy or disability rights group can change an individual's attitudes to themselves and their situation, enabling them to take control of their lives and become more effective.

The interactional approach also highlights the different ways in which the situation of disabled people can be improved. Traditional approaches to disability stress medical cure and rehabilitation. Social model approaches stress barrier removal and anti-discrimination legislation. For example, Michael Oliver has suggested that:

> the social model is not an attempt to deal with the personal restrictions of impairment but the social barriers of disability ... [It is a] pragmatic attempt to identify and address issues that can be changed through collective action rather than medical or professional treatment.
>
> (Oliver, 1996, p. 38)

However, the reality is that disabled people are affected by physical, psychological and external problems. A theory which addresses only external barriers is an incomplete response to the challenge of disability. Substituting medical or professional treatment for social change and barrier removal is also unacceptable. Both approaches are needed.

An interactional approach allows for the different levels of experience, ranging from the medical, through the psychological, to the environmental, economic and political. Rather than dismissing individual interventions as reactionary and structural change as progressive, this approach allows each option to be discussed on its merits. An interactional approach would suggest there are many different factors which could be addressed to improve quality of life: coaching or therapy to improve self-esteem; medical intervention to restore functioning or reduce pain; aids and adaptations; barrier removal; anti-discrimination and attitudinal change; better benefits and services. Given the multiple and non-contradictory options for intervention, a debate is needed as to which approach is the most appropriate or cost-effective for different impairments or specific individuals. There can be no prior assumption that one approach is automatically preferable in all cases. The notion of *appropriate interventions* suggests that judgements about how to improve individual situations are complex, and should be based on evidence, not ideology. Cases such as limb-lengthening, cochlear implants and cosmetic surgery for children with Down syndrome illustrate the contested nature of these decisions. Evaluations of particular new technologies – for example, the Ibot wheelchairs which can negotiate steps and raise individuals to reach high and make eye contact – are also relevant. Such assistive technology overcomes architectural barriers: is investment in very expensive equipment a distraction from campaigning for universal design?

Ubiquity of impairment

The interactional approach to understanding disability as a complex and multifactorial phenomenon necessitates coming to terms with impairment. Critiquing the social model, I argued that impairment was important to many disabled people, and had to be adequately theorised in any social theory of disability. Until now, only two alternatives have been offered: what Michael Oliver calls 'medical tragedy theory', and the denial or neglect of impairment within social model theory. Impairment is not the end of the world, tragic or pathological. But neither is it irrelevant or just another difference. Many disabled people are unable to view impairment as neutral, as Michael Oliver and Bob Sapey concede in the second edition of *Social Work with Disabled People*:

> Some disabled people do experience the onset of impairments as a personal tragedy which, while not invalidating the argument that they are being excluded from a range of activities by a disabling environment, does mean it would be inappropriate to deny that impairment can be experienced in this way.
>
> (Oliver and Sapey, 1998, p. 26)

Instead of the polarised and one-dimensional accounts in both traditional research and disability studies, a nuanced attitude is needed, involving a fundamental ambivalence. Disability studies needs to capture the fact that impairment may not be neutral, but neither is it always all-defining and terrible.

One way of capturing the complexity of impairment is to view it as a *predicament*. The *Concise Oxford Dictionary* defines predicament as 'an unpleasant, trying or dangerous situation'. Although still negative, this does not have the inescapable emphasis of 'tragedy'. The notion of 'trying' perhaps captures the difficulties which many impairments present. They make life harder, although this hardship can be overcome. The added burdens of social oppression and social exclusion, which turn impairment into disadvantage, need to be removed: this seems to me very much the spirit of the original UPIAS approach to disability. Everything possible needs to be provided to make coping with impairment easier. But even with the removal of barriers and the provision of support, impairment will remain problematic for many disabled people.

For example, I have restricted growth. This is a very visible impairment, but is comparatively minor. The main effect in daily life is that many people stare at me. This is because the vast majority of people do not have restricted growth and are unfamiliar with people with restricted growth. For them, and particularly for children, dwarfs are fascinating. Education can reduce but will never eliminate this natural curiosity. Therefore, I will always be stared at. This is not pleasant, even if people are not actually hostile. I cannot escape the awareness of my abnormal embodiment, however much I am happy and successful as an individual. But I do not think these reactions can easily be explained away as oppression. They are a fact of life, like the vulnerability to back problems which is another dimension of my impairment.

No amount of civil rights or social inclusion will entirely remove either of these dimensions of my predicament as a dwarf.

Similarly, many of the persistent environmental barriers discussed previously might better be theorised as predicaments. The predicament of impairment – the intrinsic difficulties of engaging with the world, the pains and sufferings and limitations of the body – mean that impairment is not neutral. It may bring insights and experiences which are positive, and for some these may even outweigh the disadvantages. But that does not mean that we should not try to minimise the number of people who are impaired, or the extent to which they are impaired.

It is not only impairment which is a predicament. For example, Zygmunt Bauman argues that 'The postmodern mind is reconciled to the idea that the messiness of the human predicament is here to stay. This is, in the broadest of outlines, what can be called postmodern wisdom' (Bauman, 1993, p. 245). Other aspects of embodiment – for example, the pains of menstruation or childbirth for women – could also be understood through the predicament concept, as could the inevitability and tragedy of death. To call something a predicament is to understand it as a difficulty, and as a challenge, and as something which we might want to minimise but which we cannot ultimately avoid. As Sebastiano Timpanaro suggests, 'physical illness ... cannot be ascribed solely to bad social arrangements: it has its zone of autonomous and invincible reality' (Timpanaro, 1975, p. 20). But this is not to fall into the trap of regarding impairment as a tragedy or an identity-defining flaw.

Some people will object to what appears to be a negative approach to impairment. They should note that I am not denigrating disabled people, nor claiming that impairment makes disabled people second-class citizens or less worthy of support and respect. Disabled people are often inferior to non-disabled people in terms of health, function or ability, but they are not lesser in terms of moral worth, political equality or human rights. The suffering and happiness of disabled people matters just as much as that of non-disabled people.

If impairment truly was neutral – or beneficial – then we could have no objection to someone who deliberately impaired a child. If impairment was just another difference, then, as John Harris (1993, 2001) points out, there would be nothing wrong with painlessly altering a baby so they could no longer see, or could no longer hear or had to use a wheelchair. Even if no suffering or pain was caused in the process, we would surely consider this irresponsible and immoral. Something would have been lost. The implication of this must be that impairment prevention should have an important role in social responses to disability. This does not undermine the worth or citizenship of existing disabled people. It suggests that because impairment causes predicaments and is limiting in various ways, we should take steps to prevent or mitigate it, where possible.

Furthermore, the connection to other embodiment predicaments underlines a commonplace observation which was made central in the work of Irving Zola (1989), and which has great significance for a post-social-model approach to disability (see also Bickenbach *et al.*, 1999). Impairment is a universal phenomenon, in the sense that every human being has limitations and vulnerabilities (Sutherland, 1981) and ultimately is mortal. Across the life span, everyone experiences impairment and limitation. Impairment is more likely to be acquired than congenital: ageing is particularly associated with increased levels of impairment. The ubiquity of impairment is underscored by the Human Genome Project which has shown that everyone has hundreds of mutations in their genome, many of which may predispose the individual to illness or impairment. In this sense, genetic diagnosis is toxic knowledge, which has the power to turn healthy people into pre-impaired people.

To claim that 'everyone is impaired' should not lead to any trivialising of impairment or the experience of disabled people. As I have stated previously, impairments differ in their impact. It is important to respect real differences – particularly the extent to which people are affected by suffering and restriction. At the extreme, as Alastair MacIntyre argues, are very severely impaired people, 'such that they can never be more than passive members of the community, not recognizing, not speaking or not speaking intelligibly, suffering, but not acting' (1999, p. 127). It would be wrong to neglect the particular needs which arise from these different differences.

Not everyone is impaired all the time. Taking a life-course view of impairment highlights the ways that impairment is manifested over time: disabled children grow up to be non-disabled adults, non-disabled people become impaired through accident or in old age. Impairments can be variable and episodic: sometimes people recover, and sometimes impairments worsen. The nature and meaning of impairment is not given in any one moment. Not all people with impairment have the same needs, or are disadvantaged to the same extent. Moreover, different people experience different levels of social disadvantage or social exclusion, because society is geared to accommodate people with certain impairments, but not others. Everyone may be impaired, but not everyone is oppressed.

The benefits of regarding every human being as living with the predicament of impairment are that it forces us to pay attention to what we have in common; it counsels us to accept the inextricable limitation of life, rather than to deny or fight against it; it suggests the need to re-evaluate disabled people; it focuses attention on the social aspects of disability. For example, if everyone is impaired, why are certain impairments remedied or accepted, and others not? Why does impairment result in exclusion in some cases and not others? These processes and choices are largely social and structural and can be changed. In policy terms, a universal approach would use the range of human variation as the basis for universal design and aim for justice in the distribution of resources and opportunities. Disabled people would not be expected to identify themselves as separate and incompetent, in order to qualify for provision.

Conclusion

The complex reality of impairment suggests that equalising the situation for disabled people will necessarily be more complex and difficult than equalising the situation for women and other minorities. As Jerome Bickenbach *et al.* (1999) have argued, disabled people experience both restrictions of negative freedom – in the form of discrimination which prevents them achieving their potential – but also restrictions of positive freedom because they cannot participate freely in society. 'The denial of opportunities and resources is an issue, not of discrimination, but of distributive injustice – an unfair distribution of social resources and opportunities that results in limitations of participation in all areas of social life' (Bickenbach *et al.*, 1999, p. 110).

Ending disablism – unfair discrimination against disabled people – will not solve all the problems of disabled people. Even if environments and transports were accessible and there was no unfair discrimination on the basis of disability, many disabled people would still be disadvantaged. For example, it is well known that some impairments generate extra costs – heating, equipment, diet (Smith *et al.*, 2005). Many disabled people require personal assistance or care. And while many disabled people could work just as productively as non-disabled people, once discrimination was fully removed, this does not apply to all disabled people. Some disabled people are unable to work a seven-hour day or a five-day week, due to fatigue. Some disabled people are unable to work at the intensity or productivity of non-disabled workers. Some disabled people are very limited in the types of tasks they are able to perform. And, of course, some disabled people are entirely unable to work.

This problem has been noted by several commentators. For example, Henley (2001) discusses the ways in which the emphasis on normalisation in policy towards people with learning difficulties in the 1980s led to the closing of day centres and other projects. In 1984 the King's Fund published *An Ordinary Working Life*, which stated that paid employment for all people with learning difficulties was an achievable aim (Henley, 2001, p. 940). While many more people with learning difficulties undoubtedly can work than were working at the time, it is unrealistic to suggest that this is an option for all:

> The lesson to be learnt from the past is that the policy of pursuing total inclusion for all people with learning disabilities and encouraging the decimation of all forms of specialist service support in the process has, in practice, proved to be fundamentally flawed.
>
> (Henley, 2001, p. 946)

Paul Abberley also notes that 'even in a society which did make profound, genuine attempts, well supported by a financial provision, to integrate profoundly impaired people into the world of work, some would be excluded' (Abberley, 2001, p. 131). Paul Hunt (1966) also challenged the focus on work, arguing that disabled people outside the labour market contributed to society in different ways, not least by challenging utilitarian values.

Analysing the Disability Discrimination Act, Gooding argues that more is required than treating everyone the same (Gooding, 2000, p. 536). Society's failure to meet the needs of disabled people cannot be accounted for simply by the concept of disablism. The strategy of promoting employment, while very desirable, will also leave a residuum of unemployed and unemployable disabled people. Disability includes intrinsic limitation and disadvantage. Societies will need to address this, by making additional investment to equalise the situation between disabled and non-disabled people – not just equal opportunities, but redistribution.

While disability studies and disability rights movements have criticised individual and medical approaches to disability, the focus on civil rights still implies a liberal solution to the disability problem (Russell, 2002). Anti-discrimination law and independent living solutions seem to suggest that the market will provide, if only disabled people are enabled to exercise choices free of unfair discrimination. But market approaches often restrict, rather than increase, choice to disabled people (Williams, 1983; Wilson *et al.*, 2000). An individual, market-based solution, by failing to acknowledge persistent inequalities in physical and mental capacities, cannot liberate all disabled people.

Human beings are not all the same, and do not all have the same capabilities and limitations. Need is variable, and disabled people are among those who need more from others and from their society. Alastair MacIntyre begins to explore the political implications of this reality:

> a form of political society in which it is taken for granted that disability and dependence on others are something that all of us experience at certain times in our lives and this to unpredictable degrees, and that consequently our interest in how the needs of the disabled are adequately voiced and met is not a special interest, the interest of one particular group rather than of others, but rather the interest of the whole political society, an interest that is integral to their conception of their common good.
>
> (MacIntyre, 1999, p. 130)

This seems as radical as, and more adequate than, a social-model denial of the persistence of impairment as a factor in creating disadvantage. Impairment is not usually a matter of individual responsibility: it arises from the random effect of genes or disease, or the socially created costs of work, warfare, poverty, or from the natural effects of the ageing process. If disabled people have equal moral worth to non-disabled people – and are viewed politically as equal citizens – then justice demands social arrangements which compensate for both the natural lottery and socially caused injury. Creating a level playing field is not enough: redistribution is required to promote true social inclusion.

Acknowledgement

Reproduced with permission of Routledge from *Disability Rights and Wrongs*, by Tom Shakespeare, London, Routledge, 2006, pp. 54–67.

References

Abberley, P. (2001) 'Work, disability and European social theory', in C. Barnes, M. Oliver and L. Barton (eds), *Disability Studies Today*, Cambridge, Polity, pp. 120–38.

Albrecht, G.L. and Devlieger, P.J. (1999) 'The disability paradox: high quality of life against all odds', *Social Science and Medicine*, 48, pp. 977–88.

Barnes, C. (1998) 'The social model of disability: a sociological phenomenon ignored by sociologists', in T. Shakespeare (ed.), *The Disability Reader*, London, Cassell, pp. 65–78.

Barnes, C. and Mercer, G. (1996) *Exploring the Divide: Illness and Disability*, Leeds, The Disability Press.

Bauman, Z. (1993) *Postmodern Ethics*, Oxford, Blackwell.

Bickenbach, J.E., Chatterji, S., Badley, E.M. and Utsun, T.B. (1999) 'Models of disablement, universalism and the international classification of impairments, disabilities and handicaps', *Social Science and Medicine*, 48, pp. 1173–87.

Bornman, J. (2004) 'The World Health Organization's terminology and classification: application to severe disability', *Disability and Rehabilitation*, 26(3), pp. 182–8.

Crow, L. (1996) 'Including all our lives', in J. Morris (ed.), *Encounters with Strangers: Feminism and Disability*, London, Women's Press, pp. 206–26.

Danermark, B. and Gellerstedt, L.C. (2004) 'Social justice: redistribution and recognition – a non-reductionist perspective on disability', *Disability and Society*, 19, 4, pp. 339–53.

Deal, M. (2003) 'Disabled people's attitudes towards other impairment groups: a hierarchy of impairment', *Disability and Society*, 18(7), pp. 897–910.

Fraser, N. (1995) 'From redistribution to recognition', *New Left Review*, 212, pp. 68–92.

—— (2000) 'Rethinking recognition', *New Left Review*, 3, pp. 107–20.

French, S. (1993) 'Disability, impairment or something in between', in J. Swain, S. French, C. Barnes and C. Thomas (eds), *Disabling Barriers, Enabling Environments*, London, Sage, pp. 17–25.

Gable, S. and Peters, S. (2004) 'Presage of a paradigm shift? Beyond the social model of disability toward resistance theories of disability', *Disability and Society*, 19(6), pp. 585–600.

Gooding, C. (2000) 'Disability Discrimination Act: from statute to practice', *Critical Social Policy*, 20(4), pp. 533–49.

Gustavsson, A. (2004) 'The role of theory in disability research: springboard or straitjacket?', *Scandinavian Journal of Disability Research*, 6(1), pp. 55–70.

Hacking, I. (2000) *The Social Construction of What?*, Cambridge, MA, Harvard University Press.

Harris, J. (1993) 'Is gene therapy a form of eugenics?', *Bioethics*, 7, pp. 178–87.

—— (2001) 'One principle and three fallacies of disability studies', *Journal of Medical Ethics*, 27(6), pp. 383–8.

Henley, C. A. (2001) 'Good intentions – unpredictable consequences', *Disability and Society*, 16(7), pp. 933–47.

Honneth, A. (1995) *The Struggle for Recognition: The Moral Grammar of Social Conflicts*, Cambridge, Polity.

Hunt, P. (ed.) (1966) *Stigma*, London, Geoffrey Chapman Publishing.

Hurst, R. (2000) 'To revise or not to revise?', *Disability and Society*, 15(7), pp. 1083–7.

Imrie, R. (2004) 'Demystifying disability: a review of the International Classification of Functioning, Disability and Health', *Sociology of Health and Illness*, 26(3), pp. 287–305.

MacIntyre, A. (1999) *Dependent Rational Animals: Why Human Beings Need the Virtues*, London, Duckworth.

Morris, J. (1991) *Pride against Prejudice*, London, Women's Press.

Oakley, A. (1972) *Sex, Gender and Society*, London, Gower.

Oliver, M. (1990) *The Politics of Disablement*, London, Macmillan.

—— (1996) *Understanding Disability: From Theory to Practice*, Basingstoke, Macmillan.

Oliver, M. and Sapey, B. (1998) *Social Work with Disabled People* (2nd edition), Basingstoke, Palgrave Macmillan.

Pfeiffer, D. (1998) 'The ICIDH and the need for its revision', *Disability and Society*, 3(4), pp. 503–23.

—— (2000) 'The devil is in the details: the ICIDH2 and the disability movement', *Disability and Society*, 15(7), pp. 1079–82.

Russell, M. (2002) 'What disability civil rights cannot do: employment and political economy', *Disability and Society*, 17(2), pp. 117–35.

Shakespeare, T.W. and Watson, N. (2001) 'The social model of disability: an outdated ideology?', in S. Barnarrt and B.M. Altman (eds), *Exploring Theories and Expanding Methodologies: Where are We and Where do We Need to Go?*, Research in Social Science and Disability, vol. 2, Amsterdam, JAI, pp. 9–28.

Sim, A.J., Milner, J., Love, J. and Lishman, J. (1998) 'Definitions of need: can disabled people and care professionals agree?', *Disability and Society*, 13(1), pp. 53–74.

Smith, N., Middleton, S., Ashton-Brooks, K., Cox, L. and Dobson, B., with Reith, L. (2005) *Disabled People's Costs of Living: 'More Than You Would Think'*, York, Joseph Rowntree Foundation.

Sutherland, A. (1981) *Disabled We Stand*, London, Souvenir Press.

Thomas, C. (1999) *Female Forms: Experiencing and Understanding Disability*, Buckingham, Open University Press.

—— (2004a) 'How is disability understood?', *Disability and Society*, 19(6), pp. 563–8.

—— (2004b) 'Rescuing a social relational understanding of disability', *Scandinavian Journal of Disability Research*, 6(1), pp. 22–36.

Timpanaro, S. (1975) *On Materialism*, London, New Left Books.

van den Ven, L., Post, M., de Witte, L. and van den Heuvel, W. (2005) 'It takes two to tango: the integration of people with disabilities into society', *Disability and Society*, 20(3), pp. 311–29.

Verdant, S. (2008) 'The who or what of Steve: severe intellectual impairment and its implications', in M. Häyry, T. Takala, P. Herissone-Kelly and G. Arnason (eds), *Arguments and Analysis in Bioethics*, New York and Amsterdam, Rodopi, pp. 243–59.

Williams, G. (1983) 'The movement for independent living: an evaluation and a critique', *Social Science and Medicine*, 17(15), pp. 1003–10.

Williams, S. J. (1999) 'Is anybody there? Critical realisms, chronic illness and the disability debate', *Sociology of Health and Illness*, 21(6), pp. 797–819.

Wilson, A., Riddell, S., Baron, S. (2000) 'Welfare for those who can? The impact of the quasi-market on the lives of people with learning difficulties', *Critical Social Policy*, 20(4), pp. 479–502.

Young, I. M. (1997) 'Asymmetrical reciprocity: on moral respect, wonder, and enlarged thought', *Constellations*, 3(3), pp. 340–63.

Zola, I. K. (1989) 'Towards the necessary universalizing of a disability policy', *The Milbank Quarterly*, 67, suppl. 2, pt. 2, pp. 401–28.

Reflective question

Drawing on your experience, consider the ways in which your organisation gathers the views of students that would inform an understanding of the barriers children face in learning and the supports they find helpful – from their own perspective. How is this information used to inform developments in provision?

Further reading

Tom Shakespeare's book *Disability Rights and Wrongs* created some interesting and often hotly contested divergences in opinion in the disability world. In order to understand these you might find it useful to read the following review symposium:

Review Symposium: *Disability Rights and Wrongs?* Reviewed by Alison Sheldon, Rannveig Traustadóttir, Peter Beresford, Kathy Boxall and Mike Oliver, *Disability and Society*, 22(2), March 2007, 209–34.
Best, S. (2007) 'The social construction of pain: an evaluation', *Disability and Society*, 22(2), 161–71.

Section 4

Policy and governance

Introduction

Hugh Lauder

(Cartoon by Ros Asquith)

In Chapter 4.1 David Hopkins outlines what he calls the 'high challenge, high support' approach to systemic reform. The idea that governments can influence 'standards' of education on a national or system-wide basis has been attractive because education is now seen to be in the service of an economy in which ideas and the manipulation of abstract symbol systems are deemed vital to competitiveness. England has gone further than any other country in seeking to develop what can only be described as a 'state theory of learning'. But the approach taken has clearly proved attractive to the federal government in the United States and in other countries. That it should do so appears quite extraordinary given the many competing theories of learning available, some of which are discussed in this book. To choose, therefore, key elements of a particular theory and to mandate them in classrooms and schools is surprising. It can be seen as a form of educational engineering on a grand scale with attendant risks if experience teaches us that it is not an effective theory.

Hopkins's chapter celebrates this state theory of learning, hailing it as a success because of the way it has been underpinned by what he calls key drivers. These drivers describe the key features of the theory: targets, accountability in relation to the targets, devolved responsibility to schools for meeting the targets, intervention where schools have not achieved the targets and access to best practice professional development.

It will be readily apparent that targets and accountability permeate the system. From the age of five children takes tests on a regular basis and on their performance teachers and schools are held to account. In primary schools the focus is on literacy, numeracy and science and the first two there have mandated forms of pedagogy. It is, in other words, a highly regulated system in which performance can be measured quantitatively by test results. The attendant theory of motivation is that teachers and pupils will be driven to improve against the state determined performance targets.

However, Hopkins recognises that such a system may generate initial early gains but that more is required to move the system from one of 'prescription' to one of 'professionalism'. This entails a greater degree of autonomy for teachers but within the context of what he calls 'intelligent accountability'. Hopkins sees this as an incremental approach but there are questions to be asked of his claim as to the success of the present system and how an incremental approach might work.

In contrast to David Hopkins's view, Harry Torrance takes issue with the idea that assessment has been used successfully to change teaching. Where Hopkins sees assessment in the cause of accountability as a success story, Torrance sees, with some qualification, the opposite. While schools are still held accountable to targets, the government manipulates the basis on which judgements about its performance can be made.

However, for teachers, the fundamental problem with a test-driven pedagogy is that it encourages teaching pupils to pass tests rather than to be educated. And Torrance argues, and Hopkins may well agree on this point, that the improvement in test results may be in significant part due to teachers training pupils to take the test. Here, the two may well move towards a consensus, for Hopkins recognises Torrance's point that, 'Central control of the curriculum and of testing may have been a short term solution ... but it will always threaten long term systemic sustainability'.

While Hopkins and Torrance may debate the successes and failure of the state theory of learning, Robinson and Stables ask more fundamental questions about both the policy process and the nature of the school.

Viviane Robinson starts from the observation that very few attempts at policy design and implementation in schools are successful. She identifies three broad problems with respect to policy. The problem that policy is designed to address may be too complex for a single or simple 'solution'. The contexts in which policy is implemented may vary; this is particularly so if the culture of the school may be different from that of the authority seeking to implement change. Finally, there may be problems of policy design and also implementation. It will be apparent from the above discussion that accountability-driven school reform may have limited use and significant unintended consequences. Robinson then uses her analysis to understand the failures of comprehensive school reform in two case studies. This analysis takes her to an important conclusion: policy requires theoretical analysis and debate. Here there may be differences between the theories held by policy makers and teachers about a particular policy intervention. Critically comparing and contrasting these theories then becomes a crucial part of a process by which policy intervention can be successful.

It will be apparent that within such a prescription lies an account of the policy process in which a top-down approach, such as that described by Hopkins's first phase of system reform, is unlikely to be successful.

While Robinson raises some important questions about the relationship of policy to practice, Andy Stables asks a fundamental question about the nature of schools. If Young has asked the question, 'what are schools for?' then Stables asks the similarly challenging question, 'what are schools?'. In the chapter by Hopkins it is clear that the state theory of learning presupposes a rather mechanical, 'system' view of schools: given the right 'drivers' or levers improvement will follow. This is no doubt the dominant policy makers' view of schools and the school system, but Stables has a radically different view of schools which challenges this official perception. He starts from the assumption that the meaning of 'school' is dependent upon actors' perceptions and that these are dependent on factors beyond the school. Rather in the same way as a nation is an imagined community in that its citizens need to project well beyond their locality and acquaintances in order to 'comprehend' the nation, so the same is true of schools. From this basis he argues that the notion of a 'good' or 'bad' school cannot be generalised, for example, from statistics because quantitative data 'cannot capture the indefinable range of experiences and indeed imaginings relating to any particular school'. Yet it is precisely this that the state theory of learning and accountability seeks to do. But from this point of departure Stables draws some surprising and certainly radical conclusions, when judged against current policy orthodoxy: what is important about a school is how it is imagined by those who imagine it and policy makers are only a tiny part of this process of imagining, with a limited engagement with it. They visit schools rarely, and no school on a frequent basis, consequently they have little understanding of how others in the school community may imagine it. Consequently, policy should be made at a decentralised level amongst those who 'imagine' their school.

4.1 Realising the potential of system reform

David Hopkins

Introduction

For a country to succeed it needs both a competitive economy and an inclusive society. That requires an education system with high standards, which transmits and develops knowledge and culture from one generation to the next, promotes respect for and engagement with learning, broadens horizons and develops high expectations. We want to ensure all young people progressively develop the knowledge, understanding, skills, attitudes and values in the curriculum, and become effective, enthusiastic and independent learners, committed to lifelong learning and able to handle the demands of adult life. This is a pretty good description of an educational system committed to ensuring that every school is at least a good school and that most are on the journey to becoming great.

Unfortunately, national policy in educational reform until recently has proved inadequate to the challenge of delivering such education systems. So much so that in the early 1990s, Milbrey McLaughlin (1990, p. 11), on the basis of her reanalysis of the extensive Rand Change Agent study, originally conducted in the United States during the 1970s, asserted that 'policy does not mandate what matters'. This mantra caught the zeitgeist and established an orthodoxy that conditioned policy, research and practice for the first half of the decade.

By the mid-1990s, however, the almost global concern over standards of learning and achievement led to a renewed interest in large-scale change. Many national and local governments were advocating programmes commonly called 'performance-based reform' in an effort to raise standards across local and regional boundaries. The general approach was to set targets for performance and then hold schools responsible for meeting them. This fairly crude approach to raising standards predictably had little positive impact on student achievement. Leithwood's meta-analysis of five such programmes noted the 'disappointing contribution that performance-base reforms have made to improving the core technology of schooling' (Leithwood *et al.*, 1999, p. 40).

Although the impact of large-scale change on student achievement is notoriously fickle, the fact that these reform strategies neglected to focus on teaching and learning and capacity building must have contributed to their inability to impact positively on student achievement. The argument that I am making in this chapter is that unless reform strategies address the context of teaching and learning, as well as capacity building at the school level, then the aspirations societies have for their educational systems will never be realised.

In making the case in this chapter for the potential of systemic reform to enable every student to reach their potential and for every school to be great, I will:

- refer to the experience of primary schooling in England as a paradigmatic example of the transition from large-scale to system-wide reform;
- clarify the central policy conundrum of balancing national prescription with schools leading reform;
- identify the four key drivers that underpin system change;
- propose the concept of system leadership; and
- suggest a model for coherent system reform.

The case of primary schooling in England

Although the reform effort in England has involved both primary (elementary education for 5–11-year-olds) and secondary schools (ages 11–16 or 11–18 for those schools with 'sixth forms') the focus of this section will reflect the performance of students within the 5–11-year age range during the first two terms of the New Labour government. The reason is that it is here where the link between reform strategy and student performance is most clearly seen.

England has since 1997 taken the opportunity to achieve high standards across an entire system of 24,000 schools and over 7 million school students. In order to move from the evidently underperforming system of the mid-1990s the government put in place a policy approach best described as 'high challenge, high support'. The way in which these principles of 'high challenge, high support' are turned into practical policies to drive school improvement is summarised in Figure 4.1.1 (Barber, 2001, p. 4).

The policies for each segment (starting at 12 o'clock) are set out in Table 4.1.1. The important point is that the policy mix was complementary and mutually supportive (Barber, 2001, p. 4).

Figure 4.1.1 The High Challenge High Support policy framework

Table 4.1.1 Complementary policies to drive school improvement

Ambitious standards	Access to best practice and quality professional development
High standards set out in the National Curriculum National Tests at age 7, 11, 14, 16	Universal professional development in national priorities (literacy, numeracy, ICT) Leadership development as an entitlement
Accountability	**Devolved responsibility**
National inspection system for schools and LEAs Publication annually of school/district level performance data and targets	School as unit of accountability Devolution of resources and employment powers to schools
Good data/clear targets	**Intervention in inverse proportion to success**
Individual pupil level data collected nationally Statutory target-setting at district and school level	School improvement grant to assist implementation of post-inspection action plan Monitoring of performance by LEA (district)

The positive influence of the National Literacy and Numeracy Strategies on student performance attracted world-wide attention. A graphic illustration of the impact that the strategies have had on the system as a whole is seen in the following series of maps (Figures 4.1.2–4). The first map gives an indication of the number of Local Education Authorities in England in 1998 where 75 per cent or more of 11-year-old students were reading at their chronological age. This by itself provides sufficient justification for introducing the strategies (the map for numeracy was similar). The situation in 2002 is illustrated in the second map and that in 2004 in the third map. The picture for numeracy in 2002 and 2004 was also similar. Although there is still progress to be made the transformation of the national picture in six years is striking.

The analysis of this success is, however, not entirely straightforward. Following an initial and significant increase over the first three years there was a levelling off in performance for the next three years, and only recently has further progress been made. This is a trend that has been noted in virtually every large-scale reform initiative. What usually happens is that early success is followed by a stalling in progress and a subsequent lack of commitment to the programme of reform.

This, however, has not happened in England, and over the past couple of years standards have continued to rise again. It is clear to me that recent progress is because in 2003 the National Literacy and Numeracy Strategies merged into a National Primary Strategy following the publication of the *Excellence and Enjoyment* White Paper (DfES, 2003). As a consequence, the reform of primary education moved from a single focus on curriculum change to a whole-school improvement effort with literacy and numeracy at its core, but which also demonstrated:

- a strong focus on Personalised Learning and Assessment for Learning;
- a re-orientation of materials to support the quality of teaching and learning and whole-school curriculum planning;

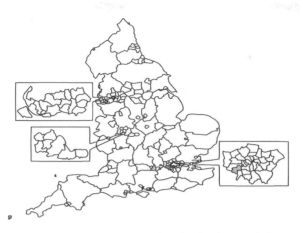

Figure 4.1.2 LEAs achieving 75%-plus level 4 English, 1998

Figure 4.1.3 LEAs achieving 75%-plus level 4 English, 2002

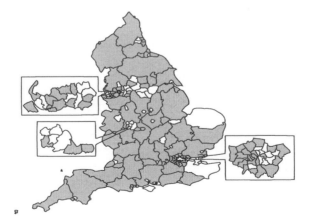

Figure 4.1.4 LEAs achieving 75%-plus level 4 English, 2004

- a move from top-down to bottom-up target-setting with an increase in moderated teacher assessment;
- a clearer identification of and support for those schools and local authorities where progress was too slow; and,
- a system-wide programme of leadership development and networking.

Let us now draw from this narrative a general lesson for large-scale/systemic reform. It is in the logic of large-scale reform that an early narrow focus on key skills produces an initial rapid increase in standards. To move beyond this plateau of achievement requires a system-wide school improvement approach that can deliver continuous improvement beyond the early gains. In other words, large-scale reform has characteristically focused on short-term objectives, whereas systemic change envisages a multi-phased process that ensures that early gains do not level off, but continue to improve as a consequence of employing strategies that at the same time raise achievement and build capacity. Still using the English experience as the point of departure, we explore the implications of this observation in more detail in the following section.

The crucial policy conundrum

The argument I am making is that there is a growing recognition that schools need to lead the next phase of reform. Using the analysis of the English experiment with large-scale reform the argument goes something like this:

- Most agreed that standards were too low and too varied in the 1970s and 80s and that some form of direct state intervention was necessary. The resultant 'national prescription' proved very successful, particularly in raising standards in primary schools – progress confirmed by international comparisons.
- But as we have seen, progress plateaued in the second term, and whilst a bit more improvement might be squeezed out nationally, and perhaps a lot more in underperforming schools, one has to question whether prescription still offers the recipe for sustained large-scale reform in the medium term.
- There is a growing recognition that schools need to lead the next phase of reform. But if the hypothesis is correct, and this is much-contested terrain, it must categorically not be a naïve return to the not so halcyon days of the 1970s when a thousand flowers bloomed and the educational life chances of too many of our children wilted.
- The implication is that we need a transition from an era of prescription to an era of professionalism, in which the balance between national prescription and schools leading reform will change.

However, achieving this shift is not straightforward. As Michael Fullan (2003, p. 7) has said, it takes capacity to build capacity, and if there is insufficient capacity to begin with it is folly to announce that a move to 'professionalism' provides the basis of a new approach. The key question is 'how do we get there?', because we cannot simply move from one era to the other without self-consciously building professional capacity throughout the system. It is this progression that is illustrated in Figure 4.1.5.

It is worth taking a little more time unpacking the thinking underlying the diagram. This is because it is fundamental to an understanding of the argument being made in this chapter. Five points need to be made.

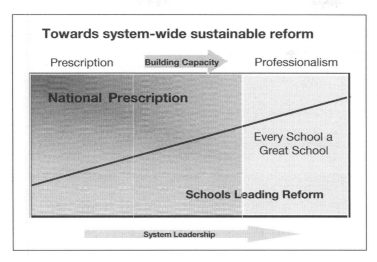

Figure 4.1.5 Towards system-wide sustainable reform

The first is to emphasise that this not an argument against 'top-down' change. It is clear that neither 'top-down' nor 'bottom-up' change works alone, they have to be in balance – in creative tension. The balance between the two at any one time will of course depend on context.

Second, it must be realised that in England in 1997 it was obvious that more central direction was needed. This reflects the balance towards national prescription as seen in the left-hand segment of the diagram. If we assume that time moves from left to right in the diagram, then in the case of England it is most probably correct to say that in terms of both policy and practice the balance is currently located in the middle segment of the diagram. This is contested terrain and there is no guarantee of an inevitable movement into the right-hand segment.

Third it should be no surprise to realise that the right-hand segment is relatively unknown territory. It implies horizontal and lateral ways of working with assumptions and governance arrangements very different from what we know now. The main difficulty in imagining this landscape is that the thinking of most people is constrained by their experiences within the power structure and norms of the left-hand segment of the diagram.

The fourth point is both complex and critical. In terms of the diagram, effective system-wide sustainable reform requires a movement from the left to the right segment, with all that implies. The left to right movement is necessarily incremental as it builds on, rather than contradicts, the success of previous phases. Yet, and this is the crucial point, the achievement of creating the educational landscape implied by the right-hand segment represents a step change from what has gone before. Yes, the difference between left- and right-hand segments represents a radical change or a transformation; but the process or journey from left to right will be incremental, building on past success and reshaping in light of learning from experience. It is in this way that the language of school improvement (logical incremental steps building on past experience) and transformation (a qualitatively different state from what was known previously) is reconciled.

To conclude this section, I emphasise that I am not suggesting that one always has to start from the left-hand side of the diagram and move in some sort of uniform way to the right.

That is just how it was in England in 1997. Other systems may well be in the middle and need to move left briefly to firm up certain conditions before rapidly proceeding into the right-hand segment. Some may believe that they are already in the right-hand segment. If this diagram has any value it is as a heuristic – its purpose is to help people think rather than tell them what to do.

Four drivers for system reform

I need to reiterate that the transition from 'prescription' to 'professionalism' is not straight-forward. In order to move from one to the other strategies are required that not only continue to raise standards but also build capacity within the system. This point is key: one cannot just drive to continue to raise standards in an instrumental way, one also needs to develop social, intellectual and organisational capital. Building capacity demands that we replace numerous central initiatives with a national consensus on a limited number of educational trends. There seem to me to be four key drivers that if pursued relentlessly and deeply will deliver both higher standards and enhanced professional capacity. These are personalised learning, professionalised teaching, networks and collaboration, and intelligent accountability.

As seen in the 'diamond of reform' (Figure 4.1.6) the four trends coalesce and mould to context through the exercise of responsible system leadership. Before elucidating the concept of system leadership let me briefly describe each of the drivers and give illustrations from policy trends in a number of different countries.

Personalised learning

The current focus on personalisation is about putting students at the heart of the education process so as to tailor teaching to individual need, interest and aptitude in order to fulfil every young person's potential. Many schools and teachers have tailored curriculum and teaching methods to meet the needs of children and young people with great success for many years. What is new is the drive to make the best practices universal. A successful system of person-alised learning means clear learning pathways through the education system and the motiva-tion to become independent, e-literate, fulfilled, lifelong learners. Obviously personalised learning demands both curriculum entitlement and choice that delivers a breadth of study and personal relevance, and which emphasises the development of the students' meta-cogni-tive capacity, in other words 'learning how to learn'. The personalisation, however, is in terms of flexible learning pathways through the education system rather than personalised goals or institutional tracking, which have often been shown to lower performance expectations for students and to provide easy ways out for teachers and schools, allowing them to defer prob-lems rather than solve them. The drive for high standards applies to all. Examples of policy options supportive of 'personalised learning' include the emphasis on formative assessment as seen in the recent OECD survey; an approach to curriculum that embraces both learning skills and content knowledge as seen in Finland; and an integrated approach to academic and vocational subjects in secondary education as seen in a number of states in Australia.

Professionalised teaching

Significant empirical evidence suggests that teaching quality is the most significant factor influencing student learning that is under the control of the school. It is also clear that

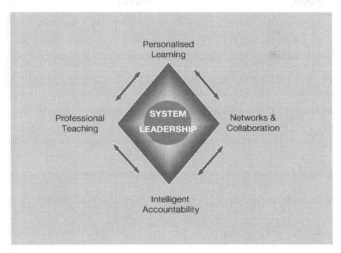

Figure 4.1.6 Four key drivers underpinning system reform

the forms of teaching that promote high levels of student learning vary in some instances quite dramatically from country to country. The phrase 'professionalised teaching' implies that teachers are on a par with other professions in terms of diagnosis, the application of evidence-based practices and professional pride. The image here is of teachers who use data to evaluate the learning needs of their students, and are consistently expanding their repertoire of pedagogic strategies to personalise learning for all students. It also implies schools that adopt innovative approaches to timetabling and the deployment of increasingly differentiated staffing models. Examples of policy options supportive of 'professionalised teaching' include teacher selection processes as seen in Finland; highly specified professional development programmes as with the National Literacy Strategy in England; and teacher promotion based on professional competence as in Canada or Sweden. Instructional and information technology may be important aspects to be considered in this context as well.

Intelligent accountability

This refers to the balance between nationally determined approaches to external accountability on the one hand and on the other the capacity for professional accountability within the school that emphasises the importance of formative assessment and the pivotal role of self-evaluation. In any debate on accountability it is important to distinguish between means and ends, methods and purpose. There are two key purposes for accountability. The first is as a tool to support higher levels of student learning and achievement; the second is to maintain public confidence. The means of achieving this will inevitably vary from country to country and from situation to situation. In general where there are high levels of student achievement and small variations of performance between schools then pressures from external accountability will be modest. In those situations where there is a need for more robust forms of external accountability it should always be designed to support teacher professionalism and the school's capacity to utilise data to enhance student performance. Examples of policy options supportive of 'intelligent accountability' include: the approaches to professional accountability developed in Finland; the use of pupil performance data and value-added analyses in England; and the approaches to school self-evaluation in Denmark.

Networking and collaboration

This relates to the various ways in which networks of schools can stimulate and spread innovation as well as collaborate to provide curriculum diversity, extended services and community support. The prevalence of networking practice supports the contention that there is no contradiction between strong, independent schools and strong networks, rather the reverse. Effective networks require strong leadership by participating heads and clear objectives that add significant value to individual schools' own efforts. Without this networks wither and die, since the transaction costs outweigh the benefits they deliver. Nor is there a contradiction between collaboration and competition – many sectors of the economy are demonstrating that the combination of competition and collaboration delivers the most rapid improvements. Although evidence of effectiveness is still accumulating, it is becoming clear that networks support improvement and innovation by enabling schools to collaborate on building curriculum diversity, extended services and professional support to develop a vision of education that is shared and owned well beyond individual schools. Examples of policy options supportive of 'networking and collaboration' include: the approaches to schools as community social centres seen in Sweden; the way in which leading schools are partnering with 'failing schools' to bring about rapid improvements in England; and burgeoning networks of schools disseminating innovative practices in the USA.

Although these key drivers provide a core strategy for systemic improvement, it is system leadership, as we will see in the following section, that adapts them to particular and individual school contexts. This is leadership that enables systemic reform to be both generic in terms of overall strategy and specific in adapting to individual and particular situations. It is system leaders who reach beyond their own school to create networks and collaborative arrangements that not only add richness and excellence to the learning of students, but also act as agents of educational transformation.

System leadership

'System leaders' are those head teachers who are willing to shoulder system leadership roles: who care about and work for the success of other schools as well as their own. In England there appears to be an emerging cadre of these head teachers who stand in contrast to the competitive ethic of headship so prevalent in the nineties. It is these educators who by their own efforts and commitment are beginning to transform the nature of leadership and educational improvement in this country. Interestingly there is also evidence of this role emerging in other leading educational systems in Europe, North America and Australia (Hopkins, forthcoming).

The proposition is simple:

> If our goal is 'every school a great school' then policy and practice has to focus on system improvement. This means that a school head has to be almost as concerned about the success of other schools as he or she is about his or her own school. Sustained improvement of schools is not possible unless the whole system is moving forward.

The first thing to say is that system leadership, as Michael Fullan (2003, 2005) has argued, is imbued with *moral purpose*. Without that, there would not be the passion to proceed or the encouragement for others to follow. In England for example, where the regularities of improvement in teaching and learning are still not well understood, where deprivation is still too good a predictor of educational success and where the goal is for every school to be a great school, the leadership challenge is surely a systemic one. This perspective gives a broader appreciation of what is meant by the moral purpose of system leadership.

I would argue therefore that system leaders express their moral purpose through:

1   Measuring their success in terms of improving student learning and increasing achievement, and striving to both raise the bar and narrow the gap(s).
2   Being fundamentally committed to the improvement of teaching and learning. They engage deeply with the organisation of teaching, learning, curriculum and assessment in order to ensure that learning is personalised for all their students.
3   Developing their schools as personal and professional learning communities, with relationships built across and beyond each school to provide a range of learning experiences and professional development opportunities.
4   Striving for equity and inclusion through acting on context and culture. This is not just about eradicating poverty, as important as that is. It is also about giving communities a sense of worth and empowerment.
5   Realising in a deep way that the classroom, school and system levels all impact on each other. Crucially they understand that in order to change the larger system you have to engage with it in a meaningful way.

Although this degree of clarity is not necessarily obvious in the behaviour and practice of every head teacher, these aspirations are increasingly becoming part of the conventional wisdom of our best global educational leaders.

It is also pleasing to see a variety of *system leader roles* emerging within various systems that are consistent with such a moral purpose. At present, in England, these are (Hopkins and Higham, forthcoming):

*   Developing and *leading a successful educational improvement partnership* between several schools, often focused on a set of specific themes that have significant and clear outcomes that reach beyond the capacity of any one single institution.
*   Choosing to *lead and improve a school in extremely challenging circumstances* and change local contexts by building a culture of success and then sustaining once low-achieving schools as high-valued-added institutions.
*   *Partnering another school facing difficulties and improving it*, either as an executive head of a federation or as the leader of a more informal improvement arrangement.
*   Acting as a *community leader* to broker and shape partnerships and/or networks of wider relationships across local communities to support children's welfare and potential, often through multi-agency work.
*   Working as a *change agent* or expert leader within the system, identifying best classroom practice and transferring it to support improvement in others' schools.

No doubt these roles will expand and mature over time; but what is significant about them is that they have evolved in response to the adaptive challenge of system change.

A model for system reform

Having described the pivotal role of the system leader it is now instructive to turn to the contribution to be made by national and local authorities in achieving system reform. A major problem here is that policy debates in many countries are often conducted with insufficient empirical evidence and policy claims are often made on the basis of tradition, aspiration or ideology. What is needed are policy frameworks that will allow countries to relate their policy choices more directly to student outcomes, to monitor the impact of changes in policy direction over time and possibly to compare policy options between countries. These are some of the issues I have been thinking through in a preliminary way with colleagues at the OECD responsible for the PISA programme.

Our initial analysis suggests that there now seem to be six 'policy drivers' that are being actively debated in many countries as being critical not just to enhancing student outcomes, but also to building capacity in the education system overall. Although these trends are often interpreted differently in different contexts, they do, however, provide the possibility of a framework in which to discuss global approaches to school change.

Three of these six policy drivers relate to teaching and learning and are consistent with the analysis already conducted in this chapter:

- teaching quality
- personalised learning
- school leadership and ethos.

The three other policy drivers relate to the approaches to reform taken at the system level:

- standards and accountability
- networking and collaboration
- choice and contestability.

With this in mind, we are now in a position to revisit the policy framework that underpinned the success of the first-term New Labour educational reforms. The broad argument was that a national education strategy based on the principle of 'high challenge and high support' – which contained a complementary cocktail of policies that linked together:

- high standards with quality materials and professional development
- demanding targets but support for schools in the most challenging of circumstances
- linked accountability with increasing devolution of responsibility

– is highly effective at raising standards in the short term.

The 'high support, high challenge' strategy was an outstandingly successful strategy for the policy objectives of the first-term New Labour government. But system-wide strategies are not immutable; they evolve with their societies and changing educational demands. The subsequent argument in this chapter has been to stress that for learning and achievement to continue to rise into the medium to long term we need a different policy arrangement because of the need to rebalance national prescription with schools leading reform. This rebalancing is necessary for building capacity for sustained improvement and leads to a trans-

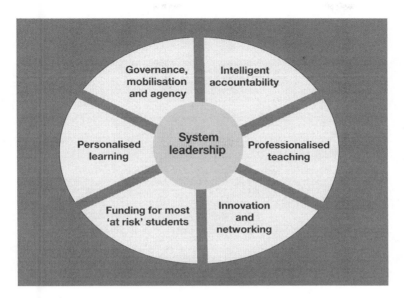

Figure 4.1.7 The Every School a Great School Policy framework

formed and reimagined educational landscape implied by the right-hand segment of our ubiquitous rectangle.

The argument that has been building throughout this chapter is that the policy framework for 'every school being great' is equally sophisticated in terms of its aspiration but is more reflective of a context that has increasingly lateral responsibilities and alignments. This framework, which should be recognisable to those who have read so far, is seen in Figure 4.1.7. In the centre is system leadership with the implication that it applies at a range of levels and roles within the system. The key policy drivers should also be familiar by now:

- the demand for personalisation requires a professional practice for teaching;
- the systemic potential of networking and collaborations requires new arrangements for governance and agency; and
- the realisation of 'intelligent accountability' within the school needs to be matched by a willingness to fund students who are most 'at risk'.

For the sake of completeness one can see that the 'every school a great school' policy framework is as appropriate for the right-hand segment of the rectangle as the original framework was to the left-hand segment in the early days of New Labour's educational reforms. This equilibrium is captured in Figure 4.1.8.

The substantive point that we have been making is that different stages of reform require different strategies. This, though, is not an 'either–or' issue, but more an evolutionary process that respects the wide degree of differentiation or segmentation within the system.

One can sharpen the point by looking at three trajectories for system reform in Figure 4.1.9. The first trajectory is the conventional straight line analysis that rarely reflects real-life situations. More usual are one of the other two trajectories numbered 2 and 3 in the

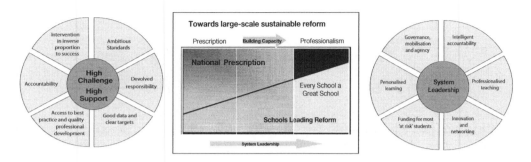

Figure 4.1.8 Complementary policy frameworks for system reform

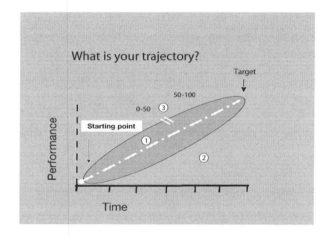

Figure 4.1.9 Three trajectories for system reform (adapted from Michael Barber)

diagram. What is clear in both cases is that an initial (slow or rapid) stage of development is followed by a second stage that is qualitatively different. One could say that the first stage takes us half-way there and the second the remaining distance.

In reflecting on this analysis it is important to remember that:

1   'everything counts' on the dimensions of system reform, it is not an *à la carte* menu;
2   there are qualitative differences between each stage;
3   the second stage, however, needs to build on the first;
4   in some cases, progress may not move beyond the first stage; and,
5   both stages need to be considered together in a long-term systemic strategy.

It is interesting to realise that this analysis is as important for individual schools or groups of schools as for national or local governments. What often happens, however, is that initiatives tend to be worked on individually; rarely is the entire framework considered at one time. What is needed is a framework to help governments (and schools) to reflect

Table 4.1.2 A 'halfway there' – 'halfway to go' analysis on 12 dimensions of school reform

Dimension	0–50%	50–100%
Standards	Apply to whole cohort	Personalised for different student groups
Targets	Top down	Bottom up
Learning	Content knowledge	Learning to learn
Curriculum	Entitlement	Choice/differentiation
Pedagogy	Explicit	Repertoire
Assessment	of Learning	for Learning
Data	Whole system	Value added and disaggregated
Professional development	External workshops	Professional learning community
Leadership	Within school	Systemic
Inspection	External	Moderated self-evaluation
System	Directive/prescriptive	Enabling but highly segmented
Government	Political passion and vision	Ever expanding guiding coalition

on how best to balance these various strategies in a comprehensive approach to systemic educational change. Figure 4.1.10 provides an example of such a framework. It seeks to identify three key elements of a coherent approach to school change. The framework also suggests how these three elements may interact and impact on the learning and achievement of students.

This educational model was developed by Michael Barber (2005) based on Thomas Friedman's analogy (in his book *The Lexus and the Olive Tree* (1999)) of a nation's economy with a computer system. Originally developed for educational systems it can also apply to schools. There is the hardware – the infrastructure, funding and physical resources as well as human and intellectual capital. There is also the software – the interaction between the school and the student, the process of teaching and learning infused by the leadership of the school. Between the two there is the operating system, or the strategy for change the school or system chooses, or not, to employ to develop itself as a whole.

Many schools, as well as ministries of education, assume that there is a direct link between the hardware and the software – as long as the resources are in place then student learning will be satisfactory. This is rarely the case and the reason is simple. We need a change strategy to link inputs to outputs: without it student and school outcomes will remain unpredictable. With it, schools will be more likely to translate their resources more directly into better learning environments and therefore enhanced learning outcomes for their students.

The same argument goes for local and national governments. The existence of such a framework allows for a more intelligent debate over the policies adopted by different countries in terms of all three elements – the hardware, the software and the operating system and their integrated impact on standards of learning and achievement.

In many ways the structure and argument of this chapter also reflect this framework. Earlier, we discussed aspects of various national policies that provide the hardware or infrastructure for system improvement. The 'drivers', especially those related to the learning

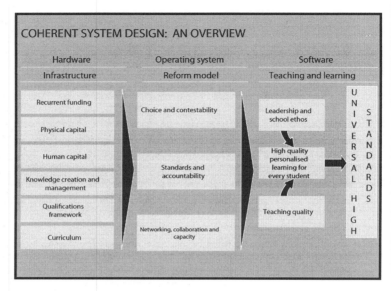

Figure 4.1.10 A coherent system design framework

and teaching aspects, reflect the software aspects of the diagram. The concepts of system leadership, accountability and networking relate to the operating system. The key issue to remember is that operating systems are, as was said earlier, not immutable; they need to reflect their context. The two policy frameworks described earlier in this section are a good example of how strategies or 'operating systems' evolve and build on each other as the system as a whole develops.

In conclusion, it is important to remember that the challenge of system reform has great moral depth to it. It addresses directly the learning needs of our students, the professional growth of our teachers and enhances the role of the school as an agent of social change. This is why I have argued that as we imagine a new educational future in line with the 'policy conundrum' analysis outlined earlier, so we require a new operating system capable of realising a future where every school is a great one. That is why the discussion on coherent system reform is so important. The operating system is not just a technical device for linking inputs to outputs; it is also a metaphor for those strategies that when implemented lead towards 'every school a great school' as well as the 'good society'.

References

Barber, M. (2001) 'Large-scale education reform in England: a work in progress', paper prepared for the School Development Conference, Tartu University, Estonia.

—— (2005) 'A twenty-first-century self-evaluation framework', annex 3 in 'Journeys of discovery: the search for success by design', keynote speech at the National Center on Education and the Economy annual conference, Florida.

DfES (2003) *Excellence and Enjoyment: A Strategy for Primary Schools*, London, Department for Education and Skills.

Friedman, T. (1999) *The Lexus and the Olive Tree: Understanding Globalization*, New York, Anchor Books.

Fullan, M. (2003) *The Moral Imperative of School Leadership*, London, Corwin Press.
—— (2005) *Leadership and Sustainability*, London, Corwin Press.
Hopkins, D. (ed.) (forthcoming) *Innovative Approaches to Contemporary School Leadership*, OECD.
Hopkins, D. and Higham, R. (forthcoming) *Report to the National College of School Leaders on System Leadership*.
Leithwood, K., Jantzi, D. and Mascall, B. (1999) 'Large-scale reform: what works?', unpublished manuscript, Ontario Institute for Studies in Education, University of Toronto.
McLaughlin, M. W. (1990) 'The Rand Change Agent study revisited: macro perspectives and micro realities', *Educational Researcher*, 19 (9), pp. 11–16.

Reflective questions

1   I have illustrated a policy framework and argued that, it is this framework that could realise the potential of systemic reform. Do you agree with this analysis of system reform? Do you think that the policy framework could realise the potential of systemic reform?
2   I have discussed system leadership and its role in systemic reform. What is your perspective on the concept of system leadership? Do you agree upon its pivotal role for system and school transformation?

Further reading

Elmore, R.F. (2004) *School Reform from the Inside Out*, Cambridge, MA: Harvard University Press.
Fullan, M. (2007) *The New Meaning of Educational Change*, 4th edn, London, Routledge.
Hopkins, D. (2007) *Every School a Great School*, Maidenhead, McGrawHill/Open University Press.

4.2 Using assessment in education reform

Policy, practice and future possibilities

Harry Torrance

Introduction

Changes in assessment policy and practice have been used to drive changes in the education system in England for more than 20 years. Other countries have engaged in similar debates and actions, notably the United States, with advocacy of 'Measurement-Driven Instruction' (Popham, 1987) and the No Child Left Behind legislation of 2001 (No Child Left Behind, 2001), but only in England has the focus on assessment been so relentless across the compulsory school system as a whole.

The arguments in favour of using assessment to change teaching essentially fall into two distinct, but nevertheless related, categories. One argument derives from educational issues and values, the other is much more orientated towards accountability and the use of political pressure to bring about change. The educational arguments revolve around the role that assessment plays in determining the curriculum; as Resnick and Resnick (1992, p. 59) have put it:

> You get what you assess; you don't get what you don't assess; you should build assessment towards what you want ... to teach.

This is very much the thinking that influenced the 'Measurement-Driven Instruction' movement in the US in the late 1980s and 1990s. Put desired objectives into testing programmes and teachers will teach those desired objectives (Airasian, 1988; Popham, 1987). A rather more complex interpretation of the same broad insight focuses much more at classroom level. Thus it is also recognised that routine, informal assessment can play a key role in underpinning or undermining the quality of teaching and learning in the classroom. How teachers assess students' work, what sorts of positive or negative feedback is given, and whether or not advice on how to improve is provided can make a great deal of difference to what is learned and how it is learned. This is the thinking which underlies the 'formative assessment' movement in England (Black and Wiliam, 1998; Torrance and Pryor, 1998), though it has also been acknowledged as potentially important for developments in the US (Shepard, 2000).

The accountability arguments are much simpler and more clear-cut, and perhaps, for that reason, are much more politically attractive. Here the claim is that education systems in general, schools in particular, must have their efficiency and effectiveness measured by the outcomes produced. Expected standards of achievement must be prescribed and tests regularly employed to identify whether or not these expectations have been met. In publicly maintained school systems which are financed out of taxation, such an argument involves governments determining what is to be taught and how it is to be tested, along with the publication of results so that the government, schools and parents can see whether or not standards are indeed rising and taxpayers are getting value for money from the system. The quality of teaching and learning in the classroom is assumed to rise if results improve. Essentially testing is a used as a 'lever' to affect the system *qua* system; the detail at classroom level is assumed to look after itself. However it is crucial to the logic and practice of such a system that the tests employed do indeed validly sample the curriculum and reliably measure student achievement. The tests must be valid indicators of quality across the system as a whole, otherwise they may 'drive' the system in the wrong direction.

In England, we are very much dealing with this latter analysis of the nature of the problem of 'educational standards' and what to do about them, though some elements of the arguments about 'formative assessment', or 'assessment for learning' as it is now more commonly known, also feature. In this respect it is interesting to note that change in the education system is unlikely to occur just as a result of compliance with government pressure and legislation. In the systemic social and institutional 'space' of education, educational arguments are likely to be deployed in policy debates in order to increase the rhetorical and symbolic legitimacy of policy and mobilise action at local level.

Policy development in England

The use of assessment to drive educational change in England dates back to the introduction of a single system of secondary school examinations, the General Certificate of Secondary Education (GCSE), for 16-year-olds (the minimum school-leaving age), by the then Conservative government of Margaret Thatcher in 1986 (with the first new exams taken in 1988). Prior to this England operated with two parallel secondary school examination systems: GCE O-level[1] for those students considered to be in the top 20 per cent of the ability range; and CSE[2] for those considered to be in the next 40 per cent of the ability range. The bottom 40 per cent were not considered capable of taking examinations at all. Such a bifurcated system derived from very outdated notions of innate ability, and more specifically the 'normal distribution' of ability in a population (Torrance, 1981). The creation of a single system of examining, GCSE, to match the aspirations of a still developing comprehensive secondary school system (first initiated under a Labour government in 1964), might be said to mark the point at which governments in England fully began to buy into human capital theory and treat education as an investment in the population as a whole, rather than as a way to select a social and economic elite. Of course education, and particularly assessment, does still play a major role in selecting and legitimating the selection of a social and economic elite. However, a full discussion of this topic would require a different chapter and it is at least now arguable that this outcome is an unintended effect of policy, rather than an overt intention.

Concerns about standards and accountability in education date back still further in England. In the 1960s and 1970s, precisely because it was not thought appropriate for all children to take secondary school examinations, there was no overall data in the system about how well schools were doing and what standards were being attained across the system as a whole. Moreover the selection test for secondary school allocation (the 11-plus) could only provide evidence that 80 per cent of pupils 'failed' their 11-plus and therefore 'failed' primary education. Even this exam was being phased out with the introduction of comprehensive secondary schools and it looked as though there would be no data whatsoever on the output of primary schools.

The Labour government of the 1970s launched the Assessment of Performance Unit (APU) to try to provide evidence of standards achieved. This employed a sampling approach, testing a 2 per cent sample of 11-years-olds and 15-year-olds in English, maths, science and modern languages. Many interesting assessment methods were developed and materials produced, some of which eventually found their way into GCSE courses and even the national curriculum. But the APU did not provide unequivocal and easily usable evidence about national standards; nor, because of its sampling strategy, could it reach into and influence every classroom. First GCSE (1986), then the National Curriculum and national testing (1988) were introduced in order to control directly what was taught and how it was taught, and to measure whether or not it was being taught effectively. The APU was also closed down by the Conservative government at this point, since it was considered unnecessary. This has meant that there has been no independent research-based check on whether or not standards have risen over time, unlike in the United States, with the National Assessment of Educational Progress (NAEP, see below).

No sooner had the first GCSE examinations been taken in 1988, than the National Curriculum was introduced in nine subjects, with national testing at ages 7, 11, 14 and 16. The curriculum was organised in four 'key stages' (KS): KS1, ages 5–7 years; KS2, 8–11; KS3, 12–14; and KS4, 15–16. The curriculum comprised nine 'foundation' subjects (mathematics, English, science, technology, history, geography, art, music, a modern foreign language starting at KS3, i.e. from age 11), plus Welsh in Wales; and was set out, subject by subject, in terms of 'attainment targets', defined in the 1988 Education Act as the 'knowledge, skills and understanding which pupils … are expected to have by the end of each Key Stage'. Additionally, attainment targets were organised into expected levels of progress, such that National Curriculum 'level 2' was the expected level to be achieved by students making 'normal' progress at the end of KS1, and 'level 4' was the expected level to be achieved at the end of KS2.

Originally national testing was also going to accompany every statutory curriculum subject. This was abandoned as the logistical implications became clear, and testing focused on English and maths at age 7 (the end of KS1); and English, maths and science (redesignated 'core' subjects) at ages 11 and 14 (end of KS2 and KS3). GCSE was retained to assess standards at age 16-plus and to provide single-subject qualifications for students at the end of the compulsory phase of schooling. Furthermore, however, when national testing was first introduced it was known as national assessment and considerable efforts were made to render the process as flexible and useful as possible to schools and teachers, through the widespread use of teacher assessment of coursework and the central provision of extended 'standard assessment tasks' (SATs) which could be completed over a period of days or even weeks. Complaints from teachers about the complexity of the system and the sheer workload involved led to the abandonment of much of this early development, and the system became more and more narrowly focused on a small number of tests in a small number of subjects (for a fuller discussion see Daugherty, 1995; Torrance, 1995, 2003).

More recently, in response to almost constant criticism of the testing of very young children, elements of this testing regime have been relaxed at KS1. Since September 2004 teachers have only had to report results based on 'teacher assessment' at KS1. These are expected to be underpinned and moderated by use of either previously used national tests, or new tests which are still produced to assist teachers, but do not necessarily have to be used. Thus for example in summer 2007 KS1 teachers could use either tests from 2005 or new tests supplied during 2006–7 to underpin their judgements. In practice, an evaluation of this development conducted by the National Foundation for Educational Research (NFER) reported that teachers are still using the nationally produced and supplied tests at

KS1 in much the same way as they have done for the last 15 years (Reed and Lewis, 2005). However, the new flexibility may be more widely exploited in the future as teachers come to understand that they do not have to use the tests at KS1. Testing has also now been abandoned at KS3.

Elements of the National Curriculum have also been relaxed as the system continues its evolution from completely planned central control to realistically workable system. The academic content of the National Curriculum at KS4 (ages 14–16) now comprises only maths, English, science and ICT, along with various social- and health-related elements including physical education, religious education, sex education, careers education, citizenship and work experience. The arts, design technology, the humanities and modern foreign languages all have to be provided by schools if students want to study them, but they are no longer legally compulsory (QCA, 2003). The corollary of a reduced statutory curriculum, however, and in particular reduced testing across the whole curriculum, is a much increased focus on that which is tested ('you get what you assess').

Much of this policy background may seem like ancient history, but it is important to revisit it and understand it as the key political problematic which continues to underpin and inform policy. It is puzzlingly difficult to find a single, coherent, integrated statement of twenty-first-century education policy in England. Continuity with the 1988 National Curriculum and testing regime is completely taken for granted, and elements of policy have been built up, layer by layer, in successive attempts by post-1997 Labour governments to try finally to realise the vision of a National Curriculum and testing system and render it operational. In his foreword to the recent Education White Paper 'Higher Standards, Better Schools for All' (DfES, 2005), the then prime minister, Tony Blair, rehearsed and claimed the history for himself, with the Conservatives conveniently omitted from the narrative:

> In the 1960s and 1970s ... there were simply not enough pressures in the system to raise standards. Lord Callaghan recognised this as Prime Minister in 1976 when he urged a National Curriculum. When it was introduced in the late eighties it was accompanied by greater accountability through national testing ... After 1997 this government extended such accountability, with literacy and numeracy reforms and targets to encourage improvements. (pp. 1–2)

Thus 'assessment policy' now comprises:

- a 'core' National Curriculum of English, maths and science with additional 'foundation' and 'entitlement' subjects;
- national teacher assessment of the whole cohort in English and maths at age 7;
- national testing of the whole cohort in English, maths and science at age 11 and GCSE at age 16 (teacher assessment replaces testing at age 14 with effect from 2009);
- national and local target setting (at school level and student level) for levels of attainment to be achieved;
- publishing of results in public performance tables (i.e. league tables of schools and local authorities);
- inspection of schools by the Office for Standards in Education (Ofsted) and publication of reports, with a particular emphasis on results obtained and trends in results over time;
- 'naming and shaming' of so-called 'failing schools', with threat of closure if improvement (as reported by Ofsted) is not evident within a year.

Benefits of National Curriculum and testing

Very little coherent policy discussion had taken place before the late 1970s with respect to what sort of overall curricular provision might be appropriate for a truly comprehensive system of education, far less how this might be assessed at individual level or evaluated at national level. Likewise, prior to 1986, the UK had one of the most decentralised and voluntaristic examination systems in the world, with many different examination boards in England and Wales, along with national boards for Scotland and Northern Ireland. Each board set individual examination papers in individual subjects, to be taken by individual students choosing to sit as many or as few papers as they wished, generally, but by no means exclusively, at ages 16 (minimum school-leaving age) and 18 (usual maximum school-leaving age prior to university entrance). Even the amalgamated GCSE remained a single-subject examination, taken voluntaristically by individual candidates and set by diverse examination boards, albeit following national criteria with syllabuses subject to approval by the Secretary of State. It was also, of course, only directly relevant to secondary schools.

So compared to what went before, the claimed benefits of National Curriculum and testing are easily stated:

- clarity of curriculum content and progression;
- clarity of outcomes;
- comparable measures of progress over time.

Since the inception of the National Curriculum there has been an enduring debate about whether or not England needs such an extensive testing system. Most recently the General Teaching Council, a professional body set up by the government to oversee teacher professional development, argued that national testing at KS2 and KS3 was unnecessary. The government response and commitment to a simple test-driven system remains unequivocal:

> A spokesman for the Department for Education and Skills said … Key Stage tests were here to stay. 'They are a non-negotiable part of school reform. They provide valuable objective evidence in the core subjects, helping inform further improvements to teaching and learning.'
>
> (BBC Education News website, 1 May 2007)

> The Department for Education said testing and performance tables were accountability measures 'essential to extending and maintaining' improvements in standards.
>
> (BBC Education News website, 10 June 2007)

Thus the analysis of the problem and the proposed solution remain the same as they were 20 years ago, although testing is now only focused on KS2, age 11.

Additionally, however, the policy focus has been further intensified by the development of the national literacy and numeracy strategies which now drive English and maths teaching in primary schools and, increasingly, in the early years of secondary school through the 'Primary and Secondary National Strategies' (DfES, 2006). These strategies prescribe curriculum content and how it should be taught in English and maths, to the point where they are included in the daily school timetable and commonly known as the 'literacy and numeracy hours'. To the crude 'lever' of national testing, combined with the control of curriculum content, has been added the development of the national strategies, which directly impact on teaching methods.

Are standards rising?

The increasingly feverish activity of post-1997 Labour governments indicates that educational standards are still a political issue about which 'something must be done', or at least be seen to be done. Test scores have plateaued since around 2000 and in so far as they indicate anything meaningful about educational standards this suggests that progress has stalled, or appears to have stalled. The particular problem for the current government derives precisely from the acceptance of the basic analysis that a National Curriculum and testing system is a good idea. It is an idea which is 20 years old, and new policy initiatives can only tinker and intensify pressure at the margins (e.g. the national strategies); new policies have not, as yet, taken the system in a different direction. Furthermore, figures indicate that tests scores have risen progressively over many years, irrespective of which government is in power, though they have levelled off recently.

Not every year's results are recorded here; rather, sufficient years are recorded to indicate trends over time along with key dates which the government has variously used and dropped as indicators of progress. The current national target is that 85 per cent of students should reach level 4 in English and maths at KS2 'as soon as possible' (DfES, 2004a, p. 4). As previous targets were set but missed (e.g. for 2002, see Table 4.2.1, footnote 5), and continue to be missed, the baseline for comparison is now routinely given by official documents as 1997, when the New Labour government was first elected (DfES, 2005, p. 7; Earl *et al.*, 2003, p. 3). Thus although targets are still used to drive the system at local level, the government no longer holds itself to account by them at national level. To do so would be to admit failure. Rather, progress since 1997 is the routinely deployed measure at national level. At first sight such progress seems significant. But closer scrutiny indicates significant improvements in results prior to 1997. Thus for example in the two years after national testing was first introduced at KS2 (1995–7) results improved by 15 percentage points in English and 17 percentage points in maths. In the *ten* years since 1997, results improved by 16 percentage points in English and 14 percentage points in maths (1997–2006), with most of this improvement being achieved by 2000.

Results for GCSE are even more instructive. They have been rising steadily since the exam was first introduced in 1988 and indeed were rising prior to its introduction. In the mid-1970s, when only the 'top 20 per cent' of students were thought capable of passing O-level, the proportion of students passing at least five O-levels or their equivalent under the previous dual system was 22.6 per cent.[3] By 1988, the first year of GCSE results, this had risen to 29.9 per cent. By the mid 1990s this had risen further to 43.5 per cent and the most recent results for 2006 indicate that almost 60 per cent of students now pass five or more GCSEs at grades A*–C. That is, 60 per cent of the school population now achieve what 30 years ago it was thought only the 'top 20 per cent' could achieve. Furthermore, taking the full range of grades into account (A*–G), as an indicator of the numbers of students gaining at least some benefit from their secondary education, almost 60 per cent gained at least five A*–G grades in 1975, while 90.5 per cent achieved five A*–G grades in 2006. Thus, to reiterate, pass rates have been rising no matter which government is in power, pursuing which policy.

Within these general trends different sub-groups perform better than others. Thus for example *c.* 75 per cent of candidates of Chinese origin gain at least five A*–Cs, while only around 35 per cent of candidates of Black African and Caribbean origin do so (Torrance,

Table 4.2.1 Percentage pupils gaining National Curriculum Assessment level 2 or above at age 7 and level 4 or above at age 11

	Age 7		Age 11		
	Eng	*Maths*	*Eng*	*Maths*	*Sci*
1992[1]	77	78			
1995[2]	76	78	48	44	
1996[3]	80	80	58	54	62
1997[4]	81/80	83	63	61	69
2000	81/78	90	75	72	85
2002[5]	84/82	90	75	73	86
2005[6]	85/82	91	79	75	86
2006	84/81	90	79	75	86

(Source: http://www.dfes.gov.uk/rsgateway[7])

Notes
1 First 'full run' of KS1 tests
2 First 'full run' of KS2 English & Maths
3 First 'full run' of KS2 Science
4 First tests under New Labour government; KS1 English results now being reported separately in terms of attainment targets (81% gained level 2 in Reading, 80% in Writing). Such details had been available previously but results were routinely reported as 'whole subject' levels. The 'Writing' score is averaged across the writing test and the spelling test.
5 First national target date: the government target was 80% of students reaching level 4 English at KS2 and 75% reaching level 4 Maths at KS2. Both targets were missed.
6 KS1 tests now conducted as 'teacher assessment' so no longer directly comparable with previous results at KS1
7 For other sources of test results data, prior to DfES online archiving, see Torrance (2003).

Table 4.2.2 Percentage of pupils gaining O-level/CSE/GCSE Equivalents 1975–2006

	% 5 or more A*–C grades	*% 5 or more A*–G grades*
1975	22.6	58.6
1980	24.0	69.9
1988 (first year GCSE results)	29.9	74.7
1990	34.5	80.3
1995	43.5	85.7
1997 (first year New Labour govt)	45.1	86.4
2000	49.2	88.9
2005	55.7	88.9
2006	59.2	90.5

(Sources: http://www.dfes.gov.uk/rsgateway; DfEE, 2000; Torrance, 2003)

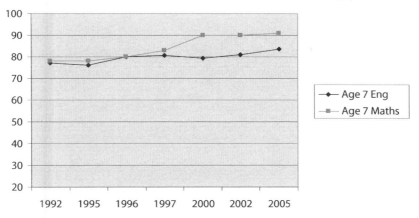

Figure 4.2.1 Percentage pupils gaining National Curriculum Assessment level 2 or above at age 7 (KS1)

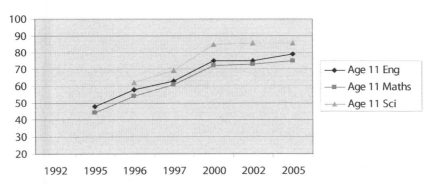

Figure 4.2.2 Percentage pupils gaining National Curriculum Assessment level 4 or above at age 11 (KS2)

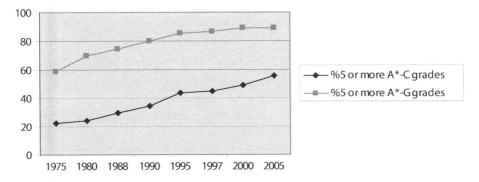

Figure 4.2.3 Percentage of pupils gaining O-level/CSE/GCSE Equivalents 1975–2006

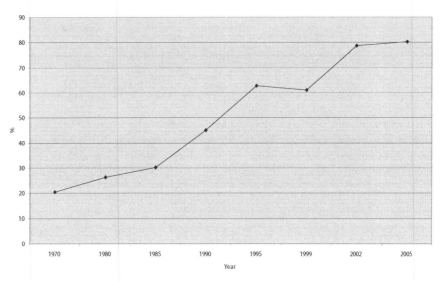

Figure 4.2.4 Percentage of cohort (18-yr-olds) obtaining a *baccalauréat* (France) (http://www.inca.org.uk)

2005). A recent Joseph Rowntree-sponsored study indicates that poor working-class white boys do worst of all (Cassen and Kingdon, 2007). These figures raise major political and educational issues, but for the purposes of this discussion, the key point is that overall pass rates have been rising for more than 30 years.

Interestingly enough, this trend is not restricted to England. Pass rates in the French *baccalauréat* examination have been rising similarly (see figure 4.2.4).

What exactly is the explanation for this international trend is difficult to discern. Some element of a genuine rise in standards is likely to be present, driven by better socio-economic conditions of students, higher expectations of educational outcomes by students, parents and teachers and better teaching. This is probably combined with and compounded by an increasingly more focused concentration on passing exams, by teachers ('teaching to the test') and students (extrinsic motivation), because of the perceived importance of educational success in institutional accountability and individual life chances.

Problems of National Curriculum and testing

In England, latterly, the evidence is that teaching to the test is by far the most likely explanation both for rising test scores throughout the 1990s and the tailing off of any further improvement post-2000. Research studies have reported an increasing focus on test preparation throughout KS2 and particularly in the final year of primary school prior to the tests being taken:

> Whole class teaching and individual pupil work increased at the expense of group work ... [there was] a noticeable increase in the time spent on the core subjects ... [and] teachers ... put time aside for revision and mock tests.
>
> (McNess *et al.*, 2001, pp. 12–13)

assessment is synonymous with testing ... assessment, narrowed to test-taking in preparation for SATs, is the main business of life in the last two terms of year six.

(Hall *et al.*, 2004, p. 804)

Such observations are confirmed by the DfES's own commissioned evaluation of the national literacy and numeracy strategies:

National targets probably skewed efforts in the direction of activities ... that were intended to lead to increases in the one highly publicized score. Many teachers acknowledged considerable test preparation, especially in the term leading up to the national assessments.

(Earl *et al.*, 2003, p. 7)

Not only does such coaching and practice raise questions about the validity of the test results produced, it also means that other aspects of the curriculum are given less attention ('you get what you assess'); something to which successive Chief Inspectors of Schools have drawn attention in speeches and annual reports compiled from Ofsted inspection evidence. Thus for example former Chief Inspector Mike Tomlinson warned that:

In some primary schools the arts, creative and practical subjects are receiving less attention than previously. This risks an unacceptable narrowing of the curriculum.

(Ofsted, 2002, Commentary, p. 1)

His successor as Chief HMI, David Bell (in a speech to the City of York Council's annual education conference, 28 February 2003), reported that: 'one of the things inspectors find is that an excessive or myopic focus on targets can actually narrow and reduce achievement by crowding out some of the essentials of effective and broadly based learning'.

Current HMI Christine Gilbert's 2006 report notes that:

In many [primary] schools the focus of the teaching of English is on those parts of the curriculum on which there are likely to questions in national tests ... History and, more so, geography continued to be marginalized ... Outside the core subjects, assessment procedures were very limited ... In [secondary] schools ... the experience of English had become narrower ... as teachers focused on tests and examinations ... There was a similar tension in mathematics ... Much weaker teaching was too narrowly focused on proficiency in examination technique.

(Ofsted, 2006, pp. 52–6)

We should not be surprised. Testing, the world over, concentrates teachers' and students' minds on test preparation. If the tests are of a very high quality and validly reflect the full range of curriculum objectives, such concentration may help to raise standards. But this is a big 'if'; and the evidence tends to be the reverse. Concentrating on test preparation may well raise test scores, but in so doing it narrows the curriculum and the educational experience of students so that as scores rise, standards may actually fall. This was certainly the conclusion of a recent study of rising test scores in Texas. Such rising scores on the state-wide Texas Assessment of Academic Skills (TAAS) partly underpinned the Bush government's commitment to the test-based No Child Left Behind legislation (No Child Left Behind, 2001). But studies indicated that the scores were simply inflated and did not reflect genuinely rising educational standards. This was revealed by the US national monitoring programme, the National Assessment of Educational Progress (NAEP), based on light sampling across states. When Texas scores on this national test programme were analysed they showed no major gains, just slight increases in line with national trends. Researchers investigating this discrepancy between TAAS and NAEP scores suggest that the explanation lies in:

> Students being coached [for] ... the statewide exam ... and ... narrowing the curriculum to improve scores ... at the expense of other important skills and subjects that are not tested.
>
> (Klein *et al.*, 2000, p. 17)

Such findings, indicating 'score inflation and unwanted test preparation' (ibid., p. 17), have been routinely reported in the American literature over many years (Atkin, 1979; Linn, 2000; Shepard, 1990) and are beginning to be discussed in the context of results emerging from the NCLB programme itself. State level NCLB test scores are rising, but equally 'Administrators and teachers have made a concerted effort to align curriculum and instruction with state academic standards and assessments' (CEP, 2006, p. 1; CEP, 2007). A recently completed study by Rand Education funded by the US National Science Foundation reported that:

> changes included a narrowing of the curriculum and instruction toward tested topics and even toward certain problems styles or formats. Teachers also reported focusing more on students near the proficient cut-score.
>
> (Hamilton *et al.*, 2007, Summary, p. xix)

I have discussed elsewhere, as have other analysts, the ways in which standards might be measured over time, and whether or not standards in English schools can or cannot be said to have risen over recent years (e.g. Meadows *et al.*, 2007; Torrance, 2003, 2006; Tymms, 2004). However, to reiterate, the most straightforward explanation is that coaching and practice had an initial major impact on scores, but this has tailed off over time as the marginal additional benefits of coaching decline. The most obvious indication of this is at KS2 (see Figure 4.2.2), where it is also interesting to note that results in science started higher and have remained higher, without the benefit (or hindrance) of a national science strategy. Given that science was a new subject for many primary school teachers in the 1990s and subject knowledge was likely to be limited, the most plausible explanation is that teachers focused on the curriculum relevant to the tests and learnt very quickly how to coach for the tests, but any benefit to be squeezed from the system by such coaching has long since been exhausted. As we have seen, such an explanation parallels similar research internationally. Linn (2000), reviewing various uses of assessment to bring about change in the American education system over many years, notes that 'the pattern of early gains followed by a levelling off is typical of ... high stakes use of tests' (p. 6). Such findings also reflect research in business management about how innovation initially brings improvement, but its impact declines over time as personnel are deskilled then reskilled by change and then become accustomed to it (Strang and Macy, 2001). The key problem with such a phenomenon in education is that it is by no means apparent that even such early improvements in scores denote any actual improvements in educational standards.

Another key issue is the quality of students' learning experiences coupled with impact on student motivation. Successive research studies over 30 years have indicated that the quality of teacher–pupil interaction is the most important factor in improving pupil learning experiences and raising attainment (Galton, Simon and Croll, 1980, Galton *et al.*, 1999; Mortimore *et al.*, 1988; Mercer, 1995). Yet this is precisely what is threatened by over-concentration on testing, especially if reinforced by very specific and fragmented curriculum content which has to be covered in initiatives such as the literacy and numeracy strategies. Reporting on studies of the impact of the national literacy strategy (NLS), English, Hargreaves and Hislam (2002, p. 24) conclude that:

> the effects of the NLS on practice in interactive teaching have been to increase the rate of pupil contributions but reduce opportunities for extended interactions ... Only 10% of observations included children's responses of more than three words.

Similarly Smith *et al.* (2004, p. 408) report that:

> teachers spent the majority of their time either explaining or using highly structured question and answer sequences ... most of the questions asked were of a low cognitive level designed to funnel pupils' responses towards a required answer.

Lord and Jones (2006), reporting 'Pupils' experiences and perspectives of the National Curriculum and assessment', derived from a research review of 'over 300 publications' for the NFER, conclude that:

> Learners tend to have a narrow view of the relevance of the curriculum, associated with perceived subject status, assessment and 'getting grades' (that is, implicit messages permeate pupils' views). (website summary, p. 1)

Returning to the impact of testing *per se*, Reay and Wiliam (1999) report a detailed study of national testing in one south London primary school, focusing on year 6. They describe the intense pressure of testing in year 6 and the anxiety this generates, as more and more time is spent practising for the tests. The curriculum is narrowed to the basics of test preparation, 'correct spelling and knowing your times tables' (p. 346) and pupils come to value themselves and construct their emerging identities in relation to these narrow definitions of academic success.

Hall *et al.* (2004) conducted case studies of the impact of national testing in two primary schools in a Midlands city and London. They likewise identify the overwhelming impact of formal testing, especially in year 6, arguing that 'SATs ... shape ... the way the school acts to position children, their parents and the teachers' (p. 802). They note the importance of national tests in the construction of success and failure for teachers and pupils alike, in the construction of notions of 'good' and 'bad' pupils, and indeed in the construction of 'happy' or 'angry' parents. They report a similar curricular narrowing to that of the research and inspection evidence reported above, including an emphasis on literacy and numeracy in the mornings, with afternoons 'left for things like Art and PE' (p. 813). Perhaps most importantly, however, they identify the subjectification of pupil identity to test activities:

> SATs and the prospects of SATs are used as a policing mechanism to keep children attentive ... pupils are relegated to the role of question-answerers ... [and] ... the ideal and most worthy pupil is someone who prioritises SATs success [and] who self-polices to this end. (pp. 805–9)

Recent findings from international comparisons of educational achievement further compound these issues. We learn for example that in the 'Progress in International Reading Literacy Study' (PIRLS), where England came 'third' in the league table, 'ten year old pupils in England have a poorer attitude towards reading and read less often for fun than pupils of the same age in other countries' (Twist *et al.*, 2003, p. vi). Thus it would appear that pupils in England *can* read, but don't want to.

Another significant problem with any national testing system is the sheer scale and cost, both financial and human, in terms of motivation and morale. Certainly in England a system is now being operated which involves tens of millions of tests being written and administered and marked every year. The Qualification and Curriculum Authority's (QCA) current 'Fact Sheet' on the examination system tells us that 1.5 million students will take examinations in the summer of 2007 (qca.org.uk/1158_2175.html). The fact sheet does not tell us which exams this figure includes but we must presume it is GCSE, A/S-level and A-level, since the age cohort is 500,000-plus and including all key stage tests would push the figure up to more than 3 million. We are also told that 5,000 separate exam papers will be sat, with 25 million examination scripts and coursework assignments being marked. Over 5.8 million GCSE results will be issued (i.e. individual grades for each subject taken by each candidate). National Testing probably doubles these totals.

Multiply these figures by at least 5 for each KS cohort to include separate papers for English (usually × 2) and maths (usually × 2) and by at least 10 at KS4 to cover multiple GCSE subjects and papers and the total number of scripts to administer in the compulsory system will be a minimum of 15 million. Add in A/S- and A-level and the total will easily top 30 million.[4]

Calculating the cost of this industry is by no means easy, since national testing is not identified separately in government expenditure figures. At the low end of an estimate we might note that the QCA had an 'operating expenditure' of £147 million in 2006 (QCA, 2006, p.34). This figure will include QCA staff salaries and payments to consortia for producing and marking the tests but does not take into account the indirect costs on local authority and teacher time. For a mind-numbingly detailed QCA 'guide to handling test papers and scripts' for head teachers and other school staff, see: http://www.naa.org.uk/downloads/naa__guide_v15_aw_lr.pdf. Of course, even the secure handling of tests and scripts does not take into account the actual time devoted to test preparation and test administration in the school, not to mention the enormous sales of test preparation booklets to parents. Neither do QCA figures include the cost of GCSE examining, which would have to be calculated from the individual fee income received from candidates by each awarding body (i.e. exami-

Table 4.2.3 Total numbers of candidates in 2006 tests

KS1	559,778
KS2	578,328
KS3	607,072
KS4 (GCSE)	594,135
TOTAL	2,339,313

(Source http://www.dfes.gov.uk/rsgateway)

nation board). It is quite probable that the total real costs of testing are at least 10 times the QCA budget, or nearly £1.5 billion per annum.

Policy options for the future

There are no simple or straightforward policy options with respect to assessment and testing. Assessment intersects with every aspect of an educational system: at the level of the individual student and teacher and their various experiences (positive or negative) of the assessment process; at the level of the school or similar educational institution and how it is organised and held to account; and at the level of the educational and social system with respect to what knowledge is endorsed and which people are legitimately accredited for future economic and social leadership.

Governments in England over the last 20 years or so seem to have only partially appreciated this, assuming that 'standards' can be measured without the process of measurement impacting on and, in key respects, distorting the system as a whole. Similarly, because educational achievement is correlated with social and economic well-being, the efforts of post-1997 Labour governments seem to have concentrated on pushing as many children as possible through as many examinations as possible. This seems to have been conceived of as part of the drive for social inclusion and improving social mobility, without reflecting on the restricted educational experience it creates for even high-achieving students, let alone the 40 per cent who still do not attain at least five A*–C grades at GCSE. Appreciating the negatives as well as the positives of assessment is an essential first step in coming to understand the trade-offs which have to be made.

An alternative vision of 'you get what you assess' would operate at classroom level, underpinning high-quality teaching by the development and use of high-quality assessment tasks which could help to structure and focus classroom activities. This is the 'formative assessment' version of 'measurement-driven instruction', focusing on clear objectives and assessment criteria, high-quality tasks and good use of criteria-related formative feedback to students on what they have achieved and how they might improve. Recent policy has made some gestures towards this, prompted by the lobbying of the Assessment Reform Group (2002). Thus 'assessment for learning' has become a significant part of the rhetoric of the revised national strategies for primary schools, with major sections of the website resources devoted to 'planning and assessment for learning' (DfES, 2004b). Interestingly no such provision has yet been made for secondary schools, despite the fact that most of the Black and Wiliam development work has been in secondary schools (Black *et al.*, 2003). However, as we have already seen, Ofsted reports that over-concentration on national testing and targets detracts from the wider development of classroom assessment skills. The 2006 Ofsted report also notes that:

> Assessment remained the weakest area of teaching … lack of detailed information on pupils' progress in foundation subjects detracted from the rigour and quality of schools' self-evaluation … The use of assessment for learning was good in only a few schools and unsatisfactory in a quarter.
>
> (Ofsted, 2006, pp. 55–6)

Moreover, recent research by the Black and Wiliam team under the auspices of the ESRC Teaching and Learning Research Programme (TLRP) reports that while some teachers have tried to implement the 'spirit' of formative assessment with respect to developing student autonomy, most have simply followed the 'letter' and used formative assessment techniques to facilitate short-term lesson planning and teaching and promote short-term grade accumulation (Marshall and Drummond, 2006). Thus, in a context which is still dominated by testing and targets, it would appear that an alternative vision of formative assessment is unlikely to gain much of a foothold in everyday teaching practices.

The key policy problem is that assessment will *always* impact on teaching and learning, the key issue is to try to accentuate the positive impact and diminish the negative impact as far as possible. It is clear that the greater the scope and scale of the testing system, the simpler and more focused the tests will become. Until recently *all* students are tested at *four* ages/stages, totalling 2.4 million candidates. Not many high-quality, expansive and challenging tasks will be produced or used in such circumstances. For example, until the move to use teacher assessment at KS1, assessing spelling at age 7 involved the use of a one-off 20-word test (QCA, 2004), and, even though it is not now mandatory, probably still does in most infant schools. Similarly if accountability is seen to be the main purpose of the exercise then quality of teaching and student experience will be subjugated to this purpose. Thus, given the overwhelming need to refocus attention on quality of learning rather than attainment of tests scores; and in so far as we might construe formative assessment as more positive than negative, the key implications of what we now know about national testing for future policy would seem to be:

- the greater the scale and scope of the testing system, the simpler the tests will be;
- the more individual student achievement is tied to system accountability the more accountability measures will dominate student experience

therefore:

- restrict testing to a politically necessary minimum;
- attend to monitoring standards by use of small national samples;
- put resources and support into developing item banks of high quality assessment tasks for teachers to use as appropriate, plus in-service training for formative assessment.

Interestingly the DfES's evaluation of the national literacy and numeracy strategies came to similar conclusions, albeit from a slightly different perspective. The evaluation team was intrigued by the question 'can large-scale reform succeed?', especially through the combination of 'high pressure and high support' (Earl *et al.*, 2003, pp. 1 and 4). They concluded that:

> In the early implementation ... pressure for compliance ... served to engage schools ... However continuing this kind of accountability for too long may result in a culture of dependence. (p. 6)

In this conclusion we seem to have both further confirmation of the reason for the levelling off of test score improvement and a warning about the loss of capacity at the periphery under the enduring pressure of government control. Central control of the curriculum and of testing may have been a short-term solution to perceived problems of teaching quality and student achievement, but it will always threaten long-term systemic sustainability, professional development and capacity building. Now is definitely the time to reinvest in local developments at local level, especially with respect to classroom level assessment skills and understandings. Posting assessment for learning material on DfES websites may be a necessary first condition for widespread dissemination, but it is by no means sufficient for effective take-up and use. The testing regime must also be relaxed so that better quality classroom level assessment can be developed.

The government has made a start by restricting testing to teacher assessment at KS1 and now abandoning testing at KS3 with effect from 2009. This would allow more time and resources to be devoted to developing better quality assessment tasks and teacher assessment at KS2, with the development of better quality materials and more in-service opportunities focused on the other foundation subjects, beyond English, maths and science. In due course an alternative model of test development and use should be produced, involving:

- central development of an item-bank of 'authentic' assessment tasks encapsulating meaningful and challenging curricular objectives, to test performance more validly and underpin high-quality teaching;
- use of these tasks by teachers to structure their own classroom work towards the end of each KS and inform their teaching more generally;
- provision of in-service support to administer and mark tasks in similar fashion, organised collaboratively in local consortia, and leading to further development of assessment criteria and local and possibly national items; i.e. teachers would be able to both draw from and add to the national resource;
- further in-service support, again organised via local consortia, to analyse patterns of pupil responses and particularly common errors and misconceptions.

In this way assessment could be modified to address the continuing political agenda while contributing to, rather than detracting from, the quality of teaching. Inspection, too, should focus far more on the quality of classroom interaction, less on 'leadership', 'management', 'outcomes' and all the other mantras of effectiveness. Indeed inspection reports which focused on the quality of classroom interaction could be fed into local consortium discussions of assessment tasks and how best to use them.

The resources are already deployed. The DfES 'Standards' website sags under the weight of the 'frameworks', 'guidance' and CPD support material which probably takes longer to download than is ever spent reading and thinking about it (always assuming that it is ever downloaded at all, the amount of material is massive). What is required is an understanding that, ultimately, quality provision of teaching, learning and assessment must be developed by local groups of teachers discussing the nature of what they do and how they do it, just as student learning is produced out of the interactions which they have with teachers and peers. This process can be supported by centrally produced materials and structured by engagement with local authorities, governing bodies, parent groups and parents' evenings to discuss the progress of individual children. The possibilities for making local discussions of assessment processes as rigorous as possible are many. But the space must first be made available for them to begin to occur so that assessment is orientated towards the development of understanding, rather than achieving compliance.

Notes

1 General Certificate of Education, Ordinary Level; GCE Advanced Level was and still is taken at around 18-plus to qualify for entry to university.
2 Certificate of Secondary Education.

3 That is the equivalent of five GCSEs at grades A*–C: the top GCSE grades of A*–C are officially accepted as the equivalent of the old O-level passes; the percentage of students gaining at least five A*–Cs is the officially and commonly accepted measure of a good secondary education; the percentage of students gaining at least five A*–Gs (the full range of grades) is the officially and commonly accepted measure of a minimally satisfactory secondary education.
4 These problems of scale led, at least in part, to the 2008 fiasco of unmarked papers and non-returned marks, which resulted in the abandonment of testing at KS3 with effect from 2009.

References

Airasian, P. (1988) 'Measurement-driven instruction: a closer look', *Educational Measurement: Issues and Practice* 7(4), pp. 6–11.

Assessment Reform Group (2002) *Assessment for Learning: 10 Principles*, see http://arg.educ.cam.ac.uk/CIE3.pdf.

Atkin, M. (1979) 'Educational accountability in the United States', *Educational Analysis* 1(1), 1979, pp. 5–21.

Black, P. and Wiliam, D. (1998) 'Assessment and classroom learning', *Assessment in Education* 5(1), pp. 7–74.

Black, P., Harrison, C., Lee, C., Marshall, B., and Wiliam, D. (2003) *Assessment for Learning*, Buckingham, Open University Press.

Cassen, R. and Kingdon, G. (2007) *Tackling Low Educational Achievement*, York, Joseph Rowntree Foundation.

Center on Education Policy (2006) *From the Capital to the Classroom: Year 4 of the No Child Left Behind Act: Summary and Recommendations*, available online at http://www.cep-dc.org/.

—— (2007) *Has Student Achievement Increased Since No Child Left Behind?*, available online at http://www.cep-dc.org/.

Daugherty, R. (1995) *National Curriculum Assessment: A Review of Policy 1987–1994*, London, Falmer Press.

Department for Education and Employment (2000) *Statistics of Education: Public Examination GCSE/GNVQ and GCE/AGNVQ in England 1999*, London, The Stationery Office.

Department for Education and Skills (2004a) *Excellence and Enjoyment: A Strategy for Primary Schools*, London, DfES, available online at http://www.standards.dfes.gov.uk/primary/publications/literacy/63553/pns_excell_enjoy037703v2.pdf.

—— (2004b) *Excellence and Enjoyment: Learning and Teaching in the Primary Years. Planning and Assessment for Learning: Assessment for Learning*, Primary National Strategy, DfES 0521-2004 G, London, DfES, available online at http://www.standards.dfes.gov.uk/primaryframeworks/literacy/assessment/.

—— (2005) *Higher Standards, Better Schools for All*, London, DfES, available online at http://www.dfes.gov.uk/publications/schoolswhitepaper/index.shtml.

—— (2006) *Primary and Secondary National Strategies*, London, DfES, available online at http://www.standards.dfes.gov.uk/.

Earl, L., Watson, N., Levin, B., Leithwood, K., Fullan, M., Torrance, N., *et al.* (2003) *Watching and Learning 3: Final Report of the External Evaluation of England's Literacy and Numeracy Strategies; Executive Summary*, Nottingham, DfES Publications.

English, E., Hargreaves, L. and Hislam, J. (2002) 'Pedagogical dilemmas in the national literacy strategy: primary teachers' perceptions, reflections and classroom behaviour', *Cambridge Journal of Education*, 32(1), pp. 9–26.

Galton, M., Simon, B. and Croll, P. (1980) *Inside the Primary Classroom*, London, Routledge and Kegan Paul.

Galton, M., Hargreaves, L., Comber, C. and Wall, D. (1999) *Inside the Primary Classroom: 20 Years On*, London, Routledge.

Hall, K., Collins, J., Benjamin, S., Nind, M. and Sheehy, K. (2004) 'SATurated models of pupildom: assessment and inclusion/exclusion', *British Educational Research Journal*, 30(6), 801–81.

Hamilton, L., Stecher, B., Marsh, J., McCombs, J., Robyn, A., Russell, J., Naftel, S. and Barney, H. (2007) *Standards-based Accountability under No Child Left Behind*, Santa Monica, Rand Education.

Klein, S., Hamilton, L., McCaffrey, D. and Stecher, B. (2000) 'What do test scores in Texas tell us?', *Education Policy Analysis Archives* 8(49), available online at http://epaa.asu.edu/epaa/v8n49.

Linn, R. (2000) 'Assessments and accountability', *Educational Researcher*, 29, pp. 4–16.

Lord, P. and Jones, M (2006) *Pupils' Experiences and Perspectives of the National Curriculum and Assessment: Final Report of the Research Review*, Slough, NFER, available online at http://www. nfer.ac.uk/research-areas/pims-data/summaries/pupils-experiences-and-perspectives.cfm.

Marshall, B. and Drummond, M.J. (2006) 'How teachers engage with Assessment for Learning: lessons from the classroom', *Research Papers in Education*, 21(2), pp. 133–49.

McNess, E., Triggs, P., Broadfoot, P., Osborn, M. and Pollard, A. (2001) 'The changing nature of assessment in English primary schools: findings from the PACE project 1989–1997', *Education 3–13*, 29(3), pp. 9–16.

Meadows, S., Herrick, D., Feiler, A. and the ALSPAC Study Team (2007) 'Improvement in national test reading scores at Key Stage 1: grade inflation or better achievement?', *British Educational Research Journal* 33(1), pp. 47–60.

Mercer, N. (1995) *The Guided Construction of Knowledge*, Clevedon, Multilingual Matters.

Mortimore, P., Sammons, P., Stoll, L., Lewis, D. and Ecob, R. (1988) *School Years: The Junior Years*, Wells, Open Books Publishing Ltd.

No Child Left Behind Act (2001) US Public Law 107–110, available online at http://www.ed.gov/ nclb/landing.jhtml and see also http://en.wikipedia.org/wiki/No_Child_Left_Behind.

Office for Standards in Education (2002) *The Annual Report of Her Majesty's Chief Inspector of Schools 2000/01*, London, Ofsted, available online at http://www.ofsted.gov.uk.

—— (2006) *The Annual Report of Her Majesty's Chief Inspector of Schools 2005/06*, London, Ofsted, available online at http://www.ofsted.gov.uk.

Popham, J. (1987) 'The merits of measurement-driven instruction', *Phi Delta Kappan* 68, pp. 679–82.

Qualifications and Curriculum Authority (2003) *Changes to the Key Stage 4 Curriculum: Guidance for Implementation from September 2004*, London, QCA.

—— (2004) *Standards at Key Stage 1: English and Maths*, London, QCA.

—— (2006) *Annual Report and Accounts 2005–06*, London, QCA, available online at http://www. qca.org.uk/downloads/TSO_annual_accounts.pdf.

Reay, D. (2006) '"I'm not seen as one of the clever children": consulting primary school pupils about the social conditions of learning', *Educational Review*, 58(2), pp. 171–81.

Reay, D. and Wiliam, D. (1999) '"I'll be a nothing": structure, agency and the construction of identity through assessment', *British Educational Research Journal*, 25(3), pp. 343–54.

Reed, M. and Lewis, K. (2005) *Key Stage 1: Evaluation of New Assessment Arrangements*, Slough, NFER.

Resnick, L. and Resnick, D. (1992) 'Assessing the thinking curriculum', in Gifford, B. and O'Connor, M. (eds), *Future Assessments: Changing Views of Aptitude, Achievement and Instruction*, Boston, MA, Kluwer.

Shepard, L. (1990) 'Inflated test score gains: is the problem old norms or teaching to the test?', *Educational Measurement: Issues and Practice*, 9(3), pp. 15–22.

—— (2000) 'The role of assessment in a learning culture', *Educational Researcher*, 29(7), pp. 4–14.

Smith, F., Hardman, F., Wall, K. and Mroz, M. (2004) 'Interactive whole class teaching in the National Literacy and Numeracy Strategies', *British Educational Research Journal*, 30(3), pp. 395–412.

Strang, D. and Macy, M. (2001) 'In search of excellence: fads, success stories, and adaptive emulation', *American Journal of Sociology*, 107(1), pp. 147–82.

Torrance, H. (1981) 'The origins and development of mental testing in England and the United States', *British Journal of Sociology of Education*, 2(1), pp. 45–59.

—— (ed.) (1995) *Evaluating Authentic Assessment: Issues, Problems and Future Possibilities*, Buckingham, Open University Press.

—— (2003) 'Assessment of the National Curriculum in England', in Kellaghan, T. and Stufflebeam, D. (eds), *International Handbook of Educational Evaluation*, Dordrecht, Kluwer.

—— (2005) 'Testing times for Black achievement – some observations from England', paper presented to Symposium 'Leaving No Child Behind: How Federal Education Agencies are Addressing Achievement Gaps for Linguistic and Racial/Ethnic Groups', American Educational Research Association Annual Conference, Montreal, 11–15 April 2005.

—— (2006) 'Globalising empiricism: what, if anything, can be learned from international comparisons of educational achievement?', in Lauder, H., Brown, P., Dillabough, J. and Halsey, A.H. (eds), *Education, Globalisation and Social Change*, Oxford, Oxford University Press.

Torrance, H. and Pryor, J. (1998) *Investigating Formative Assessment: Teaching Learning and Assessment in the Classroom*, Buckingham, Open University Press.

Twist, L., Sainsbury, M., Woodthorpe, A. and Whetton, C. (2003) *Reading All Over the World: PIRLS National Report for England*, London, NFER/DfES.

Tymms, P. (2004) 'Are standards rising in English primary schools?', *British Educational Research Journal*, 30(4), pp. 477–94.

Reflective questions

1   Is a national curriculum and testing system a 'good thing'? Identify the strengths and weaknesses as you perceive them and think about how to develop the strengths.
2   What are the key issues facing education in the early years of the twenty-first century? How might curricular provision and assessment processes be developed to address these?

Further reading

Black, P. and Wiliam, D. (1998) 'Assessment and classroom learning', *Assessment in Education*, 5(1), pp. 7–74.

Linn, R. (2000) 'Assessments and accountability', *Educational Researcher*, 29, pp. 4–16.

Torrance, H. (ed.) (1995) *Evaluating Authentic Assessment: Issues, Problems and Future Possibilities*, Buckingham, Open University Press.

4.3 Why do some policies not work in schools?

Viviane M. J. Robinson

Introduction

The main purpose of this chapter is to examine why some educational policies fail to achieve their intended impacts. I begin by providing three possible explanations for policy failure – the complexity of the policy problem, the quality of policy design and the quality of implementation. While the success or failure of a policy is often attributed to the quality of its implementation in local districts and schools, this chapter focuses on the impact of policy design on both implementation and policy outcomes. The discussion begins by contrasting three US school reform programmes. Focusing on one key aspect of policy design – the discretion afforded to teachers – I illustrate how differing degrees of discretion influence policy implementation and contribute to the success or failure of the reform. I then introduce a New Zealand literacy initiative to explore another key aspect of policy design: the level of agreement between policy makers and implementing agents around the nature of the policy problem and how it should be addressed. I show how unrecognized and unresolved differences between practitioners and policy makers around such things as the intended focus of the policy and the outcomes sought can lead to implementation failure and low impact.

The chapter concludes with a brief consideration of the implications of this analysis for policy design. I discuss the need to create a balance in policy design between local discretion and standardization. I also emphasize the need for evidence, early in the policy making process, about the match between the theory of the policy problem held by the proposed implementing agents and the theory in the proposed policy. Policy designs that do not take any mismatches into account are likely to have limited success.

Some of the questions I address in exploring how the design of a policy can influence its success include:

- Why do educational policies often fail to make an impact – is it a matter of design or implementation, or both?
- Why is fidelity of implementation considerably lower in those schools using adaptive reform policies, which allow greater degrees of teacher discretion, rather than programmatic policies that are more tightly prescribed?
- What are some of the features of good policy design that produce instructional changes in schools?
- Why is it important to treat a policy as a *theory* of a problem?

Although there is limited scope in this chapter to fully address these questions, they will be the basis of our discussion of the complex relationship between policy design, implementation and impact.

In the democratic states of the Western world, the public expects the state schooling system to make a substantial contribution to social cohesiveness and economic prosperity. As school populations in many OECD countries become more culturally and linguistically diverse, and as the demand for highly literate and adaptable workforces increases, meeting the public's expectations of the schooling system becomes a greater challenge (Firestone and Riehl, 2005).

Politicians and policy makers attempt to meet these expectations through the promulgation of educational policies. By *policy*, I mean a system-wide intervention intended to influence practices and outcomes relevant to the policy problem. Policies, therefore, are more than ideas – they are meant to change things by preventing or improving an unsatisfactory state of affairs. What is meant by *system-wide* will vary according to the scope and nature of the problem – the *system* could refer to the national or regional education system, to a sector-based system (e.g., early childhood or tertiary), or to those units (e.g., schools) that have certain features in common, such as high levels of students from minority language groups. A policy can intervene in any one of these types of systems.

Explanations of policy failure

Even though policies address problems, they often fail to resolve, or even ameliorate, them (Cuban, 1993, 1998; Elmore and McLaughlin, 1988; Elmore, 1996). Sometimes they make matters worse. The gap between policy intention and policy outcomes is such an important problem that a considerable research literature has developed about why this is the case.

In their discussion of policy failure, Rowan and Correnti (2006) summarize three possible explanations for the failure of policy to make its intended impact. The first is the nature of the policy problem itself. Some policies may be more successful than others because the policy problem they address is less complex and better understood than other policy problems. Poor literacy, for example, may be an inherently more complex policy problem than poor child dental health. This first explanation of policy failure will not be considered in this chapter.

The second possible explanation lies in the social context in which the policy is implemented. If educational policies are to work, they need to influence the practices of many different teachers and administrators working in a great variety of settings. There are a considerable number of factors within those settings that could influence the way a policy is implemented. For example, the politics and culture of a particular school or local authority may be in tension with the policy, implementing agents may not be given appropriate training and resources, or incentives associated with the policy may not be as motivating as intended.

The third possible explanation is the design of the policy. This explanation suggests the cause of policy failure may lie, not with implementing agents or the context in which they work, but with the assumptions made by policy makers themselves about the nature of the problem and what is required to address it. For example, the United Kingdom's literacy policy implemented between 1997 and 2002 incorporated a set of assumptions about the need to reduce teachers' discretion about the amount of time they spent teaching literacy and the instructional strategies they would employ. The impact of the policy was partly determined by the adequacy of these assumptions about how to improve literacy among English primary school students (Earl, Watson, Levin, Leithwood, Fullan and Torrance,

2003). There has been far less attention in the literature to this third explanation than to the social context of implementation, but, as we shall see, the quality of policy design can be a powerful determinant of the impact of an educational policy.

Table 4.3.1 provides a simplified representation of how the quality of policy design and the quality of implementation both contribute to policy impact.

The table suggests that high quality implementation is a necessary condition of moderate to high levels of policy impact. It should be noted, however, that high quality implementation can be achieved with policies that are of either high (cell A) or low (cell C) quality design. This means that the quality of policy implementation should not be confused with the quality of the policy itself. Poorly designed policies that are vigorously implemented through legislation or regulation can make as strong an impact on schools, teachers and students as well-designed policies – though, of course, the nature of the impact differs.

There are numerous complexities in determining how to locate any particular policy within the four cells of Table 4.3.1. The following brief discussion introduces rather than resolves these complexities. First, policy designs, implementation processes and policy impacts change over time. This is particularly true when policy makers work in partnership with evaluators and/or practitioners to progressively revise a policy design and its associated implementation processes on the basis of early feedback about either implementation or impact (Cohen and Hill, 2001). Judgements about the quality of each of these three aspects could change quite radically, depending on the stage at which they are being evaluated.

Second, the boundary between policy design and policy implementation is often very blurred. A policy may fail to make an impact because teachers have received incomplete or confused specifications about what is required of them. Is this a matter of design or implementation, or both? On the whole, lack of impact can be attributed to inadequate design if faulty assumptions have been made by policy makers about the cause of the problem or about how to intervene to address it. Lack of impact is attributed to faulty implementation, on the other hand, if a policy does not have the intended impact, despite the soundness of the policy ideas.

Third, important questions can be raised about what is meant by both quality of policy design and quality of implementation. Aspects of design quality have already been touched on in the preceding discussion about how to distinguish between design and implementation. In essence, the quality of policy design is about the quality of the theories incorporated in the policy about the nature of the problem and how to resolve it. It is useful to think of policies as theories because it reminds us that, like any theory, they are fallible and open to revision. This is especially the case with educational policies because both the causes

Table 4.3.1 The contribution of policy design and implementation to policy impact

		Quality of policy implementation	
		High	**Low**
Quality of policy design	**High**	A – High impact	B – Low to moderate impact
	Low	C – Moderate to high impact	D – Low impact

and possible solutions of a particular educational problem are often hotly contested. For example, high-stakes school accountability policies assume that a significant cause of the problem of poor student achievement is low levels of teacher and administrator motivation. They make the further assumption that the appropriate intervention to address this problem is the introduction of incentives and sanctions contingent on school performance levels. If either the explanation of the problem or the theory of intervention is mistaken, then the policy design is inadequate.

Most research on implementation uses the criterion of *fidelity* to judge implementation quality, meaning that a policy is implemented as intended (Correnti and Rowan, 2007). For example, a local authority might attempt to improve literacy teaching by funding teachers to conduct collaborative action research projects on their own teaching. The fidelity of implementation of this improvement policy could include the extent to which such projects (a) focused on literacy, (b) were conducted collaboratively and (c) were completed. To reiterate, if the policy is badly designed (incorporates faulty assumptions about how to improve reading levels), it will not have the intended impact (improved literacy levels) even if there are high rates of compliance on all three indicators.

In the remainder of this chapter these ideas about policy impact are further developed through discussion of two cases for which there is rich evidence about policy design, level of implementation and outcomes. As already indicated in the introduction, the emphasis will be on the impact of policy design on both the quality of implementation and impact. The cases involve school improvement policies in the United States and New Zealand. While each example can be located in one of the four cells of Table 4.3.1, the allocation is by no means clear cut and so arguments for alternative placement will also be given when appropriate.

The importance of policy design: Comprehensive School Reform (CSR)

The first case highlights the role of policy design in the success or failure of instructional interventions in schools. It involves a comparison of three different types of school reform which have been widely used in the United States to improve achievement levels of disadvantaged students. Each programme is treated as a different policy in that it incorporates a different set of ideas about how to intervene to help schools improve. Each policy is nested within and constrained by a wider federal government policy on Comprehensive School Reform (CSR) which specifies the criteria that must be met to gain federal funding. These criteria include (a) use of a teaching programme that has been proven effective through rigorous evaluation; (b) a whole-school approach to reform incorporating teaching, management, intensive professional development and parental involvement; (c) measurable goals and benchmarks for student achievement; and (d) intensive staff support and professional development including high quality external assistance (Borman, Hewes, Overman and Brown, 2003). There are currently more than 800 different CSR programmes and the three we will be discussing here – Accelerated Schools Programme (ASP), America's Choice (AC) and Success for All (SFA) – are among the most popular. These three were chosen because there is recent evidence available both about their impact (Borman *et al.*, 2003; May and Supovitz, 2006) and about the quality of their design and implementation (Correnti and Rowan, 2007; Rowan and Correnti, 2006; Rowan and Miller, 2007).

The first source of evidence about the impact of ASP, AC and SFA is a meta-analysis of 232 evaluations of 29 different CSR programmes (Borman *et al.*, 2003). The 29 programmes were classified as showing strong, highly promising or promising evidence of effectiveness on the basis of methodological criteria (quantity and quality of the evidence) and impact (whether the programme made a significant positive difference to student achievement).[1] SFA was one of only three programmes that were classified as showing the *strongest evidence of effectiveness*. America's Choice and the Accelerated Schools Programme were classified in the third category of *promising evidence*.

Subsequent evidence suggests that the impact of AC may be greater than reported by Borman *et al.* (2003). An 11-year longitudinal study in Rochester schools showed that the impact of AC on annual student gains in reading and maths in elementary and middle grades was significantly greater than in comparison schools (May and Supovitz, 2006). The authors conclude that 'on average, students in America's Choice schools learned significantly more than did other students in the district, even after adjusting for differences in student demographics' (p. 251). It seems then that both SFA and AC can be considered moderate to high impact policies.

Evidence about the contribution of policy design and implementation to these differing impacts comes from a series of studies by Brian Rowan and his associates at the University of Michigan (Correnti and Rowan, 2007; Rowan and Correnti, 2006; Rowan and Miller, 2007). Since the three reform programmes were addressing the same policy problem (unacceptably low student literacy levels), and doing so in similar contexts (primary schools serving disadvantaged students), these studies enable us to highlight the role of policy design. (To reiterate, the design of a policy is the ideas it incorporates about the nature of a policy problem and how to intervene to ameliorate it.)

Rowan and his associates determined the consequences of these three different CSR programmes for school and teacher organization and the quality of implementation through a four-year study of four matched groups of United States elementary schools. Twenty-eight schools had chosen to implement ASP, 31 schools were working with AC, and 30 with SFA. A fourth group of 26 schools, which were not involved in any CSR programme, were used as a comparison group.

The researchers studied the impacts of the programmes on school and classroom organization and on the teaching of literacy. A survey of teachers and administrators provided information about school and class organization, including the degree of *discretion* teachers experienced in the three different programmes. There are conflicting schools of thought about how much discretion should be given to teachers and administrators to adapt reforms to their local context. Policy designs which allow greater discretion are called *adaptive*, and those which are tightly prescribed are called *programmatic* (Rowan and Correnti, 2006). Information about literacy teaching was gathered from detailed logs completed by teachers after selected literacy lessons. The log was used to assess the fidelity of implementation.

The policy design of the three CSR programmes

The goal of the ASP programme was to increase authentic, learner-centred and interactive forms of instruction. It did not require a specific curriculum focus, allowing teachers to choose which curriculum areas they would develop in this manner. Nor did it specify instructional strategies, or provide achievement benchmarks.[2] Adaptation to the local setting was fostered by (a) encouraging local professional communities to discover and disseminate locally effective teaching practices and (b) giving teachers enough discretion and autonomy to adapt these practices to their own classrooms. ASP staff and facilitators 'helped local schools use a systematic process of organizational development to uncover their own unique paths toward powerful learning and to adopt locally appropriate forms of instructional practice' (Rowan and Miller, 2007, p. 259). Fidelity of implementation was promoted by inducting teachers into the underlying philosophy and values of the programme, rather than by ensuring conformity to a prespecified set of teaching objectives or techniques. The intention was that teachers' instructional choices would be constrained by the ASP pedagogical culture rather than by prescription and monitoring.

The tightly prescribed, programmatic designs of AC and SFA present a strong contrast to the more flexible, adaptive, design of ASP. The America's Choice model was based around a set of professionally endorsed standards and instructional strategies designed to help teachers and their students to achieve them. Considerably more instructional guidance and training of teachers occurred in AC than in ASP, with programme staff placed in each school to assist the principal and coach the teachers. Unlike ASP, AC had a specific curriculum focus on writing, with specified student assignments and scoring rubrics. According to Rowan and Miller (2007), teacher compliance with the programme was gained through professional control, in which expert authorities in the form of programme staff and supporting resources were used to shape teachers' understanding of and compliance with the programme.

The SFA programme was the most prescriptive of the three, with instructional routines, lesson scripts, programme materials and a strong emphasis on the supervision and monitoring of teachers by programme staff.

The consequences of design for the quality of implementation

Fidelity of implementation was considerably higher in those schools using the programmatic rather than adaptive reform policies. In the ASP schools, literacy teaching practices were indistinguishable from those used in comparison schools. In contrast, literacy teaching in the SFA and AC schools was significantly different from that in the comparison schools and showed high fidelity to programme specifications. Rowan and Miller (2007) conclude that:

> the evidence presented here suggests that the adaptive approach to instructional change … might not be as promising an approach to instructional change as current theory suggests … it had the smallest influence of all the CSR programs studied on teaching practices, hardly moving teaching practices away from the normative practices typically observed in control group schools and not moving teachers at all toward a program-specific teaching regime. (p. 288)

Rowan and his associates did not study the consequences of these differences in implementation quality for student outcomes. It would be reasonable to suggest, on the basis of the logic of Table 4.3.1, and the Borman *et al.* (2003) and May and Supovitz (2006) findings, however, that the SFA and AC programmes had a stronger impact than the ASP intervention. Rowan's research suggests that policy design made an important contribution to this differential impact because the more adaptive ASP design was inadequately implemented. Rather than blame school personnel for this failing, he suggests that the ASP's emphasis on teacher discretion and local context had produced a greatly underspecified programme.

It is important to consider the teachers' reactions to the very different patterns of organization associated with each of these three reform programmes. Rowan and Miller (2007) report that, consistent with their expectations, positive teacher attitudes were associated with reported high levels of professional community and a strong emphasis on teacher innovation. These qualities were particularly evident in ASP schools. Contrary to expectations, however, positive attitudes were also expressed by teachers who reported high levels of instructional guidance and standardization – qualities that were particularly evident in SFA schools.

In short, the adaptive ASP programme produced high levels of teacher satisfaction but little evidence of instructional change. The more programmatic approaches of AC and SFA produced high levels of programme implementation and little teacher objection to the tight supervision and monitoring of their practice. This raises the possibility that teachers are appreciative of rather than resistant to standardization, when it is accompanied by intensive support and helps their students make worthwhile achievement gains. The researchers conclude that good instructional design may be the key to producing instructional change in schools, and that we now know some of the qualities involved: i.e., targets a specific curriculum area, challenges and supports teachers in making substantial changes in their literacy instruction; continuous support by well trained on-site facilitators and strong press by school leadership for fidelity of implementation (Correnti and Rowan, 2007).

When combined with the evidence on the impact of these three approaches to comprehensive school reforms, we begin to see the inter-relationships between policy design, policy implementation and impact in schools. The more tightly specified SFA and AC programmes enabled high quality implementation and relatively high impact on student outcomes (cell A, Table 4.3.1). The loosely specified ASP was not implemented as intended, at least in Rowan's sample of schools, and this may account for its relatively low impact as reported by Borman *et al.* (2003) (cell D, Table 4.3.1).

The importance of practitioner theory: a New Zealand literacy initiative

Our second case addresses the same policy problem as the first – that is, underachievement in literacy, particularly among students from economically disadvantaged communities.

The context for the case is a New Zealand Ministry of Education national literacy initiative designed to address New Zealand's wide and persistent disparities in achievement (Ministry of Education, 2000). While international comparisons show that New Zealand students achieve, on average, well above those of most comparable countries, the variation in achievement is very wide, with high and low performance strongly associated with ethnicity and social class (Organisation for Economic Co-operation and Development, 2001).

The overarching objective of the New Zealand policy was to lift the literacy levels of the lowest performing students. The first goal involved increasing *learning-focused school leadership* so that primary school principals and senior teachers worked more closely with teachers on raising literacy levels, particularly of the lowest achieving students. The second goal was to increase teachers' use of classroom literacy assessment data so that the teaching programme could be more finely attuned to the learning needs of individual students.

Both these goals were to be achieved through teacher and principal involvement in an action research project involving (a) collecting literacy data; (b) using the data to review the teaching of literacy in their school; (c) designing a literacy intervention based on identified needs; and (d) evaluating the impact of the intervention on student achievement. Training was provided by national facilitators, and involved two one-day workshops for principals and/or literacy leaders in each school. The facilitators also made four school visits to help school leaders develop the professional communities through which the action research project would occur and to assist teachers with visiting each other's classrooms and keeping reflective diaries.

The independent evaluation involved interviews with all 19 national facilitators and data collection from 29 participating schools, which the facilitators had nominated as either the *most, somewhat* or *least* successful schools they had worked with. In all, 28 principals, 28 literacy leaders and 53 teachers were interviewed in the nominated schools. The interviews incorporated questions, based around a *teacher learning scenario*, which assessed whether participants' could recognize the conditions in the scenario that promoted or inhibited teacher learning about how to improve student achievement. Questions also assessed participants' beliefs about whose learning needs were addressed by the policy and about the implementation of the action research project.

The results revealed little evidence that the goal of improving *learning-centred* leadership was achieved (Timperley and Parr, 2005). While interviews with the 19 national facilitators showed that they clearly understood that their job was to assist principals and literacy leaders to lead their staff in evidence-informed review of the impact of their teaching, they had not successfully communicated this understanding to the principals and literacy leaders themselves. In short, the goal of developing *learning-centred* leadership was invisible to the leaders themselves. The failure to develop skills of *learning-centred* leadership was also evident from reactions to the scenario. Only about half of the interviewees recognized that some of the practices portrayed in the scenario were contrary to the approach they were supposed to have learned through the action research process.

It is likely that the overarching goal of raised literacy achievement was also not achieved. Definitive statements about student progress are not possible as, despite the requirement for an outcome-focused action research project, only 9 of the 29 schools in the evaluation could provide outcome data, and of those 9 data sets, none were interpretable in terms of shifts in student achievement (Timperley and Parr, 2005, p. 237). Analysis of the schools' standardized assessments for Year One students also suggested no shifts in reading achievement over the three years of the project, but it must be acknowledged that these standardized assessments were not tailored to the instructional focus of each school's particular project.

Explaining the failure

In the remaining discussion of this case we examine possible explanations for this policy failure. Given what has been learned about policy design in the previous case, the quality of the design of this policy is an obvious point of departure. The literacy leadership policy lacked many of the features associated with the more successful improvement policies (Correnti and Rowan, 2007). It did not clearly specify the literacy teaching practices that were to be used, because teachers were to choose the ones that would address the identified needs; it did not provide detailed rubrics or guides to support teacher learning of new practice for either literacy instruction or action research; and it did not provide benchmarks against which teachers and facilitators could monitor implementation fidelity and student progress. Consistent with the evidence on successful implementation, however, the initiative did include some implementation support (in the form of manuals and national facilitators) and focused on a narrow reform target (literacy rather than, for example, a cross-curricular intervention).

Like the less successful ASP in the previous case, this programme represents an adaptive rather than programmatic design, because the intention was for teachers to learn how to adapt literacy instruction to the needs of their own students, and it was assumed that this goal was incompatible with a tightly specified programmatic approach. A possible conclusion, therefore, is that the lack of impact is due to a design failure involving insufficient specification of the instructional strategies to be adopted. It should be noted that programmatic reforms are consistent with a range of different instructional strategies as seen in the previous discussion of the America's Choice (AC) and Success for All (SFA) school reform programmes. The tightly scripted reading skills approach of SFA would be far less acceptable in the New Zealand primary school classroom than would the emphasis in AC on the integration of writing and reading comprehension.

The evidence provided by Timperley and Parr (2005) suggests a second aspect of policy design, in addition to degree of specification, which might explain the failure of this policy. These authors provide compelling evidence that the policy was mismatched in important respects to the beliefs and values of the implementing agents, and that it was this mismatch, or at least the failure to address it, that was responsible for the implementation failure and the low impact.

Just as policy initiators have a theory about how to address a policy problem, so do the implementing agents, who in this case were principals, literacy leaders and teachers. While a policy theory is made explicit in documents, training manuals and other supporting materials, the theory of implementing agents is embedded in the daily practices that the policy is intended to change. The teachers and principals in this literacy initiative brought their own beliefs and values to the implementation process and those beliefs shaped how they interpreted and enacted the programme in which they were participating (Spillane, Reiser and Reimer, 2002).

Table 4.3.2 compares the theory held by the school practitioners (principals, literacy leaders and teachers) with those of the policy makers (ministry officials and facilitators).[3] The summary of the theory of policy makers is derived from official documents and resource materials. The practitioners' theory is inferred from the responses of the three staff groups to questions about the scenario and about how they evaluated their own projects. Since the practitioner theory column describes the beliefs and values that actually shaped implementation, it can be described as a policy-in-use (Argyris and Schon, 1996; Hatch, 1998).

The comparison between the two theories is structured around three sets of beliefs and values: who and what should change; the knowledge and skills required to make the change; and the desired outcomes and success criteria. The first row of Table 4.3.2 shows the differing understandings of the two groups about who was the focus of the policy. As already discussed, while the ministry officials and facilitators were clear that their focus was on training principals and literacy leaders so they could work more effectively with their own staff, not one member of these two groups saw themselves as the focus of the training (Timperley and Parr, 2005, p. 239).

A similar mismatch is apparent in the second row, which describes how each group believed change would be achieved. While ministry officials and policy makers saw change coming through more evidence-informed analysis of teaching impacts, the practitioners saw increased collaborative reflection on teaching as the key.

Finally, as indicated in the third row, there were substantial differences in how each group understood the intended policy outcomes and the criteria by which success should be judged. The ministry's requirement that schools conduct an outcome-based evaluation of their projects was not achieved, because while 19 of the 29 schools produced some relevant data, only 9 of the 19 collected data both before and after their intervention, and none of these 9 data sets could be reliably interpreted. As in many such intervention programmes, policy makers had considerably underestimated the gap between the assessment and evaluation skills required by their policy and the current skill level of the implementing agents. This same mistake had been made in a previous New Zealand literacy initiative designed to promote data-based reflection about the impact of centrally funded school projects on student literacy levels (Robinson, Phillips and Timperley, 2002).

Table 4.3.2   A comparison of the intervention theory of policy makers and practitioners in a national literacy initiative

Theory component	Theory of policy makers (Ministry of Education)	Theory of practitioners (principals, literacy leaders and teachers)
Who and what should change?	• Principals and literacy leaders are the focus of the policy • They need to become more data-based and learning-centred leaders	• Teachers and their students are the focus of the policy
What is needed to achieve the change?	• Principals and literacy leaders need to develop skills in collecting, analysing and using student achievement information through participation in action research projects	• Leaders do not need to develop new skills • Teachers need more opportunities to reflect together about their teaching
What are the desired outcomes & success criteria?	• Leaders will be more outcome focused in their efforts to help staff improve teaching and learning • Improved student achievement in literacy	• Teachers will be more focused and collaborative • Student achievement is already satisfactory

Note
This table is adapted from Timperley and Parr, 2005, Figure 2, p. 239.

While faulty assumptions about practitioner skill levels may account for some of the low quality implementation of the action research projects, Table 4.3.2 suggests it is also due to differences in the value each group placed on the importance of evidence and outcome-based evaluations. When principals, literacy leaders and teachers were asked to evaluate the success of their projects and to give reasons for their ratings, only 6 per cent of the reasons for their evaluations made any reference to evidence about student achievement or progress. The majority of ratings were based primarily on such affective criteria as degree of teacher collaboration, commitment and satisfaction. When there was reference to student progress, it was claimed without reference to evidence. In short, practitioners' theories of evaluation as well as their theories of intervention were substantially different from those of the policy makers.

The final and most important difference of all is that practitioners did not connect the policy problem that motivated the initiative (New Zealand's very long tail of underachievement) with the work they were doing in the classroom. The teachers in this programme were satisfied with the level of achievement of their students and there was nothing in this initiative which challenged that view. Unlike the ministry, they did not focus on the achievement levels of the lowest achievers, or if they did, they were much more accepting of them. As the evaluators put it:

> Unless these types of national concerns are debated and understood in ways that lead to their becoming local concerns, then the motivation for teachers to address such

disparities in their classes is likely to be missing. Concerns 'out there' need to be translated into concerns 'in here' if change is to be successful.

(Timperley and Parr, 2005, p. 245)

Bridging the policy-practice divide through theoretical engagement

What is problematic in this case, and responsible for the implementation and outcome failure, is a lack of public recognition of and engagement with the theoretical differences summarized in Table 4.3.2. Such mismatches are not necessarily problematic. Vigorous debate and testing of rival theories, including rival theories of practice, can lead to better theory (Kaplan, 1964; Robinson and Walker, 1999). Indeed, a subsequent initiative corrected the differences and achieved outstanding results (Parr, Timperley, Reddish, Jesson, and Adams, 2006).

There is not scope in this chapter to do any more than briefly summarize what is meant by *engagement* with theoretical difference. (A fuller account is available in Robinson, 1993; Robinson and Lai, 2006; Robinson and Walker, 1999.) It involves, first, being aware that the ideas and values that are implicit or explicit in a policy or practice represent one account or interpretation of the situation and, as such, are fallible and contestable rather than infallible and incontrovertible.

Such an epistemic realization makes it more likely that the second step will be taken of making the theory in the policy or practice explicit so that its relative adequacy can be checked. For example, if policy makers treat as a taken-for-granted truth their belief that the performance of the lowest achievers can be lifted by more skilled literacy teaching, then they are unlikely to recognize, let alone respect the fact that some teachers may not share their views. Conversely, if teachers assume that the current wide achievement disparities in their class are immutable, then they will not be open to contrary views or evidence, whether provided by policy makers or colleagues.

A third aspect of engagement involves identifying the differences that matter (such as those in Table 4.3.2) and finding mutually acceptable and rigorous ways of exploring the validity of the competing claims. In this case, one of the most important differences is the faith put in teachers' judgements about students' learning needs and progress. Why do policy makers believe those judgements need to be more firmly grounded in evidence, and why do practitioners seem to set less store by evidence? Have they asked each other these questions? Practitioners will not learn how to check their own and others' professional judgements, as intended by the literacy leadership programme, if they believe that their professional judgements are already well founded.

This particular difference could have been explored, assuming it had been identified, by inviting practitioners to test their beliefs about what particular students could do and needed to learn. The purpose of such checking is not only to learn about the validity of a claim about a particular student but to test the validity of an implicit claim about oneself (i.e., that one's professional judgements are accurate). A successful process of theory engagement would produce a new Table 4.3.2 – one which integrated those aspects of policy and practitioner theory that survived the checking process.

If differences between change initiators and implementing agents are treated as theoretical differences rather than as resistance, or as the exercise of political or personal power, then there is more chance of them being resolved in ways that improve the policy. The position taken here is not, of course, that such differences are not political or that they are always resolvable. Rather, the position is that if such differences are framed as theoretical ones, then their substance can be examined in ways that are more likely to improve policy and to bridge gaps between change initiators and implementing agents.

The question arises as to why the differences in Table 4.3.2 were not addressed during the implementation process. Although Timperley and Parr (2005) do not provide information of direct relevance to this question, their interviews of the national facilitators provide some clues. While the facilitators understood the purpose of the policy, they probably lacked the knowledge and skills required to act consistently with it and to detect and debate those aspects of practitioner theory that were in conflict with it. Evidence of the facilitators' inconsistency is apparent in the reasons they gave for nominating the three schools they worked with who were *most, somewhat* and *least* successful in implementing the policy. Over half of their reasons made no reference to the two purposes of the policy, namely, improved leadership in teaching and learning and improved student literacy. In this respect, the theories of the facilitators were more like those of the school practitioners than of the ministry officials who designed the policy, and this similarity would have made it very difficult for them to detect the gulf between the policy and practitioner theory.

If they had detected the differences, would they have had the skills to debate their implications for achieving the policy goals? Once again the evaluation provides no direct evidence about the influence processes used by facilitators, but there is considerable indirect research evidence suggesting that the answer is probably not. When theories differ to the extent of those portrayed in Table 4.3.2, norms of politeness, collegiality and professional autonomy make it very difficult for participants to engage with their differences in a productive way (Ball and Cohen, 1999; Coburn, 2001). Theory competition is productive and produces policy improvement when participants have the skills to reframe these professional norms in ways that allow differences to be named and their implications to be rigorously evaluated through either dialogical or more formal testing processes (Robinson and Lai, 2006).

The contribution of policy design and implementation to impact

In conclusion, where should this case be located? Is it a matter of a soundly designed policy that fails because it is poorly implemented (cell B) or is it poorly designed and poorly implemented (cell D)? The latter is more plausible since at least two dimensions of poor design have been identified. First, as discussed in the first case, the policy was underspecified in terms of what was involved for teachers and principals in conducting and leading an action research project on the effectiveness of their literacy teaching. The degree of discretion afforded practitioners was inappropriately high given their existing skill level in the analysis and use of achievement data in literacy and the complexity of implementing an action research project.

In addition, the failure to engage the substantial differences between the theories of policy makers and practitioners is, in part, a design flaw. This engagement should have begun at the design stage with feedback from potential implementing agents about the degree of match between the theoretical assumptions held by those planning the policy and those who would be implementing it. Such feedback could have been obtained through early articulation and critique of the emerging policy theory (as outlined in Table 4.3.2) and by using existing research evidence about teacher skill levels in evidence-based inquiry (Earl and Fullan, 2003; Earl and Katz, 2002; Robinson *et al.*, 2002). This literature tells us that those who espouse evidence-informed inquiry for practitioners underestimate its normative and technical demands. Both these sources could have provided an early alert to the gulf between the policy and practitioner theories.

The failure of this policy is also an implementation problem, because these same lessons could have been learned once the policy was in schools. Perhaps they were not learned because the adaptive design of the policy and the emphasis on team work and collaboration meant that the differences, or at least their implications for the policy goals, remained hidden. If the differences had become more overt, then the professional development could have addressed them by showing staff how to test the validity of their differing views. This would have required a more intensive and more expensive implementation phase because teachers would have been working across two theories (their own and that which was implicit or explicit in the policy). It also would have required contexts in which policy makers, practitioners and evaluators could have come together to craft a more effective and more widely shared theory of how to address the policy problem (Coburn, 2005). This eventually happened when the draft report of the independent evaluators was presented to the ministry of education.

Discussion

The two cases in this chapter provide rich evidence about the contribution of the quality of policy design and implementation to educational policy impact. The first aspect of design that was considered was the degree of discretion afforded teachers around the implementation of an instructional policy. The evidence suggests that tighter specification of instructional interventions is associated with higher quality implementation and that such prescription does not necessarily trigger a negative response from teachers.

In the light of this evidence, it is worth critically examining the arguments for more adaptive instructional policies. The argument for more discretion is usually made in terms of the need for implementing agents to adapt a policy to the needs of their particular context. Applied to the second literacy case, this argument assumes that the factors that control the literacy achievement of students are so variable from one group of students to the next that teachers need to use different instructional strategies in different contexts. The second key assumption is that teachers involved in these programmes have sufficient knowledge and skills to exercise their discretion in ways that are effective for their students' achievement.

In critically examining these two assumptions, a number of points can be made. First, it is an empirical question whether or not different approaches are needed to raise the literacy levels of students who are at the same level of achievement but differ in other ways such as language background or motivation. Second, there is something paradoxical about giving considerable instructional discretion to teachers who are participating in an improvement programme, precisely because their current practice has not led to the outcomes that they or other stakeholders desire. The technical challenge of crafting more effective teaching strategies is not only beyond many schools' and teachers' current capacities, but has also proven, as seen in Borman *et al.*'s (2003) meta-analysis of CSR programmes, to be beyond the expertise of many highly skilled and experienced professional developers and educational researchers. It is not a matter of blaming teachers but of recognizing the technical complexity of the task of designing effective instruction for students who have already failed or been failed in our schooling system.

In short, the evidence reviewed in the first case suggests that in designing effective instructional interventions, the balance between discretion and specification should lie more towards specification than discretion. There are, however, two important provisos. First, what is specified must have a strong track record of effectiveness, or else we have a case of a well implemented bad policy (cell C, Table 4.3.1). Second, the balance between discretion and specification can shift over time as a policy is implemented. If teacher professional development embeds the learning of instructional strategies in underlying theory and principles, then teachers will, with experience, exercise instructional discretion in ways that do not sacrifice instructional effectiveness. If, however, as shown in Rowan and Correnti's (2006) study of ASP, the principles are not sufficiently embedded in practice, discretion will be exercised at the cost of fidelity. Specification and standardization, in other words, should not be treated as in opposition to the development of teacher expertise and professional judgement. What these two cases suggest is the need for programmatic approaches to helping teachers make more expert, evidence-based decisions about how to adjust their teaching to increase the literacy levels of each of their students.

The second case demonstrated the importance of treating a policy as an account or theory of a problem, rather than as the problem itself. It is a *theory* in the sense that it comprises a set of claims about the nature of the problem and how to intervene to prevent or ameliorate it. A policy theory, like any theory, is contestable in terms of the validity of the claims it makes. One source of contestation is those charged with implementation, for they too have theories about the policy problem, at least as it manifests itself in their own context. Policies are more likely to work if there is engagement with rather than bypassing of competing theories of the problem. Such engagement involves testing, through dialogue or more formal means, the soundness and implications of these differing theories. Engagement is both deeply respectful and rigorous, because its purpose is theory testing and revision, not comfortable collaboration. In short, the design and implementation of sound educational policies requires attention to policy processes as well as to policy content.

While it is very difficult to separate out the relative contribution of policy design and policy implementation to the success or failure of a given policy, these two cases have drawn attention to the ways in which the design of a policy can substantially influence its success. With respect to school reform policies, there is a growing body of evidence about the design qualities associated with both more successful implementation and more successful outcomes. Those qualities include the degree of instructional standardization and discretion and the degree to which the theory in the policy matches the theory of the proposed implementing agents.

Notes

1 A fourth category included those programmes in greatest need of additional research.
2 For a summary of the characteristics of ASP and 28 other CSR programmes see Borman *et al.*, 2003, Appendix A.
3 The table focuses on the differences between the theories. There were some shared components which are not shown – notably, the need to target lower achieving students in Years 1–4.

References

Argyris, C. and Schon, D. (1996) *Organizational Learning II: Theory, Method and Practice*, Reading, MA, Addison Wesley.
Ball, D.L. and Cohen, D.K. (1999) 'Developing practice, developing practitioners: toward a practice-based theory of professional education', in L. Darling-Hammond and G. Sykes (eds), *Teaching as the Learning Profession: Handbook of Policy and Practice*, San Francisco, Jossey-Bass, pp. 3–32.
Borman, G.D., Hewes, G.M., Overman, L.T., and Brown, S. (2003) 'Comprehensive school reform and achievement: a meta-analysis', *Review of Educational Research*, 73(2), pp. 125–230.

Coburn, C. E. (2001) 'Collective sensemaking about reading: how teachers mediate reading policy in their professional communities', *Educational Evaluation and Policy Analysis*, 23, pp. 145–70.

—— (2005) 'The role of nonsystem actors in the relationship between policy and practice: the case of reading instruction in California', *Educational Evaluation and Policy Analysis*, 27(1), pp. 23–52.

Cohen, D.K., and Hill, H.C. (2001) *Learning Policy: When State Education Reform Works*, New Haven, Yale University Press.

Correnti, R. and Rowan, B. (2007) 'Opening up the black box: literacy instruction in schools participating in three comprehensive school reform programs', *American Educational Research Journal*, 44(2), pp. 298–338.

Cuban, L. (1993). *How Teachers Taught: Constancy and Change in American Classrooms 1880–1990*, 2nd edn, New York, Teachers College Press.

—— (1998) 'How schools change reforms: redefining reform success and failure', *Teachers College Record*, 99(3), pp. 453–77.

Earl, L., and Fullan, M. (2003) 'Using data in leadership for learning', *Cambridge Journal of Education*, 33, pp. 383–94.

Earl, L., and Katz, S. (2002) 'Leading schools in a data-rich world', in K. Leithwood and P. Hallinger (eds), *Second international handbook of leadership and administration*, Dordrecht, Kluwer Academic, pp. 1003–22

Earl, L., Watson, N., Levin, B., Leithwood, K., Fullan, M., and Torrance, N. (2003) 'Watching and learning 3', final report of the External Evaluation of England's National Literacy and Numeracy Strategies, Toronto, Ontario Institute for Studies in Education, University of Toronto.

Elmore, R.F. (1996) 'Getting to scale with good educational practice', *Harvard Educational Review*, 66(1), pp. 1–26.

Elmore, R.F. and MacLaughlin, M.W. (1988) *Steady Work: Policy, Practice, and the Reform of American Education*, Santa Monica, CA, RAND.

Firestone, W.A., and Riehl, C. (eds) (2005) *A New Agenda: Directions for Research on Educational Leadership*, New York, Teachers College Press.

Hatch, T. (1998) 'The differences in theory that matter in the practice of school improvement', *American Educational Research Journal*, 35(1), pp. 3–33.

Kaplan, A. (1964) *The Conduct of Inquiry: Methodology for Behavioral Science*, San Francisco, Chandler Publishing Company.

May, H. and Supovitz, J.A. (2006) 'Capturing the cumulative effects of school reform: an 11-year study of the impacts of America's choice on student achievement', *Educational Evaluation and Policy Analysis*, 28(3), pp. 231–57.

Ministry of Education (2000) *Literacy Leadership in New Zealand Schools*, Wellington, New Zealand, Learning Media.

Organisation for Economic Co-operation and Development (2001) *Knowledge and Skills for Life: First Results from the OECD Programme for International Student Assessment (PISA) 2000*, Paris, OECD.

Parr, J., Timperley, H., Reddish, P., Jesson, R., and Adams, R. (2006) *Literacy Professional Development Project: Identifying Effective Teaching and Professional Development Practices for Enhanced Student Learning*, report to the NZ Ministry of Education, Auckland, The University of Auckland.

Robinson, V.M.J. (1993) *Problem-based Methodology: Research for the Improvement of Practice*, Oxford, Pergamon Press.

Robinson, V.M.J., and Lai, M.K. (2006) *Practitioner Research for Educators: A Guide to Improving Classrooms and Schools*, Thousand Oaks, CA, Corwin Press.

Robinson, V., Phillips, G., and Timperley, H. (2002) 'Using achievement data for school-based curriculum review: a bridge too far?', *Leadership and Policy in Schools*, 1(1), pp. 3–29.

Robinson, V.M.J., and Walker, J.C. (1999) 'Theoretical privilege and researchers' contribution to educational change', in J.S. Gaffney and B.J. Askew (eds), *Stirring the Waters: The Influence of Marie Clay*, Portsmouth, NH, Heinemann, pp. 239–59.

Rowan, B., and Correnti, R. (2006) 'Reforming instruction from the outside in: rates of instructional program implementation in three CSR designs', paper presented at the Annual Meeting of the American Educational Research Association, San Francisco, CA.

Rowan, B., and Miller, R. J. (2007) 'Organizational strategies for promoting instructional change: implementation dynamics in schools working with comprehensive school reform providers', *American Educational Research Journal*, 44(1), pp. 252–97.

Spillane, J.P., Reiser, B.J., and Reimer, T. (2002) 'Policy implementation and cognition: reframing and refocusing implementation research', *Review of Educational Research*, 72, pp. 387–431.

Timperley, H.S., and Parr, J.M. (2005) 'Theory competition and the process of change', *Journal of Educational Change*, 6, pp. 227–51.

Reflective questions

1   In your experience what is the relative importance of the three explanations of the impact of an educational policy? Think of examples of either school-based, local or national education policies where success or failure can be explained using one or more of these three explanations.

2   I have argued that a policy needs to be treated as a theory of the problem itself. Think of a policy that you work with and explain how it can be treated as a theory of the problem and of its solution. What alternative theories of the problem do you find plausible?

Further reading

Coburn, C.E. (2001) 'Collective sensemaking about reading: how teachers mediate reading policy in their professional communities', *Educational Evaluation and Policy Analysis*, 23, pp. 145–70.

Elmore, R.F. (2004) *School Reform from the Inside Out: Policy, Practice, and Performance*, Cambridge, MA, Harvard Education Press.

4.4 School as imagined community in discursive space

A perspective on the school effectiveness debate

Andrew Stables

Introduction

A school, like a nation, is construed here as a complex system existing in discursive rather than physical geographical space (other than as a set of buildings). The meaning of 'school' is therefore dependent on actors' perceptions, and these are dependent on factors apparently beyond the school. Research evidence relating to such perceptions comes not as data or phenomena, in the sense of observable behaviour subject to mathematical laws, but rather as phenomenographic fragments: pieces of described experience. Although numbers can be included in such descriptions, they are thus used qualitatively. Overall evaluative judgments about school ('good school'; 'effective school') cannot therefore validly be derived from statistical models, however sophisticated, as quantitative data alone cannot capture the indefinable range of experiences relating to any particular school, particularly given a lack of absolute consensus about educational values. Research into the effectiveness of schools can thus have limited predictive validity, although reductionist approaches can certainly reveal strong specific correlations that it is tempting to regard as causes and effects, and that might be seen to endure over a period. From this perspective, given the lack of a firm evidence base, policy makers with only a researcher's interest in any institution are less well placed to make decisions about particular schools than those 'on the ground' with more sophisticated (though still inevitably incomplete) understandings of local complexity. What is important about a school is how it is imagined by those who imagine it, among whom the policy makers are inevitably a tiny constituency with very limited terms of engagement. Thus the methodological argument becomes a political argument for decentralisation.

Note: on imagination

There is a tendency in the vernacular to associate 'imagination' with the fanciful and unrealistic. What is 'imagined', thus construed, is the polar opposite of that which is 'real', and to discuss the school (or nation) as imagined community is thus to dismiss it as unworthy of study. Such a tendency is clearly at odds with the intentions of both Benedict Anderson and the present author. Modern concepts of the imagination, where the idea has been developed in the literature, are heavily influenced by the Romantic notion, expressed by Wordsworth, that to be imaginative is to 'see into the life of things', whereas to 'make things up' is rather a product of the 'fancy'. (See, for example. Wordsworth and Coleridge, *Lyrical Ballads*; Wordsworth's 'Lines Written above Tintern Abbey'.) This chapter proceeds on the assumption that what is imagined is most certainly 'there' and eminently worthy of investigation.

School as neither here nor there

> Communities are to be distinguished ... by the style in which they are imagined.
>
> (Anderson, 1983, p. 14–15)

Benedict Anderson's view of the nation as 'imagined community' has many implications, largely unexplored, for research into schools and schooling. Anderson sees how nations came to be imagined as an historical process, whereby, through more primitive systems of community and subjection, people gradually learned to 'think' the nation in terms of a broadly ethnic and geographical sense of mutual and coincident activity (p. 28). Modern times, Anderson argues, have seen a particular shift to more localised conceptions of nationhood as a reaction to the experience of empire: a trend that seems to have been confirmed since 1983 by events in the Balkans and elsewhere. Despite the experience of nation being historically determined, however, it is also retrospective: nations are imagined as sovereign, for example, because they were, not because they are (Anderson, 1983, p. 16).

Just as the boundaries of nationhood are not always clear, neither are those of schools (nor indeed of other cultural institutions, though it is research into effective schooling that is the main issue of debate within this chapter). Where do we find a school? In and among its buildings, perhaps, yet these buildings cannot of themselves constitute the school. A school only exists in relation to its being imagined: if it is the sum total of anything, it is the sum total of perceptions and experiences of it. Such perceptions and experiences are certainly refined through the school's social networks, but these are themselves indefinite and elusive, linking those who work in the institution, those who have personal connections with it and those who know it only at second or third hand. One aspect of this is that its cultural practices pay limited heed to notions of internality and externality as these relate to its buildings, or even its teachers or students. For example, students do homework and fieldwork; games are played outside the school (sometimes at other schools); books are marked at home; friendships are forged and played out within and beyond its physical confines; cigarettes are smoked in dark corners; individual and collective life trajectories are inextricably bound up with it, as are aspects of adult domestic and economic life. Even the amount of time spent within the physical boundaries of the school varies greatly between, for example, the boarding school and the liberal sixth form college (to take examples from the British context). Perhaps most importantly, schools are conceived or construed via the perceptions of those who are not presently students or teachers within them, and are often not directly related as parents of students, past or present. The imagined school, in its complexity, is a part of the imagined community within the imagined nation, each of which will be variously imagined. (Thus conceived, it is easy to understand how sensitive to broader cultural and social currents issues of schooling are: for example, with respect to religion and ethnicity.)

It might be countered, however, that Anderson's argument does indeed relate to nations and not to smaller groupings. Perhaps understandably, since nations are his concern, he is somewhat ambivalent about the degree to which other, smaller communities are imagined. For example, p. 15: 'In fact, all communities larger than primordial villages of face-to-face contact (*and perhaps even these*) are imagined' (my italics).

There are certainly aspects of Anderson's formulation that do not apply neatly to schools, including his assertion that nationhood implies a sense of 'deep, horizontal comradeship' (p. 16); it would be a rare school that could boast this, and many school leaders might not hold such aspirations. However, schools are similar to both nations and cities insofar as 'they are sociological entities of such firm and stable reality that their members can even be described as passing each other on the street, without ever becoming acquainted, and still be connected' (p. 31). (Friends of mine recall their daughter waiting for the bus to take her to her comprehensive school, happy with her friends and apparently oblivious of the behaviour of other groups of waiting students; I recall a former pupil returning to school for a day to observe classes, when considering teaching as a career, only to conclude, 'I had no idea this school was like this'.) Furthermore, all but the smallest primary schools are unlikely to bear much resemblance to the primordial village, the status of which, vis-à-vis imagined communities, Anderson seems unclear about. Nobody knows everyone else in any but the smallest schools. Even if they do, they do not live permanently at the school; there are out-of-school lives that remain private and distinct. There was no such regular escape from the primordial village community, when even the hunting party must have acted with a strong sense of mutual purpose and transparency.

To the poststructuralist, of course, all communities are imagined. In Derridean terms, the meaning of school is 'deferred' (Derrida, 1978): that is to say, not precisely spatially and temporally locatable. Just as the current experience of nation, according to Anderson, has its roots in previous contexts, so our images of schools are constructed retrospectively and from distance. Much, perhaps most, of the debate about schools, that shapes them in the public imagination, comes from those whose experience within their physical boundaries is spatially and temporally distant. By contrast, actors within schools often speak of them in the third person; school is 'it' and not 'we'. Only certain speakers, at certain times, and in certain contexts, will refer to 'my' or 'our' school; at other times, and in other contexts, participants speak of themselves in relation to 'this school'.

School, therefore, is both there and not there; it stays with us throughout the lifespan yet we are detached from it during our schooling; it both is and is not its buildings; it belongs both to some (its professionals, its students) and to all. As such, it is not easily researchable, and is best understood in terms of stakeholders' perceptions of it.

School as chimera

In one of the most cogent critiques of school effectiveness research (SER), Hugh Lauder, Felicity Wikeley and Ian Jamieson criticise the use of 'chimera' terms such as 'ethos' as causal factors and outcomes in such research (Lauder, Wikeley and Jamieson, 1998, pp. 51–69). Essentially, Lauder, Wikeley and Jamieson's argument is that the 'Received Model' of school effectiveness research takes an over-narrow view of school effects, resulting in simplistic 'checklists' that take insufficient account of social and immediate context. They see one weakness of the Received Model being its need to fall back on 'chimera' concepts such as 'ethos' to explain what a limited methodological approach has been inadequate to make sense of ('[e]thos may be a fruitful idea, but in research terms it remains suspended in the ether', p. 55). Set against this, they are also critical of Stephen Ball's Heretical Model (Ball, 1996 and 1998, pp. 70–83) for assuming 'serendipity' (Lauder, Wikeley and Jamieson, 1998, p. 65) causes school effectiveness, and they propose a Contextual Model that assumes schools are likely to perform in certain ways as a result of their 'market' positions, yet should be investigated for local factors when they do not (p. 65).

Byrne, in many ways analogously (though there is no cross-referencing between the respective texts), argues that schools are complex systems and, as such, not easily amenable to statistical analysis based on the pre-identification of variables (Byrne, 2002a, b). Byrne argues that even multi-level modelling remains linear ('describing changes of degree but not ... of kind'), nominalist ('identifying cases in terms of labels which derive from values on variables rather than the general character of the case') and analytical ('treating cases as bundles of variables rather than as complex entities) (Byrne, 2002a, p. 6). Byrne, like Lauder, Wikeley and Jamieson, proposes the classification of schools in relation to performance and social context (p. 6), with a research focus on changes over time, and the triangulation of qualitative and quantitative data.

Both Lauder, Wikeley and Jamieson's and Byrne's views remain strongly positivist, assuming that the social context of a school at a given temporal moment can be adequately accounted for. However, in discursive space there is no such clear-cut beginning or definable context. This is not to suggest that what is imagined has no coherence: rather, in discursive space, here, there, now and then are 'all of a piece'. In the *Philosophical Investigations*, Wittgenstein points out how 'the action of a machine ... seems to be in it from the start' (Wittgenstein, 1967, p. 77). Similarly, our understandings of a particular school as a whole cannot be clearly located in spatial or temporal terms, though our perceptions may differ according to the circumstances of their being 'called up', and we may remember particular points of realisation. Obviously, a school's success cannot unambiguously be held to begin with the publication of its first good set of examination results, for example. When 'school' is understood in terms of its cultural, as opposed to its physical geography, school itself becomes a chimera concept, not amenable to positivist research.

It is beyond dispute that certain hard data can be collected with respect to schools' cultural practices; these include input and output data relating to academic achievement, social class, ethnicity and gender. What these data signify depends on context and perception. It does not follow that such data, however manipulated, can attain either objective validity or sustained explanatory power as explanations of cause and effect or as evidence of the value of a school. Indeed, no empirical research can settle the ethical question of what is valuable; for this, we must turn to philosophy. As Hammersley states:

> While researchers in this [school effectiveness] field are usually careful to note that the outcome measures they use do not exhaust or measure all the goals of schooling, their work is sometimes presented and often interpreted as measuring school effectiveness *as such*.
>
> (Hammersley, 2002, p. 23; italics as original)

Haig (2000) argues that the 'proper objects of scientific explanation' (p. 292) are phenomena and not data, where 'phenomena are relatively stable, recurrent features of the world we seek to explain or predict' (p. 292), In positivist methodological terms, such data, as suggested above, may be sufficient to identify phenomena, but not to extrapolate conclusions about school effectiveness from such phenomena, or to attain predictive validity. However, many of the 'data' collected by researchers with respect to school value relate to perceptions and not to facts and figures, are less self-evidently 'observable' and cannot validly be held even to constitute phenomena.

Unfortunately, there is a strong temptation to impress policy makers by fostering, or not denying, the illusion that such phenomena and such 'data' do indeed define effective schools, and that their causal conditions can be both identified and replicated. The more reductionist the research, the more strongly it can show correlations between identified factors (though correlations in educational research are often not strong, even then), and the more it is tempting, but not valid, to interpret such correlations as causes and effects. Consider, for example, the following.

Imagine a new and unanticipated plague kills off a large proportion of the 16-year-olds in a given school year. Thus School A has only a few, deeply worried students in National

Curriculum Year 11, and they fail many of the GCSE examinations; School B, where the disease has had little impact, has many more students, who all gain passes at GCSE. It is clear that the school with more students gains more passes than the school with few. It may well be that the schools hardest hit by the disease nearly always achieve worse results, so the result is significant and generalisable, yet their failure is certainly not 'caused' by having fewer students, and may well not be caused by the disease: the effects of the disease remain open to interpretation. The generalisability of the finding promises little, therefore, in terms of predictive validity.

If SER concerns itself totally with factors within the school (as in the Received Model), the disease cannot be directly accounted for, as it is not internal, and class size may therefore appear as a key variable; perhaps students will always do better in smaller classes. (Perhaps they will!) If the view is taken that the school cannot be understood as isolated from its social context, yet reductionist research approaches are employed, it may be concluded that the key variable here is the disease, but only if the *a priori* definition of the social context does not preclude it.

Suppose, in this case as in many others, that certain schools are statistical outliers; they do not fit the general pattern. Quantitative research is generally not able to make much of outliers. Although Lauder, Jamieson and Wikeley urge that qualitative case studies should be undertaken where schools do not behave as their market positions predict they should (1998, p. 65), their Contextual Model is not geared towards picking up the disease as a key factor except where its differential impact clearly upsets the expected pattern. However, the differential impact of the disease may be quite unconnected to social context as defined by market position (though history indicates that often this may not be the case), so this effectively limits research into the effects of the disease. To sum up, the Contextual Model may only be able to look at schools insofar as the effects of the disease may have impacted on predicted performance with respect to (essentially) social class variables, which would be a partial view, to say the least, of the prevailing conditions.

Thus (as defined by Lauder, Jamieson and Wikeley), the Received Model of SER could not account for the role of the disease; the Heretical Model would be equally ill-equipped to account for it (if school effects are understood as 'loose couplings' between organisational factors at a number of levels); the Contextual Model would also prove unsatisfactory.

Plagues apart, a more common, less extreme scenario envisages that students from social class X, ethnic group Y or teaching group Z outperform all others. Again, this does not validly attribute cause to X, Y or Z. Ethnicity cannot cause university entrance, for example, other than under conditions of unlikely extremity. Of course, the research can factor in other variables, such as prior achievement, family background, number of siblings, and will then produce new, more surprising correlations. However, the list of variables can never be exhaustive, and the correlations can never clearly identify causes, single or multiple. In its complexity, such research can flatter to deceive.

In addition, quantitatively measurable outcomes are not the only valid outcomes of schooling. Whether schooling produces nice people, happiness, convenience, opportunity (whether or not taken), generational progress (see below) or fun remains a matter of individual and shared perceptions; furthermore, many such perceptions are formed long after the event, or by people with no direct experience of the school in question (in terms of its physical geography). Even in terms of hard economic models, life chances can be interpreted and measured in different ways. For example, to use Pierre Bourdieu's work in a way of which he would very likely have disapproved, it could be argued that effective schooling for many people will be assessed in terms of return on cultural capital, along the lines of 'My schooling was very good for me; I was the first member of my family to get into university' (Bourdieu, 1997; Stables, 2002). A former Labour Party leader in Britain, Neil Kinnock, indeed used this example to justify state schooling in a pre-election speech in 1992, apparently ignorant of the counter-argument that if schooling is to be assessed according to greater success than one's forebears, existing levels of social inequality could well be maintained or even increased with respect to each succeeding peer group. (Also, it may become increasingly difficult for schooling to 'deliver' against such criteria as a decreasing working population supports an increasing ageing population.)

At its most simplistic, SER claims qualitative judgments on the basis of limited quantitative evidence, and where these judgments amount to overall evaluations of a school's performance, they are invalid. Where it does not claim these, it invites policy makers to interpret the data thus. If it were to use qualitative data in the same way, it would remain invalid, but for different reasons. (Qualitative) research 'data' relating to questions of value are arguably neither data nor phenomena in scientific realist terms so cannot safely be used for the kind of theory generation that promises predictive validity. To quote Byrne: 'the elements in the hierarchy of pupil, class, school, LEA are not atoms. They are complex systems with emergent properties' (Byrne, 2002a, p. 2).

Despite this, Byrne's promotion of 'time ordered classification' (p. 6) does imply the emergence of key characteristics, though Byrne is not explicit about implications for prediction. Byrne problematises variables, but not data.

Haig (above) takes a strongly positivistic position yet is also a defender of grounded theory and qualitative research as scientific method. In Haig's case, there is an awareness of the problematic nature of these terms in the scientific realist literature, but this awareness does not extend to a critical consideration of the nature of linguistic data in terms of cultural practices and the degree to which one can predict from them. People's thoughts about a school, for example, can be logged and classified in response to a particular research question, but to extrapolate phenomena and draw theory from such data can be misleading. While it can be argued that what is heard (in interviews, for example) is as robust as what is seen, and therefore might qualify as 'data', this perspective takes insufficient account of the nature of linguistic meaning. Linguistic meaning does not exist prior to interpretation (or, at least, to 'knowing how to go on' in Wittgensteinian terms) and is not, as far as anyone can see, subject to mathematical laws. The meanings of utterances do not arise from their immediate physical and temporal (and, in that sense, observable) contexts: rather, utterances are their meanings. In scientific realist, positivist terms, patterns of data constitute phenomena in terms of their observability, and thus predictability, in space/time. However, linguistic 'data' form patterns only in discursive space. Repeated sequences of words cannot safely be held to constitute phenomena; at best, they may signal them (again, an idea used by Wittgenstein). Individual words and sounds not contextualised within utterances make no sense (this of itself problematises the issue of what constitutes a linguistic datum), and utterances make sense only within discourse practices (Fairclough, 1989, 1995). Ultimately, the relationship of signifier (the word) to signified (the concept) and referent (the 'thing') remains unverifiable, so the mathematical laws derived from, and applied to, the study of the physical world that govern positivist research cannot safely be held to apply to utterances (Culler, 1976). In the light of this confusion about the validity of utterances as data, and the problems in construing sets of utterances, or locating sets of meanings, as phenomena, qualitative data may more fruitfully be thought of as phenomenographic or perspectival fragments: pieces of expressed or described experience. Such a definition can safely be used by both realists and social constructionists, since it leaves open the possibilities both of experience itself being constituted by language, and language as representation. As with all fragments, however, it can never be certain how they relate to wholes, though it is inevitable that wholes will be constructed by interpreters from the partial evidence they provide, according to need and context. One can generalise from patterns constructed out of phenomenographic fragments, but such generalisations can relate only to practices in discursive space and not to anything 'real' that operates according to the laws of space and time. Thus generalisation does not carry predictability along with it, except insofar as patterns tend to endure for a while and then dissolve into other patterns, in ways that are themselves not predictable.

The above argument by no means implies that research has nothing to offer policy makers. Martin Hammersley (2002, p. 97) distinguishes between three sets of approaches to, and uses of qualitative research that he defines as 'models': an engineering model (in which researchers provide robust scientific knowledge), an enlightenment model (in which researchers offer critique and alternative theoretical perspectives) and a cognitive resources model (in which the researcher provides information on the understanding that this will be used in unpredictable ways). Within each of these, research influences policy, yet even the engineering model, if used sensitively, only involves research as informing policy rather than determining it.

School effectiveness as policy: the case for local control

As a complex and, furthermore, as an imagined system, the workings of a school cannot simply be explained in terms of the interaction of pre-specified variables. While research will inevitably identify common patterns between complex systems, this does not imply that variables can be abstracted and applied in terms of predictive explanatory power. 'Variable', in the abstract, might itself be a chimera. (Byrne refers to 'variate traces': Byrne, 2002a, b, his argument being that variables are credited with autonomous existence outside the complex systems within which we recognise their operations.) The preceding argument has identified two implications of this for thinking about research into school effectiveness: the first is that so-called qualitative research data are neither data nor phenomena in a scientific realist sense, and the second is that internality/externality and temporal location are contestable concepts with respect to organisations such as schools. In one sense, schools may be places to which we go to get certain things done, but as communities and organisations, they are imagined.

The implication of this in policy terms (as, indeed, of Ball's Heretical Model and, to a lesser degree, of Lauder, Jamieson and Wikeley's Contextual Model) is that those 'on the ground' in a particular school are best placed to understand its complex dynamic, albeit that complete understanding is impossible. Such understanding can be informed, but not provided, by research. This recognises 'on the ground' as a contested concept. It is clear, however, both that an imagined community can only exist in the minds of those who imagine it, and that a particular school will play a stronger role in the lives of some people than of others.

It is also, of course, not straightforward to argue for 'local' control of schools. Who, or what, is local? The term can be used in arguments for totally privatised systems, for specialist schools, for community schools, for strongly self-governing schools or for community schools under strict regulatory local control. It is not within the remit of this chapter to evaluate any of these relative to others. The present argument is that schools are best understood by those who act within, and in relation to, them (for 'within' really means 'in relation to'), and that the composite pictures derived from multiple perspectives resist closure;

furthermore, the application of large amounts of funding to generate a secure evidence base applicable to all contexts is a significant misuse of resource. It is not a matter simply of challenging the crudity of some school effectiveness research: if schools are imagined communities, they exist only in the minds of those who imagine them.

References

Anderson, B. (1983) *Imagined Communities: Reflections on the Origin and Spread of Nationalism*, London, Verso.

Ball, S. J. (1998) 'Educational studies, policy entrepreneurship and social theory', in Slee, R., Weiner, G. and Tomlinson, S. (eds), *School Effectiveness for Whom? Challenges to the School Effectiveness and School Improvement Movements*, London, Falmer, pp. 70–83.

—— (1996) 'Good school/bad school', paper delivered at the British Educational Research Association conference, Lancaster, September.

Bourdieu, P. (1997) 'Forms of capital', in Halsey, A.H., Lauder, H., Brown, P. and Stuart Wells, A. (eds), *Education: Culture, Economy, Society*, Oxford, Oxford University Press, pp. 46–58.

Byrne, D.S. (2002a) 'Beyond multilevel modelling', paper delivered at the British Educational Research Association, Leeds, September.

—— (2002b) *Interpreting Quantitative Data*, London, Sage.

Culler, J. (1976) *Saussure*, London, Fontana.

Derrida, J. (1978) *Writing and Difference*, London, Routledge and Kegan Paul.

Fairclough, N. (1989) *Language and Power*, London, Longman.

—— (1995) *Critical Discourse Analysis*, London, Longman.

Haig, B. (2000) 'Statistical Significance Testing, Hypothetico-Deductive Method, and Theory Evaluation', *Behavioral and Brain Sciences*, 23/2, pp. 292–3.

Hammersley, M. (2002) *Educational Research, Policy Making and Practice*, London, Paul Chapman.

Lauder, H., Wikeley, F. and Jamieson, I., (1998) 'Models of effective schools: limits and capabilities', in Slee, R., Weiner, G. and Tomlinson, S. (eds), *School Effectiveness for Whom? Challenges to the School Effectiveness and School Improvement Movements*, London, Falmer, pp. 50–69.

Stables, A. (2002) 'Diachronic and synchronic analysis of education: taking account of the life-history', *Westminster Studies in Education*, 25/1, pp. 59–66.

Wittgenstein, L. (1967) *Philosophical Investigations*, Oxford, Blackwell.

Reflective questions

1   If it is valid to see a school (for example) as 'imagined', how might this problematise assumptions about the relative validity of quantitative and qualitative research methods in studying such institutions?
2   If an institution (a 'structure') is 'imagined', can it have agency? In what sense, for example, might it be feasible to think in terms of 'learning organisations' or 'institutional' problems?

Further reading

Stables, A. (2005) *Living and Learning as Semiotic Engagement: A New Theory of Education*, Lewiston, NY and Lampeter, Mellen Press.

Stables, A. (2008) *Childhood and the Philosophy of Education: An Anti-Aristotelian Perspective*, London, Continuum.

Section 5

Deploying theory

Introduction

Harry Daniels

A central concern of this book has been with the role of theory in research and educational policy making and pedagogic practice. The chapters have been selected to support the development of reflective practitioners who can and do draw on the legacies of research to inform their own critical engagement with their work. In so doing they argue that they will be shaping theory in and through practice. Theory is not understood as an immutable given, rather it is understood as a repository of tools for engaging with contemporary problems. With these thoughts in mind we have brought together a collection of critical perspectives on education which we hope will help readers to reflect on the strengths that they afford and the limitations that are evident in their current manifestations. In Section 1 four chapters, in different ways, ask the reader to challenge their understandings of the place of knowledge and understandings of its production in education. Section 3 provides an opportunity to reflect on the implications of diversity in learning communities from political, sociological and perspectives. The political theme is extended in Section 4 which invites consideration of the practices of policy formation and governance.

At the end of the book we decided that we wanted to bring the processes of reflective action with and on theory to the foreground. Our concern is with the transformative effect of being a researcher, of researching. That is we wanted to present readers with accounts of why researchers have undertaken particular projects and about how they have engaged with the practice of research. Thus, in this final section of the book, we have included four chapters written by recent doctoral graduands. The purpose is to show how those who are close to practice deploy theory in their research.

Alaster Douglas's research drew on his experience as a former deputy head teacher in a large English secondary school to consider some of the impacts of departmental cultures in schooling. His primary foci were on the ways in which different secondary school subject departments work with beginning teachers implicitly and explicitly to enable them to learn about learning and the implications for teaching and the factors that influence the ways in which they set about this work. He sets the background to his study through reference to a number of sociological texts, such as Ball's work on performativity, and then moves to develop an approach based on activity theory and accounts of communities of practice. In his thesis he combines questions concerning the organisational and structural process of beginning teacher learning (context as a system) with a consideration of interpersonal relationships and practices (context as a set of relations). In so doing he ventures on the obdurate problem of the structure/agency relation which has ricocheted through social science for a considerable period of time. He does so because the problems that he sees in schooling, in part through firsthand experience, demand such a form of theoretical engagement.

Clare Morris also draws on activity theory in her professional doctorate. She is studying aspects of pedagogic practice in the field of medicine. Her aim is to develop a greater under-standing of the cultures of education and training within medicine as well as to articulate the elements of an appropriate pedagogy to underpin the work of doctors-as-teachers. This move to see a large range of professional domains as sites within which pedagogy is enacted is of growing interest amongst educators and policy makers. In so doing she teases and tests the theory and she seeks to engage with the practices which concern her. This creative interplay between theory methodology and research questions bears witness to the form of 'double move' which Mariane Hedegaard discussed in chapter 1.4, in which theoretical knowledge is brought to bear on practical experience and both shape each other and in the long term develop.

In her PhD, Sarah O'Flynn engaged with questions concerning the ways in which in the process of schooling itself or in opposition to it girls construct their desires in terms of their imagined futures. She drew on recent theorising in the fields of gender and sexuality to draw attention to mismatches between the orientation of UK government policy and the life expe-riences and aspirations of young people.

Lastly, Maria Balarin opens her chapter with a discussion of her way of understanding the role of theory in social research. She then proceeds to discuss the way in which she used theory in her doctoral study of radical education policy discontinuity in Peru. Importantly she points to how the role of theory was crucial in moving from a rather broad understanding of her problem to a clearer definition of what she wanted to study and the questions she needed to pose. Again, this exemplifies the way in which the issues flagged by Nash, Young and Hedegaard are brought to life in the context of critical inquiry. The importance of theo-retical knowledge is illustrated in what could be called the learning processes in research. Just as some of our contributors have argued the case for greater emphasis on knowledge in schooling so Maria Balarin makes a case for theory-informed research not for its own sake but for the understandings it affords when such theoretical knowledge is brought to the study of practice whether that practice is in the classroom, the clinic, the government depart-ment or the university. In her conclusion she notes an assertion that echoes the underlying drive behind this entire book: that going from an ill-structured to a clearer definition of our problems is a process that strongly relies on the use of theory. Thus we need to be aware of the theories that are in play and the problems which they lead us to articulate.

5.1 How do secondary school subject departments contribute to the learning of beginning teachers?

Alaster Douglas

Research aims

As a former deputy head teacher in a large English secondary school I have long been aware that departmental cultures can vary within schools and offer different learning environments for the teachers who work in them. The increasing involvement of schools in Initial Teacher Education (ITE) may mean that these differences have a relevance that extends beyond an individual school and its staff. I am currently completing the fieldwork for a doctoral thesis entitled 'How do secondary school subject departments contribute to the learning of beginning teachers?' I am based in one secondary school for three school terms, looking at four subject departments, and working with pre-service teachers who are participating in a one-year Postgraduate Certificate in Education (PGCE) programme.

Since the late 1980s in England schools have been given some direct responsibility for the training of beginning teachers, a responsibility that has increased over the subsequent decades. Currently two-thirds of any English secondary PGCE course is based in school, and during this time the responsibility for beginning teacher learning is shared between schools and higher education institutions.

There has been little research on how school departments contribute to beginning teacher learning, and consequently there is limited understanding of how departments might support their learning. My study aims to contribute to this area of ITE research.

Participants in the study are school and university staff involved in ITE and the student teachers who are placed in the research school. I am working in an ethnographic way, observing and attending school activities and interviewing the personnel involved about their understanding of and participation in all aspects of ITE. I am also examining relevant documentation available in schools, the university where my research is being supervised and the Teacher Development Agency (TDA), which oversees teacher preparation in England.

The findings that emerge will consider the learning processes to be found within and between the departments. I aim to compare these processes across departments and to examine how department practices are enabling beginning teachers to learn. Such detailed research and analysis into what is happening in the departments is therefore based on *what* is occurring and *how* it is occurring.

I also intend to discuss what departments might or could contribute to the learning of beginning teachers. An increased awareness of the work that is taking place in schools will ideally help the mentor development work at the university and strengthen the work of the ITE partnership.

Research questions

In order to address how secondary school subject departments contribute to beginning teacher learning, it is necessary to understand how the departments operate and why they operate in the way that they do. The data generated from interviews with tutors responsible for the curricula on the PGCE course in my MSc research (Douglas, 2005) indicated that there were differences in the notions of teaching and learning both within and between subject departments. It is therefore important to highlight the possible tensions and contradictions in the learning opportunities for beginning teachers working within subject departments. This is inherent in the first research question:

1   How do the different secondary school subject departments work with beginning teachers implicitly and explicitly to enable them to learn about learning and its implications for teaching?

The second research question seeks to explore why departments work differently and identify the reasons for this:

2   What are the factors that influence the ways in which the different departments work with beginning teachers?

The responses to these questions will describe the similarities and differences noted in the way the departments work with beginning teachers and give suggestions as to why this may be so.

Secondary school subject departments

Curriculum

The research looks at four secondary school subject departments (geography, history, science and modern foreign languages) and focuses on the work they do with beginning teachers. Research on department subcultures and the micro-politics of schools highlights the complexity of departments as learning environments in schools. The organisational structure of schools has changed little in recent decades, and this is reflected in the research done since the 1970s. However, recent interventions of government and its prescriptive strategies on the detailed processes of how and what to teach (for example the Key Stage 3 strategy) have changed the way departments approach the curriculum, and consequently debates on teaching and learning:

> As the current DfES website demonstrates, there is now a huge enthusiasm on behalf of the government to intervene in the detail of educational processes with advice on all aspects of teaching and the day-to-day running of schools (there are, for example, over 2000 model lesson plans that can be downloaded, an intervention that would have been unthinkable a generation ago).
>
> (Furlong, 2005, p. 125)

The previously fragmentary nature of departments is now overlaid by a strong national system, which is adopted by different departments to a greater or lesser extent. Beginning teachers will be aware of this, and will therefore enter departments knowledgeable about the national agenda but unsure of how the department interprets or adopts this.

Performativity

The nature of micro-politics in schools has changed in recent years with the notion of performativity, which has arisen from the modernist policies of government. When speaking about school reform at the beginning of the 1990s, Ball noted the change in the political climate:

> The market ideology of the Conservative government is clearly embedded in a broader commitment to possessive and competitive individualism.
>
> (Ball, 1990, p. 10)

School department performances are much more visible now, seen both collectively and individually by the data produced from examination results and Key Stage testing. Departments and individual teachers can be compared with other departments and teachers both within and outside of the school. Consequently, the group dynamics of teachers working together has changed, and the added pressures of meeting targets and middle manager objectives impact on their work. With the increased use and interrogation of performance data, there may be tension and an uncomfortable relationship between the collective and the individual in subject departments.

Pressures on individuals may change the nature of the work and the learning. Beginning teachers will pick up messages about what teaching and learning is from how departments and teachers within departments respond to new initiatives. They will become aware of the multi-voiced and potentially contradictory nature of departments, and see tensions within and important differences between departments. Some beginning teachers will work across departments (as in the humanities, for example), and this may add to their appreciation of department contexts.

Department subcultures and characteristics

Little research has been done on school departments but what has been described emphasises the complexity of their make-up.

Descriptions of departments as 'epistemic communities' (Esland, 1971) emphasise the separateness of subject areas and the effect this has on how teachers view pupils. The National Curriculum has dissuaded integrated project work by further defining subject areas, thereby establishing clear subject boundaries and maintaining the organisational structure of schools.

The strength of subject subcultures has been evident in research on the introduction of new subjects such as ICT (John, 2005; Goodson and Mangan, 1995) and Design and Technology (Paechter, 1995) into the curriculum.

However, the nature of subject knowledge and how it is viewed has been considered to be more complex than epistemic communities, with the identification of varied opinions about subjects and how they should be taught. Ball points out how the differences between (and within) school departments represent subcultures from both a technical point of view (the conception of subject content and structure) and from assumptions about the broader purposes of education and how children learn (1987). Bruner has explored this latter point further in his discussions of folk pedagogies, which reflect a variety of assumptions about children (1999).

Subject matter also influences instructional practice as well as how teachers think about curriculum, learning and teaching. Modern foreign languages (MFL) is seen as a well-defined subject with many connections across courses in different year groups (the learning of vocabulary and grammar, for example). The production of new knowledge in science enables it to be seen as a more dynamic subject rather than a relatively static one such as MFL. Required subjects like science often have larger departments with more accountability in the form of pupil external testing (end of Key Stage tests). Optional subjects may attract pupils who are more motivated as they have opted for the course (as in history and geography) (Stodolsky and Grossman, 1995).

Leach and Moon have explored the 'personal constructs' of teachers: 'a complex amalgam of past knowledge, experiences of learning, a personal view of what constitutes "good" teaching and belief in the purposes of the subject' (1999, p. 95).

Therefore, beginning teachers are likely to encounter a variety of beliefs and teaching styles both within and between departments. How these are mediated by staff, the mentors and the beginning teachers themselves will indicate how successfully the principles of a PGCE course designed to promote a 'conscious awareness' of preferred ways of teaching, are reflected in practice (OUDES, 2006, p. 1).

Subject departments as environments for teacher development

Although subject departments can provide a positive learning environment for beginning teachers, some research suggests that deeper thinking about pedagogical and subject beliefs is often absent (Butcher, 2000; Maynard, 2001).

The diversity of opportunities available to teachers in their department experiences is highlighted in McLaughlin and Talbert's discussion on professional communities (2001). In their research, many departments are characterised as weak professional communities where thoughts and practices are kept private. In stronger communities teachers are mutually engaged, jointly developing practice and sharing resources. Departments can differ significantly in collegiality and in beliefs about students, subject matter and good practice (Helsby, 1996; Visscher and Witziers, 2004). The importance of the role of the manager/subject leader has also been acknowledged in other research that considers departments as learning communities (Busher and Blease, 2000; Donnelly, 2000; Eraut *et al.*, 2000).

The analytic framework

A detailed exploration of how subject departments work with beginning teachers may enhance an understanding of how opportunities for learning differ between departments. This necessitates looking at what departments are offering beginning teachers and how they are receiving it, and then questioning what this contributes to their learning. An understanding of the tensions and contradictions in the environment in which beginning teachers are developing as practitioners may enhance greater appreciation of the factors influencing ITE in schools.

Activity theory

Activity theory emphasises how settings where people are working together on a shared task or common 'object' can be examined to see whether they are systems where learning occurs. What marks a setting or system as a site of learning is its capacity to allow people to

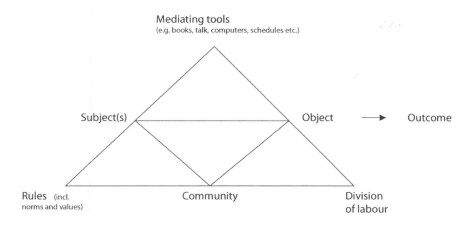

Mediating tools
(e.g. books, talk, computers, schedules etc.)

Subject(s)   Object ⟶ Outcome

Rules (incl. norms and values)   Community   Division of labour

Figure 5.1.1 An activity system (Engeström, 1999)

problematise the task, recognise the complexity in it and respond to that complexity. The result of that process is therefore not simply individual learning, but learning at a collective or systemic level in which the problem is changed and people's relationship with it is also altered. Activity theory therefore provides a device with which to look at a system of activity and can be used as an analytical tool and a way of understanding the processes of knowledge and skill construction within, for example, a school subject department. As Russell explains, the theory provides a broad context by going beyond the individual to acknowledge the social and material relations that affect complex human learning and people's interactions with others as mediated by tools (Russell, 2004).

Engeström developed activity theory by drawing on Marx, Vygotsky and Leont'ev. Whilst advocating the study of tools (which include conceptual as well as material tools) as central to human functioning, he also enlarged the activity from the Vygotsky model of subject–tool–object to include community, rules and division of labour (with the importance of analysing interactions between the system's elements). This (illustrated in Figure 5.1.1) created Engeström's second generation of activity theory.

The object or focus of the system implies an overall direction of the activity, ideally seen as a shared purpose or motive such as the professional development of a beginning teacher. By using tools, participants will act on the object in order to produce an outcome. So a teacher mentor might use a planning framework as a tool in a conversation with a student teacher. However, the object (the student teacher) may be understood differently (or even contested) by participants in the activity system, who are likely to bring many motives to a collective activity. For example the head teacher may see the student teacher as an extra pair of hands, while the mentor is focusing on the student teacher's development.

How activity theory contributes to this research

Subject departments in secondary schools are complex organisational settings for beginning teacher learning. Activity theory describes an object-orientated system, which can serve as a unit of analysis and capture the dynamics and purposes of specific departments in rela-

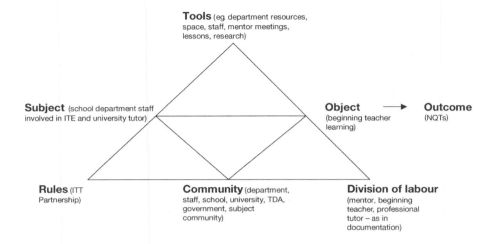

Figure 5.1.2 An activity system of school-based ITE

tion to ITE. One can examine beginning teacher learning, for example, as the object of a department ITE activity system. Therefore by framing the case study of each department as an activity system, no matter how many people there are in the department, how it is structured or how the department operates, it is possible to compare its school-based ITE activity system with other departments' school-based ITE activity systems. An activity system has been defined on the basis of the purpose of the research (Figure 5.1.2).

Activity theory is therefore being used as an analytic framework for studying departments as potential sites of learning. However, from Engeström's perspective one needs to focus on collective rather than individual learning in an activity system. This takes us only so far. For example, by examining the dynamic and contradictions in a system, I am able to identify behaviours and to try to explain their meanings in terms of the activity system in which they are produced and understood. I am also able to highlight the way the activity systems are viewed by the people involved in them, and therefore a fuller understanding of how the systems are seen becomes apparent. I can explore whether people share their understandings of what the objects and outcomes of the systems are, whether they understand the tools in the same way and how people view the significance of other communities that are part of the process of ITE.

The systems address the structure and macro-organisational aspects of beginning teacher learning in schools. This helps in exploring how and where the process of beginning teacher learning differs in the subject departments, and allows consideration of the numerous influences on the departments (for example the subject communities, central subject specific initiatives, qualification standards, the organisation of the ITE programme and so forth), as well as the numerous influences resulting from the roles department staff play in other activity systems (Figure 5.1.3).

However, activity theory will not be used as an interventionist or participatory method in order to work for change, as in Engeström's Developmental Work Research method (1991). This study will not shape opportunities for action and thinking, by working on the object

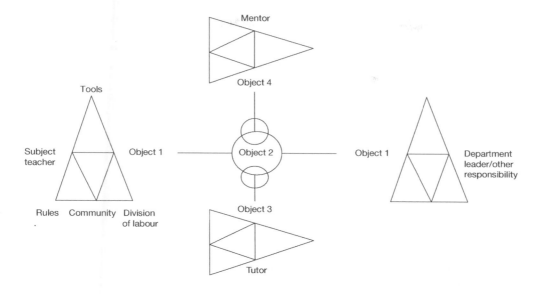

Figure 5.1.3 Third generation activity theory – school teachers

(student teachers' learning) of the activity system through expansive learning alongside the people who work in the departments. Rather, the use of activity theory will be restricted to a 'framework that has considerable potential for researchers who are interested in how conditions for learning are created, and in what is learnt' (Edwards, 2005, p. 55). Therefore, the idea of an activity system is being used as a heuristic tool for descriptive analysis before any new learning takes place.

The point of this research is not to change the system but to develop an understanding of how departments are working and the beginning teacher opportunities they are affording, and in order to fully address this, it is necessary to appreciate the systems that are operating and the nature of their action. There is no emphasis on transformation at this point but this could be the subject of future research (for example, how universities work with subject departments in order to maximise opportunities for beginning teachers).

Communities of practice

Whilst looking at a macro-structural overview of beginning teacher learning as an activity system, I am also questioning the nature of subject departments by viewing them as discrete systems. In doing this I am employing the lenses of both activity theory and communities of practice. The latter has proved useful at the level of the analysis of practices because it allows me to consider how departments' existing practices create learning opportunities for beginning teachers.

Lave and Wenger consider the kind of social engagements that provide the context for learning to take place in their book on situated learning and legitimate peripheral participation (1991). They locate professional learning in the increased access of learners to participating roles in expert performances. As learning involves not only a relation to activities but to a social community, they believe that the practice of the community creates the learning curriculum (Lave and Wenger, 1991).

Seeing student teachers as newcomers who are learning how to engage in the social practices of the department in which they are placed recognises the situated nature of learning. How this is related to the learning of general principles from, for example, staff room and mentor conversations, or visiting university tutors, can be related to Vygotsky's idea of spontaneous and scientific concepts.

> Spontaneous concepts are learned through cultural practice and because they are tied to learning in specific contexts, allow for limited generalisation in new situations; scientific concepts are learned through formal instruction and, because they are grounded in general principles, can more readily be applied to new situations.
>
> (Smagorinsky *et al.*, 2003)

The challenge for departments which offer opportunities for engagement in their social practices is to enable learners to see relationships between spontaneous and scientific concepts and to take from them experience, concepts that will enable them to interpret and work in other settings. My challenge is to capture both individual learning and the environments which shape and are shaped by it.

Lave and Wenger define a community of practice as 'a set of relations among persons, activity and world over time and in relation with other overlapping communities of practice. The social structure of this practice, its power relations, and its conditions for legitimacy define possibilities for learning' (1991, p. 98). Looking at a community as a set of relations among persons allows me to focus on individual sense-making as opposed to activity theory, which has a collective focus.

The relevance of communities of practice to this research

The research will analyse school subject departments as communities of practice and question whether they encourage participation of beginning teachers at multiple levels. Questions asked of departments should open up what participation, and what forms of participation, are allowing beginning teachers to learn. For example:

1   What forms of participation are available in shaping beginning teachers' understanding?
2   To what extent are beginning teachers encouraged to problematise how learning happens from teaching or vice versa?
3   How can transformative experiences that change beginning teachers' understanding of themselves as learners be enabled, and thus their ability to move among practices and learn from them?
4   Who defines success and failure, and how is this definition negotiated among the parties involved?

Beginning teachers who are based in subject departments for a relatively short period of time may regard the community differently from more established members, but it is still important for them to develop a sense of identity as a teacher. Possible tensions of continuity displacement may be seen when regarding communities of practice (the subject departments) in an activity system with the influences of other communities (the university and TDA, for example) as well as the beginning teachers with their current research and pedagogy interests. With this in mind, such questions as 4 above are crucial in determining how new ideas are challenged, accepted or dismissed by the community. This research specifically looks at the possibilities for action offered by existing practice, and the extent to which the beginning teachers take up these opportunities:

> Learning changes who we are by changing our ability to participate, to belong, to negotiate meaning, and this ability is configured socially with respect to practices and communities in which we shape our identities.
>
> (Wenger, 1998)

Concluding comments

By combining questions on the organisational and structural process of beginning teacher learning (context as a system) with a consideration of interpersonal relationships and practices (context as a set of relations) I aim to address how the different subject departments work with beginning teachers and identify factors that influence the ways that they work.

The two aspects of the research (researching beginning teacher learning in departments as activity systems and departments as communities of practice) are not being looked at sequentially, as data on both are being generated throughout the fieldwork period. It will be in the analysis that the elements of each will become clear.

References

Ball, S.J. (1987) *The Micro-Politics of the School: Towards a Theory of School Organization*, London, Methuen.

—— (1990) 'Education, inequality and school reform: values in crisis!', an inaugural lecture in the Centre for Educational Studies, London, King's College, University of London.

Bruner, J.S. (1999) 'Folk pedagogies', in J. Leach, B. Moon and P. Chapman (eds), *Learners and Pedagogy*, London, pp. 4–20.

Busher, H. and Blease, D. (2000) 'Growing collegial cultures in subject departments in secondary schools: working with science staff', *School Leadership and Management*, 20(1), pp. 99–112.

Butcher, J. (2000) 'Subject culture, pedagogy and policy on an open learning PGCE: can the gap be bridged between what students need, and what mentors provide?', paper presented at the European Conference on Educational Research, Edinburgh.

Donnelly, J. (2000) 'Departmental characteristics and the experience of secondary science teaching', *Educational Research*, 42(3), pp. 261–73.

Douglas, A.S. (2005) 'An exploratory study of how Oxford University PGCE curriculum tutors articulated their understandings of internship in a research interview situation', MSc dissertation, Oxford University Department of Educational Studies.

Edwards, A. (2005) 'Let's get beyond community and practice: the many meanings of learning by participating', *The Curriculum Journal*, 16(1), pp. 49–65.

Engeström, Y. (1991) 'Developmental work research: reconstructing expertise through expansive learning', in M. Nurminen and G.R.S. Weir (eds), *Human Jobs and Computer Interfaces*, Amsterdam, Elsevier, pp. 265–90.

—— (1999) 'Activity theory and individual and social transformation', in Y. Engeström, R. Miettinen and R-L. Punamaki (eds), *Perspectives on Activity Theory*, Cambridge University Press, pp. 19–38.

Eraut, M., Alderton, J., Cole, G. and Senker, P. (2000) 'The development of knowledge and skills at work', in F. Coffield, *Differing Visions of a Learning Society*, vol. 1, Bristol, Policy Press, pp. 231–62.

Esland, G.M. (1971) 'Teaching and learning as the organisation of knowledge', in M.F.D. Young, *Knowledge and Control: New Directions for the Sociology of Education*, London, Collier and Macmillan, pp. 70–115.

Furlong, J. (2005) 'New Labour and teacher education: the end of an era', *Oxford Review of Education* 31(1), pp. 119–34.

Goodson, I. and Mangan, M. (1995) 'Subject cultures and the introduction of classroom computers', *British Educational Research Journal*, 21(5), pp. 613–28.

Helsby, G. (1996) 'Defining and developing professionalism in English secondary schools', *Journal of Education for Teaching*, 22(2), pp. 135–48.

John, P. (2005) 'The sacred and the profane: subject sub-culture, pedagogical practice and teachers' perceptions of the classroom uses of ICT', *Educational Review*, 57(4), pp. 471–90.

Lave, J. and Wenger, E. (1991) *Situated Learning: Legitimate Peripheral Participation*, Cambridge University Press.

Leach, J. and Moon, B. (1999) *Learners and Pedagogy*, London, Paul Chapman.

Maynard, T. (2001) 'The student teacher and the school community of practice: a consideration of "learning as participation"', *Cambridge Journal of Education*, 31(1), pp. 39–52.

McLaughlin, M.W. and Talbert, J.E. (2001) *Professional Communities and the Work of High School Teaching*, Chicago and London, University of Chicago Press.

Oxford University Department of Educational Studies (2006) *PGCE Course Handbook*, Oxford, OUDES.

Paechter, C. (1995) 'Subcultural retreat: negotiating the design and technology curriculum', *British Educational Research Journal*, 21(1), pp. 75–87.

Russell, D.R. (2004) 'Looking beyond the interface, activity theory and distributed learning', in H. Daniels and A. Edwards (eds), *The RoutledgeFalmer Reader in Psychology of Education*, London, RoutledgeFalmer, pp. 307–26.

Smagorinsky, P., Cook, L.S. and Johnson, T.S. (2003) 'The twisting path of concept development in learning to teach', *Teachers College Record*, 105(8), pp. 1399–436.

Stodolsky, S. and Grossman, P. (1995) 'The impact of subject matter on curricular activity: an analysis of five academic subjects', *American Education Research Journal*, 32, pp. 227–49.

Visscher, A. and Witziers, B. (2004) 'Subject departments as professional communities?', *British Educational Research Journal*, 30(6), pp. 785–800.

Wenger, E. (1998) *Communities of Practice: Learning, Meaning and Identity*, Cambridge University Press.

5.2 Developing pedagogy for doctors-as-teachers

The role of activity theory

Clare Morris

Context: positioning medical education and training

Medical education in the UK has perhaps never been under such close scrutiny as in recent years. The Bristol Royal Infirmary inquiry (Department of Health, 2001) and the Shipman Inquiry (2005), among others, have resulted in a very close focus on what it means to be a doctor in the twenty-first century and significantly, on the ways in which we train doctors of the future and safeguard their practice. Such events may have put medical education in the public eye recently, but in fact the past decade has been characterised by rapid and significant reform of healthcare (see Clarke, Gewirtz and McLaughlin, 2000) and in the ways in which medical students and junior doctors are prepared for their future roles.

Ten years ago undergraduate medical education was centred in an elite group of predominantly old universities and followed a traditional technocratic model of professional education (see Bines and Watson, 1992) characterised by a 'pre-clinical/clinical' divide. Would-be doctors spent the first two years of their training in medical 'school' studying the basic sciences and then moved onto the wards and into the theatres to complete their clinical training. New graduates would then go into a relatively brief period of training for general practice or embark on the long journey (10 years or more) towards hospital consultant status by engaging in an increasingly specialist training, overseen by the Royal Colleges.

In the early 1990s the General Medical Council (GMC) published *Tomorrow's Doctors* (GMC, 1993), a far-reaching set of recommendations that signalled major curricular reform in undergraduate medical education, coinciding with unprecedented growth in new medical schools across the country. *Tomorrow's Doctors* emphasised the need to develop not only the professional knowledge of future doctors, but also their professional skills and attitudes. Most notably, recommended changes included a loss of the technocratic model by encouraging early patient contact, integration of basic and clinical sciences and, significantly, a shift to models of education and training that fostered the development of self-directed and adaptable lifelong learners. In 2004, the training of new medical graduates came under similar scrutiny and *Modernising Medical Careers* (Department of Health, 2004) has resulted in the first national, workplace-based, competency-assessed curriculum for newly qualifying doctors.

These far-reaching changes have, perhaps not unsurprisingly, resulted in an increasing 'professionalisation' of education within the context of medicine. All doctors are now expected to teach (GMC, 1999), the need to develop 'teaching competencies' is signalled in both undergraduate and postgraduate education and training, there are now specific pathways in academic medicine and 2007 has seen the creation of a new Academy of Medical Educators. Medical education units and master's programmes in medical education have proliferated as doctors in the UK increasingly struggle to reconcile their 'service' and 'teaching' roles and to understand the educational principles and practices that now characterise medical education.

The research: understanding the cultures of medical education and training

The work presented was completed as part of the EdD programme at the Institute of Education in London. The programme commences with two years of 'modules' (focused on specific areas of education and educational research), followed by an institution-focused study (IFS) and then the thesis. The work described in this chapter was undertaken as my IFS (Morris, 2005) and coincided with my taking up a new educational development role in a large London-based school of medicine. The role was to develop a programme of educational development activity for doctors and academic staff involved in teaching undergraduate medical students.

My background is not medical, although I spent the early part of my career working in hospitals (as a speech and language therapist). I have been engaged in educational development activity in schools of health and medicine for the past 10 years. I have always been fascinated by the 'men in white coats' who glide along hospital corridors and gather at the end of hospital beds, followed by a group of somewhat anxious yet observant junior colleagues. The culture of medicine has always appeared somewhat mysterious to this 'outsider looking in', and as someone charged with the role of improving medical education, it seemed to me important to at least try to unravel the mystery and to make sense of the distinct characteristics of education and training within medicine. Workplace-based learning is at the heart of medical education and training, yet is, I believe, under-theorised and poorly understood. The IFS presented here was undertaken with the aim of gaining a greater understanding of the cultures of learning in medicine and beginning to tease out an appropriate pedagogy for doctors as teachers.

Why activity theory?

In conducting some earlier EdD work, I had attempted to carry out a textual analysis of key GMC documents (such as *Tomorrow's Doctors* (GMC, 1993), *The Doctor as Teacher* (GMC, 1999) and *The New Doctor* (GMC, 1997)) in order to gain a sense of the theoretical traditions and pedagogic mores of medical education. However, this analysis was frustrated by the heavy emphasis in the texts on structures, responsibilities and lines of accountability within the medical hierarchy. There was limited attention to pedagogic issues, and where these were addressed there seemed to be tensions in relation to theories of learning and teaching. It became rapidly apparent that in order to understand medical education, it was imperative to understand its history and the contexts and settings in which it happened. At this point I started to explore sociocultural perspectives on learning. Säljö (2007) recently commented that: 'To understand learning as a socio-cultural phenomenon we must at some stage ... turn to culture, history and institutionalised patterns of communication and action' (Säljö, 2007, p. 12).

For these reasons I started to explore Lave and Wenger's work on situated learning, legitimate peripheral participation and communities of practice (Lave and Wenger, 2003). These perspectives were felt to be of potential utility when exploring medical teaching and learning practice at a micro-level, but seemed limited in their ability to capture and conceptualise the wider context of medical education. To gain this macro-level perspective I turned to Engeström's cultural-historical perspectives on learning and activity theory (Engeström, 1993, 1996). As Arnseth (2008) recently commented: 'in order to make sense of any action there is a need to examine the activity in relation to a wider cultural and material context, that is to say in relation to the activity system'.

Engeström's work on activity systems promised to provide a powerful 'theoretical lens' though which to observe medical education generally and through which to explore the 'institution in focus' for my EdD studies specifically. Activity theory was used to guide the study in four ways. First, to identify the unit of analysis for the study. Second, to theorise the 'institution in focus' by conceptualising and analysing the activity that relates to the education and training of future doctors. Third, to provide an illuminative lens through which to observe the practice of medical education (leading to the formulation of the research questions that guided the subsequent fieldwork). And finally, to provide an analytical tool to assist in the interpretation of data and to frame the concluding discussions.

What is activity theory?

Activity theory (AT) develops from the work of Leontiev and Vygotsky (see Engeström, 1996, 2001; Daniels, 2001 for detailed discussion). Simplistically, the model centres upon the relationship between subject (in this case *doctor-teacher*) and object (*future doctor*) and complex, mediated acts (*teaching and learning*). Second-generation activity theory (Engeström, 1996) extended this triangular relationship by moving from an individual to a collective focus. The mediated relationship between subject and object is placed within a complex system with its own identified traditions, practices, rules, roles and cultures.

By situating mediated relationships within activity systems (AS), second-generation AT provides a framework for looking at contradictions and tensions within AS and the potential for change and transformation over time. Whilst this model has some utility when analysing medical education, it is limited by the attention to a single activity system. The education and training of future doctors is highly complex and spans two distinct yet interacting systems

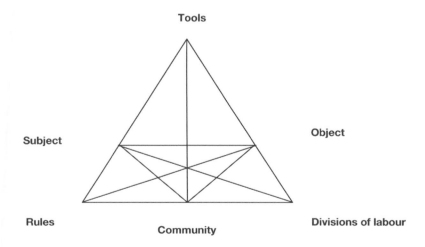

Figure 5.2.1 Activity theory model

(higher education and the NHS). The focus on a single activity system fails to provide a way of exploring the complex interactions between these two contexts and the potential 'culture clashes' between them.

Third-generation activity theory (see Engeström, 2001) expands the model further to include interacting activity systems. This model enables an analysis of complex institutions and the explicit consideration of cultural diversity opens up the possibility of looking at 'cultural clashes' within the institution and provides a framework for considering 'questions of diversity and dialogue between different traditions or perspectives' (Engeström, 2001, p. 5).

Whilst continuing to consider the roles played by historicity, contradictions and tensions in transforming activity systems over time, this model also seeks to explore the multi-voicedness of activity systems and the interactions between them.

This model was felt to provide an analytic framework to guide the study of the institution and to provide a clear way forward when identifying the primary unit of analysis for the IFS undertaken.

Identifying the unit of analysis

My work commenced with a preliminary analysis of the institution, using Engeström's third-generation activity theory as a method to guide my analysis. This work led to a realisation that rather than being one distinct entity, the school of medicine was in fact two discrete yet interacting activity systems. Further analysis focused upon an exploration of:

- the primary object (or objects) of activity in each setting (and the influence of historicity on these);
- the mediating tools and practices that characterised the education and training in each;
- an analysis of the community in each system (its multi-voicedness) and the roles community members play in supporting learning;
- divisions of labour within each system (in relation to the object of activity relating to medical education and training);
- the rules constraining and regulating the training process;
- observable tensions of contradictions within each system and across the systems.

Theorising the institution

The medical school in the research study in question has been formed over the past 15 years by the amalgamation of a number of long-established, London-based medical schools. Whilst the school has undergone some curricular reform in the light of GMC recommendations, it maintains a fairly traditional emphasis. The first two years of the programme are largely based in the university (AS1), albeit with some early patient contact and an 'integrated', 'systems-based' curriculum. In this setting they are taught mainly by academic and clinical-academic staff. In years three to six, medical students spend increasing amounts of time in NHS-based clinical attachments (AS2). During these times they are taught 'formally' by senior medical staff (i.e. hospital consultants or GP trainers) and 'informally' by more junior doctors and other members of the healthcare team.

Activity theory was used to analyse the activity that relates to the training of future doctors in both systems. The detailed analysis is outwith the scope of this chapter, and is presented elsewhere (Morris, 2005). However, in summary the activity theory analysis led to the illumination of two distinct yet interacting activity systems. In the first, academic staff are engaged in two distinct objects of activity: research and teaching. The latter is characterised by a range of historically recognised and newly emerging mediating acts and tools, including the familiar (for example, lectures), those unique to medical education (for example, dissection of cadavers) and the newly emerging (for example, learning with simulated patients). Medical students spend their early years primarily based within this activity system, with activity focused on providing a 'foundation' for future clinical and research activity. Tensions within this activity system are argued to be between the traditions of science and medicine and between the two key objects of activity undertaken, reflected in promotion strategies, resource allocation, divisions of labour and the differing status of specific mediating acts and tools used.

In the second activity system, medical teachers are also engaged in two related yet distinct objects of activity – treating patients and training future doctors. Within this activity system the emphasis is on preparing for future professional activity and extends to include junior doctors as well as medical students. As before, the training of future doctors is characterised by the continued use of historically recognised mediating acts and tools (such as bedside teaching with patients) and those which are newly emerging (such as teaching skills in simulation). Some mediating acts, traditionally the domain of AS1 (for example, lectures) are increasingly utilised within the second. Radical reform of models of medical education and the organisation of healthcare has challenged traditional roles and role boundaries and has led to changes in the divisions of labour in relation to both objects of activity. These changes have created tensions within the system that are argued to have led to the adoption of newly emerging mediating acts and tools.

Observing the practice of medical education: limitations of activity theory

By adopting an AT perspective, it was possible to theorise the institution in focus by deconstructing the complex network of interacting activity systems that make up its whole, allowing the identification of a primary unit of analysis for subsequent fieldwork in activity system 2. However, AT was not without its limitations in the context of this study. First, the absence of debate about appropriate research methods places limitations on the use of AT as a methodological tool and hindered progression. Second, whilst third-generation AT illuminates interactions between action systems, it fails to consider the ways in which 'outsiders' gain access to them. This is critical to a study exploring the ways in which future doctors gain access into AS2 but also has methodological relevance when issues concerning access to the field are explored. Third, whilst AT places great emphasis on mediation and the identification of mediating tools, acts and symbols, it fails to consider how these mediating tools and acts are used and the ways in which mediation is, or is not, successful. Finally, whilst AT has been used to conceptualise healthcare contexts (see Engeström, 1993) it has rarely been used to conceptualise medical education within the UK (the notable exception to this being Bleakley (2006), published after completion of the study). Whilst this means the work undertaken demonstrates originality, it also means it lacks precedent or a strong theoretical foundation to build upon.

Moving forward: adopting a sociocultural perspective

In order to progress the work, a pragmatic approach was therefore adopted, with the aim of preserving methodological consistency throughout. AT understands activity to be mediated, situated and historically bound, and so too must the research activity of the study. Whilst AT was the conceptual foundation for the study, it was necessary to draw upon other sociocultural theories in order to make greater sense of workplace based learning in medicine. In the absence of debate about methods, it was important to recognise the research traditions of sociocultural enquiry and to draw upon these. Finally it has been important to be mindful of the situated nature of this research and the ongoing, iterative nature of the relationship between researcher and researched.

Sociocultural theories of learning have their origins in philosophy, psychology, sociology and anthropology. The collective term 'sociocultural theory' embraces a range of theoretical perspectives each with its own distinct theoretical distinctions. In my reading of what can be loosely described as sociocultural writings (see, for example, Hutchins, 1995; Anderson, Reder and Simon, 1996; Wenger, 1998; Engeström and Middleton, 1998; Haavisto, 2002; Lave and Wenger, 2003; Saari, 2003), the aim was to pull out the core tenets of sociocultural theory to underpin and guide the development of the study. In keeping with AT, these writings emphasise the situated, mediated and historically and culturally influenced nature of learning. The emphasis on the collective nature of learning, in particular the conceptualisation of distributed cognition (the idea that knowledge and expertise is distributed across a working group rather than held by one individual within it) was also important. In a recent paper Arnseth provides an excellent critique of the parallels and distinctions between Lave and Wenger's situated learning and Engeström's activity theory (Arnseth, 2008). He argues that both offer useful theoretical frameworks that together can be '*invoked in order to leverage a critique of formal schooling*' (Arnseth, 2008, p. 14).

Together, these conceptions of learning were used to guide the development of the study in three ways. First, to guide my rereading of the medical education literatures; second, to illuminate the observed practice of medical teachers and their students in AS2; and third, to guide discussions (research interviews) with future doctors.

Sociocultural perspectives on research

Whilst the research undertaken and described was not purist in approach, it was a pragmatic attempt to 'unravel the mysteries' of medical education from a macro- and micro-perspective, with activity theory providing a backdrop to the more 'traditional' research work undertaken in later stages. The approach adopted can loosely be described as ethnographic. Ethnography is not a single research method nor does it come from one single research tradition, with differences between approaches being understood in terms of particular theoretical underpinnings or disciplinary perspectives. Ethnographic research is most closely aligned with fieldwork (classically participant observation) but embraces a range of research methods including other forms of observation, interview (conversations and discussions) and textual analysis.

The desire to explore and understand social processes and settings can be argued to be congruent with a sociocultural enquiry. However, there is a noticeable absence of discussion and debate about methods within the sociocultural literatures although the writings of Engeström, Wenger and Lave (op. cit.) suggest that fieldwork (including observation and interview method) are commonly used, albeit through a particular theoretical lens. The difficulty with classifying this study as ethnographic is that rather than seeking to identify the object of activity (as in the classic definition) the intent was clearly to explore the previously identified object of activity. Sharrock and Hughes (2002) comment that in their work, activity theory 'became the means of not only "sensitising" analysts to what they were seeing "in the field" but also imposing on that "seeing" concepts derived from activity theory itself" (Sharrock and Hughes, 2002, p. 3).

Whilst this study comes from a different ethnographic tradition to that classically described, it does have shared concerns. Critics of ethnography raise concerns about the status and authenticity of the data, the methods of observation and data recording employed, the nature of the relationship between researcher and researched and the analytic approaches adopted (see Atkinson and Hammersley, 1998; Robson, 1993). These concerns can be addressed by a transparency of approach (for example by being clear about the nature of relationships, by ensuring ethical practices), by detailing and triangulating methods and by adopting a reflexive approach that brings researcher concerns to the fore. This study, in effect, explicitly built in observational biases, with the approach being one of selective attention (to doctor-student mediated activity) and encoding (viewed through a particular theoretical lens).

In negotiating access to the field, activity theory perspectives led to a consideration of ethical issues at two levels. First, in terms of researching the system, and second when researching individuals within the system, particularly where professional identity has the potential to be compromised. In using AT to theorise the institution, explicit consideration was given to the interactions between my own activity system and that studied. This encouraged me to be more mindful of the personal nature of the research I was undertaking. The AT lens promoted identification of inner tensions and contradictions within and across AS. This type of analysis can require very sensitive handling, both during the research process but also in the writing up and dissemination of findings. One of my key ethical concerns was that both the periods of observation and the interviews may raise issues that I was unable to resolve or explicitly address. The need to make distinctions between two specific objects of activity (educational development and conducting a sociocultural enquiry) in which I was engaged was clearly important. When approaching this sociocultural enquiry ethically it was important that I did not view ethical practice simply as a formulaic application of principles or guidelines to a specific research project – rather that there was consideration of an ongoing iterative process that would require me to actively engage with my own thoughts and interpretations and to consider my place within the AS being explored and the possible impact I would have on the objects of activity undertaken.

Concluding thoughts: activity theory perspectives on medical education

Activity theory provided a powerful means to analyse medical education at a macro-level and to guide the micro-level analysis that followed. This analytic framework led to explicit consideration of the political, social, cultural and historical nature of medical education and training and a way of understanding recent changes and future developments. The study was undertaken because of its immediate potential relevance to my practice as an educational developer within medicine. The work undertaken led me to revisit perceptions of the 'medical school' being a single, unified activity system and to see it as a collection of complex, discrete yet interacting systems. In turn, it has led me to reconsider the ways in which I work with 'doctors-as-teachers' to support them in their increasingly complex roles with medical students and trainees.

In particular this research led me to be more mindful of the fact that medical teachers are drawn from a wide range of disciplines (each with their own epistemological positions) and are engaged in a wide range of teaching and learning activity within their own activity systems. It would be ill-advised to suggest that one particular pedagogy could underpin all of this, yet it is clear that doctors as teachers lack a coherent pedagogy to underpin the learning curricula of medical workplaces. Educational development activity provides a space to explore theories of learning in order to help staff identify those consistent with their world views, but also those that may challenge perceptions and lead them into new ways of working with future doctors.

It led me to be mindful, too, that educational developers in medicine need to move beyond a focus on a single AS (e.g. the NHS) or a single community (e.g. 'surgeons as teachers' or 'psychiatrists as teachers') to open up a critical dialogue between those who share the training of future doctors as an object of activity. By bringing medical teachers together, it may be possible to explore the ways in which history has shaped their current practice and how they may begin to look forward to develop their activity in new ways.

The work undertaken had considerable influence on my work with both activity systems described and has shaped the development of the master's-level activity subsequently developed in my current role in a new, equally complex organisation.

References

Anderson, J., Reder, L. and Simon, H. (1996) 'Situated learning and education', *Educational Researcher*, 25(4), pp. 4–11.

Arnseth, H. (2008) 'A critical account of the concepts of practice and situatedness in relation to activity theory and Lave and Wenger's "situated learning" – with special reference to educational research', *Pedagogy, Culture and Society*, 16(3), pp. 289–302.

Atkinson, P. and Hammersley, M. (1998) 'Ethnography and participant observation', in N. Denzin, and Y. Lincoln (eds), *Strategies of Qualitative Enquiry*, London, Sage, pp. 248–61.

Bines, H. and Watson, D. (1992) *Developing Professional Education*, Buckingham, Open University Press.

Bleakley, A. (2006) 'Broadening conceptions of learning in medical education: the message from team working', *Medical Education*, 40(2), pp. 150–7.

Clarke, J., Gerwirtz, S. and McLaughlin, E. (2000) *New Managerialism, New Welfare?*, London, Sage.

Daniels, H. (2001) *Vygotsky and Pedagogy*, New York and London, Routledge Falmer.

Department of Health (2001) *Learning from Bristol: The Report of the Public Inquiry into Children's Heart Surgery at the Bristol Royal Infirmary 1984–1995*, CM 5207, London, The Stationery Office.

—— (2004) *Modernising Medical Careers – The Next Steps: The Future of Foundation, Specialist and General Practice Training Programmes*.

Engeström, Y. (1993) 'Developmental studies of work as a test-bench of activity theory: the case of primary care medical practice', in S. Chaiklin, and J. Lave (eds), *Understanding Practice: Perspectives on Activity and Context*, Cambridge, Cambridge University Press, pp. 64–103.

—— (1996) *Perspectives on Activity Theory*, Cambridge, Cambridge University Press.

—— (2001) *Expansive Learning at Work: Towards an Activity Theory Re-conceptualisation*, London, Institute of Education, University of London.

Engestrom, Y. and Middleton, D. (eds) (1998) *Cognition and Communication at Work*, Cambridge, Cambridge University Press.

Engeström, Y., Miettinen, R. and Punamaki, R. J. (1999) *Perspectives on Activity Theory*, Cambridge, Cambridge University Press.

General Medical Council (1993) *Tomorrow's Doctors: Recommendations on Undergraduate Medical Education*, London, GMC.

—— (1997) *The New Doctor*, London, GMC.

—— (1999) *The Doctor as Teacher*, London, GMC.

Haavisto, V. (2002) *Court Work in Transition. An Activity-theoretical Study of Changing Work Practices in a Finnish District Court*, Helsinki, Helsinki University Press.

Hutchins, E. (1995) *Cognition in the Wild*, Cambridge, MA, MIT Press.

Lave, J. and Wenger, E. (2003) *Situated Learning: Legitimate Peripheral Participation*, Cambridge, Cambridge University Press.

Morris, C. (2005) 'Beyond "see one, do one, teach one": developing pedagogy for doctors as teachers', institution-focused study submitted for EdD examination, Institute of Education, University of London.

Robson, C. (1993) *Real World Research: A Resource for Social Scientists and Practitioner-Researchers*, Oxford, Blackwell.

Saari, E. (2003) *The Pulse of Change in Research Work. A Study of Learning and Development in a Research Group*, Helsinki, Helsinki University Press.

Säljö, R. (2007) 'Studying learning and knowing in social practices: units of analysis and tensions in theorising', lecture on the occasion of the opening of the Oxford Centre for Sociocultural Activity Theory Research, Department of Education, University of Oxford, 14 March 2007.

Sharrock, W. and Hughes, J. (2002) 'Ethnography in the workplace: remarks on its theoretical bases', [online], *Team-Ethno Online*, issue 1, available at www.teamethno-online.org/Issue1/Wes.html, last accessed 30 April 2005.

The Shipman Inquiry (2005) *Safeguarding Patients: Lessons from the Past – Proposals for the Future*, CM 6394, London, The Stationery Office.

Wenger, E. (1998) *Communities of Practice: Learning, Meaning and Identity*, Cambridge, Cambridge University Press.

5.3 Teacher/researcher

An unsustainable identity

Sarah O'Flynn

Preface

> 'What is this Sarah? Cos if it's a moan, I haven't got the time.'
>
> Hester, Friday 8 February 2002

The quotation above is from a participant in my research who is also one of my year-11 GCSE students. As her teacher I did indeed want 'a moan' at her for jeopardising her entire academic success by continuing to bring alcohol to school or to arrive on the premises too drunk to do anything much at all. As a researcher I wanted to observe and ask questions. As both a researcher and a teacher I wanted to understand how to support Hester and others in achieving greater academic success and future happiness, however they envisaged that for themselves. However, before I discuss the genesis of my research in more detail and while I am on the subject, I will start with 'a moan'.

My moan is about the separation brought about by this government of teaching and independent academic research. Apart from recently gaining my PhD (O'Flynn, 2007), I also work full-time as the deputy head teacher in a London authority's Pupil Referral Unit for students excluded from mainstream secondary school. I worked here throughout most of the time I was writing up my PhD, though the research participants were drawn from a mainstream secondary girls' comprehensive school. If I had had the vocational sense I was born with I would not have embarked on a PhD at all – there's not much money in it. I would have taken myself off to the National College of School Leadership and studied for an NPQH – the National Professional Qualification for Headteachers – without which I am now unable to even apply for the post of head teacher, PhD or no PhD. If I had done my NPQH rather than a PhD, I could be bringing home an infinitely larger salary by now and enjoying a more secure quality of life financially. Indeed having a PhD seems currently to be disbarring me from being sponsored by my authority to undertake an NPQH, perhaps because they consider that I might move to higher education and am not really invested in a career in secondary education or that I am now the wrong sort of person for headship anyway. Perhaps I am. The NPQH is a moulding process as much as it is a qualification, preparing one to lead a school within the government's school standards and improvement agendas. My PhD, by contrast, critiques school improvement by demonstrating the damage it does to individual young women in secondary education.

Most teachers will not in the future embark upon a PhD or indeed any independently substantive research project in education, because it will not further their careers in education. This keeps separate teachers from academic researchers and shuts down debate about the impact of school improvement at the level of classroom practice. Through further professional teacher qualifications, teacher reflexivity about student learning is brought within the terms of school improvement as if there were nothing outside that, and critiques like mine risk being considered marginal or irrelevant in the site of the school. It is important to understand my moan because it impacts upon the relationship between theory, the empirical work of my research and my continued work as a practitioner. Most of all it constrains the audiences the research can have at the level of practice and sets my identity as researcher in opposition to my identity as teacher, a point to which I will return at the end of this chapter.

Introduction

The autobiography of the question is a concept developed by Jane Miller (1995). It has methodological implications, because, unlike positivist research, it presupposes that who I am and how I got to ask the research questions – that is, my ontological position – is integral to the 'answers' I find and indeed how I set up the research to do this. In this section I briefly trace the autobiography of the question in terms of my struggle to find theoretical explanations for what I was observing in schools, which eventually led to my research questions. I will focus on three key examples here which provide insights into this process: first, the treatment in school of the pregnant teenager; second, the treatment of a young gay man; and finally the treatment of a young disabled woman.

I have always been interested in the relationship between sexuality and knowledge as it is constructed in schools and as both are embodied by learners. The government itself is interested and bemused by this relationship in some instances (though not all) where it seems to hamper educational standards. Their preoccupation with the pregnant teenager is one such example. The Social Exclusion Unit's report on teenage pregnancy seemed vaguely bemused and unable to explain why pregnant schoolgirls found themselves removed from school simply for being pregnant:

> Continuing education
> 8.22 Attention to ensuring a pregnant teenager continues to receive education is often very weak, and the Unit heard innumerable examples of pregnant girls pushed out of school on grounds of pregnancy or 'health and safety' … for many teenagers this is the beginning of permanent detachment from education.
>
> (SEU June 1999, p. 60)

Like the government's Social Exclusion Unit I was also fascinated by the ways in which the more overt presence of sexuality was often connected to poor academic achievement in school, and, conversely, why those who closeted any indication of sexuality often seemed to do much better. I wanted to move beyond common-sense explanations for this, views which are underpinned by stereotypical notions of adolescence as a time of raging, out of control hormones, to use theory to extend understanding of the complex ways in which young women's identities are positioned in relation to sexuality and knowledge. One of the first moments that made me realise just how interconnected sexuality was to knowledge in schools involved the example of a young gay man.

I started my teaching career in a large mixed suburban comprehensive school in Outer London. I became the deputy head of 'Special Educational Needs' as it was designated at the time. One day I received a referral for a year-8 pupil, Michael, who was extremely camp. He had previously come to my attention when he had asked for support to deal with homophobic bullying by other pupils. He subsequently came out as gay in year 10 (aged 14). The referral was from his maths teacher, who identified his difficulties with maths as a result of his 'femininity' (her words). I wondered whether femininity could be strictly said to be a learning need, especially as female students in the maths class were not being referred. Historically women have indeed suffered discrimination in education because their femininity was deemed to make academic study inappropriate but in 1989 it seemed anachronistic.[1] His maths teacher, a woman herself and therefore one would suppose less likely to see femininity as a stumbling block to mathematical success, made Michael's life a misery and in the end was disciplined over her behaviour, which was also clearly homophobic. Section 28[2] was in full force and this was a perfect example of the kind of homophobic behaviour that it seemed to tacitly license.

What was interesting to me was that 'femininity' performed in a masculine body could be read as a learning disability in relation to maths. It suggested that the construction of knowledge in curriculum subjects and the dominant pedagogies attached to curriculum subjects had embedded within them a requirement to learn in a particular sexualised and/ or gendered way. The performance of 'good at maths', as constructed in this school's mathematics in 1989, simply wasn't available to a young gay man, because 'good at maths' also embodied a particular form of masculinity, which was definitely not camp. Heather Mendick (2006) has argued powerfully that the pedagogy of maths is indeed masculinised. Mendick's work reveals how young people use maths to make their identities both as clever and as masculine and how young men and young women are differently positioned in relation to their study of maths. The hard knowledge of maths is associated with archetypal 'masculine' qualities of rationality, abstract thinking, objectivity and neutrality, whereas femininity is other to maths, in that it is relational, emotional, subjective and connected. In a sense, then, the teacher who said that this young man's problem in maths was that he was too 'feminine' was bizarrely correct, though it would have been more correct to have said, as Mendick has, that the problem is to do with mathematics, rather than those who are learning it.

As much as Michael's issues with maths were about gender, his failure at maths was also due to the teacher's homophobia, and the teacher's homophobia was a reaction to his homosexual performance. The actual performative aspect of his performance itself was important. If he could have just tried to act straight in maths, he might have had success as a learner. It was as if it was impossible to expect rationality from a gay male subject, a stereotype that is still pervasive in Western gay culture. I found a partial understanding of the issues involved here in terms of the Cartesian dualistic logic embedded in Western societies which constructs the binaries Mendick explores in her work. While femininity might make maths difficult, it did not threaten it in the same way as it did when embodied by a gay man. I would suggest the problem was not that Michael was too feminine, as the maths teacher suggested, but that he was mocking masculinity, which as a man was his for the taking. Instead he was treating it with disrespect.

The Cartesian dualistic logic of mind/body and rational/irrational splitting has particular relevance to the site of the school. Schools are places which are designed to produce rationality and cognitive development. Schooling is a deeply modernist project. In this context, it is unsurprising that the body is required not to draw attention to itself. The individual body becomes part of the corporate body of the school, clad in its uniform. The performance of sexuality is 'other' to the performance of learning and cognition and therefore, in simplistic terms, those who are perceived as sexual in any way are likely to be less successful than those who suppress or closet sexuality. Logically, schools educate for a delayed practice of sexuality partly because it is perceived as a practice of the body and is therefore not compatible with the development of reason. The ideal position for the secondary school pupil, logically, is to be quiet about sexuality and if possible to remain heterosexually asexual. Any active practice of sex for young people is therefore potentially undermining of academic achievement. On the other hand, Michael was not voted out of his maths class because he was having gay sex. It was because of his tendency to act gay and not to be able to closet it sufficiently, so that he was labelled as gay by others. Halley (1993, p. 85) has argued that heterosexuality is a 'default category', incorporating even homosexuality, provided that it remains covert. In short, the class of heterosexuals is 'home to those who have not fallen out of it'. As Judith Butler has remarked, '"intelligible" genders are those which in some sense institute and maintain relations of coherence and continuity among sex, gender, sexual practice, and desire' (Butler 1990, p. 23) and, we might also add, knowledge. In this instance, incoherence not only made gender unintelligible but also produced the subject as unintelligent.

Michael's case and the plight of pregnant teenagers convinced me that there was more to educational success than met the eye, that sexuality of any sort led a precarious existence in schools and that any trace of non-normative sexuality could close down the possibility of being successful in certain curriculum subjects altogether. As a teacher this was a real concern for me. It suggested that the control of adolescent sexuality was just as important in the production of educational success as any sort of cognitive development I might try to support in a classroom and that the discourse through which cognitive success materialised was intricately bound to sexuality. It suggested, too, that the control of adolescent sexuality was achieved through access to educational success. Rationing occurred when sexuality became out of control or stepped out of line. Ostensibly, schools use sex education to present an official view of sexuality to young people, that it would be in their best interests to delay sexual activity. It is presented as 'advice' (DfEE, 2000). However, a far more significant and potent way of ensuring young people's compliance with this advice is by rationing education,[3] controlling access to educational success for those who are overtly sexual, limiting access to subject choice or level or even to full-time education.

Perhaps the most important formative experience for this thesis occurred while I was working in a comprehensive, grant-maintained, over-subscribed girls' school in an Outer London borough. Helen, a young woman with cerebral palsy, was admitted into year 9 at the school at the end of the autumn term of 1998. Prior to this, she had been in a mixed school and prior to that, in a special school. The reason given for her wishing to leave the mixed school and attend this school was that she had been badly bullied by the boys at the mixed school. She only managed to remain in the school for one term and by the beginning of March she had been permanently excluded on the grounds that the school could not meet her educational needs. However, the real reason Helen could not remain in the school was that she had apparently been caught masturbating in the toilet. In many ways Helen was an example of what Shereen Benjamin suggested is 'the really disabled discourse of success' (2002a, chapter 8). As Benjamin argues, these pupils are those whose diversity cannot be valued because it is 'too diverse' (2002b, p. 132). What made Helen really different and really disabled, however, was her overt sexuality but this has to be interpreted in the context of her dis/ability, because they were productive of each other. The disability embodies the subject or rather engulfs it and there is a tendency to perceive those whose bodies are disabled as completely at the mercy of their bodies. Perceptions of disabled sexuality take to extremes the conflicting discourses of sexuality already found in schools about children's sexuality, either as unruly sexual adolescents with hormones raging out of control or as protected in a walled garden of childhood sexual innocence/ignorance. Helen's masturbation keyed into the first of these stereotypical assumptions about disabled sexuality and meant that she operated in opposition to the discourse of childhood sexual innocence. The key events in Helen's progression towards exclusion often centred on her body. Her masturbation led her to be viewed as governed completely by her body and without a mind. This served to produce Helen as ineducable.

Attitudes to masturbation underwent a considerable reworking in the latter half of the twentieth century, especially in relation to adolescents, but even in 1994 the then US president, Bill Clinton, dismissed the surgeon general, Jocelyn Elders, for suggesting that masturbation be included as a topic within sex education in public schools (*Lancet*, 1994; Irvine 2002). Helen's behaviour was seen as corrupting of others, and she had to be forcibly and permanently expelled. The most upsetting process in what happened to Helen was the production of her as incapable of reason, through her totalising embodiment. I could not understand for a long time why it was that although I kept producing evidence as her English teacher of her attainment and progress, this had no impact at all on the final judgment that the school could not meet her learning needs, a view which I did not share.

The research project

My research was born out of a desire to trace processes of inequity which were related to the presence of sexuality in adolescent pupils and which worked by constituting the presence of sexuality as also an absence of knowledge or sense. It also explains the use of post-structuralist theory subsequently in my research. The examples I use all suggest a self in process and a self constituted through key discourses about knowledge and sexuality and enshrined in dominant school effectiveness/improvement agendas. In some senses the examples that led to the research project all make 'strange' the processes at work in the schools and question the taken-for-granted assumptions through which those processes work to label pupils as difficult or impossible to educate. This is the starting point for the ethnographer, and it is no accident therefore that my research evolved as an ethnographic project (Youdell, 2006, p. 66).

It also explains why I chose not to undertake more conventional teacher-research using the model of action research. Cohen and Manion (1994, p. 186) define action research as follows:

> Action research is situational – it is concerned with diagnosing a problem in a specific context and attempting to solve it in that context: it is usually (though not inevitably) collaborative – teams of researchers and practitioners work together on a project; it is participatory – team members themselves take part directly or indirectly in implementing the research; and it is self-evaluative – modifications are continuously evaluated within the ongoing situation, the ultimate objective being to improve practice in some way or other.

The problem for me in using this method was that it could not offer a critique of the context itself. Rather it worked by attempting to improve or solve a problem 'in that context', where the context was not subjected to critical analysis. Ultimately this meant that the burden of change was left to those in the context with the support and insights of research. Pupils and teachers as the principal players in this context in my view are already impossibly burdened with the task of making school improvement or school effectiveness work. Moreover, because it appeared to me that the context of school effectiveness/improvement firstly had embedded within it assumptions about knowledge and about sexuality as the 'other' to knowledge and secondly that it also functioned as a discourse through which it constituted successful learner and non-learner identities, holding on to the possibility of envisaging a change in the context was vital. Although my research did not have the circuit of production of action research, it involved the generation of grounded concepts which led to new understandings of how young women embodied or resisted embodying sexuality in school and suggested how this might have a significant impact on their academic achievements. The research questions I asked were as follows:

- How do young people, and young women in particular, use sexuality and sexual practice in the construction of their identities as successful or failed learners?
- What are the dominant discourses of sexuality in school, how are these linked to education and how do these constrain the agency of young people in producing themselves as successful?
- Why is it that overtly (uncloseted) sexual or promiscuous behaviour in young women should so often lead to academic failure?
- What sexuality may be tolerated in young women, as compatible with academic success?

I worked with a relatively small group of about 25 year-11 pupils at a comprehensive girls' school over the course of one or two years. Of this group I worked very closely with 11 pupils, 8 of whom were from minority ethnic groups. In terms of their academic attainment eight of these pupils were poor achievers in school and five had been or were at risk of exclusion from school. Three further pupils were high achievers, though two had also had experiences of exclusion from school. One was what one might term 'a model student'.

Working with 'sexuality'

Although it is impossible to summarise my research in the scope of this chapter, what I hope to do here is explore some of the findings of the research, give insights into how young women manage their sexual selves and their academic selves in school and explore some of the costs of this self management to the self. I should perhaps say a word about 'sexuality'. The difficulty of terminology around sexuality is one that I have struggled with throughout this research. I use the word 'sexuality' always in the widest sense possible. When I am writing about sexuality I do not just mean sexual orientation, or different sexual practice, or sexual feelings or desires, or 'having sex' with others or with oneself. I also include in the definition asexuality, not having sex and sexual abstinence. I use it as a term to define broadly the ways in which individuals manage the sphere of human experience which we term 'sex'.

Much of the preparatory work of the research involved tangling with theory on identity construction (Hall, 1992), psychoanalytic accounts of sexuality (Britzman, 1998), Foucauldian work on sexuality (Foucault, 1976), the work of feminists on sexuality (Fine, 1988; Holland *et al.*, 1990; Walkerdine, 1990; Lees, 1993; Hey, 1997; Holland *et al.*, 1998), sexual theorists (Rubin, 1984; Weeks, 1985; Sedgwick, 1990; Seidman, 1993; Halberstam, 1998; Butler, 2004), and those working in the area of sexuality and schooling (Walkerdine, 1990; Mac an Ghaill, 1994; Harbeck, 1995; Unks, 1995; Hey, 1997; Valentine, 1997; Epstein and Johnson, 1998; Gordon *et al.*, 2000; Walkerdine *et al.*, 2001; Micelli, 2002) as well as sociologists on sexuality and the body (Prosser, 1998). Although the list of sources here is not comprehensive, the work of these thinkers helped me to create my own theoretical tool kit[4] to help me support and develop my interpretive frame. However, one important psychoanalytic account of learning by Deborah Britzman made a particular point, which I felt spoke to the aims of the research:

> Educators have yet to take seriously the centrality of sexuality in the making of a life and the having of ideas … educators continue to ignore the stakes of the demand to renounce instinctual pleasures, specifically as this prohibition may then also work against the capacity to risk love and work.
>
> (Britzman 1998, p. 70)

Though my research was not psychoanalytic as such, I did believe that sexuality was never taken seriously in debates around academic achievement, and that this was in stark opposition to small but established bodies of research on issues of educational success and gender, disability, class and ethnicity.

Key findings of the research

Managing sexuality

One of the most important findings of the research was the sheer hard work of identity management that young women did in relation to their sexualities in the process of making their identities as learners. In a large part sexual self-regulation was done to please us, the adults, people in authority in schools and at home, to meet our expectations. Childhood innocence was experienced as a pervasive discourse by young women, not only as a shaping influence for their sexuality but also for their cleverness. One of the high-achieving pupils, Darcy, was exemplary of this. She was entirely co-opted into the process of sexuality as irrelevant to her now, and yet in all sorts of ways she was involved in the suppression of sexuality, often by isolating herself from others and by retaining a childlike lack of knowledge about the world around her:

> So – I spose at the moment cos everybody's doing stuff – everybody's got social lives and stuff and you feel like really weird that you're like at this age and your only concern is studying whereas like everyone else is enjoying their lives – sometimes you do feel like 'oh am I doing the right thing?'
>
> (interview, July 2002)

Darcy's suppression of sexuality was only achieved by distancing herself socially from her peers and indeed from her Sikh culture and her family, as well as from any wider knowledge of what was going on in the world. She described herself as an 'alien'. She had a developing eating disorder which concerned her and her family. She had entirely absorbed neo-liberal messages about self-reliance and the need to succeed, but this was at the cost of her emotional, social, sexual and physical well-being.

Other students, less high-achieving, were often just as aware in their understandings of the links between asexual practice and enhanced academic achievement. Two Somali students, Nadjma and Nazrin, for example, clearly understood that heterosexual relationships needed to be presented as superficial:

Nazrin:	I think I want to finish my education before doing things like that [having a boyfriend, having sex]. I told my mind not to go with boys and not to do that thing until I finish my education. I mean you can have a boyfriend.
Nadjma:	Yeah yeah …
Nazrin:	But not like do the silly things … [the rest is obscured by Nadjma's interruption].
Nadjma:	No, no – you're saying it like that – but if I say I don't wanna have a boyfriend but sometimes it happen to you – cos you don't – you don't wanna have a boyfriend but who knows?
Sarah:	You meet someone?
Nadjma:	Yeah. You meet someone but if you be careful in yourself …
Nazrin:	Yeah – like more hard.
Nadjma:	Hard.
Nazrin:	Like hard on the inside.
Nadjma:	So that means nothing happen to you. You can have a boyfriend and it's not a problem.

(interview, March 2001)

These students' understanding of heterosexual sexual relationships is carefully modulated to ensure that their effect is minimised. Learning is hard and they need to be 'hard' to undertake it successfully. They work at promoting a carefully balanced identity in which they can achieve success both as heterosexual women and as learners.

Surprisingly, I found that high-achieving students did not always have histories of high achievement and they had learned various techniques subsequently to manage sexuality successfully after experiencing school failure. Mataia, for example, explained how following her permanent exclusion from another school for homophobic bullying of a teacher and a rebellious attitude to learning, she had set about recreating herself as an intellectual. Part of this involved taking up more fundamentalist Islamic attitudes and wearing a jilbab. She spoke at length about Islam, presented a sustained and cogent critique of Western globalisation but also intellectualised sexuality and demonstrated a wide cultural knowledge about sexual practice. Mataia also invested considerable time and effort in contrasting a past life for herself in which she had a more overt sexuality and her new identity as a Muslim woman, in which she did not. In this way she was able to present herself as at once sexually knowledgeable rather than naïve, but also as a sexually innocent good Muslim woman, with regard to sexual practice. This was a successful strategy for managing both sexual and learner identities in school and helped her to achieve highly academically.

What became clear from the research, I think, was that education operated disingenuously in relation to young people and their sexualities, because sexuality was not something that young people could choose to manage or not. By acting as if it was by, for example, suggesting it could just be advantageously 'delayed' (DfEE, 2000), a burden was placed on young people to manage their sexual selves in ways that we approve of but without our support, and if they failed, then we ensured that the education system punished them. With alarming regularity anyone who was overtly sexual or who 'did girl' inappropriately and in unfeminine ways, or who did not do heterosexual girl, found themselves excluded from school or displaced from school or confined to certain spaces in the school; effectively marginalised.

Excluding sex from the school

Four students I worked intensively with were all excluded at various times from a school and in each case their exclusion centred on sexuality or their performance of gender. For example, although Ann had never been in trouble in school previously and was a high achiever, her lesbian desire for a teacher in year 11 simply could not be managed by the school. She had to leave. Her desire was distressing for the teacher, and because there were no strategies in place to manage such an event, Ann could not remain in school. She attempted suicide and received psychiatric support but her lesbian desire was always in danger of being constituted as a psychiatric illness. When Ann spoke to me about what had happened, there were clearly psychoanalytic processes occurring both in relation to her early childhood attachments and the similarities she saw between those attachments and the teacher object of her crush. It was also a means by which she could displace or park her sexuality onto someone who was academically successful. It was an attempt by Ann to manage her sexuality in school and also revealed teaching itself as a potentially seductive process.

One of the problems for teachers, however, is that they are often unsure how to talk about sexuality or gender nonconformity in school in relation to pupils or their own practice. This was clear for the teacher who was the recipient of Ann's desire, but also emerged as an issue for other staff. Better teacher education around sexuality, and in particular around the psychoanalytic processes involved in learning and teaching, would enable strategies to be evolved with greater confidence, which might increase young women's well-being and their educational success at school. At the moment teacher education programmes pay very little attention to sexuality within education. The Teacher Development Agency website details 48 key professional standards which a teacher must meet in order to gain qualified teacher status (QTS). Nowhere is the word 'sexuality', or 'sex', mentioned, even once.[5] This, in turn, makes it very unlikely that trainee teachers will ever have lectures or seminars on the importance of sexuality to learning or to teaching. It is unlikely that, even minimally, young people's sexuality will be acknowledged.

For those not excluded as such, I found that exclusion was avoided through internment or displacement, as in Carol's case. Carol had been excluded from her previous school for 'doing boy' through fighting and violence. Carol regularly 'passed' outside school as male. Indeed she preferred this. Carol confessed to me that she thought she was a boy really, that her father spoke to her as if she were a boy and over the course of the year she worked very hard to make her appearance even more masculine than it already was by wearing classic schoolboy uniform and by shaving off her hair. She also constructed her learner identity as masculine, preferring maths to English, practical subjects to those that were theory, or content-led and excelling in PE. Carol's school file from her previous school indicated such a difficult history in education that when she first arrived the head teacher decided that she should attend no lessons at all but spend all week in alternative education, of which I was in charge. She was placed on work experience two days per week in a car mechanic's workshop and studied for all her subjects in the alternative education unit initially, though she eventually became able to attend maths, PE and art classes in the main school. It was what I called 'benevolent internment'. It did allow her some success and it protected her from a trans-phobic and homophobic school population but it also protected them from her. Carol's case raised wider issues potentially. Her presence caused anxiety amongst other students, who seemed worried about the fact that she might 'fancy' them but also perhaps that they might fancy her. It also called into question statistics about the differences between girls' and boys' achievement. When girls start being boys one is forced to ask how to include them in statistics about gendered learning. Whilst researchers have observed that 'sissy' boys – those boys whose studiousness aligns them with forms of femininity – experience considerable homophobia in school (see, for example, Epstein and Johnson, 1998) the treatment of pupils who practise female masculinity is also punitive or ostracising, making it difficult for them to participate in school successfully. By focusing on girls who 'do girl' very differently or present sexualities that are not normative, or who don't do girl at all, we would be able to give a fuller account of the range of subject positions taken up by young women in school. By making these visible we could also provide a more detailed account of the ways in which gender and sexuality make a difference to educational success.

Being a teacher/researcher: exposing contradictions

'I didn't even know you *could* study that.'
(Hester, fieldnotes September 2001, on the occasion of my explaining to her that my PhD was about young women's sexualities)

I found that pupils often led closeted sexual lives or imagined sexual futures that were not in line with government education policies to raise standards and career expectations, policies which consequently misaddressed them. Being a teacher/researcher here was a perfect position from which to experience the contradictions of government policy. As a teacher I had to implement such policy but as a researcher I uncovered reasons why it could not work.

Mercedes, for example, as a young Traveller woman, was the object of considerable attention in government policy around inclusion. However, while policy tried to raise Mercedes's expectations of success and her career expectations, she was busily planning her own future, making herself more central in the Traveller community through marriage to a Traveller and a child by the time she was 18. Whilst initiatives such as the government's Aim Higher programme tried to lift Mercedes out of the material poverty of her community through education, Mercedes was vowing to me that she would never leave that community and would never have a professional career because 'snobby' people would not understand her. Her main priority was that such professionals kept out of her 'business' because they were 'too nosey' and that if she had any power the first thing she would do was reduce the numbers of police, teachers and social workers.

Bringing sexuality openly into the school as research and hence a legitimate subject for sustained inquiry and discussion and my openly declared identity as a lesbian fractured boundaries about what was knowledge and what was not, the status of pupil experience and whether it could count as knowledge. Could their ontologies be used to make new knowledge? Interestingly, after her initial disbelief that sexuality could be a topic for research, Hester came back into my office two days later to ask me if you could study 'women' at university, because if so she wanted to do a course which was just about women's literature, history, science and medicine and so on 'but only women's'. She had clearly been thinking about what might count as knowledge in other academic but non-school settings. She was delighted when I told her about women's studies courses. There were instances throughout the research such as this, when an engagement with sexuality led to a re-envisaging of whether one could, after all, make a successful learner identity.

However, although Hester wanted to do this and eventually to become an MP, her academic achievements meant that she was considered a more appropriate candidate for a vocational path into the caring profession. A career for her in the caring profession was practically assured and yet she 'chose' to throw it away. In order to convince everyone that it wasn't after all right for her, she set about remaking her sexuality, so that it was the very antithesis of caring femininity. As much as I tried, as her teacher, to support Hester to gain GCSEs, to encourage her to think about how to be an MP, there was always this big plan for Hester waiting in the background: the training scheme, the vocational work-placement waiting to take her on, because she would make a good carer. Hester was already a good carer. She used her sexuality as much to unmake a carer identity, as she did for her own pleasure. Indeed, her own pleasure was not really ever achieved and there were considerable costs to her sanity.

If we look at it in this way, then we might argue that in Hester's case at least, the stereotype of the adolescent at the mercy of libidinous energy and hormone imbalances was produced by and through her education. It was her education which conjured it into existence. Her sexuality was socially and institutionally produced as well as being a psychological production by Hester. It was not her body and the out of control hormones running round it that caused her to behave in this way, it was a psychological resistance to what schooling offered her which mobilised sexuality as resistance.

Conclusion

The title of my PhD was 'Testing Times: The Construction of Girls' Desires through Secondary Education'. I wanted to draw attention to the fact that adolescence is perceived to be a testing time for young people and also to allude to the target and auditing culture of New Labour neo-liberal education policy, in which young people are constantly engaged in an endless round of assessment and target setting. I also wanted to suggest that it is partly through the process of schooling itself or in opposition to it that girls construct their desires in terms of their imagined futures and that learner and sexual identities are always in 'construction'. One of the most disenchanting aspects of the research was the regularity with which government education policy seemed to fail these young women either by creating educational success but at the cost of individual health, or by misaddressing them but more fundamentally by failing to acknowledge young people as subjects with sexuality and sexuality itself as important for education. I still believe that we are failing to recognise the implications of this for schooling and that we continue therefore to produce failure by attempting vainly to expel sexuality from the site of the school. But now I risk ending up back at my moan where there seems no way for my researcher identity to influence policy at the level of classroom practice.

Notes

1 Further reading would suggest that femininity does indeed make success more difficult. See, for example, Benjamin, 2002; Leathwood, 1998; Walkerdine, 1988.
2 Section 28 was the infamous amendment to the Local Government Act of 1986, brought into force in 1988, which forbade Local Authorities from 'promoting homosexuality' or promoting 'the teaching in any *maintained school* of the acceptability of homosexuality as a pretended family relationship'. It was finally repealed in November 2003.
3 For further discussion of the concept of 'Rationing Education' see Gillborn and Youdell, 2000.
4 For a 'tool kit' for academic writing see Boden *et al.*, 2005.
5 See Teacher Development Agency website, accessed 30 December 2006: www.tda.gov.uk/teachers/professionalstandards/currentprofessionalstandards/qtsstandards.aspx.

References

Benjamin, S. (2002a) *The Micropolitics of Inclusive Education: An Ethnography*, Buckingham and Philadelphia, Open University Press.

—— (2002b) 'Reproducing traditional femininities? The social relations of "special educational needs" in a girls' comprehensive school', *Gender and Education*, 14(3), pp. 281–94.

Boden, R., Epstein, D. and Kenway, J. (2005) *The Academic's Support Kit*, London, Sage Publications.

Britzman, D. P. (1998) *Lost Subjects, Contested Objects: Towards a Psychoanalytic Inquiry of Learning*, New York, State University of New York Press.

Butler, J. (1990) *Gender Trouble: Feminism and the Subversion of Identity*, New York, Routledge.

—— (2004) *Undoing Gender*, New York and London, Routledge.

Cohen, L. and Manion, L. (1994) *Research Methods in Education*, 4th edn, London and New York, Routledge.

DfEE (2000) *Guidance on Sex and Relationship Education*, London, Department for Education and Employment.

Epstein, D. and Johnson, R. (1998) *Schooling Sexualities*, Buckingham, Open University Press.

Fine, M. (1988) 'Sexuality, schooling, and adolescent females: the missing discourse of desire', *Harvard Educational Review*, 58(1), pp. 29–53.

Foucault, M. (1976) *The History of Sexuality, Volume One: An Introduction*, London, Penguin Books.

Gillborn, D. and Youdell, D. (2000) *Rationing Education: Policy, Practice, Reform and Equity*, Buckingham and Philadelphia, Open University Press.

Gordon, T., Holland, J. and Lahelma, E. (2000) *Making Spaces: Citizenship and Difference in Schools*, Basingstoke and New York, Macmillan.

Halberstam, J. (1998) *Female Masculinity*, Durham, NC and London, Duke University Press.

Hall, S. (1992) 'New ethnicities', in J. Donald and A. Rattansi (eds), *'Race', Culture and Difference*, London, Sage Publications, pp. 252–9.

Halley, J.E. (1993) 'The construction of heterosexuality', in M. Warner, *Fear of a Queer Planet: Queer Politics and Social Theory*, Minneapolis and London, University of Minnesota Press, pp. 82–102.

Harbeck, K.M. (1995) 'Invisible no more: addressing the needs of lesbian, gay, and bisexual youth and their advocates', in G. Unks, *The Gay Teen: Educational Practice and Theory for Lesbian, Gay and Bisexual Adolescents*, New York and London, Routledge, pp. 125–33.

Hey, V. (1997) *The Company She Keeps: An Ethnography of Girls' Friendship*, Buckingham and Philadelphia, Open University Press.

Holland, J., Ramazanoglu, C., Scott, S., Sharpe, S. and Thomson, R. (1990) *'Don't Die of Ignorance' – I Nearly Died of Embarrassment: Condoms in Context*, London, Tufnell Press.

Holland, J., Ramazanoglu, C., Sharpe, S. and Thomson, R. (1998) *The Male in the Head: Young People, Heterosexuality and Power*, London, Tufnell Press.

Irvine, J.M. (2002) *Talk about Sex: The Battle over Sex Education in the United States*, Berkeley and Los Angeles, University of California Press.

Lancet (1994) 'The politics of masturbation', *The Lancet*, 344, pp. 1714–15.

Leathwood, C. (1998) 'Irrational bodies and corporate culture: further education in the 1990s', *Inclusive Education*, 2(3), pp. 255–68.

Lees, S. (1993) *Sugar and Spice*, London, Penguin Books.

Mac an Ghaill, M. (1994) *The Making of Men: Masculinities, Sexualities and Schooling*, Buckingham, Open University Press.

Mendick, H. (2006) *Masculinities in Mathematics*, Maidenhead and New York, Open University Press.

Micelli, M.S. (2002) 'Gay, lesbian and bisexual youth', in D. Richardson and S. Seidman (eds), *Handbook of Lesbian and Gay Studies*, London, Sage, pp. 199–204.

Miller, J. (1995) '"Trick or treat?": the autobiography of the question', *English Quarterly*, 27(3), pp. 22–6.

O'Flynn, S. (2007) 'Testing times: the construction of girls' desires through secondary education', unpublished PhD thesis, Cardiff University.

Prosser, J. (1998) *Second Skins: The Body Narratives of Transsexuality*, New York, Columbia University Press.

Rubin, G.S. (1984) 'Thinking sex: notes for a radical theory of the politics of sexuality', in C.S. Vance, *Pleasure and Danger: Exploring Female Sexuality*, London and New York, Routledge and Kegan Paul, pp. 267–93.

Sedgwick, E. K. (1990) *The Epistemology of the Closet*, London, Penguin Books.

Seidman, S. (1993) 'Identity and politics in a "postmodern" gay culture', in M. Warner, *Fear of a Queer Planet*, Minneapolis and London, University of Minnesota Press, pp. 105–42.

SEU (June 1999) *Teenage Pregnancy*, Wetherby Yorkshire, Social Exclusion Unit.

Unks, G., ed. (1995) *The Gay Teen: Educational Practice and Theory for Lesbian, Gay and Bisexual Adolescents*, New York and London, Routledge.

Valentine, G. (1997) 'Ode to a geography teacher: sexuality and the classroom', *Geography in Higher Education*, 21(3), pp. 417–24.

Walkerdine, V. (1988) *The Mastery of Reason*, London, Routledge.

—— (1990) *Schoolgirl Fictions*, London and New York, Verso.

Walkerdine, V., Lucey, H. and Melody, J. (2001) *Growing Up Girl: Psychosocial Explorations of Gender and Class*, Basingstoke, Palgrave.

Weeks, J. (1985) *Sexuality and Its Discontents*, London, Routledge.

Youdell, D. (2006) *Impossible Bodies, Impossible Selves: Exclusions and Student Subjectivities*, Dordrecht, Springer.

5.4 Using theory in social research

Reflections on a doctoral study

Maria Balarin

The word *theory* is central to the process of doing research. It is, however, often understood in very different ways that range from the idea of theory as something more or less rigid to more dynamic understandings of theory and theorising that highlight the importance of developing new explanations through research. Grappling with the idea of using and developing theory when pursuing a project of one's own can often be daunting, as one faces questions about the originality and relevance of one's explanations. But the role of theory is crucial from the first moments of defining a research problem and the set of related questions, as well as in gathering relevant data and in developing explanations for the problem under investigation.

Understanding the role of theory in social research has to do with some very fundamental questions in relation to how we understand the process of doing research itself, and which we can start to deal with by asking 'when does theory come into the research process?' Is it at the beginning, at the end, or is it present all the way through the research? Responding to such questions, rather than a practical matter, requires dealing with some of the most delicate conceptual issues surrounding the process of doing research. It involves defining whether we understand research as a process of formulating a set of more or less definite hypotheses which we then try to 'test' through empirical data; or as a more inductive process by which we collect data and then try to elaborate a theory on what the data 'tell us'; or, indeed, whether it has components of both.

Addressing such questions can lead us to focus on discussions about the way in which we understand the world, whether it is an entity with more or less fixed properties that we can investigate (rather neutrally), or, whether, while the world is independent from us, we always come to know it in a way that is mediated by our interpretations. For empiricists, for instance, who believe that research is a way of tapping into the 'world out there' and reporting on what we find, the role of theory is much less important than for those of us who believe that we actually come to know the world through theory, and that developing better knowledge is equivalent to developing better theoretical explanations for the problems we encounter. This discussion involves complex issues about the extent to which we can have access to the world out there, or whether we live in a world of mere interpretations. Each of these positions has particular assumptions and implications. In the first case, the assumption is that our knowledge corresponds to the world, it mirrors it; in the latter, if one is not careful, there is an open door towards relativism, a position in which any kind of knowledge seems equally plausible (Pryke *et al.*, 2003).

Defining one's position in relation to such problems requires a careful articulation of ideas that is beyond the limits of the present chapter. Some things, however, must be said, and will hopefully become clearer in the course of the coming pages. The empiricist position that claims the possibility of developing knowledge actually *corresponds* to 'the world out there' has been thoroughly criticised from various strands of philosophy, which, more recently aided by developments in the biology of cognition, support the idea that our knowledge of the world is always mediated by our perspectives and by the particular interpretive frameworks through which we organise our perceptions. This, however, does not mean that our knowledge does not open to the world at all. It does (Clark, 2003). The problem is that while we can go on trying to know and understand the world, our representations and our knowledge of it have certain insurmountable limitations. They will always be incomplete and fallible.

This implies that criteria for judging between theories cannot rely on the correspondence between our theories and the world, which cannot be determined in a definitive way, but rather on the robustness of our theories to actually explain social or natural phenomena, and on other criteria such as the degree of coherence of our explanations, their capacity to explain what other theories don't while at the same time explaining what they do, their plausibility, etc. (Sayer, 1992; Steinke, 2004). It is important to bear in mind that while we might not be able to know the world precisely and absolutely, the world does have a certain structure and certain characteristics which are more or less stable and definitely independent of our thought processes. This sets limits to the explanations we can come up with, as the world will simply not allow any kind of interpretation (Sayer, 1992).

From this standpoint, theory is not something that comes in at specific moments of the research process, nor does it refer to a set of fixed ideas that we test against the world. Rather, theory comes in at the very beginning, from the moment when we start asking questions and formulating a particular problem that we want to focus on. By theoretically engaging with such questions the borders of our research problems start to become crisper, we begin to ask more precise questions and it is thus that we can actually begin to define the more technical matters of how to go about gathering relevant data. In the latter, theory is also fundamental, as we begin to develop explanations from the first moments we set foot on the field, and when we make decisions about new information we want to gather to help us refine our questions. Thus, while theory and theorising are maybe more clearly present when we are interpreting data and attempting to arrive at more coherent explanations about our research problems, the role of theory is continuous.

What follows will attempt to illustrate these ideas with the use of an example from a research study carried out as part of a doctoral degree, which focused on the radical nature of policy discontinuity in Peru.

Using theory in a study of radical education policy discontinuity in Peru

The problems that concerned me when I embarked on this piece of research had to do with the ways in which educational reforms in Peru are usually handled (Balarin 2006). I became interested in this during the time in which I worked in the Ministry of Education of Peru, at a moment in which a very comprehensive reform was being planned and set in motion with the financial help of international organisations such as the World Bank and the InterAmerican Development Bank. A couple of years into the beginning of this reform process, the policies that it involved began to change, responding not to technical considerations, nor to specific demands or new information about the specific problems being addressed, but, rather, to what appeared as very particular political decisions in relation to the existing government's attempts to perpetuate itself in power. The latter increasingly came to replace the reform aims. And while that government was to collapse as a result of the deep corruption that it gave rise to, the more democratic and transparent government that followed continued with this style of policy making, led by the particular views of some individuals in power. The problem that aggravated this, and which gave rise to radical degrees of policy discontinuity, was that policy makers (i.e. ministers and heads of ministerial offices) were constantly changed in response to the shifts in the usually delicate balance on which governments depend.

While the complexities of this process of constant policy change were to become clearer once I started researching it, this was where my initial interests focused. At the beginning, though, it was a rather ill-defined problem that simply pointed the direction in which I was to go, but which still lacked definition. I already had some ideas, some initial theories as to the reasons that might lie behind the problem of radical education policy discontinuity. After leaving the Ministry of Education I was involved in several educational research projects, and the issue of radical discontinuity – although not necessarily described in those terms – was a constant reference in people's comments about the failure of reforms. It also became increasingly clear that it was not a recent problem, but that it had marked the history of educational change in the country, and was also a characteristic of other countries in the region. All this gave me some initial hints as to the nature of the problem and where to start thinking about it.

The role of theory was crucial in moving from this rather broad understanding of the problem to a clearer definition of what I wanted to study and the questions I needed to address. I began reading texts about education policy, many of which focus on the forces that are at play in the definition of policies and increasingly refer to the effects of globalisation on educational change. Many of these texts stress the way in which policy agendas are shaped by economic change. I increasingly came to think that the problems I found in Peru had to do with even more fundamental issues. In the more advanced nations in which most of the education policy literature had emerged, there were certain assumptions about the way in which the policy machinery operates, and the interaction between different social, economic and political forces that did not appear to follow the same circuit in a developing country like Peru.

This marked the first area of theoretical exploration that I was to focus on. I had to theorise the differences and particularities that I found in the Peruvian system, in the way in which the state had developed, and which explained the characteristics of the public administration, as well as the often complicated relations between education, society and national development. What marked this moment as well as other stages in which theory became crucial for the research was a kind of friction between the problem I was interested in and the theories currently available to explain the most common features of education policy making. There was a need for explanation that was not covered by current theories and which therefore required elaboration. This was a first step towards achieving a clearer definition of the research problem.

The exploration of this area led me to clarify what were the particularities of the Peruvian state system that I found interesting, and which appeared to be related to the styles of policy making that had emerged in the country and led to the radical levels of discontinuity. I began by focusing on rather broad bodies of theoretical thought, such as conflict and consensus theories of the state, which, in different ways, provided descriptions and explanations for the particular ways in which states, their administrative apparatuses and their relations with social demands operate (Lauder *et al.*, 2006). Different theoretical approaches focused on particular issues, with some stressing the power relations between different factions in society, others suggesting that political interests are structured in a more open and competitive way, and yet others emphasising the ways in which the organisational apparatus of the state (the way in which it has developed to administer different areas of social life) has a certain autonomy from specific economic or political interests.

What became clear through these and other readings was that configurations of state power and administrative organisation have to be understood in relation to the ways in which different states have historically developed. This led me to focus on a complementary area of theoretical ideas coming from post-colonial theories of the state. The latter offer relevant explanations for the developmental routes followed by countries once under colonial rule, and which have often maintained some of the deep social cleavages established during colonial times. Here, I found, one could begin to find some of the explanations for both the way in which the institutions of the state have developed, how the interests of different social groups have become politically articulated (or not) and the role played by social policies such as education in national development.

As the research problem began to get into focus I found other more specific areas of theoretical exploration. One of them had to do with understanding policy processes, how they operate and the arrangements that regulate them. Again, it became clear that particular ways of formulating policies have to do with the characteristics of different state formations. My readings, therefore, also had a strong focus on Peru, and more specifically on available historical and sociological discussions of the ways in which the state has developed.

It was by engaging with these more theoretical discussions that I could refine both the research problem and the research questions. This also allowed me to define the way in which I was to go about the data collection. The specific decisions I made in relation to the latter emerged from the research questions, just as these had emerged from the different areas of theoretical discussion that I had embarked upon.

As it appeared, the problem of policy discontinuity was related not to the way in which micro-political forces (such as school-level decisions) impinge on and modify initial reform aims – which is a frequent source of policy change (Ball, 1987) – but rather to the way in which high-level policy makers make decisions about the need for changes in policy directions. The focus of the data collection was thus on a sample of policy makers (ministers, their close advisers, heads of ministerial offices) and other relevant policy actors (members of the Teachers' Union and of the National Council for Education) who were interviewed in depth. While there was an initial identification of subjects, the final sample was completed through a snowballing technique common in policy studies, whereby new individuals were identified through the initial interviews (Goldfinch, 2000).

The specific areas on which the interviews focused were also theoretically driven. While an open-ended and conversational approach to interviewing was used (Holstein and Gubrium, 2004), the initial preparation of the interview schedules included the definition of certain topics that appeared to be important in the light of theoretical discussions. Most of these had to do with the institutional arrangements that frame and regulate policy making, such as the characteristics of the bureaucracy, the formal rules for policy making, the extent to which different sectors coordinate when making decisions, the role of international agencies in the definition of policies, etc.

While this selection of areas was theoretically driven, the interviews were open enough to let new elements come up. In this way, it soon became clear that very rich data offering interesting explanations for the radical levels of discontinuity were emerging from the less structured and more narrative accounts provided by the interviewees (Riessman, 1993). These took the form of personal stories that included reflections on how they reached positions of power, as well as accounts of the decisions they made and the difficulties they encountered.

While some of these overlapped or added to the pre-defined areas of enquiry, they offered important new information with which to understand radical discontinuity. Through their stories the interviewees were presenting themselves in particular forms that served to explain and justify many of their decisions. By noting this, and seeing how it could contribute to the theoretical explanations of the problem, I soon began to give more space in the interviews for the narrative elaboration.

A clearer picture began to emerge from these accounts of the difficulties of steering a sector such as education in an institutional context like that of Peru. Issues such as the lack of a civil service career, the lack of a more or less structured party political system, the absence of a culture of accountability, the extremely intricate regulations that often slow down decision making and hinder policy consolidation, were among the issues that would later help me develop a more complete set of explanations for the problem under study.

Although I had already defined some of the areas for theoretical elaboration while collecting the data and, later, when analysing it, new areas of interest started to appear. The final analysis thus combined a discussion about both the interview themes and the policy narratives, which together provided a view of the institutional context of policy making, and of the particular cultures that emerge within it. The latter were characterised by highly individualistic decisions, which were attributed to the lack of structuring rules to limit and bind policy decisions. Coming up with this was not a straightforward process, but more like a coming and going with ways of presenting the analysis until I was more or less satisfied with the explanations I was providing.

In this process, it became increasingly clear that while institutional elements could help explain radical policy discontinuity, the latter was also deeply related to the kind of developmental path assumed by the Peruvian state, which had historically maintained a deeply divided social structure. Public education, which had emerged as an attempt to extend social provision, had increasingly developed as a service for the poor – particularly in recent years, when private provision of educational services has been on the rise. This meant that solving the problem of radical discontinuity would not only require institutional changes, but also a different approach to development, more focused on extending citizenship and opportunities to all.

The data collection and analysis were thus characterised by an interplay between the emerging findings and the theoretical explorations that I had originally pursued, which I complemented as the research went by. Rather than applying a set of theories to a particular case – or attempting to test them – the theory guided the research, but without constraining it. In the end, the contributions of the study were not only the particular findings, but also, and maybe more importantly, the ways in which such findings were used to refine existing theories. The research process itself, in this respect, can be seen as a sort of permanent conversation between the researcher and the theoretical resources available to her.

The view which I have tried to convey reflects not only my personal experience and understanding of what doing research is about, but fits also with those of other researchers. Layder (1998), for instance, makes it clear that 'theorizing should ... be regarded as a continuous feature of research' (p. 28), where the researcher adapts, transforms and adds to existing theoretical bodies. Taking this into account implies leaving behind more traditional approaches to research, which often have a clear-cut definition of research stages (identifying a problem, mostly in terms of gaps in the literature reviewed; defining a set of questions and methodological strategies for data collection; collecting data; analysing it; and arriving at conclusions). What emerges then is a somewhat more chaotic, though no less rigorous, view of the research process in which the formulation of the problem and the research questions, as well as the data gathering and analysis, remain open to transformation and refinement as the research develops and as we formulate better theories to explain the problems that concern us. As Layder (1998) suggests, 'there may be no end-point to the formulation of the research problem', but the research itself resembles 'a rather haphazard "evolution" characterized by a series of oscillating phases of relative confusion and clarity rather than an immaculate conception' (p. 30). This view also coincides with Haig's (1995), who suggests that 'because our most important research problems will be decidedly ill-structured, we can say that the basic task of scientific enquiry is to better structure our research problems'.

It is precisely this process that I have tried to illustrate through the account provided above. Going from an ill-structured to a clearer definition of our research problems is a process that strongly relies on the use of theory. The latter is not 'an end-product of the research process' (Layder, 1998), nor is it limited to a 'tightly formulated' set of assumptions, but is a crucial element that helps us define and redefine our research questions and problems in what is more like a to-and-fro process of going from theory to data and vice versa, until we find a set of explanations that address the problem of study and at the same help us define it more clearly. In this sense, the goal of social research can be seen as much in terms of defining new problems as in terms of generating new theories (explanations) for them. Pre-existing theory is crucial in this process, as it marks some of the ways in which we are to go. Our contributions will stem from the particular ways in which we engage with such theories, and from our ability to come up with views and explanations of our own.

References

Balarin, M. (2006) 'Radical discontinuity: a study of the role of education in the Peruvian state and of the institutions and cultures of policy making in education', PhD thesis, University of Bath.

Ball, S.J. (1987) *The Micro-Politics of the School: Towards a Theory of School Organization*, London, Methuen, Routledge.

Clark, N. (2003) 'The play of the world', in M. Pryke, G. Rose and S. Whatmore, *Using Social Theory*, London, Sage and The Open University, pp. 28–46.

Goldfinch, S. (2000) *Remaking New Zealand and Australian Economic Policy: Ideas, Institutions and Policy Communities*, Wellington, Victoria University Press.

Haig, B. (1995) 'Grounded theory as scientific method', in *Philosophy of Education 1995: Current Issues*, Urbana, University of Illinois Press, pp. 281–90.

Holstein, J. and Gubrium, J. (2004) 'The active interview', in D. Silverman, *Qualitative Research: Theory, Method and Practice*, London, Sage, pp. 140–61.

Lauder, H., Brown, P., Dillabough, J. A. and Halsey, A. H. (eds) (2006) *Education, Globalization and Social Change*, Oxford, Oxford University Press.

Layder, D. (1998) *Sociological Practice: Linking Theory and Social Research*, London, Sage.

Pryke, M., Rose, G. and Whatmore, S. (eds) (2003) *Using Social Theory: Thinking Through Research*, London, Sage and The Open University.

Riessman, C. (1993) *Narrative Analysis*, London, Sage.

Sayer, A. (1992) *Method in Social Science: A Realist Approach*, London, Routledge.

Steinke, I. (2004) 'Quality criteria in qualitative research', in U. Flick, E. von Kardoff and I. Steinke, *A Companion to Qualitative Research*, London, Sage, pp. 184–90.

Index